W9-DBK-415

Chicago, 1910-29

*Publication of this volume was assisted
by a grant from the Graham Foundation for
Advanced Studies in the Fine Arts*

CHICAGO

1910-29

Building, Planning, and Urban Technology

WITHDRAWN

MORTON COLLEGE LRC
CICERO, ILLINOIS

Carl W. Condit

The University of Chicago Press Chicago and London

The University of Chicago Press, Chicago 60637
The University of Chicago Press, Ltd., London
© 1973 by The University of Chicago
All rights reserved. Published 1973
Printed in the United States of America
International Standard Book Number: 0–226–11456–2
Library of Congress Catalog Card Number: 72–94791

Carl W. Condit is professor of history, urban affairs, and art at Northwestern University. He is an acknowledged authority on urban architecture and has published many books and articles on the subject.

1973

Contents

52592

Illustrations

Preface

My purpose in writing this book might best be explained by first describing its genesis in my own mind. I originally intended to write a history of commercial and public building in Chicago from about 1910 to the present, thinking of the work as a kind of sequel to my *Chicago School of Architecture*, published in 1964. There are several aspects of twentieth-century building in the city that deserve the serious attention of the architectural and urban historian—the extravagant yet brilliantly designed works of the final phase of ornamental eclecticism, the new "purified" skyscraper of the twenties, the leading civic institutions, the emergence of a second distinguishable Chicago movement in the boom that followed World War II—enough to warrant an architectural and technological study in its own right. I had not progressed far in my research, however, when I realized that it is not possible to talk meaningfully about modern urban building without examining its role both as causal factor and as consequence in the physical process of urban history. This is especially true for Chicago, first, because one cannot treat building in the city since 1900 without considering the Chicago Plan of 1909, usually called the Burnham Plan, and second, because the city that emerged in mid-century presented a perfect paradox of brilliant technological and architectural achievement standing beside the failure to produce a decent human environment for the majority of its citizens. And this failure exists in the face of all the devices that were thought to be capable of producing the livable city that steadily eludes us.

I was thus compelled to broaden my aims and to attempt a kind of urban history that to the best of my knowledge has not been previously written. Whether I was dealing with the promise of urban planning or the reality of urban disaster, it seemed to me that I could not escape describing the development of the whole domain of urban technology—that is, all those human activities that together provide the physical basis of organized community existence. Perhaps another way to look at the history I have essayed is to regard it as the technical biography of the city in the period of its maturity and of its troubles and decline. I chose 1910 as my starting point primarily because it marked the acceptance of the Burnham Plan as the official plan of the city, but for the equally valid reason that by historical coincidence the physical plant of the city had been established by that year in all its fundamental elements, except for the facilities of air transportation. But since one cannot pick up the narrative of urban growth at any date other than its beginning without considering the earlier evolution, my first chapter constitutes a descriptive-historical panorama of Chicago as it took its shape in the roughly seventy-five-year period that extends from 1837, the date of its charter, to 1910. My ultimate aim in the subsequent chapters is to describe the continuing evolution of the physical city while also attempting to evaluate what has been achieved in the light of the all-embracing criterion of how well this achievement has answered the needs of those who have lived and worked in the city.

MORTON COLLEGE
VERITAS
1924
WITHDRAWN
LIBRARY

Acknowledgments

An undertaking of this magnitude always involves the assistance of many individuals and institutions, and now that I have assembled what I hope is the complete roster, I am surprised at how many friends, associates, and students I have depended on. The gathering and tabulation of statistical data, the most tedious and exacting task in the preparation of the book, was almost entirely the work of Patricia Wishart. Some of the bibliographical material and tabular details were assembled by Marilyn Mollman, Sandra Page, Elizabeth Dull, Rosanne Maine, Susan Hull, and Lucy Shaffer. Among the librarians to whose patience and willing cooperation I am indebted are the following: Joseph Benson, former director of the Municipal Reference Library of Chicago; Joyce Malden, the present acting director; Candace Morgan, a staff member of the same library; Pauline Steffens, former director of the Chicago Park District Library; Benjamin Jacobson, director of the Transportation Library of Northwestern University; Mary Roy, his assistant librarian; and Janet Ayers of the library of the Northwestern Technological Institute. For answers to numerous and varied questions about the architectural history of Chicago, along with many conversations as useful as they were pleasant, I could always count on Wilbert Hasbrouck, executive director of the Chicago chapter of the American Institute of Architects, editor of the *Prairie School Review*, and director of the Prairie School Press. Information on rail traffic at Union Station was made available to me by Robert E. Clarkson of the Burlington Railroad's Industrial Engineering Department, and much valuable material on the Chicago Transit Authority and its predecessors was provided by George Krambles, director of the CTA's Research and Planning Department. Architectural plans and voluminous tabular data on Chicago schools were placed at my disposal by Francis Lederer, superintendent of physical plant and equipment, and Saul Samuels, chief architect, both of the Chicago Board of Education. Among those who provided photographs and drawings, I must single out for special thanks Richard Nickel, who gave his life for the preservation of Chicago's architectural heritage, Betty Ritter of the Perkins and Will Partnership, Jack Schaffer of Skidmore, Owings and Merrill, and Ben Weese of Harry Weese and Associates. Photographers, architects, libraries, and other institutions that provided photographs, drawings, and various prints are indicated in the list of credits for illustrations, and all sources of quotations are given in the notes.

The considerable expenses of fieldwork, travel, research assistance, and the assembly of illustrative material were borne by a number of organizations. I am indebted to Professor Scott Greer and the Center for Metropolitan Studies (now the Center for Urban Affairs) of Northwestern University for the largest single grant made in support of this work. Next in generosity was the Committee on Research Funds of the university, which provided me with annual grants over a period of five years. Finally, parts of recent grants from the American Philosophical Society and the National Science Foundation covered a share of the costs, chiefly of travel for comparative study in the field.

I think that anyone who labors in his home at what we are pleased to call scholarly work owes a special kind of continuing seven-day-a-week gratitude to the members of his family—in my case to my children, as much for their intermittent but apparently genuine expressions of interest in the uninteresting activity of authorship as for their willingness to forego conversation when it would be an unwanted interruption, and to my wife Isabel for patience, good humor, much useful criticism, and that belief in the validity of one's work that a man's ego can seldom survive without.

Chicago in 1910

1. The City in Its Natural Setting

The Early City and Its Geological Background

Chicago was legally recognized as a town on 4 August 1830 when the surveyor James Thompson made the first map of the community, whose area was then less than half a square mile, and it was incorporated as a city under the laws of Illinois on 4 March 1837. For the first century of its existence the growth of the city exhibited a rhythmic pattern of remarkable uniformity, in which the changing rate of population increase, from rapid acceleration to steady deceleration, coincided with a shifting pulse beat in the expansion and reconstruction of its physical fabric.[1] There have been four distinct phases in the history of the city's building. The first extended from the founding of the urban community in 1830 to the fire of 1871, a disaster which very nearly required that Chicago begin its material growth all over again. The second began with the reconstruction following the fire and continued until the brief interruption of World War I and the depression that followed; it was perhaps the most important of all the phases because it saw the emergence of a unique architectural and urban style. The third was short and hectic, for it was concentrated in the boom of the 1920s that ushered in the new skyscraper age and thus wrought a third transformation of the urban core and the lakefront. The extravagant act ended with a crash, to be succeeded by a twenty-year hiatus of depression, war, and postwar recovery. The fourth phase, beginning in 1950, quickly established a baffling mixture of paradoxes—boom and decline, social troubles and renewal, confidence and fear.

The spatial counterpart to the uniformity of temporal growth is the physical form of the city, which is predominantly a rectangular grid that fills the interstices of an enormous pattern of radial and concentric arteries, the whole vast geometry extending seemingly without end and with monotonous repetition to the limitless horizon. The spatiotemporal regularities that stand in strong contrast to the social violence of Chicago's history were established, possibly to an unparalleled degree, by the natural, economic, and technical factors underlying the modern industrial city. The term may be taken as a convenient shorthand for any commercial and manufacturing city that was established or acquired its present character chiefly since the Industrial Revolution of the eighteenth century. Chicago had no natural feature that stood in its way, so that its setting, combined with the extreme economic pressures that energized it, compelled it to recapitulate the entire history of this kind of urban complex in a few generations.

Three broad classes of operating factors have together played the decisive role in shaping the modern city. First and most fundamental is the geographical, the primary elements of which are water, topography, precipitation, and the agricultural potential of the surrounding area. Second are the economic factors, the city's role as a market and a manufacturing center being of paramount importance. The third class is the technological, which is properly to be considered as composed of all those techniques necessary to provide the physical basis of organized community existence. This last group of factors grew progressively more potent as determinants of the modern industrial city until they became dominant at the end of the nineteenth century. When we say this, however, we ought not to suppose that technology—a collection of utilitarian inventions and their applications—necessarily acts as a prime causal agent in urban development. A fully exploited technology is an instrument energized by social, cultural, and economic activities and used well or ill to meet the challenges of the urban site, to surmount the geographical limitations, and thus to realize the economic potential of the region.

For approximately the first half of its life the modern industrial city had no means of horizontal transportation other than foot and horse, and no means of vertical travel other than climbing stairs. These limitations, which lasted until well into the nineteenth century, effectively prevented the city from expanding either horizontally or vertically, so that it could only grow interstitially into a compact mass. The city outgrew this phase when a broad galaxy of fundamental inventions suddenly became available to make possible an enormous expansion of the urban fabric in all directions. The first phase of development, which we might characterize as the horse and pedestrian city, began to give way around 1860 to the railroad and elevator city, and this in turn around 1920 to the automobile city. The technical developments that emerged during the decades around the mid-nineteenth century provided the city builder with the tools he needed to break out of the traditional form. The most important of these had to do with transportation, construction, and energy transformation—the steam railroad and the street railway; the internal iron frame for buildings; fireproof construction and the power-driven elevator; methods of excavating, dredging, filling, and tunneling with power-operated tools; hydraulic control and sanitary systems; and the generation of electric power. These constitute the primary elements of urban technology, that complex of interrelated techniques that constitutes the material basis of the new metropolitan life. Chief among them in the history of modern city building are the railroad, high-rise building technology, and the whole domain of water control, but transportation and water have ordinarily been the most decisive factors.

Chicago was born and lived through its youth near the end of the foot-and-horse age, so that it passed through the early part of its extremely concentrated development in uncomfortably close contact with its natural setting of marsh grass, lake, and sluggish streams. The overburden above the bedrock of the region is a mixture of sand, clay, and gravel of glacial origin, the various layers of clay ranging in consistency from a tough plastic state to a gravel-bearing hardpan almost as resistant as a true conglomerate. The bedrock that underlies the glacial materials is Niagara limestone, a dolomitic limestone of Silurian origin that is dense, hard, and fine grained, possessing a softly scintillating gray white color in its buried state but weathering to a darker gray on exposure. The original shore of the glacial lake (designated Lake Chicago by the geologists) at its maximum area extended to the western edge of the Des Plaines River valley and to an irregular line a few miles south of the Little Calumet River. This great body of water drained into the Mississippi through a continuous waterway roughly following the present courses of the Des Plaines and the Illinois rivers. In the immediate area of future Chicago the water flowed out of the lake through two broad channels, one following a diagonal passage along the line of the present Sanitary and Ship Canal, the other somewhat to the south, along the east-west line of Calumet-Sag Channel.[2] Two islands once broke the lake surface near the shore, their ancient presence retained in the modern place names of Blue Island and Stony Island.[3] The two channels that drained the lake were eventually dammed by a moraine, which left only the Des Plaines River of the original westward-flowing drainage system; the present streams flowing through the city itself are entirely postglacial.

Old Lake Chicago receded by stages, leaving a succession of beach terraces and the present lake plain on which the city now stands. At its maximum width the plain extends about fifteen miles west of the present shoreline, but it narrows rapidly north of the city. Between Winnetka and Waukegan it has been eroded away by waves and flooded, with the consequence that the moraines that lie at intervals across the plain terminate at the water's edge, forming the high bluffs of Highland Park and Lake Forest. Elsewhere the plain is broken by a series of low ridges which are the remains of beach terraces and spits left by the receding lake. In the level region of Chicago even these slight changes in elevation are conspicuous features, and the more prominent of them are clearly visible in the northeast part of the metropolitan area, along Ridge Avenue, Gross Point Road, Waukegan Road, and the Milwaukee Railroad line between Morton Grove and Glenview.

Except for these minor topographic changes the lake plain is relatively low, close to the water level of Lake Michigan, and extremely flat, a consequence of the leveling and filling action of repeated glacial movements. The various moraines lie roughly parallel to the lakeshore or follow the contours of its curved south end, the valleys between them providing the natural courses for the new drainage pattern of the region (fig. 1). The Des Plaines River lies far enough west to remain in the Mississippi system, but the rest of the streams rise close to the lake and flowed into it as long as they followed their natural gradients. The system that converges on the city proper consists mainly of two pairs of rivers: one the North and South branches of the Chicago River, which flow together to form the short east-west stem that once terminated at the lake; the other pair the nearly parallel Grand and Little Calumet rivers, the confluence of which forms the Calumet proper that also once flowed into the lake. Joined to the Calumet River as a huge saclike embayment is Lake Calumet on the far South Side of the city. The one inland geological feature of importance is the low limestone ridge west of the city that separates the Lake Michigan and the Mississippi drainage systems.[4]

The Chicago setting, if we exclude Lake Michigan, was a rather unprepossessing area that at first showed little promise; but over the horizon, so to speak, there lay enormous advantages, and the city was quick to realize them. Although the weather has the harsh quality typical of the prairie climate, it has a fairly predictable regularity and a moderate total precipitation (normal precipation, measured as rain, is 33.18 inches per annum, based on averages up to 1968), with snowfall very much lower than in the Great Lakes area east of Lake Michigan. The geographical location, at the farthest interior penetration of the Great Lakes–Saint Lawrence system, placed the city in the agricultural heartland of North America and at the same time gave it immediate access to the greatest body of interconnected inland waterways in the world, one that extends westward to the plains and eastward to the sea itself. The level prairie setting meant that the city could expand radially in all directions except east, but this expansion was hampered in the early years of the pioneer community by the need to drain and fill the low marshy tracts that lay between the moraines and near the lake. It was the advantageous natural factors, however, that determined the location of the original settlement and hence of the central business district of the mature city. The site of that settlement lay close to the mouth of the main river, set back a little way from the marsh and beach area along the shore. What was later to become the heart of the city was thus established by nature as a rectangular area bounded by the lake, the main river, the South Branch of the river, and a vaguely defined line running east and west between the lake and a point where the river curves to the southwest (somewhat below the present Roosevelt Road).

Commercial Building

Until the end of the nineteenth century the actual working core of Chicago was always somewhat smaller than the area defined by the natural features. The retail center

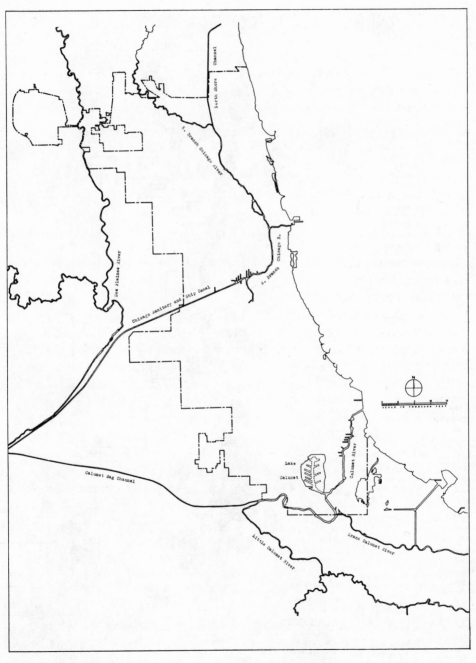

Fig. 2. The Forest Preserve District of
Chicago and Cook County in 1967.

1. Spring Creek Preserve
2. Deer Grove
3. Ned Brown Preserve
   Busse Forest
4. Potawatomi Woods
   & Lake
5. Dam No. 1
6. Allison's Woods
7. River Trails Nature
   Center
8. Lake Avenue Woods
8A. Beck Lake
9. Camp Pine Road
10. Lions Woods
11. Big Bend Lake
12. Northwestern Park
    Woods
13. Belleau Lake
14. Camp Ground Road
15. Iroquois Woods
16. Somme Woods
17. Turnbull Woods
18. Erickson Preserves
19. Willow Road Woods
20. Glenview Woods
21. Harms Woods
22. Northwestern Golf
    Course
23. Linne Woods
24. Wayside Woods
25. St. Paul Woods
26. Miami Woods
27. Clayton F. Smith
    Preserve—Bunker Hill
28. Clayton F. Smith-
    Caldwell— (Swim-
    ming Pool)
29. Edgebrook Golf Course
30. Edgebrook Woods
31. Billy Caldwell
    Golf Course
32. Indian Road Woods
33. Forest Glen Woods
34. Labagh Woods
35. Axehead Lake
36. Dam No. 4
37. Robinson Woods
38. Schiller Woods
39. Che-Che-Pin-Qua
    Woods
40. Fullerton Woods
40A. Indian Boundary
    Golf Course
41. Evans Fields
42. Thatcher Woods
43. Trailside Museum
44. Maywood Woods
45. George A. Miller
    Meadows
46. Schuth's Grove
47. National Grove
48. McCormick Woods

49. Brookfield Woods
50. Chicago Zoological
    Park (Brookfield Zoo)
51. Twenty-sixth Street
    Woods
52. Westchester Woods
53. Brezina Woods
54. Possum Hollow Woods
55. LaGrange Park Woods
56. Bemis Woods-Meadow
    Lark Golf Course
57. Zoo Woods
58. Flank Road Meadow
59. Cermak Woods
    (Swimming Pool)
60. White Eagle Woods
61. Ottawa Trail Woods
62. Stony Ford
63. Chicago Portage
    (National Historical
    Site)
64. Arie Crown Woods
    Lake Ida
65. Buffalo Woods
66. Willow Springs Woods
67. Columbia Woods
68. Maple Lake
69. Bullfrog Lake
70. Pulaski Woods
71. Red Gate Woods
72. Wolf Road Woods
73. Black Partridge Woods
74. Saganashkee Slough
75. Spears Woods
76. Hidden Pond Woods
77. Country Lane Woods
78. Hickory Hills Woods
79. Little Red School
    House (Nature Center)
80. Belly Deep Slough
81. White Oak Woods
82. Crooked Creek Woods
83. Pioneer Woods
84. McCloughry Springs
85. Paddock Woods
86. Palos Park Woods
87. Forty Acre Woods
88. Winter Sports Area
    Swallow Cliff
89. Teasons Woods
90. Cherry Hill Woods
91. Swallow Cliff Woods
92. Papoose Lake
93. Duffy Preserve
    Tampier Slough
94. McGinnis Slough
95. Elizabeth A. Conkey
    Forest
96. Carlson Springs
97. Burr Oak Woods
98. Turtle Head Lake
99. Tinley Creek Woods
100. Bachelor Grove Woods
101. Rubio Woods
102. Yankee Woods
103. St. Mihiel Reservation
104. Dan Ryan Woods

105. Eggers Grove
106. Whistler Woods
107. Pipe O'Peace Golf
     Course
108. Calumet River Boat
     Dock
109. Calumet Grove
110. Kickapoo Grove
111. Beaubien Preserve
     and Boating Center
112. Powderhorn Lake
113. Burnham Golf Course
114. Shabbona Wood
     (Nature Center)
115. Green Lake Woods
     (Swimming Pool)
116. Wampum Lake
117. Sweet Woods
118. Zenders Woods
119. Jurgensen Woods
120. Lansing Woods

121. North Creek Meadow
122. Brownell Woods
123. Glenwood Woods
124. Joe Orr Woods
125. Woodrow Wilson
     Woods
126. Indian Hill Woods
127. Sauk Trail Woods
128. Schuberts Woods
129. Calumet City Playfield

was concentrated on State Street, within the north and south boundaries of the future elevated Loop, while the financial institutions grew up along LaSalle Street, three blocks to the west. Between these two arteries and for a block to the east and west of them there multiplied, in ever increasing density, a heterogeneous assortment of office and governmental buildings, small stores, warehouses, hotels, saloons, and various service establishments. The open spaces lay mostly along the southern edge of the core, along Jackson Boulevard and below, where the ragged edge of the commercial city began to give way to the railroad city, which consisted of scattered terminals extending from Van Buren south to Polk Street. Along this line the irregular pattern of stations and tracks turns, even to this day, into a solid belt of railroad lines that blankets the area from State Street westward to Canal. Nearly all the structures in the entire core area were demolished by fire on 8 and 9 October 1871, and the already flourishing city, with a population of nearly 300,000 persons housed in everything from the costliest of stone mansions to the dirtiest and flimsiest of jerry-built shacks, a major hub of manufacturing, milling, slaughtering, and transportation, totally unplanned, boundlessly rapacious and ambitious, was suddenly faced with the necessity of beginning all over again. Housing, sanitation, and civic amenities lagged, as they always do in a nation that places aggrandizement before life itself, but commercial building expanded in prodigious and violently irregular spurts. All office space was wiped out in 1871, but more than 300,000 square feet were opened to use within a year, a feat that was not to be repeated until 1885.[5] The total area of new office construction was to rise to nearly a million square feet for the year 1892, and to pass a million square feet by 1910.

The innovations in building technology came in the large commercial blocks of the core, and it was here that Chicago architects and engineers created the modern steel-framed skyscraper in the marvelously prolific decade of the 1880s. In the twenty-five years between 1885 and 1910 the creative figures of the Chicago school explored the functional and aesthetic possibilities of the new structural system so throughly as to develop an architectural style free at last from historical influences. The underlying principles of the Chicago movement were broad enough to give the architect great latitude in the design of individual buildings, but they were also precise enough to give rise to a coherent body of work clearly expressing the philosophy from which it grew.

The first principle was the most important: a building had to be designed in such a way as to satisfy all the economic, utilitarian, and environmental requirements of the completed functioning structure. Given the space available, the location, and the needs and resources of the owner, the architect's task was to plan the building so as to secure these results to the fullest possible degree and with the utmost economy.

His engineering associate, at the same time, had to design a supporting structure that would embody most efficiently, safely, and durably all the features of the plan and all the uses to which it would be put. For a high building, this structure would most naturally be a steel or reinforced concrete frame carrying all gravity loads and adequately braced against the wind. The last step in the process was the design of an external form that was to grow organically out of the functional demands and the structural solutions, and to express these characteristics in its overall appearance and in the detailed pattern of its elevations.

Out of this organic approach imaginative architects like Root and Sullivan, concerned with aesthetic and emotional possibilities as much as functional, could produce an astonishingly rich vocabulary of forms. The supreme creations of the two men among commercial structures are the Monadnock Building (1889–91) and the Carson Pirie Scott Store (1899, 1903–4, 1906), the sources respectively of the two chief streams of modern architecture. Root's Monadnock is the ancestor of the plastic-sculptural wing of contemporary design, with its emphasis on the mass and fluidity of concrete or masonry bearing walls; Sullivan's store, on the other hand, is the leading example of the clarity and articulation of steel framing, in which the ornament, rich as it is, is carefully subordinated to the precise rectilinear geometry of the underlying cage. Outside the new style of the Chicago school the city's architects were capable of creating impressive designs that fell into every category from the radically new to the strictly traditional. As a matter of fact, the same architect could command both ends of the spectrum: Charles B. Atwood of D. H. Burnham's office, for example, designed the huge but superbly integrated Fine Arts Building for the Columbian Exposition in pure Greco-Roman Imperial style, and in the following year produced the elegant glass tower of the Reliance Building. A transitional work, half in the Chicago commercial style and half in the classical, is the Marshall Field Store of the Burnham office (1902 et seq.), and a thoroughly functional interior presented in a classical exterior is the office and headhouse building of LaSalle Street Station (1901–3), designed by Frost and Granger.[6] At the far right end of the spectrum was the Baroque-domed monument of the Federal Building and Post Office (1896–1905), the work of Henry Ives Cobb, which filled the whole block bounded by Adams, Dearborn, Jackson, and Clark streets before its demolition in 1965.[7] In this eloquent statement of an honorable civic tradition Cobb forced interior functions into the mold of arbitrary exterior form, thus making it impossible to preserve the grand building in the face of changing requirements.

The mechanical equipment of buildings, as we know it today, was introduced chiefly in the period of the Chicago and the Prairie schools. Most of the large buildings were heated by steam generated in their own boiler plants, lighted by gas until it was progressively superseded by electricity after 1887, and provided with water supply and drainage by means of cast-iron pipe, all the plumbing fixtures being centralized in stacks. Both flexible and rigid electrical conduits lay in the future, and so wires had to be imbedded directly in plaster, with the result that they could not be drawn for repair or replacement but had to be removed by breaking out partitions. Radiant heating in the form of coils mounted forty-five feet above the floor appeared in the Oak Lawn Shops of the Chicago and Eastern Illinois Railroad in 1903, but its use in floor slabs was not to become common until after World War II. Ice cooling of air in association with electrically driven ventilating fans was introduced by Adler and Sullivan in the Auditorium Building, but true air conditioning or even uniform air cooling could come only after the fundamental inventions made by Willis Carrier in the early years of the new century. There were many experiments in air cooling around 1910, and various systems began to appear in the hotels of the time. The Kroeschell Brothers Ice Machine Company began to manufacture refrigeration machines using carbon dioxide as a refrigerant in 1897 and installed a 150-ton machine to cool the Pompeian Room of the Congress Hotel in 1906. The cooling of air by water sprays was developed mainly by William G. R. Braemer of Camden, New Jersey, who made a number of installations in Chicago, notably in the Blackstone and the Planters hotels in 1911.

Schools and Universities

There is a great deal of evidence, offered by the surviving structures themselves, that Chicago has always lavished far more architectural and technological imagination on the big commercial buildings than on its housing, schools, and civic institutions.[8] The facilities of public education scarcely existed before the fire of 1871, and the few structures that had been erected were largely obliterated in the catastrophe. Like the commercial and industrial city, the educational plant and the present board of education are products of the post-fire period, although the original founding of the board occurred in 1854. The available records indicate that the city built 169 schools between 1871 and the end of the century, of which 117 were still standing and in use in 1969.[9] The rate of construction increased slightly during the decade follow-ing 1900, when the board placed 72 new schools in service, but it was hardly enough to keep pace with the growth of population. The practice in the design of schools was to establish a given school as a type, its form based mainly on the number of rooms, and to repeat it wherever similar requirements existed. This approach, adopted by the Chicago board in 1879, still persists. Although the practice tends toward repetition of form and inhibition of architectural imagination, it also opens the design and construction of schools to the methods of systems analysis, which the United States is only now beginning to use.

Grade schools in Chicago up to 1910 were nearly always constructed with exterior bearing walls of red brick and with interior bearing partitions for the lower buildings or interior iron framing for the four-story structures. The whole design was extremely simple: narrow windows were placed in separate openings spaced too widely for adequate light; brick arches and trim were in the Romanesque style up to the 1890s and in the Gothic up to the adoption of the classical mode around 1910. The big high schools, among which Lakeview (1897–98) at 4015 North Ashland Boulevard is the handsomest, were generally built with full iron framing and red-brick bearing walls, grouped windows in the Tudor style, and a nicely executed stone trim. This adequate but uninspired program was suddenly revolutionized in 1905 when the board of education appointed Dwight Heald Perkins staff architect. His brief tenure of five years was terminated when the board demanded his resignation on the grounds of incompetence and insubordination—the first charge being a grotesque distortion of the truth, while the second possibly possessed some validity in view of Perkins's independent spirit. By 1910 he had created a modern scholastic architecture and had given Chicago five schools that are unique in the excellence and originality of their design.[10]

Aside from elementary and secondary schools, the foremost works of public building in Chicago before 1910 constitute the initial group of the city's celebrated institutions devoted to the aesthetic and intellectual life. The buildings that house them all stand today, monumental structures revealing at a high level of design the shifting tides of architectural taste near the turn of the century. The need for a big theater to house opera performances, spectacles, public entertainments, and ceremonies led to the construction of the most famous of all these cultural institutions, Adler and Sullivan's Auditorium Building, built in 1887–89 at Michigan Avenue and Congress Street. The Art Institute, founded in 1879, constructed its own museum in 1891–93 on Michigan Avenue at the foot of Adams Street, the Renaissance design of its main block being the work of the Boston architects Shepley, Rutan and Coolidge. The first Public Library to replace the facilities destroyed by the fire came a few years later (1895–97), when the same architects again used Renaissance precedents for the building that faces Michigan Avenue between Randolph and Washington streets. The establishment of the Chicago Symphony Orchestra in 1891 eventually required an auditorium adequate to the acoustical and spatial demands of the audience, a need which was satisfied with the construction of the present Orchestra Hall, designed by D. H. Burnham and Company and erected in 1904 on Michigan Avenue between Adams Street and Jackson Boulevard.[11] Outside the city's core the most impressive individual work of public building is the Walter L. Newberry Library, a Romanesque masterpiece by Henry Ives Cobb, constructed in 1891–92 on Walton Street near North Dearborn.

Of all the educational and cultural institutions that were established in Chicago during the marvelously prolific period that centered around the decade of the nineties, none acquired the international influence and prestige of the University of Chicago. The forerunner of the present university was a Baptist college founded in 1858 on Cottage Grove Avenue between 33rd and 35th streets, where the ten-acre tract for the campus had been donated to the church in the previous year by Senator Stephen A. Douglas. The little college struggled through financial difficulties for thirty years before closing its doors in 1886. Two years later the American Baptist Educational Society approved the establishment of a second college in Chicago and took the step necessary to assure success in such ventures: its officers turned to John D. Rockefeller, a stalwart communicant of the denomination, who pledged $600,000 to the endowment fund on condition that another $400,000 be raised by 1 June 1890. The next step was almost inevitable in Chicago when raising money was the issue: the Baptist Society approached Marshall Field, who gave them land near the site of the Columbian Exposition worth about $125,000. Since piety and wealth have always worked well together in America, the whole enterprise succeeded in ways that all universities have subsequently envied. The wisest act on the part of the trustees (among them Rockefeller, Field, Frederick T. Gates, and Thomas F. Goodspeed) was the election as first president of William Rainey Harper, who was to assume his duties on 1 June 1891. Rockefeller immediately added $1,000,000 to the endowment on the condition that the Baptist Union Theological Seminary in Morgan Park be transferred to the Midway as the university's Divinity School, a proposal that the trustees were happy to act upon.

Construction of the Quadrangles that compose one of the few distinguished campus plans in the United States began on 26 November 1891, under the design and direction of the talented Henry Ives Cobb. The rate of expansion of the physical plant was probably unmatched in the history of American universities: by the end of the century eighteen buildings had been completed; by 1910 another fourteen were added; before the depression year of 1930, thirty-five more were opened for a total of sixty-seven buildings. Before Harper died in 1906 the new university acquired a Medical School

(1898), a School of Education (1901), and a Law School (1902), and had assembled a faculty (among them John Dewey and Thorstein Veblen) to match in intellectual activity the architectural and civic quality of Cobb's plan. The two Quadrangles that constitute this plan occupy the two-block area bounded by 57th and 59th streets on the north and south and by University and Ellis avenues on the east and west. The closing of 58th Street and Greenwood Avenue within these boundaries made it possible for Cobb to treat the entire four-block area as a unit. Each of the main Quadrangles, balanced on either side of a broad central walkway, is in turn divided into two smaller quadrangles which both enclose and are separated by nicely land-scaped courts that focus on a circular walkway at the geometric center of the whole system. The architectural treatment of the numerous buildings is strongly unified through minor variations on the Tudor Gothic style. Cobb designed the first seventeen buildings, and Shepley, Rutan and Coolidge, following the Cobb precedent, were responsible for the next eight.[12]

The excellence of the individual designs, the adaptability of the various buildings to changing requirements, and the harmonious relations of the structures among themselves and to the site plan place the Quadrangles in the front rank of civic art, and thus make them perfectly appropriate to their setting along Olmsted's classic design for the Midway Plaisance. The best tribute to the university group came from Eero Saarinen, who himself made distinguished contributions to the expansion of the campus after World War II.

Wandering n the University of Chicago today, one is amazed at·the beauty achieved by spaces surrounded by buildings all in one discipline and made out of uniform material [limestone]; where each building is being considerate of the next, and each building—through its common material—is aging in the same way . . . . It is significant that on a small court on the University of Chicago campus built between 1894 [sic] and 1930, three different architects, Henry I. Cobb, Shepley, Rutan and Coolidge, and Charles Klauder, built the four sides of the court. All are in the Gothic style, and the court today gives us a beautiful, harmonious visual picture.[13]

Although the University of Chicago came late to the collegiate scene in Chicago, its rapid expansion, unified planning, and attractive location on the Midway, where visitors to the Columbian Exposition could hardly fail to notice the construction of its first halls, quickly gave it a prominence that eclipsed the other universities. The oldest among them is Northwestern, which seemed far from the urban center through-out the nineteenth century, when only the Chicago and North Western Railway pro-vided transportation between the central city and distant Evanston. But Northwestern was a going concern nearly forty years before Rockefeller's lavish gifts made the University of Chicago possible: the older school was chartered in 1851 and acquired its first permanent building in 1855. Old College, in active use today as the home of the university's School of Education, is a timber-frame clapboard-siding work built in the style of the Greek Revival from the design of John Mills Van Osdel, the first architect to practice in Chicago. Northwestern grew slowly and steadily, depending on its early association with the Methodist Church for some of its support, but by the turn of the century it was clearly established as a major secular institution. After Old College came University Hall (1869), the most charming example of the Gothic Revival other than the Water Tower on Michigan Avenue. The continuation of the high standards of design promised by these early buildings suffered a long delay when a succession of nondescript structures in red-brick Romanesque filled out the superb lakeshore setting. The campus was rescued from these architectural doldrums by George W. Maher, who designed two buildings that were erected in 1908–9, one the original Patten Gymnasium, a great work that was needlessly replaced, and the other Swift Hall, which still stands as the center for the biological sciences. The major and drastic expansion of Northwestern University, one that transformed it into a metro-politan institution, was to come with the creation of the Chicago campus in the mid-twenties.[14]

Water and Sanitation

The use of buildings by human occupants in an urban environment, whether for commerce, dwelling, education, or recreation, is impossible unless the city can satisfy the vital need for water. The various supply systems designed to answer this need fall into three broad categories that differ according to the nature of the water source. If the supply flows in relatively small streams at some distance from the city, impound-ment is necessary and water must be conveyed in aqueducts and in conduits which may have to function as pressure siphons where drastic changes in elevation occur. The New York system is the foremost American example of this most costly and elab-orate type, although of course ancient Rome had pioneered in the use of gravity aqueducts. If the city is on a broad waterway with a steady current, water may be drawn off directly into the purifying and pumping facilities, as in Philadelphia or Saint Louis. The third situation arises when the community lies on a large body of fresh water, from which the supply is drawn by gravity flow into a vertical supply tube, and through a tunnel in the bed of the lake to pumping stations on the shore.

In level regions reservoirs often must be high tanks or standpipes so that gravity may insure a regular flow to individual consumers. Chicago falls in the third category, and in this respect it is not only the most fortunately located of all the great cities of the world, but has done more than any other to exploit its natural hydraulic advantages.

The frontier town began to draw on the lake for its water supply in 1842, when the Chicago Hydraulic Company built a steam-driven pumping plant (its reciprocating engine rated at twenty-five horsepower) and two elevated wooden tanks at the foot of Lake Street and laid a system of wooden mains under some of the downtown streets.[15] An adequate water supply was the first necessity to be recognized as the responsibility of public bodies, and Chicago waited only ten years to replace the private installation with a municipal plant. The first was built in 1852–54 at the foot of Chicago Avenue. It included an intake crib situated six hundred feet offshore to reach pure water, since the city then discharged its sewage into the lake, a storage tank, and a distribution system of cast-iron water mains. The original pumping capacity was about 2,000,000 gallons per day, but this was increased to 3,000,000 gallons within three years and to 6,400,000 in 1863, when the present system of distant intakes was inaugurated. In that year the city engineer, Ellis S. Chesbrough, proposed that the city locate the intake crib of its new plant two miles from the shore on the line of Chicago Avenue (800N) to escape the increasing pollution along the margins of the lake. The crib of masonry and timber construction and the associated brick-lined tunnel were built in 1864–66 but were not opened to service until March of the following year. The masonry water tower and pumping plant, characterized by a delightfully exuberant medieval design, were constructed in 1868–69 at the intersection of Michigan and Chicago avenues, where they stand today as the city's only monuments to its pre-fire past. Brick-lined water tunnels gave way to concrete in 1900, and electrically operated pumps superseded the steam-driven forms at about the same time, but the system contained no filtration plants until 1942, the water being subjected only to settlement and chlorination. The initial installation was steadily expanded over the years as Chicago built up the largest water supply system in the world and the first to exceed the hydraulic capacity of imperial Rome.[16]

Sanitation had always been a problem for every city, but in the nineteenth century it reached disastrous proportions as both the total urban population and the population density expanded at an exponential rate. The trouble arose mainly from the contamination of the domestic water supply by pathogenic organisms associated with human wastes, and as a consequence typhoid and cholera epidemics grew in frequency and virulence in the major cities of Europe and America. The nature of the problem was at last understood through the pioneer investigations of Henle, Pasteur, and Koch, but the technological solution was delayed by the limited capacity of natural waterways to dilute the sewage, oxidize it, and carry it off to the sea and by the absence of municipal institutions that could make use of the new technical resources. In Chicago the situation was acute because its natural water supply, which also served as the repository of its sewage, has no currents that can carry away the accumulated pollution. The first step in coping with the problem was typical of American municipalities, where political indifference is always profitable to those who hold power: a citizens' association was established in 1880 to demand the action that the municipal government failed to provide. The specific occasion that finally brought results was a flood in the Des Plaines River in the summer of 1885. Although it was a minor inundation, it caused the floodwater to back up through the Illinois-Michigan Canal into the South Branch of the Chicago River, which was laden with effluent from the stockyards, and thence into Lake Michigan and the city water supply.

The threat of a disastrous epidemic was enough to induce the city council to appoint a committee in the fall of 1885 to inquire into the possibility of remedies. This committee, in its report of the following January, proposed the creation of a Drainage and Water Supply Commission, which was immediately established by Mayor Carter H. Harrison.[17] The report that the commission issued in January 1887 was staggering in the magnitude and far-reaching consequences of its recommendations. The problem faced by nearly all cities on the shores of the Great Lakes is that they lie on the rims of huge basins, of which most of the area is occupied by the lakes themselves, so that the direction of flow in the various drainage regions must inevitably be toward these large and relatively static bodies of water. Chicago alone enjoyed a topographic setting that made it possible to escape from the trap, as the promoters of the Illinois-Michigan Canal had seen as early as 1809.[18] Rudolph Hering and his fellow commissioners accordingly recommended, first, that the city dig a waterway of generous cross-sectional area from the Chicago River to the Des Plaines River through the limestone ridge separating the Mississippi and the Lake Michigan drainage regions and, second, that it establish a sanitary district to be directed by a public body responsible for maintaining adequate standards of sanitation in the metropolitan area. On the basis of the commission's report the state legislature (known as the general assembly in Illinois) followed the usual agonizing procedure of appointing another committee to study the question, to hold hearings on the matter in the Chicago region, and to report a bill. The deliberations in this instance proved immensely valuable, for they laid the foundations of an enterprise that was eventually to create the largest and most effective sewage treatment system in the world.

The bill that was submitted to the legislature in February 1889 was without precedent at the time and thus proved to be one of those model works of legislation on which major political institutions are established. The act combined in a single agency, known as the Chicago Sanitary District, the necessary authority to create and operate both drainage and water supply systems; it made the district an independent body presumably beyond politics by granting the popularly elected trustees the authority to levy and collect taxes and to administer the physical plant free of political interference. Finally, the legislative committee drew up the bill so expertly that it has withstood all lawsuits aimed at testing its constitutionality. After the turn of the century the district expanded into a metropolitan body independent of municipal agencies and extending far beyond the city's jurisdiction. The provision of freedom from political interference, however, turned out to be an ideal impossible to attain: any elected body in or associated with Chicago is likely to be subject to corruption, and with elected trustees the Sanitary District proved to be no exception.[19]

The first and most gigantic single step in carrying out this grand program was the construction of the Sanitary and Ship Canal. Planning for the waterway that unites Lake Michigan with the Des Plaines River began in 1890, less than a year after the district was established, and was carried to the point where initial contracts could be let in about two years (fig. 1). Construction began on 3 September 1892 and was completed for the admission of water on 16 January 1900, the result being a waterway unique not only for its reversal of a natural river but also for its multipurpose civic character. The primary aim was to prevent the contamination of the municipal water supply as a consequence of raw sewage flowing into the lake; the second was to carry surface drainage and waste away from the city and into the Illinois River; the third, to maintain clean beaches and shore waters for recreational purposes; and the fourth, to provide a commercial waterway connecting the Chicago and Illinois rivers via the Des Plaines which would replace the outmoded Illinois-Michigan Canal. The new canal thus sprang from moral as well as economic considerations, and its most dramatic consequence was an immediate and drastic reduction in the death rate from diseases caused by waterborne organisms. None of these ends could be realized, of course, without a parallel and continuing construction of underground sewers.[20]

Parks and Forests

Chicago not only was fortunate in possessing an inexhaustible supply of water, it also enjoyed access to an unlimited area of land, which—true to the spirit of the

West—it proceeded to devour in reckless fashion. When the city received its charter in 1837 it adopted the phrase *Urbs in horto* as its motto, for the expression exactly described the situation at the time: on one side of the rectangular area lay the lake, while on the other three stretched endless vistas of trees, meadowland, and flowers. This proximity to nature, manifested in the presence of sheer space bounded by the sky and the horizon, made the city indifferent to open space within its own limits, so that by the time of the Civil War, with a population of well over 100,000, it had only six little parks, on an average smaller in size than a city square. The original one of this group covered the site of the future Public Library, on Michigan Avenue between Randolph and Washington streets. Even more disgraceful was the condition of the lakefront: from the river south it had been preempted by the steel industry and by the Illinois Central Railroad, whose tracks were carried along the central area of the city on a timber trestle about two hundred feet offshore; at the mouth of the river stood warehouses and docks, and above it stretched a sandy waste of scrub oak, juniper, and dune grass.

The first step in the direction of a decent park system was the city's acquisition in 1864 of the North Side shoreland and an adjoining cemetery. These were partially cleared, drained, and landscaped, as far as a $10,000 appropriation would stretch, and designated Lake Park. This first lakefront park, extending for a mile from North Avenue (1600N) to Fullerton Avenue (2400N), was renamed Lincoln Park after the assassination of President Abraham Lincoln in April 1865. It was a modest beginning, but four years later, with the establishment of the park district system of Chicago after the enabling act passed by the general assembly on 27 February 1869, the city, by itself and in cooperation with its southern neighbor Hyde Park, initiated what proved for a time to be the foremost program of park and boulevard development in the country. In the cooperative program with Hyde Park, Frederick Law Olmsted was engaged as the chief landscape designer. This ambitious undertaking rapidly achieved results, so that by 1880 Chicago was second only to Philadelphia in the ratio of park area to population. These first parks, however, were mainly landscaped areas lacking recreational facilities for either adults or children. To remedy this failure the city council created the Special Park Commission in 1899, appointed Dwight H. Perkins, Chicago's most energetic and effective conservationist, as commissioner, and specified that the body was to develop and act upon a systematic plan for meeting the city's space and recreational needs, with the emphasis on creating playgrounds for children, beaches, pools, public baths, and parkways. This plan was supplemented by a parallel cooperative program inaugurated by the Outer Belt Commission, established by the Cook County Board in 1903.

With the zealous and idealistic Perkins in a key administrative position, and with the creative talents of Olmsted, Jensen, and Cleveland available for landscape design, the qualitative results of all these efforts were considerable—enough for Frank Lloyd Wright to praise Jensen and Chicago "for our wonderful park system; a system that together with our small playgrounds is one of the finest civic urban features of the world; a recreation ground beyond compare. No small-hearted city, no city except Chicago could have established it or would have made the sacrifices necessary to maintain it."[21] By 1900 the large parks included not only the usual wooded areas, shrubs, meadows, picnic grounds, walks, and drives, but a full complement of lagoons for boating, flower gardens, baseball diamonds, golf links, tennis courts, and various indoor recreational facilities as well. The small neighborhood parks—of which there were too few—were well equipped with play apparatus, sandlots, shelters, wading pools, running tracks, and in some cases, tobogganing and skating areas. The crown pieces of the big parks were the zoo and aquarium in Lincoln Park and the conservatory in Garfield Park.[22]

In the heroic spirit that characterized the period from 1869 to 1910 the several park districts were thus engaged in numerous projects involving civic enterprise and design on a very high level. The area comprehended by Lincoln Park offered the greatest extent of open land, and it was here that the city first concentrated its energies on the task of creating parks out of wild shoreland. For nearly forty years after its establishment in 1865 the Lincoln district was occupied with clearing and landscaping the area it originally possessed and building recreational structures with their associated facilities. Because of the rapidly increasing value of contiguous land, the district was unable to expand its area by purchasing property along the landward boundaries of the park; its only alternatives, as a consequence, were to reclaim marshland by drainage and to increase acreage by filling the lake along the shore. By 1910 the district had added 294 acres to the park by filling in a large rectangular area extending at a maximum 1,800 feet outward from the shore and more than a mile north and south from Fullerton (2400N) to Belmont Avenue (3200N). This operation included the construction of a yacht harbor at Diversey Avenue and the dredging of the associated narrow lagoon that extends southward from this harbor for about three-quarters of a mile. The Lincoln Park commissioners proposed to continue the program to the north city limits, thus anticipating Burnham's scheme in the Chicago Plan of 1909.[23] The process of filling, reclamation, and landscaping was accompanied by an equally ambitious program of beach improvement and new construction, the latter embracing not only numerous recreational buildings but also two of the city's major cultural institutions, the Chicago Academy of Sciences and the Lincoln Park Zoological

Garden. The ruling mediocrity of the park's architectural design is relieved by two buildings from the hand of Dwight Perkins: the refectory known as Cafe Brauer (1907–8), and the Lion House at the zoo (1912), for which Perkins received the gold medal of the American Institute of Architects.[24]

The West Park District, which was the second of the park systems to be established under the legislation of 27 February 1869, was to achieve the highest level of landscape art after the appointment of Jens Jensen as landscape architect. The general plan for the location and size of the big parks in the system was completed shortly after the fire, and the formal design of the specific parks (Douglas, Garfield, and Humboldt) was the work of William Le Baron Jenney, who probably undertook the task shortly after his return from the University of Michigan in 1876. The undistinguished landscaping was poorly executed, and the parks deteriorated steadily during the next decade. It was a situation that offered immense opportunities and formidable challenges to the man who possessed the courage to face municipal cynicism and corruption in Chicago. The necessary combination of moral character and creative imagination quietly appeared one day in the person of the most remarkable man in the history of American landscape art. Jens Jensen came to Chicago from his native Denmark and began his thirty-four-year association with the Chicago parks as a common gardener for the West Park District. He rose to the position of superintendent of Humboldt Park in a few years, but lost it in 1900 as a consequence of the principle that regards park superintendencies as political plums to be awarded to the faithful servants of the machine, whatever their incompetence and dishonesty. Jensen was deeply impressed by the floral beauties of the prairie, which became the basis of his highly personal romantic-naturalistic art. His great opportunity came in 1905, when Bernard A. Eckhart, founder of the Eckhart Milling Company and a man of genuine civic vision, was appointed chairman of the West Park Commission. His most important act was to appoint Jensen to the dual position of superintendent and chief landscape architect of the entire district. Humboldt was the first park to exhibit the fruits not only of Jensen's talents but of the architect Hugh Garden's as well, and was succeeded in the fourteen years following Jensen's appointment by three more masterpieces, Douglas, Garfield, and Columbus, of which the last is one of his wholly new creations.[25]

In addition to its landscaped areas and its recreational facilities, the West Park District embraced the north half of the most extensive boulevard system in Chicago and also a number of specialized structures associated with botanical exhibits. Humboldt Park is full of architectural gems by Hugh Garden—entrance pylons, light standards, and above all, the pavilion and boathouse of 1907 that stands between the two rowing ponds. Garfield Park is distinguished by one of the largest groups of botanical conservatories in the United States; the five interconnected structures were designed by Hitchings and Company of New York City and built in 1905–7 to take the place of smaller conservatories in the individual parks. The most spacious enclosure of this complex is the Palm House, constructed as a segmental vault forming a somewhat flattened Gothic arch in cross section. The armature of thin bars and purlins that carries the glass is in turn supported by a series of transverse steel ribs, the whole envelope representing a handsome and airy variation on the form originally developed in 1836 by Joseph Paxton and Decimus Burton for the Great Conservatory at Chatsworth, England.[26]

The South Park District, established in 1869 like Lincoln Park and West Park, contains the two best-known parks in the Chicago system, Grant and Jackson, the former carefully preserved as the city's showpiece, the latter outrageously disfigured by irresponsible maintenance and the vandalism of traffic engineers. Jackson was part of the extensive park and boulevard system planned and built cooperatively by Chicago and Hyde Park, with the landscape and boulevard design under the charge of Frederick Law Olmsted and Horace Cleveland. The planning of the system began in 1869, the same year the indefatigable Olmsted laid out the plan for the suburban community of Riverside, and construction on various parts of the program was initiated two years later. The marshy site of Jackson Park involved difficult problems of drainage, impoundment, and dredging for the lagoons, so that although the first operations were undertaken in 1874, the area was little improved by the time of the Columbian Exposition in 1893. The park was not finally completed until about 1905, when this masterpiece of Olmsted's romantic style began to emerge into something like the mature beauty of its lagoons, woodlands, meadows, and islands. The subsequent treatment of the park is one of the most revolting examples of the destructive rage that has become an inherent characteristic of the American economic system.

Grant Park, symmetrically balanced in its stiff axial formality, is the classical antithesis to the romantic Jackson, but for the first thirty years of its history it was little more than bare fill and grass. Except for the Illinois Central trestle, which the city had persuaded the railroad to build in order to acquire shore protection without cost to the taxpayer, the site was open water until 1871, when the municipal officers found that they could simultaneously create a downtown lakefront park and dispose of the debris left from the fire by using it to fill in the strip of dirty water between the railroad line and the shore. This base of rubble and junk was then steadily enlarged with sand and clay dredged from the river and the outer harbor, deposited in accumulating basins by scows, and finally transferred to the park site by hydraulic dredges, all at a unit cost of ten cents per cubic yard. The remainder of the area, extending in width at the maximum from the original shore along Michigan Avenue to the outer edge of the Illinois Central yards above Randolph Street, was filled out with spoil taken from excavations for new buildings, at no cost whatsoever to the city. In this way 180 acres were reclaimed up to the turn of the century, and the entire area of 202 acres was completed by 1909. The landscaping came after 1910, much of it dating from the New Deal's public works program of the 1930s. The importance of Grant Park to the civic design of Chicago was first fully appreciated by Daniel Burnham, who regarded it as the primary focus of any plan for the urban core as early as 1896.[27]

Yet in spite of all this activity in the creation of parks and beaches, the initial impetus was spending itself in the early years of the new century, so that the quantitative achievement was discouraging. By 1909 Chicago had dropped to seventh place in park area per unit of population, with an average of one acre of park for 510 residents as against the planners' and recreationists' recommendation of one acre for 100 persons. Worse than the low average was the ominous fact that parks were not where they were needed: in the Stockyards area and other slums the ratio was an acre to 5,000 persons—foreshadowing Chicago's continuing failure to provide decent living and neighborhood conditions for its racial and economic ghettos. Compared with New York, however, the city was doing rather well: by 1908 the various metropolitan park boards were spending a total of $6,000,000 per annum, for a per capita expenditure of $1.43, against a comparable figure of $0.83 for New York. The entire system was organized in an antiquated and cumbersome way in which jurisdiction was divided among eleven separate districts, although about 90 percent of the park area was held by the three largest and oldest districts. In 1910 the total acreage was about 4,600, for a population somewhat above 2,000,000. The chief scandal of the time was the failure of the city to exploit the unparalleled scenic and recreational potential of the lakefront. Except for Jackson Park, interrupted stretches of lower Lincoln Park, and raw, unfinished Grant Park, it was an asset that the city had yet to discover, as an anonymous French visitor was quoted as saying in 1902.[28]

If Chicago had had to depend on its internal parks alone for nonaquatic recreational activities, it would soon have had one of the worst records of all major American cities in this respect. The internal area, however, was supplemented by the beach system and eventually eclipsed by the immense woodland areas of the Forest Preserve District. The city was fortunate in having the potential of an outer park system readily available in the unbroken bands of forest that extended along the main waterways from the moraine and lake terrace region of Glencoe at the Cook-Lake county line southward to the Calumet rivers and the moraine along the future course of the Calumet-Sag Channel (figs. 1, 2).[29] The idea of preserving these wooded areas permanently for recreational purposes must be attributed to a number of people active around the turn of the century, among whom Jens Jensen and Dwight Perkins were the leaders. Jensen made a personal survey of the woodlands around Chicago in 1901–2, taking many photographs along the way, and gave an illustrated lecture at the Chicago Academy of Sciences in 1902 urging the preservation of these lands for public uses. The lecture, which brought the proposal wide attention and influential backing, led to Jensen's being appointed a member of the Metropolitan Park Commission, the public body that was most effective in persuading the Illinois General Assembly to pass the bill that authorized the establishment of the Forest Preserve District of Chicago and Cook County. Perkins played an equally valuable role in this activity. He was one of the group that in 1904 founded the Prairie Club, which quickly became the most potent private organization in lobbying for the creation of the forest preserves. The assembly acted in 1909, and passed the far-sighted legislation that authorized the establishment of forest preserve districts in all Illinois counties. Under this authorization a majority of the voters in the special county election of 1910 approved the specific proposal to establish the Cook County Forest Preserve Commission, but because of a constitutional technicality, the original act was nullified in the courts. Thus the whole tedious process had to be repeated; the second effort, however, which was greatly helped by the lobbying of the newly created Chicago Plan Commission, eventually brought success.[30]

NOTES TO CHAPTER 1

1. For the growth of Chicago's population and area, see table 1 (all tables are at the end of the text).
2. For these waterways, see chapter 2.
3. Blue Island is a suburban community off the southwest corner of Chicago along the line of 130th Street. It stands clear of the surrounding flatland on an eminence that is roughly rectangular, though now much cut away along the flanks by railway lines and yards. The second name is preserved only in Stony Island Avenue, a broad north-south thoroughfare in the southeast area of the city. Its original raised elevation was long ago leveled for streets, buildings, and rail lines.
4. The direction of flow in the entire waterway system of Chicago was reversed through an immense program of canal construction (1891–1922); see pp. 18, 27–28, 247.
5. For the expansion of office space in Chicago, see table 2; for the number of dwelling

MORTON COLLEGE LRC
CICERO, ILLINOIS

units constructed annually, table 3; for the dollar value of new construction by year, table 4.

6. For further discussion of LaSalle Street Station and its participating railroads, see pp. 46–47.

7. The present Federal Center took the place of this building.

8. As a matter of fact, the high standards of architectural and structural design exhibited by the Chicago school were applied mainly to office buildings and hotels, which enjoyed the maximum capital investment. In other buildings careless design and cheap construction invited various kinds of disaster that the enforcers of the city building code and its associated system of inspection seemed unable or unwilling to prevent. The most appalling of these catastrophes for loss of life was the Iroquois Theater fire of 30 December 1903. During the matinee performance of *Mr. Bluebeard* a muslin hanging caught fire, producing at first only a minor blaze, but the set began to burn, and smoke and flame billowed out over the orchestra. The asbestos curtain was lowered, but the mechanism failed, leaving the curtain fixed at the halfway position. The inevitable panic resulted in the death of 596 persons in fifteen minutes. The investigation revealed that although rather little of the theater burned, there was a very high loss of life from suffocation, smoke inhalation, and crushing, these in turn the consequences of an insufficient number of exits for the capacity of the house and of the fact that some exit doors were inoperable from long disuse.

9. For the inventory of Chicago schools, see table 5.

10. The schools designed by Dwight Perkins, in chronological order, are the following:

    Albert G. Lane Technical High School, Division Street and Sedgewick Avenue, 1906–8. (The board of education *Annual Reports* are dated by academic years; consequently, the dates I have given indicate that the construction of the school was begun in the academic year 1906–7 and completed in 1908–9.) This school was replaced by the present building on Addison Street in 1934.

    James H. Bowen High School, 89th Street and Manistee Avenue, 1908–9.

    Carl Schurz High School, Addison Street and Milwaukee Avenue, 1908–9.

    Lyman Trumbull Elementary School, Foster Avenue and Ashland Boulevard, 1908–9.

    Grover Cleveland Elementary School, Byron Street and Albany Avenue, 1909–10.

    Project, commercial high school, Harrison Street and Plymouth Court, 1908–9. If it had been built, this would have been the first inner-city skyscraper public school, since the projected height was fifteen stories. The present Jones Commercial High School represents the contemporary realization of Perkins's novel proposal.

11. On the completion of the Michigan Avenue–Grant Park "cultural center," see pp. 186–205.

12. Buildings and architects of the University of Chicago Quadrangles, 1892–1910, arranged by designers and dates of completion:

    I. South Quadrangle
        1892, Henry Ives Cobb: Blake, Cobb, Gates, Goodspeed
        1893, Henry Ives Cobb: Beecher, Foster, Kelly, Walker Museum
        1896, Henry Ives Cobb: Haskell Museum
        1899, Henry Ives Cobb: Green
        1904, Shepley, Rutan and Coolidge: Law School

    II. North Quadrangle
        1893, Henry Ives Cobb: Snell
        1894, Henry Ives Cobb: Kent, Ryerson

1897, Henry Ives Cobb: Anatomy, Botany, Culver, Zoology
1903, Shepley, Rutan and Coolidge: Hutchinson, Mandel, Mitchell Tower, Reynolds
(for post-1910 buildings, see pp. 222–26).
13. Quoted in Michael Sorkin, "The Grey City," *Chicago Maroon*, 8 March 1968, p. 2.
14. For the prominent buildings of Northwestern University erected after 1910, see pp.
226–29.
   The smaller colleges and universities of Chicago were all established by 1910. Chief
among them are the two Roman Catholic universities: Loyola, on Sheridan Road in
the area of the Devon Avenue–Broadway intersection, was founded in 1870, and its
first building on the Sheridan campus, Loyola Academy, was opened in 1909; DePaul,
centered at Webster and Seminary avenues on the North Side, began instruction as
Saint Vincent's College in 1898 and was chartered as a university in 1907. The two predecessors of Illinois Institute of Technology, Armour Institute and Lewis Institute, were
founded in 1893 and 1896.
15. The foot of Lake Street was then at Michigan Avenue, but until the Illinois Central
Railroad and the city began the long process of filling along the shore, the lateral street
terminated at the water's edge.
16. The physical plant of the Chicago water system includes four separate parts, other than
distribution mains: intake cribs, pumping stations, storage tanks, and connecting tunnels.
Because of the great size of the system, the water department eventually divided its
operations into three districts designated as north, central, and south. The following
outline of stages in expansion to 1910 comprehends cribs, pumps, and tunnels, arranged
chronologically by type of facility.
   I. Intake cribs
      1. Chicago Avenue, 1867; timber construction; abandoned and demolished. Central
District.
      2. Four-Mile, 1892; timber and masonry construction; standby service for summer
use only. Central District.
      3. 68th Street, 1894; timber and masonry construction; not in service. South District.
      4. Carter H. Harrison, off Chicago Avenue, 1900; timber and masonry construction;
not in service. Central District.
   II. Water tunnels
      1. Chicago Avenue, 1867. Length 2 miles; depth 60 feet below lake level; interior
diameter 5 feet; brick-lined. Replaced.
      2. Second Chicago Avenue and extensions, 1874. Length 6 miles; interior diameter
7 feet; brick-lined.
      3. Lake View, 1892. Length 2 miles; interior diameter 6 feet; brick-lined. Not in
service.
      4. Four-Mile, 1892. Length 6.45 miles; interior diameter 6 and 8 feet; brick-lined.
Standby service.
      5. Northeast, 1900. Length 2.66 miles; interior diameter 10 feet; concrete-lined.
Not in service.
      6. Chicago Avenue Pumping Station Land, 1904. Length 0.13 mile; interior diameter
6 feet; concrete-lined.
      7. Polk Street Land, 1907. Length 1.42 miles; interior diameter 7 feet; concrete-lined.
Standby service.
      8. Blue Island Avenue Land, 1909. Length 3.1 miles; interior diameter 8 feet;
concrete-lined. Not in service.
(The table indicates that most of the tunnels built before 1900 were replaced by

others built in the decade of 1900–1910, and these in turn were largely replaced by still newer facilities.)

III. Pumping stations built up to 1910
  1. Chicago Avenue, original 1854, replaced 1869. Original steam-driven reciprocating pumps replaced by electrically operated centrifugal pumps in 1903. Capacity of six pumps 260 million gallons per day (hereafter abbreviated mgd).
  2. 22nd Street, 1876. Original steam reciprocating pumps replaced by electrical centrifugal pumps in 1912. Retired from service in 1959.
  3. Harrison Street (later Cermak), 1889. Original steam reciprocating pumps converted to electrical centrifugal pumps in 1936.
  4. Lake View, 1889. Steam-operated.
  5. 68th Street, 1889. Original steam reciprocating pumps later converted to electrical centrifugal pumps. Capacity of five pumps 250 mgd.
  6. Central Park Avenue, 1900. Steam-driven reciprocating pumps. Capacity of five pumps 360 mgd.
  7. Springfield Avenue, 1901. Steam-driven reciprocating pumps. Capacity of five pumps 360 mgd. (For water facilities built after 1910, see pp. 248–49, 291–92.)

17. The Carter H. Harrisons, father and son, were elected to five terms as mayor of the city. The commission appointed by the elder Harrison included Rudolph Hering as chief engineer and Samuel G. Artingstall and Benizette Williams as consultants.

18. For the construction of this canal, see pp. 30–31; for the geological and topographical setting, pp. 3–6.

19. The official name of the district was eventually changed to the Metropolitan Sanitary District of Greater Chicago to reflect its expanded status. The city's Department of Water and Sewers is independent of the district but must work so closely with it as to constitute its municipal arm in matters of planning, design, and construction. The original area of the sanitary district covered the central area of Chicago and a few of the western suburbs, the boundaries being Devon Avenue (6400N), Harlem Avenue (7200W), 87th Street (S), and the lake. This area was expanded in 1903 to include the rest of the city and the northern suburbs up to and including Northbrook and Glencoe.

20. The date of 16 January 1900 marked the opening of the control gates in the South Side of Chicago that allowed the Chicago River to flow into the canal, thus reversing its natural flow into the lake. Final completion of all facilities came in 1901.

Physical data on the construction and dimensions of the canal:

Maximum number of men engaged in construction	8,500
Volume of excavation	41,819,000 cu. yds.
Earth	29,558,000 cu. yds.
Rock (dolomite)	12,261,000 cu. yds.
Length of canal	28 miles
Depth	24 feet
Width	160–220 feet
Gradient, Chicago to Lockport, mean	1 ft. in 30,000 ft.
Minimum	1 ft. in 40,000 ft.
Maximum	1 ft. in 20,000 ft.
Capacity	20,000 cu. ft. per sec.
Rate of flow	1.5 miles per hour
Factor of dilution (fixed by act of 1889)	3.3 cu. ft. per sec. for each 1,000 persons
Cost	$60,000,000

The machines and techniques of excavation developed for the Chicago project demonstrated the feasibility of digging the Panama Canal (1906–14).

The primary interceptor-sewer system was constructed in 1900–1907, with the main trunks extending chiefly along the waterways.

21. Frederick Gutheim, ed., *Frank Lloyd Wright on Architecture*; quoted in Leonard Eaton, *Landscape Artist in America* (Chicago: University of Chicago Press, 1964), p. 52.

22. For details of these institutions, see under the individual parks, pp. 20–22, 28–29.

23. The lakefill program was carried out in two stages: the first, begun in 1893, involved the construction of a rubble seawall close to the shore from Burton Place (1500N) to Fullerton Avenue (2400N), behind which earth and rock were placed to an area of 60 acres; the second, undertaken in 1906, was accomplished by more elaborate techniques which added 234 acres between Fullerton and Belmont (3200N). The method required the construction, first, of a rock-filled, timber-walled groin 1,800 feet outward into the water along the line of Fullerton Avenue, and second, a rubble-stone dike running roughly parallel to the shore from the outer end of the groin northward and westward for 6,500 feet. The rubble was composed of blocks of limestone taken from the spoil banks left after the excavation for the Sanitary and Ship Canal. The dike had the conventional trapezoidal section with a base width of 140 feet. The enclosed rectangular area within the groin and the dikes was filled with sand and clay dredged from the lake bottom, the process representing the pioneer phase of the highly mechanized technique by which the tremendous Burnham Park fill was made in the 1920s (see pp. 195–96). The engineer in charge of the Lincoln Park project was Arthur S. Lewis.

24. Chronology of the chief Lincoln Park improvements to 1910:

Refectory Building, 1882 (superseded by Cafe Brauer).

Conservatory, Stockton Drive near Fullerton Avenue, 1892. Joseph Lyman Silsbee, architect. Addition, 1904; renovation, 1925.

Chicago Academy of Sciences, Clark Street at the foot of Ogden Avenue, 1893–94. Patton and Fisher, architects.

Beach improvement, North Avenue (1600N) to Newport Avenue (3432N), 1891–99.

Lincoln Park Zoological Garden, between Stockton and Cannon drives south of Fullerton Avenue, 1868 et seq. Existing structures:

Animal House I, 1888
Monkey House I, 1892
Animal House II, 1902
Bird House, 1904
Lion House, 1912

The so-called Animal Houses now shelter a variety of small mammals, and the inhabitants of the Lion House include several species of Fissipeda other than lions. The zoo has been expanded repeatedly since 1912, some of the buildings changing in usage along the way (see p. 208).

25. Jensen and Eckhart are two examples among many of how profoundly indebted Chicago is to the German and Scandinavian people who settled in the city during the nineteenth and early twentieth centuries. Humboldt Park is a fitting memorial to the tradition they established, since it was named by the city's German community after the great naturalist and geographer who flourished in the long and turbulent period that stretched from the French Revolution to the age of Louis Napoleon. But the tradition that named parks after scientists and adorned them with statues of poets left a legacy that Chicago has used most shabbily.

26. In addition to the Palm House, the conservatory group of Garfield Park originally included the Aquatic, Conifer, New Holland, Show, and Economic houses, the last reserved for plants with an economic value, such as edible fruits, but the first four have changed in function over the years and are now designated as the Fernery, Aroid House, Cactus House, and Horticultural Hall. The dimensions of the Palm House are 85 × 250 feet in plan and 60 feet in overall height (50 feet clear from the springing to the crown). The main structural ribs of this enclosure have the curious distinction of being the deepest and longest sections to be cold-bent from mill-rolled beams. The structural systems of the smaller houses represent a variety of steel rib and truss frames. (For the boulevard system of the West Park District, see pp. 32, 53.)
27. The acreage given for Grant Park does not include the southward extension required for the Field Museum, Shedd Aquarium, and Adler Planetarium (see pp. 186–205). The South Park District also includes a boulevard system; see pp. 32, 53.
28. The multidistrict park system survived until the unification of 1934. The eleven districts of 1910 included the big three, namely, South Park, West Park, and Lincoln Park, the Special Park Commission, and seven small districts designated as Calumet, Fernwood, Irving Park, North Shore, Northwest, Ridge, and Ridge Avenue. The numbers, locations, names, and areas of the major parks have changed little since 1910, although the city's population has increased about 75 percent since that date. The chief parks in the three large districts in 1910, with acreage, were the following:

    South Park District: Bessemer, Calumet, Gage, Grant, Hamilton, Jackson, Marquette, McKinley, Ogden, Palmer, Sherman, Washington, and eleven small parks and squares. Total area 2,495 acres.

    West Park District: Columbus, Douglas, Garfield, Humboldt, Union, and ten small parks. Total area 1,035 acres.

    Lincoln Park District: Lincoln Park and various small parks. Total area 700 acres. (This district enjoyed the greatest increase in later years through successive northward extensions of Lincoln Park.)

    Grand total area of the three districts, 4,230 acres. The distribution of acreage corresponded to the distribution of population in 1910, which was concentrated on the South Side.
29. The chief belts of forest land, in order from north to south, are the following: moraines and terraces around Lake-Cook and Green Bay roads; Skokie River (dammed at Willow Road in Winnetka to form Skokie Lagoons); North Branch of the Chicago River extending into the northwest corner of the city at Caldwell Road and Devon Avenue; Des Plaines River, from the Cook-Lake county line south to below Riverside; on roughly east-west lines along the Calumet rivers and their tributaries; east and west along Calumet-Sag Channel; scattered areas in Chicago and the suburbs, chiefly along Flag and Stone creeks west of the city.
30. For the establishment of the permanent Forest Preserve District and its program, see pp. 211–13.

2. The Transportation Network

Waterways

In the first century of its existence Chicago built up the greatest multilayered network of transportation arteries in the world. Its geographical location with respect to the nation as a whole and to the continent, its site at the south end of Lake Michigan, the level land that stretched around it for hundreds of miles—these virtually guaranteed its role as the hub of the North American system of waterways, highways, railroads, and airlines. Water was there by natural circumstance from the very beginning, and it was the waterway system that provided the first avenues of commerce. Eastward lay the access to the sea, through four of the five Great Lakes and the Saint Lawrence River, although the waterways were rendered impassable by ice for the four and one-half months from the beginning of December to mid-April. The extensive rapids of the Saint Lawrence and the immense cataract of the Niagara had to be bypassed by canals, but British and Canadian builders had placed these in operation before Chicago emerged as a city. Sailing vessels were regularly carrying cargo on the lakes from the beginning of urban development, and the schooner *Dean Richmond* inaugurated Chicago's history as an international port in 1856 when it made the eighty-day voyage to Liverpool with a cargo of wheat. In the following year the *Madeira Pet* completed the first return voyage, but regularly scheduled service lay nearly eighty years in the future. The total tonnage expanded at an extremely rapid rate with the establishment and growth of the iron, steel, and petroleum industries, and of lumbering, agriculture, and mining, all of which require bulk-cargo shipment of a kind that can be most economically provided by the lake freighters. Passenger service came shortly after freight shipping, and up to 1930 the docks of the Chicago River and Navy Pier were lined with passenger-carrying as well as cargo vessels.

The early entrepreneurs of the city were quick to see that a through water route to the Mississippi River was entirely feasible even with the modest resources of the newly founded state, since the construction of the necessary canal could be simplified by excavating parallel to the Des Plaines River, thus avoiding the low and relatively narrow limestone divide that separates the South Branch of the Chicago River from the Des Plaines.[1] The canal would thus unite the lake with the Mississippi and supplement the natural waterway system formed by the Calumet River and the two branches of the Chicago. Various federal acts of the 1820s empowered the state of Illinois to acquire land, appropriate the necessary funds, establish a canal commission, and eventually proceed with construction. Excavation of the Illinois-Michigan Canal and a number of feeders began in 1836, and the completed waterway was opened to use twelve years later. The early canal was much longer than the Sanitary and Ship Canal that succeeded it, since the former extended from near 26th Street and Western Avenue in Chicago to a confluence with the Illinois River at La Salle, Illinois, for a total length of ninety-seven miles. The completion in 1852 of the Illinois-Mississippi Canal, which united the Illinois River at La Salle with the Mississippi River at Rock Island, gave Chicago two water routes between the lake and the vast Mississippi-Ohio-Missouri system. These early canals suffered acutely from the competition of the Chicago and Rock Island and the Chicago and Alton railroads, but they continued to play a minor role as commercial arteries until they were entirely superseded by the present Illinois Waterway, a continuous stream composed of the Chicago Sanitary and Ship Canal and the canalized Des Plaines and Illinois rivers. The location of the various waterways, along with the railroad lines, was the prime determinant in the distribution of heavy industry, lumber and coal yards, and bulk-commodity storage facilities, which thus tended to concentrate along the far South Shore, the Calumet River, and the Sanitary Canal.

Streets and Street Railways

Since it was unnecessary to adapt the street system of Chicago to topographic features, the city and most of its surrounding communities were free to build a rigid gridiron pattern without inhibition and without bounds, with only the rivers, rail yards, and enclaves of heavy industry interrupting the monotonous rhythm. This gridiron is overlaid by an extensive system of diagonal arteries, many of which were originally roads that connected the city with other towns of the region, such as Milwaukee, Elgin, Joliet, and Aurora. At first through fortuitous circumstances of growth and physiography and later by design, the practice grew up of establishing the streets at half-mile intervals as the primary thoroughfares, built to run through a considerable length or breadth of the urban area and to serve as the axes or boundaries of neighborhoods.[2] The streetcar routes of the Chicago Surface Lines and its predecessors were laid down on the half-mile and diagonal arteries, thus forming a system of near-perfect regularity, exact, coherent, monotonous, but thoroughly efficient for economy and circulation. The result of this growth pattern in the street railway network was that commercial development in the form of neighborhood stores and service facilities came to be concentrated along the main arteries, producing the most extreme form of ribbon development in the United States, with an attendant stratification of land

Fig. 3. The rapid transit and chief surface lines of Chicago.

values and land uses. The most intense concentration of commercial institutions, including large department stores, restaurants, and theaters, occurred at the nuclei formed by the intersections of the arterial streets, especially those three-way intersections composed of a diagonal and two rectangular thoroughfares that are peculiar to Chicago.

The street layout of Chicago was little more than thirty years old when the city, again in cooperation with its southern neighbor, Hyde Park, undertook an ambitious program of boulevard construction. The joint South Side system of the two communities was planned first by Frederick Law Olmsted and Calvert Vaux in 1869–70, and by Horace Cleveland after 1872. Grading and macadam paving on the first two drives began during the planning stage, and by the turn of the century the system was essentially completed with respect to locations, lengths, and dimensions of boulevards as it exists today. The standards for the major thoroughfares had been previously worked out by the far-sighted Olmsted for the Central Park project in New York: the maximum width was two hundred feet; parkway strips at the sides were landscaped with trees, shrubs, and grass; the broad center roadway was designed for through traffic, and the narrow side pavements were restricted to local traffic. The South Side boulevards formed two major patterns, the smaller one a gridiron system near the lake, the other a long westward and northward extension of interior drives designed to meet the south end of the West Park system.[3]

Far more extensive in scope and impressive in landscaping features is the continuous boulevard pattern of the West Park District, which was designed to form, in conjunction with the two westernmost drives of the Hyde Park system, a great interior ring extending in an irregular rectangle from Lincoln Park at Diversey Avenue (2800N) to Jackson Park at the Midway Plaisance (5950S). Although most of the drives in this circuit followed the standard width of 100 to 200 feet, a few were extremely generous in area: variable dividing strips expanded Humboldt Boulevard to a breadth of 315 feet in places; a parklike space between the twin drives pushed Palmer Square to 400 feet, and a similar feature at the Humboldt Park Natatorium stretched Sacramento to 572 feet.[4]

The third of the city's three boulevard systems is made up of Lake Shore Drive and the associated local and access drives in Lincoln Park. The ancestor of this most celebrated of all urban parkways was Lincoln Park Drive, which was originally laid out through the south end of the park in 1893 as a scenic drive and was gradually extended south to Ohio Street (600N) and north to Belmont Avenue (3200N) between 1893 and 1910. Progressive construction of supplementary interior drives and the present Lake Shore Drive came with the civic program that followed the acceptance of Burnham's plan.

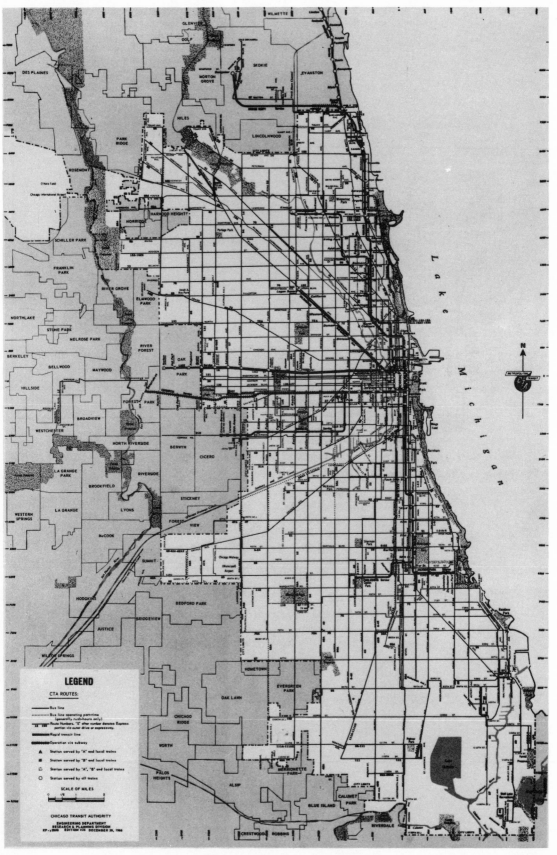

Fig. 4. Railroad lines and freight yards of the Chicago Switching District.

Fig. 5. Railroad terminals and yards in the core area of Chicago. The map shows clearly how the core area of the city is embraced by a rectangular ring of tracks and stations.

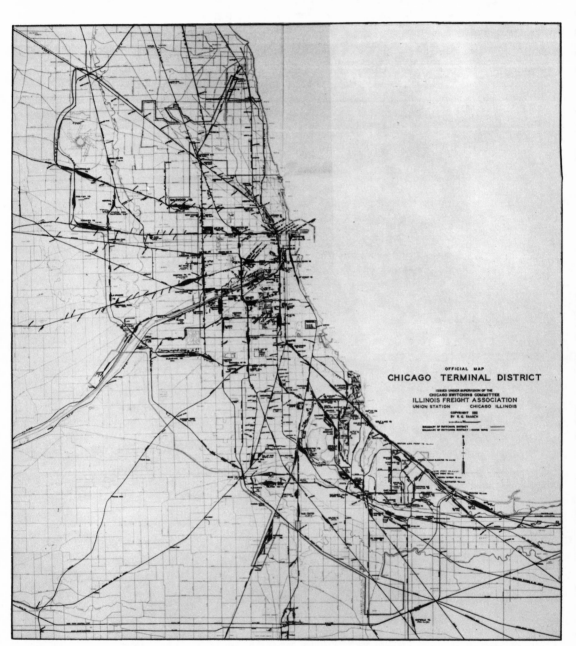

OFFICIAL MAP

CHICAGO TERMINAL DISTRICT

ISSUED UNDER SUPERVISION OF THE
CHICAGO SWITCHING COMMITTEE
ILLINOIS FREIGHT ASSOCIATION
UNION STATION   CHICAGO ILLINOIS

COPYRIGHT 1911
BY R. G. RAACH

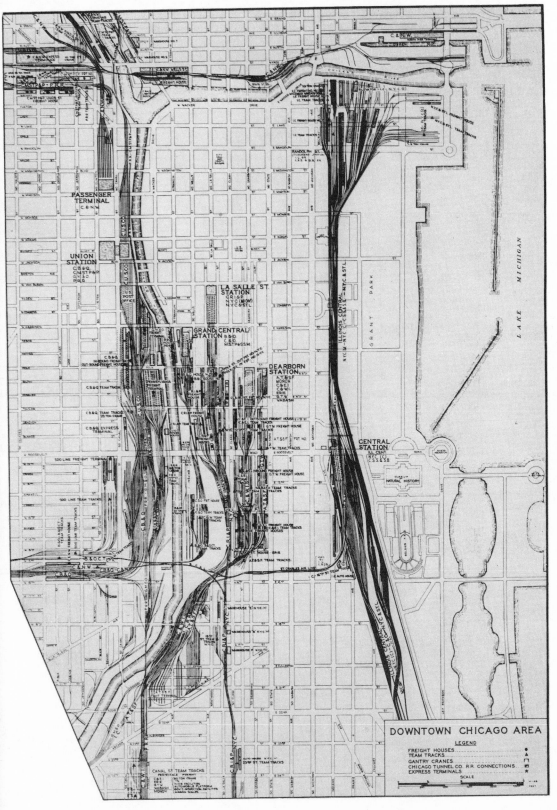

DOWNTOWN CHICAGO AREA

LEGEND

FREIGHT HOUSES..........
TEAM TRACKS............
GANTRY CRANES..........
CHICAGO TUNNEL CO. R.R. CONNECTIONS
EXPRESS TERMINALS........

SCALE

Fig. 6. Railroad terminals, transit lines,
street pattern of the inner city, and
downtown harbor development, as
proposed in the Plan of Chicago.

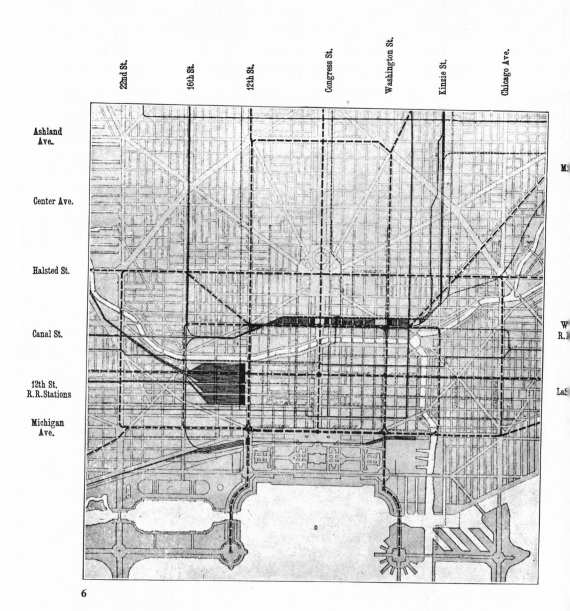

As late as 1920 the boulevards were still thought of primarily as scenic drives, and most weekday movements to and from the city and all commercial traffic were restricted to the conventional streets. Until the widespread dependence on the automobile that emerged in the mid-twenties, the street railway and the rapid transit systems were the chief intracity carriers and hence the main determinants in fixing the commercial pattern of Chicago (fig. 3). The establishment and expansion of both of them could come about only as a consequence of fundamental developments in the technology of transportation that occurred during the late nineteenth century. Yet the street railway made its appearance toward the end of the period characterized by what we have called the horse-and-pedestrian city. Horse-drawn streetcars were introduced in Chicago as early as 1859, when the Chicago City Railway began its operation on State Street, which was soon to become the central shopping artery of the whole metropolitan area. Cable cars appeared on the same car line in 1882, to be replaced within a few years (1890) by cars equipped with electric traction motors drawing power from an overhead trolley-wire system. The street railway constituted the most widespread application of the electric motor to transportation, but its use in this respect was feasible only because of the prior development of electric-power generation, which was initiated in Chicago in 1887 by the Chicago Edison Company. Both street transportation and the power generation on which it depended grew at a rate unparalleled in the history of technology. By 1910 the basic street railway system of Chicago had been laid down on the half-mile gridiron streets and on the diagonal arteries, requiring only extensions at the ends of the various lines as the city expanded. By the same date the electric power industry was serving an area with a population of more than 2,000,000, and the number of its customers was rapidly approaching 250,000.[5]

Rapid Transit Lines

Equally decisive in determining urban population movement and commercial development was the rapid transit system, which in Chicago had a peculiarly complex and potent effect on the city's core (fig. 3). Although a mass-transit rail service operating on a separate right of way antedates both the cable and the motor-driven streetcar, a much broader confluence of technical innovations was necessary for the successful exploitation of the earlier form. Electric power was not a requirement in the beginning, since the first motive power consisted of steam locomotives, but it soon became highly desirable for economic reasons as well as for the clean and relatively quiet operation that was essential in densely built urban areas. Girder rails and rigid street paving were enough for the street railway, but roofed cuts, lined tunnels, and long iron viaducts were necessities for the rapid transit systems. Structures composed of simple deck girders or trusses had to be brought to the level of predictable scientific design for elevated lines, and these had to be supplemented by continuous forms for special kinds of crossings. The close headway of trains made the automatic block signal a valuable safety feature on elevated lines and an absolute necessity in subways. Numerous junctions and crossings made the mechanical and later the electropneumatic interlocking essential for two reasons: first, as with the steam railroad, junctions and crossings of main lines required the positive control of all switches and signals in such a form as to make it physically impossible for the towerman to line up conflicting routes; and second, on the narrow rapid transit viaducts, it was extremely hazardous for operators to throw switches by hand at the trackside. By 1890 all the mechanical and electrical inventions were available, with the profound consequence that the modern spread-out metropolis could now evolve, superseding the earlier city that had been shaped by the process of interstitial growth. A comparable evolution of building technology and elevator transportation underlay the vertical expansion that took place in the core of the new commercial-industrial city.[6]

The rapid transit system of Chicago began its chartered history on 4 January 1888 with the incorporation of the Chicago and South Side Rapid Transit Company, although operations over its original 3.6-mile line did not commence until 1892. The company extended its track to Jackson Park in the following year to capture a share of the Columbian Exposition traffic and reached its maximum extent in 1908, after the Englewood and Stock Yards branches had been added to the Jackson Park line. The original motive power consisted of twenty compound tank locomotives, which ordinarily handled trains of six cars. These engines were replaced in 1898 by open-platform electric cars designed for multiple-unit operation, the initial fleet supplemented in 1902 by the first closed-platform cars, many of which stayed in service until the Chicago Transit Authority began to operate the system in 1947.[7] The second rapid transit line, the Lake Street Elevated Railway, began operation with steam locomotives in 1893, electrified its line in 1896, and reached Oak Park and its greatest extent five years later. Another western line came with the Metropolitan West Side Elevated Railroad, which was electrified from the opening of the initial line in 1895, but the company did not reach the far western suburbs of Berwyn, Maywood, and Westchester until 1926. The three companies maintained separate terminals in the downtown core until 1897, when the Union Elevated Railroad ended this awkward arrangement by building a continuous elevated structure in the form of a closed rectangle over Wells, Van Buren, Wabash, and Lake streets. This double-track ring, first known as the "Union Loop" and eventually simply as the "Loop," made it possible for trains to be operated in a continuous movement without reversal in the downtown terminal area. The completion of the basic rapid transit system came with the opening of the Northwestern Elevated Railroad from the Loop to Wilson Avenue (4600N) in 1900. The company acquired the Union Elevated Railroad in the following year and extended its line to Evanston in 1908 and to Wilmette in 1912, its right of way from Wilson Avenue to Central Street in Evanston having been leased from the Milwaukee Railroad.[8]

In 1911 the four separate companies were unified under a single management, and in 1913 they began to provide through service without transfer from the north city limit to Englewood and Jackson Park on the South Side. At the time of the Chicago Plan of 1909 the city enjoyed one of the best rapid transit systems in the world, one which not only provided reliable unified service to outlying communities and neighborhoods then in existence, but in places, most notably on the North Side above Wilson Avenue, lay in open prairie land still awaiting the development that transit service powerfully stimulated. Unfortunately, this excellent system, experiencing the usual financial difficulties, remained fixed in extent for the next sixty years, except for the abandonment of the Stock Yards and Westchester branches and the opening of the Skokie line. The chief consequences of rapid transit service up to 1930 were the rapid growth of certain inner suburbs and the concentration of commercial activity along the transit lines beyond the level fixed by the street and street railway patterns, thus intensifying the inflexible ribbon form of this development.

The construction of the Union Loop had results without exact parallel in the history of the American city. We have already noted how the pattern of waterways had the effect of fixing the urban core in the rectangle bounded on three sides by the lake and the two branches of the river. The construction of the railroad terminals closed this rectangle on the south side, while the Loop threw a tight ring around the inner heart, so to speak. This extreme compaction offered valuable advantages that proved to be potent factors in the development of the central business district from the beginning to the present day and will undoubtedly continue to be in the future. All elements of the core—all offices, stores, theaters, and other commercial and recreational facilities, all financial, administrative, and municipal institutions—lie within a ten-minute walk of one or another of the ten Loop stations. The elevated structure made possible the building of covered pedestrian bridges to special second-floor entrances in the annexes of various department stores along Wabash Avenue and Van Buren Street and to the waiting-room level of LaSalle Street Station on Van Buren. The blessings, however, were not unmixed: the iron ring had a strangling effect, producing so high a density of building that the mixture of pedestrian, streetcar, truck, automobile, and wagon traffic eventually made certain Loop streets impassable during rush hours and on popular shopping days. Worse was the blighting effect of the elevated structure and the noisy trains on property along the four boundary streets. With a few exceptions such as the rear elevation of the Palmer House and the annexes of the Field, Carson, and Mandel (now Wieboldt) stores, the buildings along the elevated structure are low-rent blocks whose deterioration no one is interested in arresting. Yet the subways that came around World War II added further to the advantages of the Loop, and the building boom of the 1960s, much of it compacted around the very geometric center of the rectangle, was a direct consequence of these riches of public transit.[9]

Steam Railroads and Rail Terminals

In no city of the world has the railroad played a more pervasive role, extended its sheer physical presence to a greater magnitude, offered more possibilities for economic growth, or created more serious and refractory problems than in Chicago. The Chicago Switching District, which is somewhat smaller than the metropolitan area but similar in shape, covers four hundred square miles and embraces nearly six thousand miles of track forming what appears to be a pattern of bewildering confusion but in fact represents a relatively coherent and rational order imposed on a good deal of internal operating chaos (fig. 4). The main rail lines of Chicago constitute a radial and concentric pattern in which through movements tend to be restricted to the radial lines and transfer movements to the interstitial or concentric lines. This geometry was less a matter of design than of the geographic location of Chicago and the physiography of its region. The other urban centers, the waterways, and the productive regions lay around it in a ring, and the level terrain allowed the construction of railroads in a vast spider-web shape, the main-line radii knitted together by the concentric segments of the belt and transfer companies.

The construction of this web began in 1848, when the Galena and Chicago Union Railroad operated its first train between the central city and Oak Park. A second western line, the Aurora Branch, offered service in 1852, the Michigan Southern and Northern Indiana and the Michigan Central in the same year united the city with communities to the east and northeast, and the Illinois and Wisconsin Railroad built northwest toward Madison in the following year. The Chicago and Rock Island reached the Mississippi River in 1854; the Chicago, Burlington and Quincy (successor to the Aurora Branch) joined the towns of its corporate title in the following year, and the Illinois Central reached the Ohio River at Cairo before another year had passed. The first large-scale mergers of these little capital-hungry companies came around the time of the Civil War: through service to Pittsburgh by way of a single company followed the establishment of the Pittsburgh, Fort Wayne and Chicago Railroad in 1858, and a similar route to Cleveland and Buffalo was provided by the Lake Shore and Michigan Southern in 1869. Both these companies were created by mergers of numerous smaller lines built up over the years after 1852. The most important event in this irregular process of expansion and financial difficulty was the completion on 10 May 1869 of the first transcontinental railroad. The connection between the Union Pacific and the Chicago, Iowa and Nebraska at Council Bluffs put Chicago at the hub of an ocean-to-ocean railroad line, as the Illinois-Michigan Canal twenty years earlier had placed it at the heart of the longest inland waterway system. Water and rail thus fixed the pattern of American economic development until the rise of air transportation and the electronics industry after World War II, and for eighty years Chicago was at the strategic focus.[10]

Up to 1900 the railroads located freight yards and freight-handling facilities anywhere in the city where open land was available and land prices were not prohibitive. As both the area and the physical density of the city grew, however, and as freight traffic increased, these small scattered stations with their associated trackage, built up in piecemeal fashion, became hopelessly inadequate, especially for the classification of freight, a process that reached astronomical magnitudes in the Chicago area. The trunk lines accordingly were forced to adopt the practice of building huge classification yards in open areas beyond the city limits where land values were minimal, the various installations thus lying in a series of rings ten to twenty miles from the urban core. The largest of all these is the main freight yard of the North Western at Proviso, a western township on the company's Galena Division, but similar facilities of the New York Central, Milwaukee, Illinois Central, and Santa Fe are close to it in area and capacity.[11] In addition to the main classification yards, various subsidiary yards, team tracks, and industrial spurs, the principal trunk lines also operate in-town freight terminals for merchandise and less-than-carload tonnage. These are for the most part along the approach tracks close to the passenger terminals in the Loop area. They were once joined together and connected with store and office buildings of the core by a narrow-gage electric freight-handling railroad situated far below grade in a network of elliptical concrete-lined tunnels that still remains, although the service itself was long ago abandoned. With the loss of most less-than-carload traffic because of truck competition, however, the freight houses have declined in importance and have been progressively transformed into warehouses. Many of these stations are old by Chicago standards—that of the Illinois Central on South Water Street, for example, dated from pre-fire days and survived until 1970; among the few built since 1910 are those associated with the vast Union Station project.[12]

The practice among the trunk lines in Chicago, growing up over the years as traffic, commerce, and urban density increased, has been to separate freight from passenger traffic by building separate tracks for the two kinds of service. This technique made it possible to handle the enormous volume of tonnage together with a passenger traffic that had reached 1,300 trains per day by 1910, while at the same time facilitating the construction of an interconnecting network of belt and transfer lines.[13] These railroads function primarily to transfer freight by car or train-load from one trunk line to another, or from one yard or freight terminal to another, thus avoiding the traffic chaos and congestion within the urban area arising from switching at the junction points of main lines. The major transfer line within the city proper is the Belt Railway of Chicago, which is owned by the twelve companies that are its primary users and which unites all their freight tracks in the city through the elongated L-shape of its main lines.[14] Lying mainly outside the city limits in similar L- and U-shaped patterns are the Indiana Harbor Belt, owned three-quarters by the New York Central and one-quarter by the Milwaukee, and the Baltimore and Ohio Chicago Terminal, the extensive belt and terminal subsidiary of the Baltimore and Ohio. Supplementing these metropolitan belt lines are a number of independent companies or branches of larger systems that function in the combined capacities of belt, bypass, and bridge routes. Lying near the periphery of the metropolitan area are the Joliet Branch of the Michigan Central, which provides a straight-line bypass from Gary to Joliet, and the Elgin, Joliet and Eastern, a line-haul subsidiary of the United States Steel Corporation that extends in a great crescent from Lake Michigan at Waukegan back to the lake at Gary. South of the city a succession of bridge routes lie at regular intervals across northern Illinois; north of it a similar connecting and bypass function is provided by combinations of railroad lines and Lake Michigan car ferries.[15]

The growth of this vast system of trunk, belt, switching, and transfer lines operated as both cause and effect in fixing the traditional pattern of industrial development in the Chicago metropolitan area. Heavy industry, requiring either rail or water or likely to benefit from both, grew up in dense belts in the great rail-water complex of the Lake Michigan–Calumet River area in the far southeast corner of the city, while a similar though more extensive and less concentrated belt of manufacturing and bulk storage emerged along the South Branch of the river, the Sanitary Canal, and the contiguous rail lines. A smaller enclave was dominated by the Pullman Company between Lake Calumet and the Illinois Central Railroad tracks. The Stockyards, dating from 1865, constituted a nexus of its own, filling a square bounded by 39th and 47th streets on the north and south, and by Halsted Street and Ashland Avenue to the east and west, an area of an exact square mile as densely laced with rail lines as living tissue with its blood vessels. Extensive inner corridors of the West Side were given over to warehouses and smaller factories, distributed in broad belts along the numerous railroad embankments. But even manufacturing establishments that did not need rail transportation were restricted by zoning ordinances to streets contiguous to the tracks, so that ribbons spread along the main lines of the inner North and entire Northwest sides. The overall consequence of this process was a ribbon development of industry comparable on a much larger scale to that of stores and services along the streets, except that the former was dictated by the radial and concentric pattern of the rail lines rather than the arterial gridiron. It was all a dirty, noisy, and pollution-generating tangle that flourished prodigiously up to 1930, but depression, war, and postwar economic changes have left parts of it grim areas of rusty tracks, derelict buildings, and vacant weed-covered land, worse in appearance and effect than the busy factories and slaughterhouses of the once prosperous manufacturing city.

The grand pattern of railroad lines and freight facilities throughout the metropolitan area reveals a certain coherence and order, but that is more than one can say of the passenger terminals and their associated trackage in the core. The six through-train stations and the three suburban stations of the Illinois Central along Michigan Avenue formed an open U or horseshoe that fitted mostly between the two rectangles outlined by the waterways and by the elevated Loop, and thus constituted the intermediate of the three rings that determined the shape and location of Chicago's core (fig. 5). What led to the confusion of the downtown rail pattern was the forty-year period of initial growth in which the many different companies competed for strategic locations and minimum land costs, the older companies naturally enjoying the advantages whereas the latecomers had to settle for what was left. Beyond these obvious factors there were many occasions when decisions affecting line location were made in the light of local and immediate exigencies or short-term advantages that led in later years to unnecessary expenses, irrational forms of rail operation, and urban disloca-tions. The bad results of unplanned growth and the multiplicity of separate corpora-tions took two forms: one was the manifest absurdity of eastern railroads using West Side stations and of northern lines using South Side stations or stations with track layouts opening to the south; the other was the contrast between the direct-line approaches of the older or richer companies and the tortuous wanderings of the newer or less well endowed, the latter in some cases straying so far from the right direction as to suggest that their builders had no idea of their intended destinations.[16] Long-established individual companies, most notably the Illinois Central and the predecessors of the North Western, held exclusive title to all their tracks and terminals within the city, while others, like the Pere Marquette and the Big Four, operated entirely by trackage rights over still other railroads. All these intricate arrangements, hopelessly entangled over a century of construction, reconstruction, and mergers, are still in effect, although the ring of tracks began to crumble in 1971 with the abandonment of Dearborn and Grand Central stations.

Any attempt to provide a coherent historical description of the rail passenger terminals of Chicago thus presents insoluble difficulties. Chronological, spatial, corporate, or station-by-station approaches to the task all lead to unavoidable confusion that can be overcome only through long familiarity with the rail pattern of Chicago and with its evolution over the seventy-seven years between the opening of the first station in 1848 and the completion of the newest terminal in 1925. An arbitrary but reasonably convenient way of dealing with the problem is to begin with the station used by the eventual successor to the first rail line and to take up the remainder counterclockwise around the ring. North Western Station thus offers a plausible starting point by virtue of its position at the northernmost corner of the terminal group and because its original ancestor, the Galena and Chicago Union Railroad, was the first to provide rail service to and from the city. Although the present North Western Station and its immediate predecessor have been the only terminal facilities used exclusively by a single company, the entire history of station construction is the most complex of all because the North Western Railway and its numerous ancestors have built a total of eleven terminal stations in Chicago. The many scattered stations, constructed for the most part along the north bank of the main river and on the west bank of the North Branch in the area of Wells and Canal streets, were replaced by a unified operating entity in 1880–81, when the North Western built the Wells Street Station at Kinzie and Wells streets, the site of the present Merchandise Mart. The extremely rapid growth of both through and suburban traffic compelled the company to replace the spacious Wells Street facility with the vastly expanded terminal at Canal and Madison streets in less than thirty years.[17]

Two blocks south of North Western Station, along Canal between Adams Street and Jackson Boulevard, stands the so-called Union Station, which at the maximum served five of Chicago's twenty-four passenger-carrying railroads. The original station, which occupied a small part of the extensive site now covered by the headhouse buildings and the associated track and platform layout, was built by the Fort Wayne and Chicago Railroad (predecessor of the Pittsburgh, Fort Wayne and Chicago) in 1858 at the southeast corner of Canal and Madison streets, from which its baggage and express facilities extended south to Adams Street. Three years later the newly incorporated Chicago and Alton Railroad entered the station as a tenant. The simple timber structures served the two roads until the fire of 1871 wiped out all the train and engine facilities, which were then replaced by makeshift temporary quarters that survived in a disreputable state for eight years. Something at least suggesting the possibilities of a union terminal began to take shape when the Fort Wayne company entered into an agreement with the Milwaukee, the Burlington, and the Chicago, Saint Louis and Pittsburgh to build a permanent structure at Adams Street. The mansard-roofed red-brick building, with its Gothic windows and immensely long train shed on iron Pratt trusses, was constructed in 1879–80, although the Burlington did not divert its trains from Central Station until the following year. Its plan was unique among rail facilities: the whole complex was designed as a through station but was actually operated as two stub-end terminals placed back to back, the trains of the Fort Wayne, Burlington, and Alton railroads entering from the south and those of the Milwaukee and the Chicago, Saint Louis and Pittsburgh coming in from the north, with the latter company owning the jointly used right of way from Western Avenue to the station. The architect of the building and its appurtenances, William W. Boyington (1818–98), was Chicago's leading designer of rail passenger stations during his busy career of more than half a century. Given a train shed a thousand feet in length, the practice of entry from both ends worked well enough from the standpoint of mechanical operations, but the single-level plan for concourse and tracks, along with the frequent overrunning of the center line by trains entering from two directions, resulted in considerable confusion and danger to both employees and passengers. The Victorian structure was a perfect expression of the railroad style and aura in the nineteenth century, and it survived for forty-five years before it was replaced in 1925 by the present Union Station.[18]

Grand Central Station, at the southwest corner of Harrison and Wells streets, followed its single predecessor in little more than a year. The Wisconsin Central Railway in 1888 extended its line into the city from a junction with the Chicago, Saint Paul and Kansas City in Forest Park and simultaneously built a small terminal at Polk and Wells streets. The little station immediately proved to be inadequate for the two roads, and the owners began building a new and much larger terminal one block north of the original site during the following year; but it was the newly organized Chicago and Northern Pacific Railway that completed the enterprise in 1890. The handsome headhouse and clock tower, designed by Solon S. Beman in collaboration with the engineer Willis S. Jones, were constructed in the usual combination of masonry bearing walls and interior iron frame, but the balloon shed was in its day an impressive work of vaulted roofing on wrought-iron arched trusses. The station was not used to capacity for twelve years, since the original participants carried a relatively modest passenger traffic and the Northern Pacific project proved abortive. This road was organized by Henry Villard to extend his Pacific line from Saint Paul into Chicago by trackage rights over the Wisconsin Central, but financial difficulties forced the connecting company into receivership in 1897, with a consequent fore-closure sale of the local properties to the Chicago Terminal Transfer Railroad. An active life commensurate with the station's size and straightforward, thoroughly functional plan was at least promised at the turn of the century: the Baltimore and Ohio, shifting operations from the Central Station, became a tenant in 1902, and the Pere Marquette joined it in the following year. The larger company acquired the station with the properties of the Transfer line in 1910 and used them as the nucleus of the Baltimore and Ohio Chicago Terminal Railroad, an operating subsidiary whose extensive belt lines account for the circuitous route of the Baltimore and Ohio and Pere Marquette passenger trains in Chicago. The terminal complex, except for the substitution of electrical interlocking and color-position light signals for the original mechanical system, remained unchanged since its opening in 1890.

LaSalle Street Station, at the southwest corner of LaSalle and Van Buren streets, is unique in two respects: it is the only station that stands contiguous to the elevated Loop and hence the only one with direct access to the rapid transit line, and the headhouse includes not only the usual terminal facilities but an office building of skyscraper proportions for the date of its construction. The fourth station on its site and the seventh of its participating companies or their predecessors, LaSalle Street Station was erected in 1901-3 after the plans of the architects Frost and Granger and the engineers Edward C. and Ralph M. Shankland. The first station built by the original proprietary roads—the Northern Indiana and the Chicago and Rock Island—was constructed in 1853 at 12th Street (now Roosevelt Road) on the line of LaSalle, but the Rock Island had built an independent terminal on 22nd Street (now Cermak Road), at the city limit, the previous year. What followed was an incredible succession of new constructions, demolitions, and replacements strongly suggesting complete innocence among the various railroad executives with respect to planning, civic foresight, and the traffic which their companies rapidly generated. A temporary station was quickly erected on Jackson Boulevard at the very moment when the first permanent station was built at LaSalle and Van Buren streets (1853–54). The latter structure attracted some attention for its vaulted train shed carried on arched timber Howe trusses of 116-foot clear span. It was replaced by a handsome building of rough-faced stone masonry in 1868, but the fire and expanding traffic compelled its replace-ment in turn by a substantially larger structure in 1872. By this date the Lake Shore and Michigan Southern had been formed out of many little Michigan, Indiana, and Ohio companies, and had established a through connection at Buffalo with Cornelius Vanderbilt's newly created New York Central and Hudson River Railroad. The traf-fic increased at an even more rapid rate, augmented somewhat by the later tenancy of the Nickel Plate Road, with the consequence that another LaSalle Street Station had to be built within thirty years. By 1910 the three roads were operating about two hundred trains a day on eleven tracks, a feat made possible partly by the four-track straight-line approach from 63rd Street. The whole track and platform layout was originally spanned by a huge barrel-vaulted shed on steel bowstring trusses with a Pratt web system and steeply cambered bottom chords, but this eventually gave way to an uninteresting flat slab.[19]

Dearborn Station, on Polk Street at the foot of Dearborn, is the oldest of the Chicago group and the oldest metropolitan terminal in the United States, exceeded in its antiquity only by the surviving remnants of the Central of Georgia station at Savannah and the Union Depot at Chattanooga, Tennessee. The station was con-structed in 1883–85 by the Chicago and Western Indiana Railroad, a terminal com-pany specifically organized by the Chicago and Eastern Illinois to undertake the project and thus provide entry into the city. By the time the station had reached the planning stage in 1882, four other companies had joined the Chicago and Eastern Illinois in the venture, assuring the construction of a station that would rival Union Station in elegance and size.[20] Meanwhile, the usual construction of urban extensions and temporary quarters kept the new company busy: the first necessity was building a line from Dolton, Illinois, into the city to provide trackage for the Chicago and Western Indiana and its tenants; next came the usual makeshift stations, the first at Archer Avenue near State Street, the second at 12th and State. The extension from 12th Street to Polk was undertaken in 1883, after the city had agreed to extend Dear-born Street south from Van Buren to Polk, and the permanent station was erected during the next two years.[21] The headhouse was designed by Cyrus L. W. Eidlitz as a three-story red-brick building in the Romanesque style, the central feature of which is a high, slender clock tower at the center line that was once capped with a steeply pitched Flemish Gothic roof. The train shed is primitive even by the standards of the 1880s: a central gable and two flanking lean-to roofs together spanning ten tracks are carried on timber and wrought-iron trusses of a kind that appeared at the very beginning of railroad architecture. The shed remains unchanged, but the station in-terior, signaling, interlocking, and appurtenant structures have been repeatedly altered and extended over the years. In 1887 the Santa Fe became the sixth and final tenant-owner when it acquired the properties of the Chicago, Santa Fe and California Railroad to close the remaining gap in a new transcontinental rail line.

Central Station, constructed in 1892–93 at Michigan Avenue and 11th Place, was the second of the Illinois Central terminals in Chicago. The first of these, known as Great Central, had been opened in 1856 at Randolph Street and the lakeshore, a work of Romanesque primitivism by Otto H. Matz which was chiefly noteworthy for an immense vaulted roof of wood sheathing supported by arched timber Howe trusses with a clear span of 166 feet. Although it was the easternmost of the city's rail terminals—so far to the east, in fact, that the approach tracks lay on a pile-and-beam timber trestle in the lake—the Burlington and the Galena and Chicago Union were among the early tenants, reaching the Illinois Central over a crosstown extension that is still known as Saint Charles Air Line.[22] Great Central Station burned in the fire of 1871, but its owner cheerfully went on using the roofless hulk for twenty-two years, until its replacement was opened at the south end of Grant Park in 1893. The new structure was designed by Bradford Gilbert, a New York architect, and John F. Wallace, who was associated with him as chief engineer. It is a handsome Romanesque building distinguished by a particularly formidable clock tower and, for many years, by a grand vaulted ceiling over the waiting room—now hidden by a cheaply constructed false ceiling set for minimal headroom above the floor.

A number of tenants have come and gone at Central Station over the years, but only the Michigan Central and the Big Four maintained a long relationship that extends back to the days of the earlier facilities at Randolph Street.[23] The presence of these two heavily traveled affiliates of the New York Central, along with the only direct rail line to Memphis and New Orleans, meant that the station and its approach tracks carried a high density of through passenger traffic. The same right of way provided access to a suburban terminal that was eventually to serve 60,000 passengers a day and to an extensive freight yard with its associated loading, unloading, and storage areas. This huge volume of every type of rail traffic, at one time exceeding 800 trains every weekday, required a separate but contiguous main line for each type: there were two tracks for freight-train movements, two for through passenger trains, and six from Roosevelt Road to 67th Street for the suburban trains of the South Shore Railroad and the Illinois Central, but four tracks of the total group were subsequently abandoned. This ten-track corridor, the widest railroad main line in the world and as broad as a modern expressway, still lies like a permanent geological formation down the east front of the city from the river to Jackson Park. Air rights construction may some day bury it under lakefront skyscrapers.

Our survey indicates that the rail terminal and main-line pattern of Chicago had been laid down in all but minor extensions and interconnections by 1910.[24] The six terminal stations, reflecting in their design the changing architectural fashions of the long period in which they were built, form an irregular U-shaped group around the Loop, a second iron ring between the elevated structure and the encompassing waterways. The various buildings hold considerable interest for the architectural and urban historian, but in their number, their location, and the distribution of rail lines among them, they have constituted an endless confusion to travelers, an immovable obstruction to the orderly growth of the city, and a devourer of many hundreds of acres of increasingly unproductive land. The United States has never developed a national railroad system or a coherent and rational transportation policy. The consequence of this peculiar backwardness is nowhere better exhibited than in Chicago. The multiplicity of stations required an even greater multiplicity of coach yards, engine terminals, and associated service facilities, whose numerous tracks and structures extended in an unbroken belt south of the Loop between State Street and Canal. The haphazard expansion of railroads, their administrative officers locating stations wherever open space, financial exigencies, and corporate relations dictated, produced the civic and technological absurdity in which lines extending east of the city used stations on the west side of the terminal group, western lines terminated on the east side of the area, and northern lines extended southward from south-facing train sheds. Only the North Western and the Central stations could be regarded as having been located in accordance with the geographical direction of the rail lines they were built to serve.

The chief operating result of this internal chaos has been a vast proliferation of multiline crossings, all of which at one time were single-level, guaranteeing a high proportion of delays and accidents. The most complex of these, such as the great ganglion at Canal and 14th streets, or its outlying counterpart at Grand Crossing on the far South Side, were eventually disentangled by completely separating the grades of the different rail lines and the streets by three-level intersections. Others have remained as grade-level crossings at which only the signaling and interlocking systems have been improved. The largest of these is near Archer Avenue and 21st Street, where the tracks of the Chicago and Western Indiana, the Santa Fe, the Illinois Central, and the Pennsylvania form a bewildering pattern of switches and frogs. The worst of all, however, were the intersections of main lines and yard leads, for which interlocking systems were never devised and signals remained manually operated. Crossings of this kind require safety stops—the absolute stopping of all trains from whatever direction to await a signal clearance. In spite of their primitive character, a number of such crossings remained until 1970 on passenger-carrying main lines, the most conspicuously irritating being those on the lines of the Baltimore and Ohio Chicago Terminal and the Gulf, Mobile and Ohio (successor to the Alton).

By 1910 train movements on most of the main lines in the Chicago Switching District were governed by automatic block signals operated by electric motors controlled in turn by track circuits. On branches, transfer lines, and the more lightly traveled mains, however, trains were operated in accordance with manual block systems or written train orders. The great majority of home signals at those junctions and crossings under interlocking control were mechanically operated, although the electrical forms were becoming common at the newer and larger installations. Signals were the standard upper-quadrant three-position semaphores on the eastern and southern lines, but the less efficient lower-quadrant type was dominant on the western roads. Color- and position-light signals, cab signals, reverse-direction signaling, automatic stop, centralized traffic control, and radio communication all lay in the future. These improvements were to come for the most part in the great period of rail reconstruction between 1910 and 1930.[25] For all the handicaps imposed by the heterogeneous standards of operation and construction that obtained in 1910, however, the Chicago railroads transported an extraordinary and rapidly increasing number of passengers, totaling at the time about 175,000 per day distributed among 1,300 trains. At the high point of passenger traffic in 1920 the respective figures had increased to more than 270,000 passengers and 1,500 trains on an average weekday.[26]

The economic effects of expanding rail suburban service were broadly similar to those of the street railway and rapid transit systems, but the precise physical impact was somewhat different. The commuter lines did not foster the ribbon developments that lay along the streets, but rather chains of commercial nuclei that grew up in the vicinity of the stations, these nuclei in turn surrounded by the local residential areas. This pattern of radiating suburban chains is most conspicuous along the lines of the major commuter carriers, notably those of the North Western Railroad in the northwest quadrant, the Burlington to the west, the Rock Island to the southwest, and the Illinois Central to the south.

Electric Interurban Railroads

The vast network of surface, rapid transit, and standard rail lines in the Chicago metropolitan area was rounded out with the establishment of a high-speed intermediate-run interurban system which, for all the brevity of its active life, once played a large and valuable role in the movement of passengers to and from the suburbs and the neighboring cities. The first of the three companies that once extended to Milwaukee, Aurora, and South Bend was the Chicago, North Shore and Milwaukee Railroad, founded as a single-track car line in Waukegan, Illinois, in 1894, when it was known as the Bluff City Electric Street Railway. By progressively extending its line north and south from Waukegan, it was able to offer through service, predominantly in single cars (the traditional interurban standard), between Evanston and Milwaukee by 1908. The operation of multiple-unit trains expanded with the purchase of suitable rolling stock, but the road was handicapped in reaching the traffic potential of the North Shore because the terminal was at Evanston, then far from the developed residential areas of Chicago's North Side. This frustration was removed in 1919 when the interurban company negotiated an agreement with the Northwestern Elevated Railroad that provided the former with trackage rights over the rapid transit line to a terminal at Roosevelt Road. The results of this direct entry into the core of the city were immediate and drastic: in the six-year period from 1916 to 1922 the number of passengers increased five and one-half times, from 2,775,000 to 15,205,000 per annum. The major expansion of line and train service came in the 1920s, with Samuel Insull's Midland Utilities Company providing the capital, but the date proved to be precariously close to the time when the automobile and the depression of 1930 combined to wipe out most interurban lines and render the rest mortally sick.[27]

Electric car and train service to Michigan City, Gary, and South Bend came with the incorporation of the Chicago and Indiana Air Line Railway in 1901. Like the North Shore, the eastern road was handicapped by being forced to terminate its operations at 115th Street on the far South Side of Chicago, where its line joined that of the Illinois Central. The two roads negotiated a similar agreement in 1913 whereby the trailer cars (as opposed to motor cars) of the Indiana line were hauled to the Illinois Central's suburban terminal by the latter's steam locomotives. The electrification of the Illinois Central Suburban lines in 1926 ended this oddity in favor of the direct operation of the electric trains by trackage rights. Meanwhile, the Indiana company had passed through the corporate vicissitudes of many capital-hungry interurban systems. Two reorganizations transformed the title of the original line successively into the Chicago, Lake Shore and South Bend and the Chicago, South Shore and South Bend, its present designation. The second reorganization came in 1925, again with Insull's Midland empire providing the money for the renewal of the run-down property.

The third of the interurban group was the Aurora, Elgin and Chicago, which was founded in 1902 and was once part of an extensive utility, trolley, and third-rail traction system that united Chicago with the western communities of Aurora, Elgin, Geneva, Saint Charles, and Batavia. The Aurora line gained access to the Loop as early as 1905 through another trackage-rights agreement, in this case with the Metropolitan West Side Elevated Company, and constructed its own terminal at Quincy and Wells streets at the same time. The company passed through the usual reorganization in 1922, when the name was changed to Chicago, Aurora and Elgin, which it retained throughout the remainder of its history. Four years later it too was acquired by the Midland Utilities Company to round out the Insull holdings in electric railways. Unlike the North Shore and the South Shore, which required extensive rebuilding or new construction to bring them up to the best interurban standards, the Aurora track was laid down as a first-class high-speed line at the beginning: the ruling grade was 1 percent, the maximum curvature three degrees, and eighty-pound rail, rock ballast, and steel bridges were the rule, the whole constituting a heavy-duty railway designed for train operations at seventy miles per hour. On the other hand, the Aurora company maintained a high proportion of old cars, some of which remained throughout the history of operations, and in this respect it was inferior to its northern and eastern counterparts.

NOTES TO CHAPTER 2

1. The passage had served the Indians as a portage between the two drainage systems, and it was used and described as such by Jolliet and Marquette as early as 1673. The extensive marshes along the Chicago, Des Plaines, and Kankakee rivers made it possible in time of high water for laden barges to pass directly from the Chicago to the Des Plaines River. It was this, known to the Indians and rediscovered by the French military engineer Victor Collot, that suggested the idea of a canal to various members of Congress as early as 1809.

2. The geometric simplicity of the street pattern made it possible for Chicago to institute a rational house-numbering system that is a model of clarity. The primary street spacing was fixed at eight equal intervals to the mile, with a range of one hundred numbers to the block, or eight hundred to the mile. Madison Street was established as the east-west base line, the numbers thus ranging north and south of it, and State Street as the corresponding north-south line. The primary arteries on the North Side are Chicago (800), Division (1200), North (1600), Armitage (2000), Fullerton (2400), Diversey (2800), Belmont (3200), etc.; on the South Side (where uniformity of spacing is interrupted by rail lines) they are Roosevelt (1200), Cermak (2200), 31st, 35th, Pershing (3900), 43rd, 47th, 51st, Garfield (5500), 59th, 63rd, etc.; on the West Side, Halsted (800), Racine (1200), Ashland (1600), Damen (2000), Western (2400), etc. Since many of these arteries run unbroken through the city, some of them are immensely long tangents: Halsted Street, for example, extends without curves or angles for 22.25 miles, and Western

Avenue for 24.5 miles, the latter claimed to be the longest continuous street within city limits in the world.

3. The gridiron portion of the Chicago–Hyde Park boulevards embraces three east-west drives, Oakwood, Hyde Park, and Midway Plaisance, and three running north and south, South Parkway (now Martin Luther King, Jr., Drive), Drexel, and the southward leg of Hyde Park. The western extension, which joins the West Park system at its north end, consists of Garfield and Western boulevards. Michigan Avenue was converted to boulevard status for a length of nearly six miles shortly after 1900. The initial proposal to expand it into a grand shore drive along Grant Park, with landscaped dividing islands as well as parkway strips, was made by the architect Jarvis Hunt at a meeting with the South Park commissioners in 1904. This proposal became a central feature of Burnham's plan for the downtown arteries (see p. 75). Bituminous resurfacing of all drives began in 1910.

4. The complete circuit from Diversey to the east end of the Midway is made up of eighteen end-to-end boulevards, from north to south as follows: Diversey (E-W); Logan (E-W); Kedzie (N-S); Palmer Square (E-W); Humboldt (N-S); Sacramento (two segments, N-S); Franklin (E-W); Central Park (N-S); Independence (N-S); Douglas (E-W); Marshall (N-S); 24th (E-W); California (N-S); 31st (E-W); Western (N-S); Garfield (E-W); Morgan (SE-NW); Midway Plaisance (E-W). A number of these drives are boulevard segments of much longer streets. There are eight other boulevards in the West Park system, of which Washington, Warren, and Jackson are the primary east-west thoroughfares that carried most of the Loop traffic until the completion of the present expressway system.

5. The astonishing proliferation of little street railway companies in Chicago paralleled on a small scale the construction of the steam railroads: with available capital inadequate for large undertakings, the intermittent flow of money led to the building of great numbers of short lines each serving no more than a few neighborhoods. By 1900 these had been merged into ten companies in Chicago, seven operating north of 22nd Street (Cermak Road) and three south of it. The seven northern lines were consolidated in two steps (1903, 1908) into the Chicago Railways Company. The southern group consisted of the Chicago City Railway, the Calumet and South Chicago Railway, and the Southern Railway, of which the first was the pioneer with the State Street horsecar line. All the companies were merged into the Chicago Surface Lines in 1914.

   The power industry followed a much simpler corporate history, chiefly because the wide distribution of usable electrical energy was less costly than the building of street railway lines and partly because of Thomas Edison's early preemption of the field. As a consequence, the Chicago Edison Company, which secured its franchise in 1887, enjoyed a monopoly for the first decade of its history, having no competitor until the Commonwealth Electric Company was granted a parallel franchise in 1897. In another ten years power generation was again in the hands of a single utility: in 1907 the two original firms were consolidated into the present Commonwealth Edison Company.

6. The chronology of inventions that made possible the creation of mass transportation will have to be established in detail before an adequate technological history can be written. Structural inventions, with their long pragmatic ancestry, came first: the iron-truss bridge appeared in 1840 (Earl Trumbull in the United States), and the iron-grider form in 1841 (Robert Stephenson in England). The block signal operated automatically by a closed electric track circuit was available near the beginning of rapid transit construction, having been invented in the United States in 1871 by William Robinson. The mechanical

interlocking was invented in England by John Saxby in 1856 and first patented in the United States by Ashbel Welch in 1870. The first electropneumatic interlocking was developed by the Westinghouse Company in 1883 and installed at various railroad junctions throughout the United States during the following year. The electric traction motor was applied to street railway operation in 1884 in Frankfurt, Germany, and introduced into transit systems for the first London subway in 1890. The first electric railroad locomotive was placed in service by the Baltimore and Ohio in 1895 for the Howard Street tunnel in Baltimore, by which date the multiple-unit operation of cars was at least understood in theory, if it was not an actuality, although the historians of technology have yet to establish the precise dates.

7. The steam locomotives of the South Side company were the kind invented by Mathias Forney, who gave his name to the type, and had an 0-4-4T wheel arrangement. The construction of the line to Jackson Park (1892–93) required an iron viaduct extending from the Loop to Stony Island Avenue at 63rd Street. This is a straightforward work of simple-grider construction except for the handsome and precisely designed continuous-girder bridge that carries the line over the broad expanse of Garfield Boulevard and its parklike median strip. The shapes of girders and columns, suggesting a proto-rigid frame, nicely reflect the distribution of bending moments in the various members. The Garfield crossing may be the earliest American bridge to reveal this form.

8. For a few years after 1909 the Milwaukee Railroad operated suburban trains between Union Station and Evanston over this line, which is a northward extension of the in-industrial-switching branch that originally terminated at Wilson Avenue (4600N). The elevated line to Evanston is probably unique among urban rapid transit systems in two respects: it is carried on a walled fill rather than a structure from Wilson Avenue to the north city limit at Howard Street (7600N), and it provides switching service by means of two electric locomotives to a number of sidings and coal yards along the way. In Evanston the tracks lie on a conventional sloped fill.

9. The boom of the twenties broke through the iron ring to North Michigan Avenue, but surprisingly enough, in the long run the Loop proved to be the more powerful attraction.

10. The eventual corporate status of the pioneer Chicago railroads is as follows: the Galena and Chicago Union became the Chicago and North Western, Galena Division; the Michigan Southern and Northern Indiana became part of the Lake Shore and Michigan Southern, which merged in 1914 with the New York Central and Hudson River to form the New York Central; the Michigan Central was leased to and merged with the New York Central; the Aurora Branch became the Chicago Burlington and Quincy; the Illinois and Wisconsin became the Chicago and North Western, Wisconsin Division; the Chicago and Rock Island became the Chicago, Rock Island and Pacific; the Pittsburgh, Fort Wayne and Chicago was leased to and merged with the Pennsylvania. (For a complete inventory of Chicago railroads as they existed in 1910–70, see table 6.)

11. The main freight yards of the principal trunk lines and their location, listed from north to south, roughly counterclockwise, are the following:

Minneapolis, Saint Paul and Sault Sainte Marie (Soo Line). Schiller Park; 16 miles northwest of terminal area near Irving Park Road.

Chicago, Milwaukee, Saint Paul and Pacific. Bensenville Yard, Bensenville and Franklin Park; 16 miles northwest of terminal area along Irving Park Road.

Chicago and North Western. Proviso Yard, Melrose Park, Bellwood, Berkeley, and Northlake; 14 miles west of terminal area along Lake Street.

Chicago Great Western. West end of city, 8 miles from terminal area along Congress (Eisenhower) Expressway.

Chicago, Burlington and Quincy. Hawthorne Yard, Cicero; 10 miles west of terminal area along Ogden Avenue.

Pennsylvania. Several small yards along company's lines in Chicago, Calumet City, and Hammond, Indiana.

Chicago and Alton (Gulf, Mobile and Ohio). Forest View; 10 miles southwest of terminal area along line of 47th Street.

Wabash. Western Avenue at 75th Street; 11 miles southwest of terminal area.

Atchison, Topeka and Santa Fe. Corwith Yard; 7.5 miles southwest of terminal area along Stevenson Expressway. This is the newest yard in the Chicago Switching District and the only one in the intermediate area of the city.

Baltimore and Ohio. Barr Yard, near Riverdale; 17.5 miles south of terminal area near Halsted Street.

Chicago, Rock Island and Pacific. Blue Island Yard, Blue Island; 16.5 miles south of terminal area at 127th Street.

Illinois Central. Markham Yard, Markham; 20 miles south of terminal area at 159th Street.

New York Central. Gibson Yard, East Chicago, Indiana; 21 miles southeast of terminal area.

12. For the various freight facilities built in connection with Union Station, see pp. 000–00. The freight-handling tunnels of the core area are unique to Chicago (fig. 59). Construction of the system was begun in 1901 by the Illinois Telephone and Telegraph Company as an underground passageway for telephone and telegraph wires and cables. In 1903, after about twenty miles of tunnels had been completed, the property was sold to the newly organized Illinois Tunnel Company, which planned to install tracks in the tunnels and operate trains primarily to transport packages between stores, warehouses, and delivery points, and secondarily to haul rubbish to barges and wagons for disposal. The company was reorganized in 1904, when it established the Chicago Warehouse and Terminal Company as an addition to its properties. The system was expanded to serve rail freight terminals and office buildings, and by 1909 the two corporations had completed sixty-two miles of tunnel, installed a track of two-foot gauge, electric trolley lines, and elevators for lifting cars in freight stations, and purchased a fleet of electric locomotives. The cost of all this subterranean work was understandably high, amounting to about $30,000,000 by 1910, or $300,000,000 at the 1971 price level, and the inevitable second reorganization came in 1912, when the corporate title was changed to the Chicago Tunnel Company. At the time of its peak traffic the little trains moved 70,000 cars of freight per year, or about 235 per working day.

13. For a complete list of belt and switching companies, see table 6.

14. The north-south line of this L extends along Cicero Avenue (4800W) from approximately North Avenue (1600N) to 67th Street, and the east-west line eastward from Cicero along 75th Street to a junction with the Chicago and Western Indiana tracks near Halsted Street (800W), then southeastward to a yard immediately east of the Illinois Central line along 95th Street. The Belt Railway operates a huge classification yard in Bedford Park, at the elbow point in its two lines.

15. Chief of the bridge routes that function mainly to move freight from one trunk line to another around the Chicago terminal area are the so-called Kankakee Belt Line, a long

branch of the New York Central extending in a shallow arc from South Bend through Kankakee to Zearing, Illinois, and the Toledo, Peoria and Western, now jointly owned by the Pennsylvania and the Santa Fe, and lying in a straight line between Kentland, Indiana, and Keokuk, Iowa. The railroad companies originally operating car-ferry routes were the Ann Arbor, Grand Trunk Western, Pennsylvania, and Pere Marquette (now Chesapeake and Ohio), but the Pennsylvania eventually abandoned its lake service.

16. The extreme examples, respectively, of direct-line and circuitous routing are the lines of the Chicago and North Western and the Grand Trunk Western. The three main passenger lines of the first are perfectly straight for most of their length throughout the city and radiate from the main junctions on the terminal approach along the compass points, north, northwest, and west. The Grand Trunk, on the other hand, extends northeast from Chicago to Port Huron, where it connects with the parent Canadian National for Toronto and Montreal, but that is the last impression one would receive from the location of its tracks in the metropolitan area. An outbound train travels south from Dearborn Station to 47th Street, west to Central Park Avenue (4.5 miles *west* of the terminal), south and southeast to Griffith, Indiana (13 miles *south* of the southern tip of Lake Michigan), before turning in the northeasterly direction likely to take one to Battle Creek, Lansing, and Port Huron. (For a list of passenger-carrying railroads distributed by station, see table 6.)

17. The three original predecessors of the Chicago and North Western corresponded to the three main passenger lines that radiate from the Madison Street terminal: the Galena and Chicago Union became the Galena Division (west), the Illinois and Wisconsin, the Wisconsin Division (northwest), and the Chicago and Milwaukee, the Milwaukee Division (north). A number of transformations in corporate status and title occurred before the ultimate merger.

    The first railroad station in Chicago was the initial Galena and Chicago Union terminal, constructed in 1848 at Canal and Kinzie streets. This structure was enlarged in 1849 and replaced in 1851 by facilities at Wells and North Water streets, the latter in turn being enlarged in 1862–63 and replaced in 1871. The original Illinois and Wisconsin station, built at Kinzie Street and the North Branch in 1854, was replaced in two years. The Chicago and Milwaukee stations followed each other in equally rapid succession after the completion of the first one in 1855. The unified Wells Street Station opened in 1881, and the present structure at Canal and Madison streets in 1911 (for details of the Madison Street terminal and associated improvements to freight and passenger lines, see pp. 253–60, 298).

18. For the design and construction of Union Station, see pp. 264–84. The Chicago, Saint Louis and Pittsburgh was one of the five lines merged in 1890 to form the Pittsburgh, Cincinnati, Chicago and Saint Louis Railroad, later leased to, then merged with, the Pennsylvania.

19. The only structural change in the LaSalle Street complex was the replacement of the vaulted shed.

20. The terminal was originally conceived by the Chicago, Danville and Vincennes Railroad, the predecessor of the Chicago and Eastern Illinois in the Chicago area. The tenants of the Chicago and Western Indiana up to 1881, other than the Chicago and Eastern Illinois, and the dates of their affiliation, were the following: Wabash, Saint Louis and Pacific, 1879 (Wabash); Grand Trunk Junction, 1880 (Grand Trunk Western); Chicago and Atlantic, 1880 (Erie); Louisville, New Albany and Chicago, 1881 (Chicago, Indianapolis

and Louisville, then Monon). The Danville company terminated at Dolton, from which it entered the city by trackage rights over the Chicago, Saint Louis and Pittsburgh, using the latter's original station at Clinton and Carroll streets (this company became one of the participants in the Union Station project). Dearborn Station was closed in 1971, when the remaining trains were transferred to Union Station.

21. Two details are noteworthy in connection with the numerous proposals for terminal unification that began with the Burnham Plan of 1909: first is the number of roads that temporarily terminated at 12th Street, in fortuitous anticipation of Burnham's proposal for a union station along 12th; second is the association of civic improvements with railroad construction in the core area, the one reinforcing and necessitating the other in an urban symbiosis.

22. The origin of this curious name goes back to the beginning of rail history in Chicago. Among the more ambitious projects of the mid-century was one planned to connect Chicago with the Mississippi River on a direct route, an aim that was reflected in the impressive corporate title of Chicago, Saint Charles and Mississippi Air Line Railroad. The Galena company in 1854 bought what little property it possessed, and in 1855–56 the Burlington, Galena, Illinois Central, and Michigan Central built a short crosstown connecting line approximately on the latitude of 15th Street to join the Galena's newly acquired trackage west of the river with the Illinois Central on the lake. These historical antecedents survive in the truncated designation of Saint Charles Air Line, which is now jointly owned by the Illinois Central, Burlington, and New York Central. Except for the Illinois Central's portion of the east end, it is used only for freight transfer movements.

23. After the departure of the Galena (1857) and the Burlington (1881), the tenants since 1874 have included the Baltimore, Pittsburgh and Chicago (Baltimore and Ohio), the Nickel Plate Road, the Wisconsin Central, and the Chesapeake and Ohio. The Michigan Central acquired its trackage rights at the very beginning of the Illinois Central's operations in Chicago, and the Big Four in 1886, but only the latter remains today. Central Station was closed as an operating entity in the spring of 1972, when the remaining trains of the Illinois Central and the former Big Four were transferred to Union Station, to realize at last the dream of a genuine union terminal in Chicago.

24. The Chicago Switching District probably reached its maximum extent in 1920 or shortly thereafter, at which time it had an overall length, between Des Plaines, Illinois, and East Chicago, Indiana, of 38 miles, embraced 400 square miles of area, and included 5,717 miles of track, 160 freight yards, 73 freight stations, six through-passenger terminal stations, and one suburban terminal. The volume and character of rail traffic have changed so drastically over the years that much of this trackage eventually became useless or could easily have been abandoned with a consequent gain in overall efficiency. The shrinking proportion of rail to total traffic and the loss of nearly all merchandise and less-than-carload freight have been the chief factors in the progressive changes in operating procedures. The declining proportion of freight handled by rail since the turn of the century is revealed in the following figures indicating the railroad share over the years: 1910, 95 percent; 1945, 67.2 percent; 1958, 46.0 percent; 1967, 41.8 percent. The total movement of freight measured in ton-miles has increased steadily to the present except for the decline that occurred during the depression of the 1930s and the sudden, extraordinary increase of World War II, but total passenger traffic has just as steadily declined, again except for the artificial expansion of the 1940 war. The high point came in 1920, when the number of passengers was more than double that at the turn of the century, as the accompanying table shows.

Railroad Passengers and Passenger-Miles

Year	Passengers Carried	Passenger-Miles
1900	584,695,935	16,313,284,471
1910	998,735,432	32,388,870,444
1920	1,234,862,000	46,848,668,000
1930	703,598,000	26,814,825,000
1940	452,921,000	23,762,359,000
1950	486,194,000	31,760,001,000
1960	325,872,000	21,257,969,000
1970	283,923,000	10,770,000,000

25. For the program of grade separation, line elevation, new construction, signaling, and other operating improvements, see pp. 000–00.
26. Reliable figures for number of trains and passengers at the various Chicago stations are difficult to secure, and for long periods simply nonexistent. The accompanying table, based on statistics gathered in 1912, provides some idea of rail passenger traffic by station around the time of the Burnham Plan.

Rail Passenger Traffic by Station

Station	Through Traffic		Suburban Traffic		Total	
	Trains	Passengers	Trains	Passengers	Trains	Passengers
North						
Western	121	16,811	189	32,583	310	49,394
Union	169	19,145	112	16,323	281	35,468
Grand						
Central	34	3,175	4	470	38	3,645
LaSalle	80	10,384	111	24,718	191	35,102
Dearborn	104	9,968	42	8,337	146	18,305
Central	85	10,140			85	10,140
Illinois Central						
Suburban			288	40,757	288	40,757
Total	593	69,623	746	123,188	1,339	192,811

After 1920 the number of through passengers declined steadily except for the artificial inflation of World War II, whereas the number of suburban passengers increased irregularly to a grand total more than double that of 1912 (about 260,000 in 1969).

27. On the subsequent history of the North Shore and the other Chicago interurban companies, see pp. 239–40.

3. The Chicago Plan

The Antecedents

Two great motivating factors underlay the metropolitan plan that Daniel Burnham and Edward Bennett created in 1906–8 and that the city adopted in 1910 as the official guide to its economic growth and civic development. One was the essential problem as Burnham grasped it: the building of a harmonious city which would provide, first, an encompassing aesthetic order in its public spaces and, second, the arteries necessary for the convenient and efficient movement of the traffic that was rapidly becoming immobile in the core area. The other motivating factor was the solution, and Burnham saw it on the urban scale in the boulevards, squares, monuments, and river promenades of Haussmann's Paris, and again on the scale of the microcity in the ordered spaces and buildings of the World's Columbian Exposition of 1893. Moreover, as chief of design of the fair and hence closely associated with the architects of the various buildings and with Frederick Law Olmsted, the chief landscape architect, Burnham had firsthand knowledge of the process by which this vision was translated into reality. Whatever the ultimate judgment on its architectural character, there can be no question that both its site plan and its various buildings were brilliantly designed to achieve two ends: to allow the easy circulation of crowds measured in the hundreds of thousands and to offer them the spectacle of the highest civic art constructed on a scale adequate to the immense number of daily visitors and hence to the new industrial city itself.[1]

The damage alleged to have been done by the architectural design of the fair may have lasted half a century, as Sullivan predicted, but the influence of its best buildings and of its site plan was immensely beneficial to the development of American civic art. For a panoramic description of its general planning excellence, that of Talbot Hamlin is still unsurpassed.

It was the compelling effect of its formal plan, rather than the accident of its superficial style, which was largely responsible for its [architectural] popularity. For the first time, hundreds of thousands of Americans saw a large group of buildings harmoniously and powerfully arranged in a plan of great variety, perfect balance, and strong climax effect. . . .

One entered through a railroad station into a sort of vestibule court, a preparation for the grandeur that lay beyond. From there, one either progressed through the Administration Building, or passed by it . . . into the great court; here the lagoon filled most of the area; buildings which balanced, although they were not symmetrical, were ranged on each side; an open colonnade stretched across the far end, and between its columns one was conscious of the level horizon of Lake Michigan beyond. Part way down the length of this major court an axis at right angles to it opened up; at the end of that axis, on the right, was a building of great richness and, on the left, an open view over an informal inner lake, with its green shores and the white masses of the Fine Arts Building as a minor climax. This connecting of the more informal part of the Exposition with the more formal by means of the waterway between the lagoon and the inner lake was most brilliantly handled and gave a needed variety to the whole impression. The way in which the waters of Lake Michigan itself were woven into the whole composition—their broad sweep made an integral part of the Exposition—was also a stroke of genius. . . .

All through the Chicago Exposition of 1893 the handling of climaxes, both major and minor, was outstanding. From a distant view in one direction the dome of the Administration Building formed a climax. But within the central court more intimate and human climaxes were furnished by the great fountain at the inshore end of the lagoon and by the colossal figure of the Republic, backed by the Triumphal Arch on the axis at the end toward the lake. Everywhere the visitor found views, intimate or distant, which were satisfactorily balanced, with climaxes proportionate to their importance and with the balance so arranged as to suggest the correct progress through the Exposition. The whole formed a group plan of superb general composition.[2]

It was this vision, over whose creation he himself presided, that left a profound and ineradicable mark on Daniel Burnham, and however much he was smitten by the classical decor, he correctly saw the lessons in this grand design. He wanted space for compositional effects and for large numbers of people, and he wanted ease of circulation for whatever useful ends, but above all he wanted visual unity, a need that accounts for his idolatry of classicism and his distrust of what he called "incoherent originalities." As he put it,

The influence of the Exposition on architecture will be to inspire a reversion toward the pure ideal of the ancients. We have been in an inventive period, and have had rather contempt for the classics. Men evolved new ideas and imagined they could start a new school without much reference to the past. But action and reaction are equal, and the exterior and obvious result will be that men will strive to do classic architecture. . . . The intellectual reflex of the Exposition will be shown in a demand for better architecture, and designers will be obliged to abandon their incoherent originalities and study the ancient masters of building. There is shown so much of fine architecture here that people have seen and appreciated this. It will be unavailing hereafter to say that great classic forms are undesirable. The people have the vision before them here, and words cannot efface it.[3]

But it is no longer so easy to condemn this passion for antiquity as it once was, especially in view of the new knowledge of urban history and the hopeless state of the contemporary urban milieu. Burnham's essential point was sound: whether architects had to confine themselves to the classical mode was arguable, but the chaos of the city made functional coherence and visual order, at least in the major civic areas, a matter of necessity. The prime example of the value of order, one that was just then coming into being, was the Quadrangle group at the University of Chicago. Montgomery Schuyler, a literate and searching critic who was in no way tied to a revivalistic scheme of architectural design, saw the excellence and the civic value of the fair both in its unity and in its magnitude—in its great size combined with harmony and scale. Thus its importance lay in the structural and architectural design of individual buildings as well as in expert planning, for both taught the architect valuable lessons in the efficient handling of large crowds without sacrifice of formal amenities. Perhaps the foremost structures in this respect were the Agricultural Building of McKim, Mead and White, its great length controlled by a central portico and dome, the huge Manufacturers Building of George B. Post, which was roofed by an immense vault on three-hinged arches, the extreme length dominated by an entrance arch repeated on smaller scale at the corners, and the immensely elongated Fine Arts Building of Charles B. Atwood, where the length was strongly contained and drawn into unified focus by means of advancing end wings. These and other structures of the fair exercised a compelling and beneficent influence on the design of big public buildings. As Christopher Tunnard wrote,

The architecture and city planning of the Fair actually influenced European cities, which in some cases were about to build new civic centers and open up new squares. As the distinguished critic Talbot Hamlin has pointed out, it was a classicism which sought aesthetic, not archaeological, harmony. It leaned much more to the Roman than to the French Renaissance, yet it used Renaissance forms freely. It was a flexible style, which could make a unity of a building by combining boldness of plan with refinement of detail. It made possible the handling of entirely new building types, frequently of great scale, that a growing democracy required. These were the new state capitols, the railroad stations, and the public libraries, which are part of America's contribution to world architecture.[4]

The first person to see the necessity for a Chicago plan and the possibility of realizing it appears to have been James F. Gookins, an obscure graphic artist who was born in Indiana, studied in Munich, lived part of his earlier life in Cincinnati, and acquired his reputation mainly for battle sketches of the Civil War executed for *Harper's Weekly* and *Leslie's Illustrated Weekly*. He moved to Chicago at the end of the war and helped to found the art society in Crosby's Opera House that was one of the forerunners of the present Art Institute. Like Burnham, he was impressed by the orderly planning of the fair and shocked by the contrasting congestion and chaos of Chicago, and he recognized in consequence that the major need was for expanded transportation facilities organized into a rational circulatory system. The plan that he drew up in the decade between 1893 and 1903, which now seems to be known only from a few secondary accounts, was reduced to workable dimensions, and he estimated that it could be realized at a total cost of $225,000,000 (at least $2,850,000,000 in construction costs in 1971). His first step in carrying out this scheme was to found a construction company and secure at least the encouragement if not the outright backing of various executive officers of the Illinois Central Railroad. He went to New York in 1903 to arrange for further financial backing, apparently because of a less than enthusiastic response from the Chicago financiers, and adopted the curious device of dividing his potential backers into groups of banks and insurance companies, no one of which possessed a complete knowledge of the plan, although he seems to have made an exception for the assessment and evaluation staffs of the insurance companies. The only question Gookins had not satisfactorily answered was whether the Chicago City Council would pass the necessary enabling legislation, but before he could find out he suddenly died of a cerebral hemorrhage during his New York visit, and the whole scheme collapsed.

There are several incredible aspects to this odd episode in urban history, but the plan itself, although restricted entirely to the problem of circulation, had a number of features to recommend it. Among modern cities, certainly, there has been no other case in which a private individual, with little financial stake in the community, without political and financial influence, without the backing of powerful public bodies or even publicity, could organize an extensive urban plan and encourage the executives of railroads, banks, and insurance companies to consider underwriting it. With respect to streets, Gookins proposed the widening of all through arteries, the joining of the disconnected segments of the various shore drives, and the unification of the whole system through the construction of a high-level boulevard bridge over the river at the former mouth, with warehouses to be built into the abutments of the structure. The river was to be closed to navigation at the meeting point between the Sanitary and Ship Canal and the former natural waterway (approximately at the intersection of Western Avenue and 26th Street) and the necessary turning basin provided at that point. In this way all street and rail crossings over the river could be fixed rather than movable bridges. All docks were to be restricted to the lake front, but the exact locations are not given in the available summaries of the plan. Proposals for rail travel included a complete subway system in the core area and presumably a union station, although this is by no means clear, and electric power for public uses was to be generated in a single municipally owned plant.[5]

Burnham seems to have known Gookins as an artist and may very well have known of his plan, but whether he was influenced by it has never been determined. In both cases, however, the chief reason the two men proposed their schemes was the realization that a solution to the city's traffic congestion was essential. Other associations and experiences were more decisive factors in the preparation of Burnham's own plan. In 1894, some years before Gookins completed his program, the South Park commissioners proposed the improvement of the south lakeshore from Grant Park to Jackson Park, where the tracks of the Illinois Central lay close to the water's edge behind riprap protection. Burnham submitted a plan in 1896 for a system of scenic drives, beaches, lagoons, and peninsulas much like that proposed in the comprehensive plan of 1909. This scheme was presented to a gathering of merchants and industrialists at a dinner in 1896, where it was received with enthusiasm: George M. Pullman agreed to donate the riparian rights he held near his South Side home, and even the cautious Marshall Field was willing to admit that the idea had possibilities. The Merchants Club undertook the project in 1906, but by that date Burnham had begun to work on his own grand design.

By far the most important experience in the preparation for the Chicago Plan, however, was Burnham's appointment in 1901 to the chairmanship of the Park Commission of the District of Columbia, with Charles F. McKim, Augustus Saint-Gaudens, and Frederick Law Olmsted, Jr., as the associate members. The commission was established by the Senate Committee on the District of Columbia, whose chairman, Senator James MacMillan of Michigan, made the appointments. This powerful commission was largely responsible for the modernization of Major Pierre L'Enfant's Washington Plan of 1791 and hence for the present character of the monumental areas of the city. What was perhaps most decisive for Burnham's Chicago work was the tour of Paris and Versailles that he and his fellow commissioners made during the summer of 1901 as preparation for the Washington plan. Since L'Enfant's design shows the unmistakable influence of the Versailles scheme, both of Burnham's greatest achievements were directly and indirectly indebted to French precedents.

In Chicago, architects, civic officials, and business executives had been meeting at the Commercial Club and the Merchants Club for about a dozen years, from 1893 to 1905, to discuss the rebuilding of the city along the lines suggested by the fair. The specific plan that eventually emerged from these meetings and that came to be known officially as the Chicago Plan was prepared by Daniel Burnham and Edward

H. Bennett in 1906–8, with the assistance of Charles H. Moore, who edited the text, Jules Guerin, who made the illustrations, and Charles Norton and Frederick A. Delano, who offered various kinds of advice on the preliminary versions. The plan was substantially completed by 1908, when the two organizations merged under the single name of the Commercial Club, and was published in complete form by the club in the following year. Coincident with its publication came the establishment of the Chicago Plan Commission, which was at first a group of private citizens organized to urge the adoption and the implementation of the plan and to enlist the cooperation of the building industry in the new construction it proposed. The first chairman was Charles D. Norton and the vice-chairman Charles H. Wacker, who was eventually honored for his civic contributions when Wacker Drive was named after him. In 1910, under the mayoralty of Fred A. Busse, Burnham's handiwork was submitted to the voters and approved by a comfortable majority, as a consequence in good measure of the campaign of public education carried on by the commission and undoubtedly because of happy financial as well as visual memories of the fair itself. Following the adoption of the plan by the voters the commission became a public body appointed by the mayor, with the rather unwieldy number of 328 members, among whom were the mayor ex officio, the city council, the heads of the municipal departments, the planning staff, and various private citizens. The commission's first act was to elect Wacker permanent chairman. For obscure legal and political reasons, however, the document was not adopted by the council as the official plan of Chicago until 1917, during the first of two successive administrations of William Hale Thompson (1915–23), although most public works authorized in the intervening seven years were carried out in accordance with Burnham's program.

The Chicago Plan: General Purpose and Regional Character

The full historical importance of the Burnham plan far transcends its local reference: not only was it the first metropolitan plan, and hence the first to be predicated on an understanding of the unity of the city and its metropolitan context, but it also marked the transition between the strictly geometric planning of the Renaissance and Baroque periods and the three-dimensional, organic, and functional planning of the present day. It represented the next logical stage after Haussmann's plan for Paris (1853–69), and was thus the first plan conceived on a scale necessary for a city of 2,000,000 inhabitants and a metropolitan area of close to 3,000,000. It was the first to be concerned with the problem of circulation in the automotive-electric rapid transit age, to provide an adequate answer to the recreational needs of the modern industrial city, and to pay more than passing attention to the conditions of dwelling and daily work. Burnham and Bennett were among the earliest planners to recognize the need for land-use control and to recommend that land be reserved outside the city against the future requirements for recreational space, streets, and community services. Yet paradoxically enough, the Chicago Plan at the same time marked the last phase of the geometric, Neo-Platonic planning of the Renaissance, with balance, axiality, and monumental vistas deployed in a hierarchical arrangment—the surviving symbols of the mathematical harmonies underlying the divine order, a cosmos in which mankind by the nineteenth century had ceased to believe.

The economic and dynamic character of metropolitan Chicago constituted the foundation on which Burnham's whole program was constructed, as the authors made explicit at the very beginning of their first chapter.

The plan frankly takes into consideration the fact that the American city, and Chicago pre-eminently, is a center of industry and traffic. Therefore attention is given to the betterment of commercial facilities; to methods of transportation for persons and for goods; to removing obstacles which prevent or obstruct circulation; and to the increase of convenience. It is realized, also, that good workmanship requires a large degree of comfort on the part of the workers in their homes and their surroundings, and ample opportunity for that rest and recreation without which all work becomes drudgery. Then, too, the city has a dignity to be maintained, and good order is essential to material advancement. Consequently, the plan provides for impressive groupings of public buildings, and reciprocal relations among such groups. Moreover, consideration is given to the fact that in all probability Chicago, within the lifetime of persons now living, will become a greater city than any existing at the present time; and that therefore the most comprehensive plans of today will need to be supplemented in the not remote future. Opportunity for such expansion is provided for.[6]

With the general character of the work established, the authors devoted their second chapter to an illustrated outline of city planning in ancient and modern periods, in which it is obvious that Burnham was most influenced by the boulevard system and the electric railway terminals of Haussmann's Paris. It is in the third chapter that the focus is directed to Chicago, which is seen with acute insight as the midwestern metropolis bound in an intricate and unbreakable web of relations with the elements of its regional and suburban context. The unparalleled expansion of the city had to be a matter of prime concern: during the second half of the nineteenth century its population had increased from 30,000 to 2,000,000, and no one could predict anything but continued growth at the same rate. By the middle of the new century the population could be expected to reach a maximum of 13,250,000.[7] But the toll exacted by this expansion was appalling, especially in the inner city: long before the horrors of the contemporary ghetto, economic rapacity and civic indifference had combined to leave an ever widening trail of slums, overcrowding, unsanitary conditions and ill health, crime, and endemic lawlessness. Metropolitan Chicago formed a perfect cross section of life in the United States—the promise and the failure, the power of a few and the misery of multitudes.

The whole picture emerged only by means of an overview of the region: Chicago at the turn of the century, far more than at present, was the financial, manufacturing, transportation, cultural, and entertainment center of the Midwest, and hence the magnet which drew people and towns into the dense though widespread pattern of its metropolitan area. A tight symbiotic interdependency among all the communities and between the outer communities and the central city was and continues to be the primary fact of life of this area, and the whole was bound into a single web by the balanced transportation network of 1910—the steam railroads, the electric inter-urbans, the trolley lines, and the new automobiles on old streets. Some suburbs, like some parts of the city, were ordered, harmonious, pleasing in their architectural dignity; others were squalid and ugly, or at best meretricious, rendered so by the two chief sources of maldistributed wealth—financial manipulation and real estate speculation. This contradictory pattern has grown more extreme with the passing years. The primary need, as Burnham saw it, was to undo the damage of the past, where this was possible, to plan for future expansion, and to lay down principles guiding the development of the peripheral as well as the central area, making adequate provision at the same time for future public services.

Burnham somewhat arbitrarily defined the metropolitan area of Chicago as lying within a radius of sixty miles from the Loop, a distance that corresponded roughly to the outer limits of rail suburban service and the electric interurban lines, and a two-hour drive by automobile. He predicted that all the towns lying within this circumference would eventually by incorporated into the city, an irony that might provoke laughter were it not for the tragic imbecility of fragmented political jurisdic-tions in the modern urban conglomerate. To knit this area into a tighter physical unity, at the same time providing adequate highway transportation, initially required two programs of public construction: first, the improvement of existing radial thor-oughfares and, second, the building of a system of circumferential arteries to connect the outlying towns and the radial highways. The proposal for improving the spokes of the wheel, so to speak, proved to be remarkably farsighted. Burnham argued that the best location for the arterial roads is contiguous to the railroad lines, and that the improvement of the roadway should include the separation of through and local traffic, with the local confined to the pavement immediately adjacent to the rail line. This wise provision, which has been followed in the design of Chicago's expressway system, offered a number of advantages to the city and the suburbs: except in areas zoned for and sought after for industrial development, land costs are generally at a minimum along railroad tracks; the routing usually provided the shortest distance into the city because the main rail lines lie on long tangents; residential dislocations could be kept to a minimum; and harmony rather than conflict could be maintained between the two modes of transportation.

The specific proposals for a circumferential system included a through lakeshore highway extending from Wilmette to Milwaukee which would supplement the existing and tortuous Sheridan Road, and an elaborate pattern of four concentric ring highways to be constructed by connecting existing disconnected pieces of suburban roads and upgrading them to the best arterial standards.[8] The circumferential and radial highways were to be supplemented by suburban extensions of the main trolley lines, which were to be constructed, like the electric interurbans, on their own rights of way paralleling the highways at the margin opposite to that of the steam railroad lines, where the latter lay adjacent to the road. Locations were planned to minimize interference with vehicular traffic, and borders were to be laid out in grass and lined with trees and shrubs, so that the ugly billboards and the vile commercial strips would be replaced by landscaped corridors. In this way the whole transportation system could be make to look like the handsomely designed station and associated landscaped grounds of the North Western Railway at Kenilworth or the Burlington at Riverside, to name two conspicuous examples; but this simple and perfectly attainable vision proved beyond the reach of Chicago and indeed of all America, which could only exploit for further financial profit the economic stimulus that always comes with the building of good highways.

Parks and Recreation

Except for the problem of traffic congestion no defect in the urban fabric impressed Burnham more than the relative decline of the city's recreational facilities and the failure to exploit the unparalleled potential of the lakefront. For this reason the fourth chapter of the plan, the first in which the authors considered the city proper rather than the whole metropolitan area, is concerned with parks. The proposals they advanced rested on two kinds of distinctions: the primary one was between large parks offering full landscaping and recreational possibilities and small neighborhood parks which were conceived as recreational plots primarily intended for children; the other had to do with location, whether inland or lakeshore, and hence with the type, since the latter would be composed predominantly of beach area and its appropriate vegetation. The guiding principle in the distribution of large parks was to locate them on boulevards, thus assuring easy access while at the same time uniting all major parks with green corridors. The basis for the detailed proposal was chiefly the report of the Special Park Commission issued in 1904, and to a certain extent the park systems of London, Paris, Boston, and Washington, which Burnham and Bennett reviewed before presenting their own proposals.

The primary consideration was the lakefront, and it was here that the authors exhibited perhaps their finest artistic and planning imagination. The entire shoreline from Evanston to the Indiana state line at 103rd Street, a distance of 23.5 miles, was to be opened to recreational purposes and scenic promenades except for the dock strips immediately north of the Chicago River and at the Calumet River (fig. 6). The most brilliantly conceived feature was the division of the shoreland into two parallel elements, the outer one a succession of peninsulas and narrow islands created by filling along a line following the profile of the shore, and the inner a necklace of lagoons protected by the filled areas. Thus the outer shore could be given over to sand beach, strips of green vegetation, and the natural protection afforded by beaches, against which the most destructive waves will harmlessly spend themselves, while the narrow, and in places winding, lagoons could be used for calm-water boating and scenic promenades. The two lines of peninsulas and islands, extending respectively along the north and south shores, terminated at both ends of Grant Park to form a broad protected harbor for pleasure craft. At the north side of this protected enclosure were the passenger docks and slips for cargo vessels, while a scenic drive ending in a lighthouse and pavilion were to occupy the fill along the south side. The whole scheme, as costly as it seemed, actually rested on a very nice understanding of hydrodynamic and economic realities. The narrow filled areas paralleling the shore would have duplicated in shape and location the numerous spits and bars that naturally form on the bed of the lake as a result of the action of waves and shore currents. The process of filling itself was a cheap and relatively simple operation: the city annually conveyed 1,000,000 cubic yards of immersible and uncontaminating waste into the lake, enough to raise twenty acres of material seven feet above the water surface in a depth of twenty feet, all of which could be readily deposited behind coffer-dams, shore walls, or beach fills. The shore currents can be counted on to deposit their traction load of sand where they are slowed and deflected at the north edges of the peninsular fills, in this way forming beaches by the natural action of the moving water. The lagoons, with their landscaped banks, Burnham visualized as being lined with restaurants and "pleasure pavilions" on the European model. With the exception of Dwight Perkins's Cafe Brauer in Lincoln Park, and in spite of the beer garden tradition of Chicago's German and Scandinavian population, this happy scene went unrealized. The proposed yacht harbors and the extensive pleasure drives along the inner shores of the lagoons, however, have been built to some degree as the plan depicted them.

In addition to the numerous neighborhood parks and children's playing fields, the interior park system was to include three immense fully landscaped reserves in the central part of the North, West, and South sides. Varying in area from 800 to 1,000 acres, they were to be the nodal points of the entire inner system: the northern was to be along the North Branch of the Chicago River at Graceland Avenue (now Grace Street, 3800N); the western near the intersection of Congress Street and Austin Avenue (6000W), and the southern at Western and Garfield boulevards (2400W–5500S). The three were to be connected by a semicircular parkway about fifteen miles in overall length. Supplementing the city parks were the outlying forest lands of the still embryonic Forest Preserve District of Chicago and Cook County, for which Burnham proposed an expansion well beyond the goal the founders had fixed.[9] The area was to include the marshes and woodland along the Calumet River, Lake Calumet, and Wolf Lake, the eastern half of which lies in Hammond, Indiana, but except for the Wolf Lake Wildlife Preserve, the lands bordering these bodies of water have been devoted entirely to industry and railroad lines. The total area of existing and proposed parkland and forest preserve was to be 50,000 acres, or the equivalent of 1 acre per 100 inhabitants for a metropolitan population of 5,000,000. The authors of the plan were confident that this area would provide adequate recreational space through the year 1985; the metropolitan area, however, reached a population of nearly 7,000,000 in 1968, so that only the expansion of the Forest Preserve District to 59,000 acres kept the recreational lands reasonably near the standard of 1 acre per 100 persons.

Transportation and Circulation

The treatment of railroad terminals for freight and passengers, their associated track arrangements, and harbor facilities involved the most extensive changes and additions to the physical fabric of Chicago, with the consequence that the proposals offered in the fifth chapter of the plan are the most complex of all. As the administrator of one of the largest architectural firms in the United States, Burnham had enjoyed extensive firsthand experience with the design of big railroad terminals, chief of which are the Pennsylvania Station in Pittsburgh (1898–1901) and Washington Union Station (1903–07), the latter a major feature of the Washington Plan. He thus had every reason to feel qualified to make thoroughgoing recommendations for the seemingly insoluble problems of rail coordination that Chicago offered. It was more than a matter of trackage, as tangled as that was: at the turn of the century the railroads handled 95 percent of the freight traffic, the balance moving by water, and nearly 100 percent of the intercity passenger traffic, the electric interurban car and the automobile both lying in the very near future. The overriding problem was the inability of the railroads to carry all the freight that was offered to them because of congestion at terminals and yards arising from the chaotic, inefficient, and sometimes makeshift character of these facilities. The ironic result was that the rail companies were unable to use their own motive power, rolling stock, and main tracks to full capacity—in short, bad planning and shortsighted construction frustrated mechanical technology. Part of the trouble arose from the railroad practice in large terminal areas of transferring freight from one line-haul carrier to another in the inner city or at main-line junction points instead of using belt, transfer, and bridge lines already in existence.

For all these reasons Burnham was chiefly concerned to establish a union freight yard or clearing center to function as a common classification, depositing, warehousing, and reloading facility for all freight other than that destined for local city and suburban consignees. Its location was determined to a great extent by the lines of the Belt Railway Company, which is itself a union belt railroad owned by twelve of the trunk-line companies in Chicago.[10] Since the main tracks of the Belt extend in an L-shape through the West and South sides of Chicago and intersect all the through lines entering the city proper, Burnham logically proposed that the union freight yard be located at the elbow of the L, approximately where the transfer company built its clearing yard, immediately southwest of the intersection of Cicero Avenue (4800W) and 65th Street. But the existing transfer lines were to be supplemented by a great extension of the belt system in the form of four rectangular loops located between the elevated Loop in the core and the suburbs immediately outside the western and southern city limits.[11] This circumferential system was to be built by extending, straightening, and piecing together existing rail lines, of which the innermost would presumably lie in tunnels, although this is not clear from the text and the maps in the plan. Burnham thought that future industrial expansion in Chicago would be situated along loop C, the Sanitary and Ship Canal, and the great corridor laced by railroad lines and waterways southwest of the city. Inner-city stations for the handling of merchandise and less-than-carload freight would be along loop A. The entire rail freight system was to be thoroughly integrated with the proposed harbors for waterborne freight at the lake ends of the Chicago and Calumet rivers (fig. 6 shows the plan of slips at the Chicago River). The docks and warehouses for cargo would be connected to the metropolitan railroad lines by electrically operated narrow-gage rail tunnels constructed as an extension of the existing Chicago Tunnel Company's network.[12]

Nothing in the history of civic works in Chicago has been more tedious and ultimately fatuous than the proposals, presented almost yearly, for the unification of railroad passenger terminals. Burnham's plan was essentially sound, although it called for drastic surgery: the six existing stations, with their approach tracks, coach yards, and service facilities, were to be swept away and replaced by three big terminals, one of which was so large as to require the division of the headhouse into separate enclosures; all trains using these stations were to be operated electrically (fig. 6). Central Station would be replaced by a new and much larger structure on the same site, but its approach tracks and those of the Illinois Central Suburban station at Randolph Street were to be screened by depressing them below the grade level of the new lakefront parks. On the West Side an integrated complex embracing Union and North Western stations would occupy an elongated site between Clinton and Jefferson streets (540–600W), extending north and south from Fulton Street (300N) to Taylor (1000S), a distance of 1⅝ miles. Between these two, stretching for four blocks along the south side of Roosevelt Road (1200S) from State to the line of Franklin Street (300W), was the grandest of all, the renderings in the plan suggesting that the vast headhouse complex was to consist of three separate buildings. Associated with the construction of the South Side and West Side stations were two major civic works: one was the straightening of the eastward curving crescent in the Chicago River between Van Buren and 21st Street, and the other the widening of Roosevelt Road between Michigan Avenue and Canal Street (400W) and its elevation to the level of the passenger concourse in the new station.[13]

The main criticism of Burnham's essentially valid scheme is that he held an exaggerated idea of the area of trackage required to handle Chicago's admittedly enormous rail traffic.[14] In 1910 the railroads of the city operated about 1,300 trains per day, a total which could be readily accommodated on forty-four station tracks with a six-track approach, or on fifty tracks at the maximum to allow for the increase in rail traffic that occurred during the next decade. Since about 40 percent of these trains, however, used the Illinois Central Suburban terminal and the new North Western Station, the remainder could be handled on twenty-five tracks, or seven less than the number at Saint Louis Union Station, which is the maximum constructed on a single level. The restriction of the largest stations to areas south of Roosevelt Road and west of Canal Street was the primary aim of Burnham's plan, and the attendant reduction in the area and number of stations conferred the greatest civic benefits. The immense area lying between Van Buren Street and Roosevelt Road, and between State and Canal streets, would have been freed of the railroad properties that still cover the major part of it and released for general commercial and public uses, thus very nearly doubling the space available for building and circulation in the high-density core. The expansion of the elevated Loop into a complete overhead circuit serving the rail stations, the addition of surface car lines and a streetcar subway system following the same route, with subway extensions north of the river, south of Roosevelt Road, and west of Ashland Avenue (1600W), as Burnham proposed, would have enormously improved the circulation of the core area for an indefinite period in the future (certainly far superior to what it is now). The whole plan would have led to the creation of a new Loop bounded by the river on the north, Roosevelt Road on the south, and Michigan Avenue and Canal Street on the east and west. A ring subway system on something like this routing at last reached the planning stage in 1969.

Rail, rapid transit, and surface lines constitute three dimensions of the urban transportation network, but the crucial element in Chicago is the street system that composes the vital fourth. Pedestrian and vehicular congestion in the city's core had reached the point by 1905 where a new and enlarged means of circulation was a necessity for the future growth of the urban area, even if that growth were simply a matter of numerical increase without improvement in the quality of community life. The sixth chapter of the plan, which deals with the street pattern, opens with a bold passage on how the character and scale of the Chicago setting act with population growth as prime determinants in shaping the physical city.

Chicago has two dominant natural features: the expanse of Lake Michigan, which stretches, unbroken by islands or peninsulas, to the horizon; and a corresponding area of land extending north, west and south without hills or any marked elevation. These two features, each immeasurable by the senses, give the scale. Whatever man undertakes here should be actually or seemingly without limit. Great thoroughfares may lead from the water back into the country interminably; broad boulevards may skirt the Lake front, or sweep through the city; but their beginnings on the north, or on the south, or on the west must of necessity be points that move along determined lines with the growth of population. Other harbors have channels winding among islands or around jutting promontories until the landlocked basin is reached; but Chicago must throw out into the open water her long arms of piled-up rock in order to gather in safety the storm-tossed vessels. Other cities may climb hills and build around them, crowning the elevations with some dominating structure; but the people of Chicago must ever recognize the fact that their city is without bounds or limits. Elsewhere, indeed, man and his works may be taken as the measure; but here the city appears as that portion of illimitable space now occupied by a population capable of indefinite expansion.[15]

It was precisely this level and illimitable space that made it possible for Burnham to project a rational arterial pattern that combined the geometric clarity of Renaissance planning with the requirements of modern traffic circulation. The original gridiron pattern, with its uninterrupted straight lines, had to be supplemented by a diagonal system for direct access to the core from peripheral neighborhoods and outlying suburbs. Chicago had several such arteries from the beginning, most of them the original roads uniting the city with outlying towns, such as Milwaukee and Lincoln avenues on the North Side, and Archer and Blue Island on the South. Burnham proposed a considerable extension of the existing system: the primary was to consist of seven diagonal arteries extending northwestward from the inner city and three extending southwestward; in addition to these there was to be a secondary group of diagonals extending across the primary in the form of a latticelike pattern overlying the basic gridiron—that is, diagonal arteries on the North Side would lie in parallel lines from the Lincoln Park area toward the southwest, and a similar group would extend from the south lakeshore parks toward the northwest. Everywhere in the entire street system through traffic was to be separated from local residential traffic in order to maintain safety and quiet surroundings in dwelling areas and to protect the residential property from the deterioration attendant upon future commercial development. Because of these distinctions in traffic character there were to be three classes of streets: the conventional street serving all local traffic generated by residential areas and neighborhood commercial facilities; the avenue, designed for through traffic; and the boulevard with landscaped parkway strips, combining the corridor park and the drive.

This admirable scheme, perfectly sound throughout for our own day as well as in Burnham's time, was to be built little by little as the outward expansion of the city and its traffic required it. Every street was to be bordered by grass and trees except where commercial deliveries made this impossible, and all utilities, including electrical conduits, were to be placed underground.[16] It was obvious that an efficient circulatory system was essential to the future growth of the city, and the question was whether this was to be built haphazardly, with the usual chaos as a result, or whether it was to be done with the foresight that would yield maximum benefit to all concerned. "That task belongs to the city itself," Burnham and Bennett wrote, "and the only way in which it can be accomplished is by the preparation and adoption of a plan for platting all those lands adjacent to the city which are reasonably certain to be included within the enlarged boundaries."[17] The implication in this passage of land reservation and control for future use marks the introduction of this concept into the building of American cities, although the idea had long been applied in certain European cities. Burnham failed to reckon, however, with the intransigence of the modern suburb, and there is an ironic naivete in his valid and understandable belief that the natural western boundary of the city would be the Des Plaines River.

Various end-to-end boulevard systems and specially widened streets were planned as a series of circuits at increasing distances from the city center. The outermost, or Grand Circuit, as we noted previously, was conceived as a semicircular drive uniting the three great interior parks and sweeping in an arc from the middle North Side to an opposite point on the South Side. This not particularly useful scheme could also be regarded as a semicircular ribbon of parkland uniting the expanded park areas in the outer quarters of the city. The intermediate circuit was to be composed of the widened and newly landscaped segments of the West Park and South Park boulevards that had been gradually planned and layed out over the years from 1869.[18] The inner circuit was L-shaped, consisting of improved and greatly widened commercial arteries, namely, Chicago (800N), Halsted (800W), Union Park on a diagonal, Ashland (1600W), Roosevelt (1200S), Halsted, and 22nd (Cermak), among which Roosevelt Road was to be elevated between Michigan Avenue and Canal Street. The innermost was a smaller duplicate of the preceding system, beginning with Washington Street in the Loop and extending to Roosevelt Road via Canal, Congress, and Halsted streets. Two South Side boulevards, Michigan and South Parkway, were to be extended across the river and through the North Side to a connection with North Lake Shore Drive at the south end of Lincoln Park. A special boulevard system, clearly derived from the river promenades of Paris, was planned for both banks of the widened, straightened, and deepened river, from the "mouth" at the lake, westward to the turning basin, northward along the North Branch to North Avenue (1600N), and south-southwestward along the South Branch to Halsted Street. These were to be double-deck arteries, the lower of the two providing access for commercial traffic to the docks and warehouses along the rivers. Very nearly all of this program was realized except for the outer park and river drives; among the latter only Wacker Drive exists today to provide some realization of the aesthetic potential inherent in the highly urbanized river.

The Urban Core

The vision of monumental grandeur evoked by the White City of the fair was most fully embodied in Burnham's proposals for Chicago's core area, which are presented in the seventh chapter as the end point of a plan that moves inward from the encompassing region to the working heart of the city. Burnham defined the administrative, shopping, financial, and transportation center as the rectangular area bounded by the lake and Halsted Street on the east and west and by the main river and Roosevelt Road on the north and south, but he predicted that it would soon expand to Chicago Avenue (800N) on the north, Ashland (1600W) on the west, and 22nd Street (Cermak) on the south.[19] In the smaller space the public activities of the entire city converged, with the obvious consequence that a substantial proportion of the middle-class population entered, moved within, and left it every working and shopping day. The overriding problem in this extremely concentrated enclave was—as it is today—the movement of both wheeled and pedestrian traffic.

The first and most effective step was the reconstruction of Michigan Avenue, since it was not only a major commercial thoroughfare, its west side lined with office buildings, hotels, large houses, and expensive shops, but also the site of many institutions that constituted the city's intellectual and artistic center—the Public Library, the Art Institute, Orchestra Hall, and the Auditorium were the foremost among them. Burnham proposed that the street be rebuilt into a great landscaped boulevard, bordered by planted strips and fountains, its pavement divided by grass-covered islands into separate lanes for through and local traffic. From Randolph Street north to Erie (658N) Michigan was to be elevated to a sufficient height above grade to accommodate a lower level reserved for commercial traffic serving the docks along the river and the spur of the North Western Railway lying on the north bank. This brilliant proposal, which has been extensively realized, required a double-deck movable bridge over the river.

Second to Michigan in its importance at the time and in its need for improvement was Halsted Street (800W), the twenty-two mile tangent length of which very likely made it the longest commercial street in the world. The first necessity was widening and dividing the paved area to handle the immense volume of street railway, wagon, and recently appearing automotive traffic; the second was the separation of the street and railroad grade levels. The seemingly endless thoroughfare passed over two major commercial waterways, crossed eleven railroad lines and their associated yards, passed through numerous industrial, warehouse, and outdoor bulk-storage areas, lay along commercial developments that extended for unbroken miles, and carried every kind of wheeled traffic moving at every rate of speed. Grade separation was thus a matter of desperate urgency, for safety and for the circulation of the city's lifeblood. But Halsted Street meant more than this: congestion, slums, and traffic chaos were combined with air pollution and surface dirt to present the vision of the urban inferno in all its horror, and it was a scene that inspired Burnham and Bennett to write one of the most prophetic passages in the plan. The ugliness in their day reached its most concentrated and hence most repulsive form at the intersection of Halsted Street and Chicago Avenue (800N), and if anything were to be done to make the city a decent human habitation it was there that the maximum effort would have to be focused.

There the smoke from railroad shops and yards and from standing locomotives combines with the soot sent up by nearly four hundred trains that come and go each day. Steamships, tugs, and other river craft add their contribution; the near-by tanneries and the garbage wagons contribute their odors; the great coal docks, with their noisy buckets and intermittent engines, increase the din; and the streets are covered with the sawdust, coal, and dirt spilled from the thousands of wagons that constantly use this crossing. Close to this intersection is a cosmopolitan district inhabited by a mixture of races living in surroundings which are a menace to the moral and physical health of the community.[20]

Burnham clearly recognized the evil as one that transcended the problem of moving goods and people, for in many places the city had become the enemy of life itself, and in a single passage he and Bennett proposed what they hoped would be the solution for slums as well as dirt and chaos.

The electrification of railways within the city, which cannot be long delayed, will serve to change radically for the better the dirt conditions in this neighborhood; but the slum conditions will remain. The remedy is the same as has been resorted to the world over: first, the cutting of broad thoroughfares through the unwholesome district; and, secondly, the establishment and remorseless enforcement of sanitary regulations which shall insure adequate air-space for the dwellers in crowded areas, and absolute cleanliness in the street, on the sidewalks, and even within the buildings. The slum exists today only because of the failure of the city to protect itself against gross evils and known perils, all of which should be corrected by the enforcement of

simple principles of sanitation that are recognized to be just, equitable, and necessary. . . . In respect to street cleanliness and adequate air-space, Chicago may well
take a lesson from Berlin, where the streets are kept clean by daily washings, and
where a property owner may build on only two-thirds of his land, leaving the remainder for a court.[21]

After this brief but pregnant digression on urban blight, Burnham returned,
perhaps anticlimatically, to his program for the improvement of circulation in the
core. From Halsted Street, at the west boundary of the inner area, he turned eastward
into the Loop. He proposed the widening of LaSalle Street, the financial artery of
Chicago, northward from Van Buren Street at the south edge of the elevated circuit
to North Avenue (1600N), expanding the block between Van Buren and Congress
into a plaza which would be the center of the financial strip.[22] We have here another
of several proposals for the movement of various centers of urban ecology to areas
south and west of the Loop, on land freed of rail trackage.

It was in Grant Park, on the east side of the core, however, that Burnham offered
his second-grandest scheme for the creation of civic monuments and the enhancement
of urban life. The park was conceived in effect as a cultural center set in a vast landscaped surrounding. The Art Institute was already there, and so Burnham saw no
reason why the intellectual and aesthetic life of the city should not be rounded out
with the establishment of the Field Museum of Natural History at the park end of the
Congress Street axis and of the Crerar Library between the two museums. The construction cost of the library, estimated at $1,000,000, he thought would be borne
primarily by funds provided by the South Park Commission, under whose jurisdiction
Grant Park fell.[23] While these new structures were being built, the Art Institute was
to be expanded through the addition of a new gallery and a separate school building.
The museums, the library, and the new Central Station at the south end of the park
were to form, as we might expect, a monumental classical composition of the kind
Burnham loved.

The park was conceived not only as a landscaped center for cultural institutions,
but equally as the background and inner boundary of an immense harbor development
extending nearly two miles from the river to the line of Roosevelt Road (1200S).
At the north and south sides the rectangular harbor area was to be enclosed by peninsular fills extending for a maximum of a mile and a half into the lake (fig. 6). Both
peninsulas were to end in circular embayments carrying lighthouses and ring drives,
with numerous recreational facilities along the way—promenades, restaurants, band
shelters, and the like—and streetcar lines to provide full public access at all times.
A broad meadow embracing athletic fields, gymnasiums, and beaches was to extend

southward from Roosevelt to 22nd Street. The south fill would have been devoted strictly to pleasure and scenic vistas, but the north, in addition, was to terminate in a ring of radial docks for passenger vessels and to constitute the south boundary of a large protected harbor containing slips for cargo vessels. The whole scheme was princely in its magnitude, highly sophisticated in its urbanity, and yet marked by a scrupulous attention to details of function and design: it would have commanded permanent attention, because not even great harbor cities on the sea could show this magnificent balance between commerce and recreation, the two lying side by side but in no way intruding on each other.

The landward counterpart of the harbor development was an east-west axis in the form of a great boulevard created out of old Congress Street, its east end in Grant Park and its west at the Civic Center proposed for the intersection of Congress and Halsted streets. Again we see how this element of the civic design was predicated on the expansion of the central business district southward to the new line of rail terminals on Roosevelt Road, since the central east-west axis of that district would then be shifted roughly to the line of Congress at 500 South. This avenue, it was hoped, varying in width from 200 to 300 feet, was to be lined with public buildings, theaters, smart shops, and the most elegant hotels. The Civic Center at its west end was the grand climax of the whole composition, a vast pentagonal plaza from which six avenues would radiate on the diagonal directions and four on the cardinal points of the compass. It was the unifying element of the whole core plan—indeed, the hub and focus of the vast city spread out around it—and Congress Parkway was thus at once a geometric axis and the cord that united the institutions of art and science in Grant Park with those of government in the Civic Center. The specific buildings, all of them elevated on terraces, were to stand in three groups, respectively those of the municipality, the county and state, and the federal government, with the great domed City Hall, rivaling the United States Capitol in height, at the center of the complex. The plan was generous in its proposal for municipal facilities, which were to include separate buildings for the city administration, the departments of public works and public health, the city hospital (including a mental hospital), the city records, and the courthouse. The proposal for a unified federal enclave was particularly farsighted: the domed Federal Building completed as recently as 1905 was already out of date, and the promise of a genuine federal center did not come until 1960, but a decade later the city was still waiting for its completion as the federal government poured its resources into military programs.

The authors of the plan have been frequently assailed for the monumental extravagance of the Civic Center and for its distant removal from the inner heart of the city.

But Burnham and his colleagues knew very well what they were doing, and they had good reason for their location as long as they could believe that the city would cooperate with the plan commission in relocating the railroads.

The population in Chicago [they wrote] has stretched itself along the Lake shore; but the center of density has moved steadily in a southwesterly direction. . . . The line of density of population passes through the present location of the City Hall and the Court House [block bounded by Clark, LaSalle, Randolph, and Washington streets], thence a little to the south of the proposed civic center. Moreover, the point selected for the civic center is the center of gravity, so to speak, of all the radial arteries entering Chicago.[24]

As for the monumentality, although we have understandably lost sympathy for the classical expressions of institutional power, Burnham was searching for something that the foremost cities of Europe and Asia possessed but that all American cities save Washington lacked, and he thought that classicism best proclaimed the symbolic and the functional role of buildings and plazas in the civic center.

They typify the permanence of the city, they record its history, and express its aspirations. Such a group of buildings as Chicago should and may possess would be for all time to come a distinction for the city. It would be what the Acropolis was to Athens, or the Forum to Rome, and what St. Mark's Square is to Venice,—the very embodiment of civic life. Land should be acquired in quantity sufficient to carry out a plan commensurate with Chicago's needs, and with her dominating position in this region. This plan first should be worked out by the architects, and then should be realized by the concerted action of the community.[25]

The vision was essentially a true one, but unfortunately the American—and particularly Chicago's—experience gave it a bitter, ironic quality: by 1970 the city was mortally sick, its problems overwhelming, and its primary aim was to heal rather than to memorialize itself. Burnham correctly saw, however, that the monumental center was more than a group of symbolic buildings serving the functions of government.

Important as is the civic center considered by itself, when taken in connection with this plan of Chicago, it becomes the keystone of the arch. The development of Halsted Street, and Ashland and Michigan avenues, flanked by the great thoroughfares of Chicago Avenue and Twelfth Street [Roosevelt Road], will give form to the business center; while the opening of Congress Street as the great central axis of the city will at once create coherence in the city plan. Nowhere else on this continent does there exist so great a possibility combined with such ease of attainment. Simply by an intelligent handling of the changes necessary to accommodate the growing business of Chicago, a city both unified and beautiful will result. The Lake front will be opened to those who are now shut away from it by lack of adequate approaches; the great masses of people which daily converge in the now congested civic center will be able to come and go, quickly and without discomfort; the intellectual life of the city will be stimulated by institutions grouped in Grant Park, and in the center of all the varied activities of Chicago will rise the towering dome of the civic center, vivifying and unifying the entire composition.[26]

In view of what life in Chicago became for a high proportion of its citizens, these words constitute perhaps the saddest irony in the history of civic art.

The final question Burnham and Bennett had to face was the tedious but essential business of the cost of carrying out their plan and of how it could be met. The realization of the whole vast program, of course, was dependent on the continuing growth of the city's economy. There were many factors that made the authors of the plan supremely confident. First was the reasonable expectation that the rapid increase in the assessed value of real estate, and in the annual value of manufactures and of wholesale and retail trade, would continue indefinitely in the future, providing an economic basis for bond issues and direct annual expenditures well beyond the cost of putting the plan into effect. Further, it was assumed, again on good ground, that the implementation of the plan would greatly stimulate urban commerce, thus making the total cost smaller in proportion to the income of the metropolitan area. Finally, there was need for extensive legislation enacted in the Illinois General Assembly and the city council to enable the municipality to undertake numerous operations which lay outside the scope of its normal activity. Chicago had an impressive tradition of great public enterprises—the park and boulevard system, the Sanitary and Ship Canal, the Columbian Exposition—and of establishing cultural and educational institutions of the first rank—the Symphony Orchestra, the Field Museum, the Art Institute, Newberry and Crerar libraries, Chicago and Northwestern universities. These accomplishments, added to the reconstruction of the entire commercial area of the city after the fire of 1871 and the concomitant creation of a new urban architecture, argued persuasively that Chicago had had more than its share of experience in the successful undertaking of the most ambitious artistic, educational, civic, and engineering works. There was every reason to believe that the citizens of Chicago would accept the plan once its benefits were made clear, and they did, with a substantial majority, in the year following its publication. Once again Burnham's experience with Paris proved to be decisive, for the French capital offered a concrete example of the feasibility of public works on the greatest scale: with fewer than 1,000,000 residents and with economic prospects far below those of Chicago, the city had undertaken a street improvement program estimated to have a total cost of $260,000,000 and had seen it through to successful completion in thirty-five years.[27]

There were serious legal obstacles to an immediate full-scale implementation of the plan, and it is another credit to Burnham's thoroughness that he concluded the document with an appendix by Walter L. Fisher entitled "Legal Aspects of the Plan of Chicago." Here the essential problems were explored in terms of the legal possibilities and difficulties associated with the various aspects of the plan: how much of the program could be carried out under existing laws; how much of it required additional legislation; the extent to which new legislation might require changes in the Illinois constitution, which was antiquated even at that date. Ironically enough, the fewest obstacles stood in the way of rail terminal unification; yet this was one part of the plan that remained wholly unrealized. Both Fisher and the authors of the plan realized that "rigid constitutional restraints" in the United States tied the hands of municipal governments, effectively preventing them from carrying out works that had been readily accomplished in Europe, sometimes by "arbitrary though effective methods of . . . city planning." What they failed to see is that the constitutional and legal restraints in the United States operate to give the business community and especially the real estate interests a free hand in the exercise of their rapacity. The most obvious and immediate limitation was that placed on Chicago's capacity to raise capital for large public works. The city's bonded debt was and continues to be restricted by the Illinois constitution to a maximum of 5 percent of the assessed valuation of property, and the city was then allowed to levy an annual tax for corporate expenses not to exceed 2 percent of this valuation, exclusive of the taxes levied to retire bond issues. The property valuation of 1908 was $477,190,399, fixing the debt limit at $23,859,520 and the tax yield at $9,543,808.[28] The city had a little margin for increasing its bonded debt, but the overriding problem was and remains the fact that the legislature can authorize a higher tax but cannot increase the municipal debt limit without a constitutional amendment. Legal obstacles, the rural backwardness of the Illinois legislature and other state institutions, the failure of the city to maintain anything like an adequate rate of economic growth, depression, militarism—these ultimately proved disastrous to the full realization of Burnham's brave vision.

NOTES TO CHAPTER 3

1. Some part of the fair's success in handling great crowds must be attributed to the suburban service of the Illinois Central Railroad and to Atwood's design of the special station

at the fair entrance. The record traffic came on 9 October 1893, when the railroad transported 541,312 passengers in twenty-four hours, apparently with no higher toll than the usual lost children and frayed nerves. The figure also indicates that the Chicago railroads could probably have carried ten times the number of suburban passengers actually transported around 1910.

2. Talbot Hamlin, *The Forms and Functions of Twentieth Century Architecture* (New York: Columbia University Press, 1952), 2: 578–81.

3. Originally quoted in Montgomery Schuyler, "Last Words about the Fair," *Architectural Record*, 1893; reprinted in William A. Coles and Henry Hope Reed, Jr., *Architecture in America: A Battle of Styles* (New York: Appleton-Century-Crofts, 1961), p. 198.

4. Christopher Tunnard, *The Modern American City* (Princeton: Van Nostrand, 1968), pp. 47–48. Tunnard's thesis is illustrated by the fact that the five leading railroad stations in the United States reveal this combination of great spatial enclosure and effective planning with scale and control, and all were built in the first quarter of the twentieth century. They are Union Station, Washington (1903–7); Pennsylvania Station, New York (1903–10; now demolished); Grand Central Terminal, New York (1903–13); North Western Station, Chicago (1906–11); and Union Station, Chicago (1916–25), to which there might be added Cincinnati Union Terminal (1929–33), the only one in the modern style but obviously indebted to the classical precedents.

5. Certain features of this plan deserve detailed comment. The valuable proposal for a bridge at the "mouth" of the river was unusually farsighted: it was not realized until the completion of Link Bridge in 1937. The idea of closing the river to navigation in the core and inner-city railroad areas had been first advanced about 1880 by a former mayor of Chicago, De Witt C. Cregier, in order to put an end to what for many years were intolerable obstructions to rail and street traffic occasioned by the repeated openings of movable bridges. Over the years, however, the problem took care of itself as truck transportation gradually superseded rail and water transport for merchandise freight, and as manufacturing and warehousing facilities moved out of the city center to open land along the canal. The consequence has been that bridges above the north end of the canal are seldom opened, the few vessels using the river proper being tankers and river tugs with superstructures low enough to clear the bottom chords of the bridge trusses. Finally, the only rail bridges in this length of the waterway are those of the Pennsylvania Railroad at 21st Street and the Baltimore and Ohio Chicago Terminal and Saint Charles Air Line at 15th Street, and traffic on them has declined markedly with the reduction in the number of through passenger trains and inner-city freight transfers.

6. Daniel Burnham and Edward H. Bennett, *The Plan of Chicago* (Chicago: Commercial Club, 1909), p. 4.

7. These figures explain in good part the confidence of the business and political establishment in the city's ever increasing prosperity. It is necessary to keep them in mind in order to understand the extravagant programs of public works undertaken up to 1930 as well as the irony of these optimistic convictions. The high point of the city's population —3,620,962—came in 1950 (see table 1).

8. The four circumferential highways were to lie on the following routes, in order from outermost to inner: (1) Kenosha–McHenry–Sycamore–Morris–Kankakee–La Porte–Michigan City (ca. 55-mile radius); (2) Waukegan–Elgin–Aurora–Joliet–Crown Point–Hobart, and Joliet–Gary (ca. 35-mile radius; the second almost exactly corresponds to the line of the Elgin, Joliet and Eastern Railway); (3) Winnetka–Des Plaines–Elmhurst–Hinsdale–Harvey–Gary (variable 16- to 25-mile radius); (4) Evanston–Niles Center

(now Skokie)–Riverside–Chicago Ridge–east to lake on the line of 103rd Street (ca. 14-mile radius).

It is important to bear in mind that all this was proposed before state and federal highway departments had been established. The only questionable idea in Burnham's scheme is the location of a lakeshore highway through the residential areas of the North Shore.

9. For the establishment and early expansion of the Forest Preserve District, see pp. 211–12.

10. For the ownership of the Belt Railway, see table 6, part 2.

11. The innermost rail loop or belt, designated A in the Plan, surrounded the Loop approximately at the river on the north, Canal Street on the west, and Roosevelt Road (1200S) on the south. Next beyond A was loop B, essentially a westward extension of A along the lines of Lake Street and Roosevelt Road to Western Avenue. The third, loop C, was much more extensive, its three sides lying close to Armitage Avenue (2000N) on the north, Cicero (4800W) on the west, and 75th Street on the south. The last, loop D, lay outside the city limits approximately on the line of the Indiana Harbor Belt Railroad.

12. The tunnel system is concentrated mainly in the core area. The concrete-line tunnels, which still exist, contain a track of two-foot gage and the associated electrical distribution system.

The numerous switching and transfer companies built in Chicago realized to some extent the proposals of the Plan, and the construction of cargo-handling harbor facilities at Navy Pier and Lake Calumet closely followed Burnham's recommendations. In other respects, however, the detailed plans for a rail belt system proved to be largely irrelevant because of radical changes in freight transportation: over the years trucks came to carry nearly all local and less-than-carload freight, while the railroads concentrated on long-haul bulk commodities, making greater use of belt and bridge lines in order to bypass crowded terminal areas. The introduction of piggyback freight is changing the picture once again, and the need for a coherent pattern of integrated rail-truck facilities is now as essential as ever.

13. Roosevelt Road (formerly 12th Street) was to be expanded to a plaza 250 feet wide in front of the station buildings, and to a thoroughfare 180 feet wide throughout the remainder of its length, crossing the river on a double-level bascule bridge. The river was eventually straightened, but since the station was never built the elevation and widening of Roosevelt Road were considerably reduced in extent.

For the West Side station along Clinton Street several schemes were proposed by various engineers working independently of Burnham and Bennett. The proposals were about equally divided among grade level, elevated, and depressed track areas, but all had the disadvantage of sharply curving approach tracks at the north and south throats of the double-ended terminal. Those at the north end were required to swing the tracks into the east-west alignment of the Pittsburgh, Cincinnati, Chicago and Saint Louis-Milwaukee Railroad approach, and those at the south to swing the tracks eastward to the original alignment of the Pennsylvania Railroad approach.

14. A terminal station of standard design, with at least eight tracks, an interlocking plant, and an adequate approach, can easily handle thirty trains per track per day, but the density may be increased for short periods during rush hours if there are at least four approach tracks. (For the basis of this principle, see under North Western Station, pp. 260, 294–95.)

15. Burnham and Bennett, *Plan of Chicago*, pp. 79–80.

16. With typical thoroughness Burnham and Bennett even specified street widths: for resi-

dential traffic, 20-36 feet (the latter now standard); for heavy commercial traffic, 70-90 feet; for similar traffic in congested retail districts, 80-100 feet; through arteries and boulevards varied considerably, from 120 to 250 feet.

17. Burnham and Bennett, *Plan of Chicago*, p. 91.
18. For the intermediate boulevard system, see pp. 32, 53.
19. The core area of a city can seldom be defined exactly in geometric terms; yet however we establish its shape and size in Chicago, there is no question that Burnham's confidence in its future growth was not borne out by subsequent developments. The northward expansion along Michigan Avenue ultimately extended to Oak Street (1000N), but redundant rail facilities, derelict industrial and commercial areas, Skid Row, and similar deteriorated neighborhoods effectively bottled up the core area on the west and south sides. It was not until 1969 that major capital investments characteristic of the commercial heart began to appear in the inner edges of the blighted West Side, immediately west of Canal Street.
20. Burnham and Bennett, *Plan of Chicago*, p. 108.
21. Ibid., pp. 108–9. Once the *Plan of Chicago* was launched, concern with the ethical ends of urban planning grew in proportion to the economic, technical, and aesthetic concerns, in great measure under the influence of the Hull House program, the physical plant of which had been completed in 1908. A speaker at a dinner given by the Commercial Club for members of the Plan Commission on 8 January 1910 described the human problem in more emphatic terms than Burnham did.

> The physical and moral deterioration of the human race under bad conditions of city life is one of the great problems of the age. That city life is producing a physically and morally deficient life is apparent, especially in old cities where the process has gone on longer. Chicago's problem is to check this tendency before it has a fixed type of physical and moral inferiority. If you will consult the deficient and delinquent records of Chicago, as well as the records of premature mortality . . . , you will find certain black spots on the map representing districts in which misery, vice and early death seem congested. . . . Proper housing, proper sanitation, air and sunlight are the first rights of humanity, and when we permit them to be denied, we must accept responsibility for the inevitable result. [Quoted in *Wacker's Manual of the Plan of Chicago*, prepared by Walter D. Moody under the auspices of the Chicago Plan Commission (Chicago, 1912), pp. 89–90].

> The prescription might seem a little too simple and naive to an age that has experimented on the grand scale with renewal and public housing and seen all of the experiments fail; yet the establishment of an adequate code, coupled with its ruthless and equitable enforcement, is a sine qua non for urban improvement. An extension of precisely the same proposal offered in the original *Plan of Chicago* was presented in city council in spring 1969 by an independent alderman, Leon Despres. As a method of preventing further deterioration of buildings in blighted areas, and on the assumption that the city would provide an adequate number of building inspectors and housing court judges, he offered a four-point program: (1) frequent, thorough, systematic building inspection in aging neighborhoods; (2) heavy fines levied against landlords who violate the code; (3) early rehabilitation receivership with adequate resources to repair deteriorated buildings; (4) establishment of administration hearing boards in the slums to reduce the load on the housing court. In spite of lessons taught long ago, nothing has been permanently learned, and the United States remains the only industrially mature country in which slums constitute a steadily growing feature of urban life.

22. This scheme is meaningful only if we recall the previous plan to demolish LaSalle Street

Station after the construction of the new union rail complex on Roosevelt Road (see pp. 71–72).

23. For the construction of the Field Museum, see pp. 188–94. The John Crerar Library of Science and Technology was founded in 1894 under the terms of a bequest left by John Crerar, who provided the major part of its endowment of $3,400,000 in his will. The library acquired its own quarters in a new building constructed at Michigan Avenue and Randolph Street in 1920, and was merged with the library of Illinois Institute of Technology in 1963.

24. Burnham and Bennett, *Plan of Chicago*, p. 115. By "line of median density" the authors meant the median line of population distribution.

25. Ibid., p. 117.

26. Ibid., pp. 117–18.

27. The 1971 replacement value of the street and boulevard system planned by Haussmann would probably be about $3,750,000,000 at United States price levels.

28. The 1971 equivalents of these figures, based on comparative building costs, are as follows: valuation, $5,640,000,000; debt limit, $282,000,000; tax yield, $112,800,000. Some idea of the capacity of the largest corporations for capital investment comparable to that for municipal public works may be gained from the fact that the total investment in Pennsylvania Station in New York (1903–10) was carried on the company's books at $112,000,000, or nearly a billion dollars at the present time. Clearly, the largest cities were less well off.

Expansion and Boom

4. Buildings of the Commercial City

Office Buildings

In 1910 Chicago had every reason to be confident of its future prosperity and to believe unquestioningly in the realization of the grand vision that Burnham had set before it. Although the city's population increase of 24 percent in the coming decade marked some reduction from the 29 percent of the previous one, the rate of increase was still unparalleled for cities whose populations numbered in the millions.[1] The expansion of wealth measured in manufactured products and total income exceeded the growth in population, so that per capita income steadily rose. The growth in all forms of rail traffic was spectacular: passenger traffic, for example, continued to climb at such a rate that the number of passengers more than doubled in the first two decades of the new century. Behind this phenomenon lay many social and economic factors—increasing mobility and wealth, the continental distribution of markets and manufacturing, increasingly rapid expansion of the metropolitan area, the rise of the suburbs, and the growing interdependency among cities and between cities and agricultural regions. The rapid transit system, although relying exclusively on elevated structures rather than on subways like the more advanced systems in New York, London, and Paris, was nevertheless comparable to these larger organizations in capacity and efficiency.

For the design and construction of all types of buildings, the organization of the building industry, and the volume of new construction measured against population, Chicago had no serious competitor other than New York. In 1910 alone the city opened to use nearly a million and a quarter square feet of office space and 17,500 dwelling units, divided between apartments and individual houses by a ratio of four to one. Both figures were to increase irregularly but steadily to the high point that came in the years 1927 to 1929.[2] The Burnham Plan was as yet too new to be tested through practical realization, but it had already given Chicago the great distinction of possessing the first metropolitan plan in the world. Civic, cultural, and educational institutions stood in the front rank, and at least one of them, the University of Chicago, had already attracted international attention, especially in philosophy and the natural sciences.

At the same time, there were unpleasant realities, and one did not have to look far to see them. The city was unbelievably dirty: the hydrocarbons and carbon oxides of automobile exhaust lay in the future, but the smoke from high-sulfur Illinois bituminous coal poured daily out of thousands of homes, skyscrapers, factories, and locomotives. Soot and cinders in the air, sewage far beyond the oxidation point in the Sanitary Canal, the excrement of horses covering the streets, ashes and rubbish around the rail yards and engine terminals, the junk accumulating from abandoned machines, containers, and other metal objects—these features characterized the whole working city, and if some progress was made in getting rid of one of them, there were other forms of ugliness and dirt to take its place. A high and unchanging proportion of the citizens, possibly as many as one-third, lived under conditions of poverty and squalor, in slums and other areas of urban blight that have resisted the few attempts to reduce their area.

The black ghetto, which was the deliberate creation of race prejudice and the real estate and financial practices that pandered to it, had been established as an endemic, growing, and so far ineradicable element of the city by 1910. The first black settlements in Chicago grew up in the area roughly bounded by South Saint Lawrence Avenue (600E), South Parkway (400E), and 40th and 45th streets. Up to the end of the nineteenth century it could be regarded as one ethnic enclave out of many, for the city was made up of numerous little ghettos—Irish, German, Scandinavian, Italian, Polish, Greek, Lithuanian, Jewish—each relatively self-contained and with rather little intercourse among them. But these European peoples were eventually assimilated to varying degrees into the economic, social, and political life of the city; the black ghetto, on the other hand, was built up over the thirty years from 1890 to 1920 as a true medieval enclave, walled in by social and economic pressures that prevented integration with the white areas. The process, learned so well in the years before World War I, was to be repeated for Mexican, Puerto Rican, and Indian peoples after the Second World War. The race riot of 1919 should have provided ominous warning of a potentially fatal sickness. It went unheeded, of course, and the only solution forthcoming was the escape of white people to the suburbs, a movement that was already under way in 1910, when the metropolitan population began to increase more rapidly than the urban.[3] If the immense productive powers of Chicago's building industry and its vast technical resources could have been used to satsify the material requirements of all its citizens, the American Dream might have been realized in an urban context; as it was, however, although the city could provide water for everyone, the capacity of the building industry and the talents of the designing professions were devoted to serving the centers of economic and political power rather than humanity.

The volume of new construction during the decade following 1910 was radically affected by the economic dislocations of the First World War and the depression that followed it. The area of new office space placed in service year by year varied from a maximum of nearly 2,000,000 square feet in 1912 to a minimum of about 74,000 square feet in 1918. The pattern exhibited by the annual construction of dwelling units was somewhat more stable, but the decline caused by the war, though coming later, was equally drastic: the maximum of more than 24,000 houses and apartments came in 1916; two years later the total fell to 1,946.[4] The physical character of the large multistory building and its role in the urban economy represented a continuing development up to about 1922 of techniques of design, construction, and management that had been evolved in the marvelously innovative period following the fire of 1871. The creation of the skyscraper in the densely packed area of the urban core had very nearly reached the stage of an exact science: caisson foundations; riveted steel frames, usually in straightforward column-and-girder forms but with truss and cantilever systems appearing where special exigencies required them; the mechanical and electrical utilities of internal environmental control; fireproofing and fire-control devices; curtain walls; high-speed elevators; external architectural design combining with increasing skill the image of corporate power with maximum utility and economy— these characterized the working fabric for the great majority of big buildings.

Beyond structural and architectural planning, the large office block in the crowded urban core posed peculiarly difficult problems that lay beyond the traditional province of building design. Growing most rapidly in sheer bulk, complexity, and cost was the mechanical and electrical plant on which the inhabitants of the twentieth-century office tower increasingly came to depend. The elevator was quickly seen to be a necessity if the building was to grow in height, and by 1900 the business community had come to regard the electric light and the telephone as equally essential to the conduct of its affairs. Far more fundamental in its necessity, however, is the high-pressure water system required for the operation of flush toilets, lavatories, and drinking fountains, without which the most elegant building would be unfit for human occupancy. The maintenance of a stable interior environment was recognized as a highly desirable ideal at the very moment that the iron-framed skyscraper had reached its maturity. Heating a big multistory building was a difficult enough problem, but as the walls increasingly dissolved into glass and as building density along the street steadily grew, wind turbulence, with changing patterns of light and shade, exaggerated and unpredictably altered the temperature differential that already existed between sunlit and shaded, windward and leeward sides. Steam boilers and furnaces, pressure plumbing, water heaters, storage tanks, intricate electrical circuits, and power-driven ventilating machinery required basement and roof spaces, stacks, ducts, conduits, cables, and pipes of such individual size and multiplicity that by the time of World

War I the major part of building design was devoted to locating these organs and arteries of the functioning edifice while still preserving adequate space for its inhabitants.

But even more than this was involved if a building was to play a remunerative and useful role in the activities of business administration. The entire complex of requirements was nicely summarized in the mid-twenties by Leo J. Sheridan, a leading member of the management profession.

The problems involved in the creation of a modern office building are numerous and difficult. Selection of the most appropriate site; choice of architect and general contractor; formulation of general and detail plans for an improvement that will mean the most effective utilization of the site; developing an efficient, flexible organization to collaborate with architects and contractors; supervising of construction to see that the owners' ideas as reflected in the plans and specifications are being carried out with fidelity and dispatch; inauguration of a renting and publicity campaign which will assure maximum occupancy by tenants of the desired kind as soon as possible after completion of the building; the selection and training of a building organization which will assure efficient service to the tenants from the opening day; these are some of the major tasks which confront the owner-builder in the year or year and a half following the inception of his project.[5]

The office buildings erected up to the war were of a shape that we would not today associate with the skyscraper, chiefly because we have come to think of it since the late twenties either as an extremely high, slender tower or as a slablike form. But the skyscrapers of the years immediately preceding World War I were blocklike masses, filling out their sites to the lot lines and seldom more than twenty stories in height, the form dictated mainly by the zoning and height-limiting ordinances of the time. Associated with each of the major phases of Chicago building has been a new urban scale in the core area and along the lakefront: before the fire it was the modest scale of the pedestrian city, with its four-story office and store buildings; this was rapidly expanded in the period 1880–1900, when the height rose from a maximum of ten to more than twenty stories, and total volume spread out to areas of half a block or more. That scale persisted until the mid-twenties, when the core of the city was radically transformed by the sudden appearance of slender towers, with setbacks to increase their apparent height, which rose to forty-five stories. The boom following World War II saw another expansion of building dimensions, in bulk to block-long elevations, and in height to sixty stories. Thus the history of the city can be read in the scale of its working center, and the buildings of the early twentieth century indicate to us that they belong to the economic and technical milieu of the the nineteenth.

Office-building design around 1910 was so thoroughly dominated by the architectural firm of D. H. Burnham and Company that their works remain representative of the whole volume of construction until 1920. The Peoples Gas Company Building, a creation of the Burnham office and the structural engineer Joachim G. Giaver, was erected in 1910–11 at 122 South Michigan Avenue to take the place of the company's earlier headquarters, which had begun their existence as the Brunswick Hotel (1883) of Burnham and Root. The newer structure is so richly clad and so overpoweringly dominated at the base by a row of immense monolithic granite columns that we can infer its steel frame on hardpan caissons only from its twenty-story height. The distinguishing feature of its structural system is that the exterior walls on Michigan Avenue and Adams Street are carried on huge cantilever girders at the second-floor line in order to free the highly polished columns from the wall and floor loads above them. It was a case of a strictly aesthetic decision dictating a costly structural expedient, and it was to arise repeatedly as long as decorative systems were derived from historial precedents.

More impressive in its size and the discipline of its classical detail is the Insurance Exchange, which eventually covered the entire block bounded by Jackson, Sherman, Van Buren, and Wells streets (fig. 7). Another product of the collaboration between Burnham's office and Joachim Giaver, it probably remains the foremost concentration of insurance offices in the world, and in spite of its twenty-two-story height, it was until the late sixties the largest office building in Chicago. The addition of 1927–28, designed by the enormously prolific firm of Graham, Anderson, Probst and White, brought the total rentable area to 1,320,000 square feet, with other spaces and facilities sufficient to serve 11,000 employees and a daily traffic of 60,000 visitors. The first floor of the Exchange once included the downtown ticket offices of most Chicago railroads, but the decline of rail passenger traffic forced the various companies to close all of them over the years following 1950. The genesis of the highly profitable building might prove instructive to architects who have made enough money to accumulate a portfolio of investments. The Insurance Exchange project was organized by the corporation lawyer Max Pam and by Ernest R. Graham, a partner in Burnham's firm and founder of the two successive offices that inherited Burnham's practice, Graham, Burnham and Company (1912) and Graham, Anderson, Probst and White (1917). The architect died in 1936 rich enough to endow the Graham Foundation for Advanced Study in the Fine Arts, much of whose income is derived from earnings on the stock of the Exchange held by the Graham estate. Even during the depression the big building remained profitable, and it was one of the few Loop properties that were not forced into receivership. A high occupancy rate and low maintenance costs are both factors in the rate of the building's return, and the Insurance Exchange was well designed in the latter respect: its steel frame is covered with enameled brick and terra-cotta impervious even to the destructive acids of Chicago's badly polluted air.

The City National Bank, at 208 South LaSalle Street, proved to be the last building to come from the drafting tables of Burnham's office, for he died in the year the building was placed under construction. Erected in 1912–14 to serve originally as the chief banking and administrative center of the Continental and Commercial National Bank, the structure later became the property of the City National Bank and Trust Company, which was organized in 1932 by Charles Gates Dawes, vice-president of the United States under Calvin Coolidge. The building constitutes the perfect example of the kind of commission that Burnham sought and regularly enjoyed in unprecedented numbers. It occupies one of the largest landholdings in the Loop, with a long elevation of 325 feet along Adams Street; it stands the usual twenty stories in height, and its standard riveted steel frame, again the work of Joachim Giaver, is well hidden under granite and terra-cotta sheathing on the upper floors and under the polished red-granite columnar shells of the base. The outer elevations are heavy and monumental, done in the grand manner that Burnham loved, but the interior reveals features of much greater spatial and structural interest. The main banking room occupies the entire second floor and extends upward to the sixth floor for a total height of four and one-half stories. The area above the sixth floor forms a central light court around which the office enclosures are disposed in an open rectangle. The banking floor is bounded by marble-sheathed columns and was originally covered by an immense glass skylight whose most impressive element was a glazed barrel vault set in steel ribs over the central area of the floor; but, as in nearly every other case, this magnificent sweep of glass, with the warm diffused light that fell through it, was replaced by a conventional roof and ceiling. The great open area of the floor is articulated and defined by locating the shafts for elevators and stairways in such a way that they penetrate the space near but separate from the four corners.

Burnham was the high priest of the classical movement in Chicago, and his authority continued with little challenge for at least ten years after his death. A majority of the big office blocks were carried by steel frames on rock or hardpan caissons, heights ranged from nineteen to twenty-two stories, and the ornamental system varied only in details, while the window size ranged from the small independent opening that

Fig. 7. Insurance Exchange, 175 West Jackson Boulevard, 1911–12, 1927–28. D. H. Burnham and Company; Graham, Anderson, Probst and White, architects.

Fig. 8. *Left:* Wrigley Building, 400 North Michigan Avenue, 1919–21, 1924. Graham, Anderson, Probst and White, architects. *Right:* Tribune Tower, 435 North Michigan Avenue, 1923–25. Raymond Hood and John Mead Howells, architects.

7

8

Fig. 9. *Left:* 333 North Michigan Avenue, 1927–28. Holabird and Roche, architects. *Center right:* London Guarantee and Accident (now Stone Container) Building, 360 North Michigan Avenue, 1922–23. A. S. Alschuler, architect. *Right:* Mather (now Lincoln Tower) Building, 75 East Wacker Drive, 1927–28. Herbert H. Riddle, architect. *Far Right:* Executive House, 63 East Wacker Drive, 1956–58. Milton Schwartz, architect.

9

implied the solidity of masonry construction to the baywide group or broad "Chicago window" that made possible an articulated wall more in the spirit of the Chicago school.[6]

The only other firm comparable to Burnham's in size if not in the number of commissions was the durable and prosperous office of Holabird and Roche, which flourished over the forty-five years from 1883 to 1927. Their largest work is the huge City Hall and Court House on Clark Street between Washington and Randolph, but the commercial structure that most fully preserves the spirit of the Chicago school is the third Rand McNally Building, erected at 538 South Clark Street in 1911–12.[7] Another volume with the great horizontal dimensions typical of Chicago, the ten-story structure fills the entire block bounded by Clark and LaSalle streets on the east and west and by Congress and Harrison on the north and south.[8] Since the building was designed to house the printing plant as well as the administrative center of the nation's largest publisher of maps, the steel frame was calculated to support the high floor load of 250 pounds per square foot on all floors except the fourth, where heavy machinery required a unit load of 375 pounds. The treatment of the elevations, all four of which face well-traveled thoroughfares, represents a handsome example of the articulated wall that Holabird and Roche developed at the beginning of their practice: the simple composition of piers and spandrels has a finely drawn clarity, warm in color and materials, and its Gothic detail is restrained in a way befitting a sober commercial and manufacturing block. The bay spans are relatively short, 16 feet 6 inches parallel to the long elevations and 24 feet on the transverse, reflecting the heavy floor loads, and as a consequence the continuous piers impart a strong rhythm to the 300-foot length of the east and west walls. The sheathing of the base, the flattened Tudor arches that terminate the bays at the top story, the coping, and other elements of the trim are composed of light tan terra-cotta, and the remainder of the opaque wall areas are sheathed in buff brick. The whole building forms a hollow rectangle in plan, with a generous central light court that was a necessity at the time for the fine work of engraving and printing maps. The Rand McNally Company moved its operations to Skokie in 1952, and the building, which still compels attention in the grimy setting of South LaSalle Street, became one of the many properties of the federal government in Chicago.[9]

The World War brought a delayed but potent stimulus to building in Chicago, first through the immense productive effort itself and second because of the necessity to defer the construction of commercial space as the nation poured its resources into military activity.[10] A positive factor peculiar to Chicago that increased the pressure of unsatisfied demand was the completion in 1921 of the Michigan Avenue Bridge, to break through the double barricade of the Loop and the river and to open North Michigan Avenue to commercial development of maximum prestige. The effect was immediate and striking, as the Wrigley Building was the first to demonstrate, and in less than a decade the extension of Michigan Avenue northward to its termination at Oak Street (1000N) was to be totally transformed into a new kind of urban boulevard.

The celebrated tower that inaugurated this process was built as a profitable investment and a dazzling corporate advertisement as well as the headquarters of the chewing-gum empire founded by William Wrigley, Jr. (fig. 8). It represents a major innovation in the design of the Chicago skyscraper, and its genesis tells us much about its role in the planning and rebuilding of the Near North Side. The proposal of the Burnham Plan for river promenades in the core area undoubtedly suggested the unique potential of the waterway for commercial development, and the particular advantages of the Michigan Avenue crossing appeared to a few farsighted men even before construction of the bridge began. In 1918 Wrigley, in association with B. M. Winston, founder of the office-management firm of Winston and Company, and the builder Andrew Lanquist, chose the site at 400 North Michigan as the most impressive location for the building that was to outclass all others in its splendor. The choice revealed a sound understanding of civic design: the river and the broad thoroughfare provided generous foreground; and the eastward displacement of Michigan along the line of former Pine Street required that the axis of the bridge and the plaza at its north end be set at a slight angle to that of the boulevard, so that a building at the northwest corner of the river crossing, when viewed from the south, would stand freely and prominently displayed, as though it were in the middle of the street. Having selected the site, Wrigley and his associates in 1919 commissioned Graham, Anderson, Probst and White to prepare the architectural design in collaboration with the structural engineer William Braeger. The building was constructed in 1919–21 by Lanquist and Illsley, and was so expertly managed by Winston and Company that its space was fully leased by the time the first office was opened in 1920.

The Wrigley is a steel-framed building on bedrock caissons that differs markedly from its predecessors because it consists of two distinct but thoroughly unified parts, an isolated main block of seventeen stories and a slender tower rising above it for an additional eleven floors. The idea of a tower, which is prefigured in the central shaft and flanking wings of Adler and Sullivan's Garrick Theater Building (1891–92), arose from the belief that the prestige conferred by height could be further enhanced by separation from lower or surrounding offices, and that rents in this desirable space could thus be proportionately increased. In the Wrigley the columns of the tower are collinear with those of the main block, thus eliminating the costly necessity of introducing distributing girders for offset columns. The exterior design of the building is a work of expertly controlled extravagance whose details were suggested to Pierce Anderson by the Giralda Tower of Seville Cathedral, a curious though brilliant work of the Spanish Renaissance containing Moorish elements derived from an earlier minaret (the tower dates from 1568). The curtain walls of the Wrigley rise from a strongly articulated three-story base with a vaulted entranceway and broad windows nearly filling the structural bays. The main block that stands above the belt course at the third story is characterized by a subdued vertical emphasis achieved through the continuity of the pierlike bands and the thin mullions. A highly ornamental cornice and parapet terminate the upward movement of the main walls, and setbacks at the eighteenth and twentieth stories provide a transition to the slender tower. The clocks on the four faces are surrounded and topped by an extremely rich concentration of ornament, which gives way to a ring colonnade and cupola that brings the entire volume to its conclusion.

Anderson, who was in charge of the design, adapted this extravagance of detail to the requirements of a high office building with a skill and *esprit* that have seldom been duplicated. Since everything visible above the twenty-fourth floor serves a decorative end, the maximum density of ornament occurs at the top of the building, and the distance from the ground allows an otherwise suffocating redundancy to remain delicate and playful. The building stands free on all sides, and its entire surface except for the windows is covered with a white-enameled terra-cotta that is impervious to dirt. This shining envelope is made to glow at night more dazzlingly than it does during the day by a system of illumination that is probably the most extensive of its kind in the world. The Michigan Avenue elevation of the building is lighted by a bank of 321 floodlights set on a framework somewhat east of the boulevard on the south bank of the river. The intensity of the light, like the various shades of white in the terra-cotta sheathing, is graded to provide increasing brilliance of reflected light from bottom to top.[11]

The Wrigley was a great success from the beginning, and nothing revealed its triumph more emphatically than the construction in 1923–24 of an annex that stands immediately north of the original building, at 422–28 North Michigan Avenue, and that contains twice the floor area of its predecessor. The two are joined by a thin screen of glass set in a steel armature covered with glazed terra-cotta that harmonizes with the wall surfaces on both sides. An early installation of air conditioning in 1936 and the construction of a little plaza between the main block and the annex have kept the Wrigley as profitable in its return as it is brilliant in its appearance.

Any attempt to repeat this tour de force on the same terms would have been a disaster. When the London Guarantee and Accident Company chose the second of the four corners of the Michigan Avenue Bridge for its office building, the architect wisely decided to use relatively simple detail and to cover the frame with a sheathing of gray Indiana limestone (fig. 9).[12] The twenty-one-story building, structurally typical in its steel frame and rock caissons, was erected in 1922–23 after the plans of the architect Alfred S. Alschuler and the structural engineers Edward C. and Ralph M. Shankland. The exterior design is derived from Renaissance precedents, but these are confined entirely to base and top. Engaged fluted columns of the Corinthian order flank the entrance on Wacker Drive; smooth-shafted columns distinguish the top three stories, and a belvedere in the form of a ring colonnade topped by a cupola and a lantern stands above the roof. The emphasis throughout the height of the street elevations is on the masonry sheathing, which is rusticated for the first five stories, but continuous piers suggest the unbroken column lines of the steel frame. The Guarantee has an odd pentagonal plan because of the lot shape that was originally dictated by the alignment of the river: above the base the eastern third of the building is divided into two unequal wings separated by a deeply indented light court; since the main block behind the wings is turned at a slight angle to their axes, the facade along Wacker Drive curves in a shallow concavity facing the narrow plaza at Wacker and the bridge, providing the most pleasing visual feature in the overall mass. The restrained classicism of the design and the concern to relate the building to Burnham's river plan brought A. S. Alschuler the Gold Medal of the American Institute of Architects in 1929. Good design and a superb site have kept the Guarantee prosperous in spite of vicissitudes that included the sale of the property by its original owners to the Michigan-Wacker Building Corporation and its subsequent conversion to the headquarters of the Stone Container Corporation.

If Michigan Avenue and Wacker Drive saw the liveliest activity in the years immediately following the depression of 1919–20, the interior of the Loop was not neglected. The renewed passion for towers, once a nineteenth-century obsession, reached some kind of culmination in the Chicago Temple Building, designed by Holabird and Roche in collaboration with the engineer Henry J. Burt and constructed at 77 West Washington Street in 1922–23. The chief function of this curiosity has been to house the central offices and various chapels of the Methodist Episcopal Church, which had owned the site since 1845. The twenty-one-story main block continues upward at the street corner in an eight-story Gothic spire terminating in a cross whose tip stands 568 feet above the sidewalk level. This novelty, which would now be regarded as amusing or absurd, according to the seriousness of one's convictions, required a complex system of offset columns, distributing girders, and bracing to carry the steel frame of the spire above the flat roof frame of the office block.

While Holabird and Roche devoted the talents of their productive staff to these lively sensations, the office of Graham, Anderson, Probst and White showed unswerving devotion to the classical canon. The Illinois Merchants Bank Building (later the Continental Illinois Bank), erected at 231 South LaSalle Street in 1923–24, is a nineteen-story block typical of the sobriety thought to be appropriate to the great financial artery. For its design William Braeger was again the structural engineer. On Michigan Avenue, however, a princely extravagance was regarded as essential, not merely acceptable, and in the Straus Building Graham and his associates enjoyed the grandest opportunity to exploit their unparalleled talents for Renaissance magnificence. Designed in collaboration with the engineer Magnus Gunderson, the building was constructed in 1923–24 at Michigan Avenue and Jackson Boulevard (310 South Michigan) for the investment banking firm of S. W. Straus and Company, which retained it until it became a property of the Continental Companies in 1943.[13] The Straus Company specialized in financing large building projects of every description throughout the United States and was understandably prominent in high-level real estate operations in Chicago, roles which gave it additional incentives to insure the most commanding and profitable use of its expensive site. The company, therefore, engaged the Planning Service Committee of the National Association of Building Owners and Managers to examine the plans of the architects and engineers and to make recommendations for their improvement. The outcome of this collaboration is a prize work in all respects, among them a substantial increase in rentable space at a reduction in the cost of construction of $250,000.[14]

The overall height of the steel-framed building on rock caissons is divided into the fashionable main shaft and tower, the lower rising twenty-one stories and the upper nine, for a total height of 475 feet above grade level. The two top stories of the tower are set back less than a full bay and hence required offset columns supported by distributing girders. The tower is surmounted by a pyramid roof in the terrace form somewhat like that of a ziggurat and is framed by means of inward-leaning posts at the corners carrying a dense array of light horizontal beams, one ring for each level of the pyramid. On the little square that constitutes the roof of this pyramid stands a sculptural and structural complex whose iconography probably eludes the pedestrian far below on Michigan Avenue: within the square are chimes that sound the "Cambridge Quarters," copied from those in the Metropolitan Tower in New York; at the corners stand four stone bison representing the continental area of America in which the Straus Company carried on its business; on their necks rests a steel-framed glass enclosure in the shape of a beehive, the symbol of thrift and industry, which originally contained four beacons pointing in the cardinal directions but now houses a prominent blue light installed in 1954. The Indiana limestone sheathing that covers the building frame up to the beehive represents the sober classical decor that was always chosen to suggest the imperial power of a large financial institution. The two-story base on the facade (Michigan Avenue) was originally opened to large arched windows extending up the full height of the base to light the banking room, but these were replaced by separate rectangular openings when Continental converted the room to offices. Above this arcade and the arched entrance, topped by a statue of Mercury and flanked by rusticated masonry, rises the main shaft, neutral in its emphasis up to the belt courses, cornices, and pilasters at the setbacks.[15]

Except for the golden-bronze window frames on the Jackson Boulevard elevation, the exterior of the Straus Building suggests restraint in the spending of money, but this caution was cheerfully abandoned in the design of the grand banking room that extended over most of the second floor and was probably unparalleled for sheer commercial opulence. The main access to the room was provided by an immense marble stairway that rose from the Michigan Avenue entrance and was lighted by lamps with crystal panels set in a metal framework finished in antique gold. The banking room had the form of a three-aisled basilica with an overall area of 160 × 170 feet and a ceiling height of 45 feet. The floor was paved with Tennessee marble, the walls sheathed in travertine, and the ceiling of hexagonal coffers was finished in bronze, gold, iridescent blues, reds, and greens. The steel columns that supported both the ceiling and the trusses above it and defined the aisles of the banking room were sheathed in Hauteville marble with Corinthian capitals of Belgian black marble. All railings were wrought and cast iron covered with gold leaf, and the metal elements of the two huge chandeliers suspended from the ceiling were finished in antique gold and bronze. The wall at the west end of the room opened into a window 14 × 24 feet in area, which was done in the Florentine manner showing a sixteenth-century ship (suggesting commerce) flanked by allegorical figures of Art and Justice, the colors of the glass being amber (dominant), red, blue, and green. In the spandrels of the window arches there were gold medallions representing Greek coins, and at the very center of the floor, where these surrounding symbols of the antiquity of coinage would appear most prominent, there was a raised salesmen's platform floored in Belgian black marble and surrounded by a travertine parapet.[16]

In this work of sumptuous architecture only the richest and costliest materials were used, and only those with the most honorable traditions in the building art.

Fig. 10. Tribune Tower. *Top:*
Construction view showing the framing
of the tower and buttresses. *Bottom:*
Sections showing the framing with the
offset columns at various levels.

Fig. 11. Project, Tribune Tower
competition, 1922. Eliel Saarinen,
architect.

10

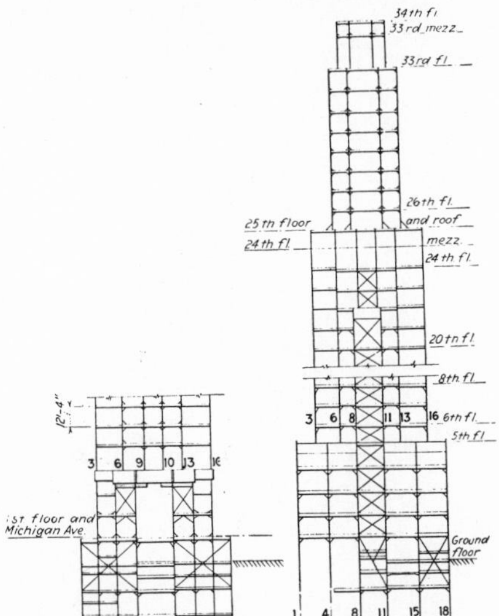

11

Fig. 12. Jewelers (later Pure Oil, then North American Life) Building, 35 East Wacker Drive, 1924–26. Giaver and Dinkelberg, Thielbar and Fugard, architects and engineers.

Fig. 13. Palmolive (now Playboy) Building, 919 North Michigan Avenue, 1928–29. Holabird and Root, architects.

12

13

Fig. 14. Daily News (now Riverside
Plaza) Building, 400 West Madison
Street, 1928–29. Holabird and Root,
architects. The Butler Brothers
Warehouse is in the right background.
(Courtesy Chicago Historical Society.)

Fig. 15. Daily News Building. Sections
showing the framing of the wings over
the Union Station tracks.

14

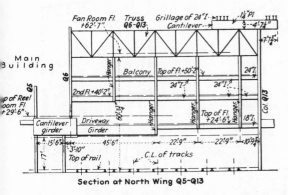

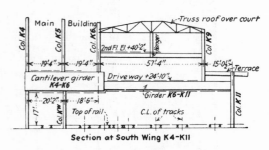

Section at North Wing Q5-Q13

Section at South Wing K4-K11

15

Fig. 16. Civic Opera (now Kemper Insurance) Building, 20 North Wacker Drive, 1928–29. Graham, Anderson, Probst and White, architects.

Fig. 17. Civic Opera House. Plan of the main floor.

16

17

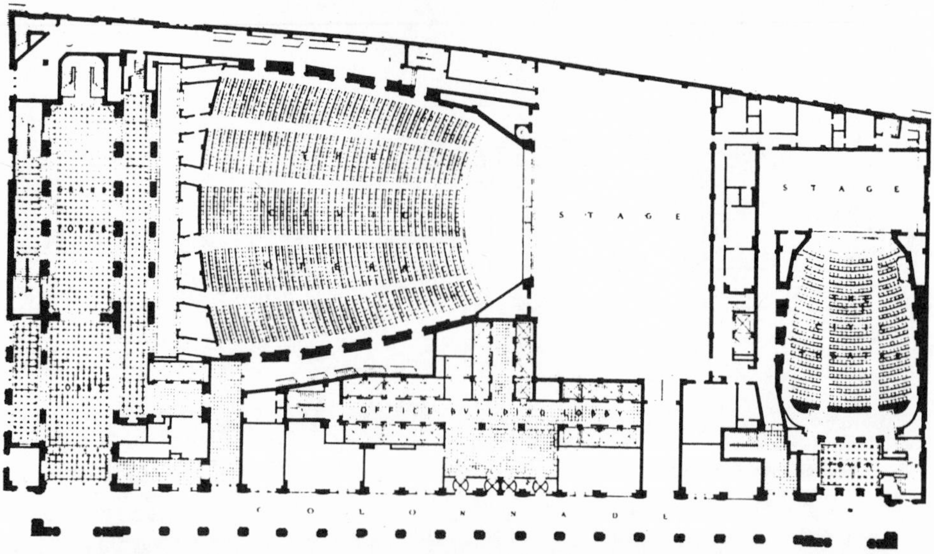

Fig. 18. Civic Opera House. *Top:* Plan of the trusses over the Civic Opera Auditorium and the Civic Theater. *Bottom:* Longitudinal section, looking toward the river.

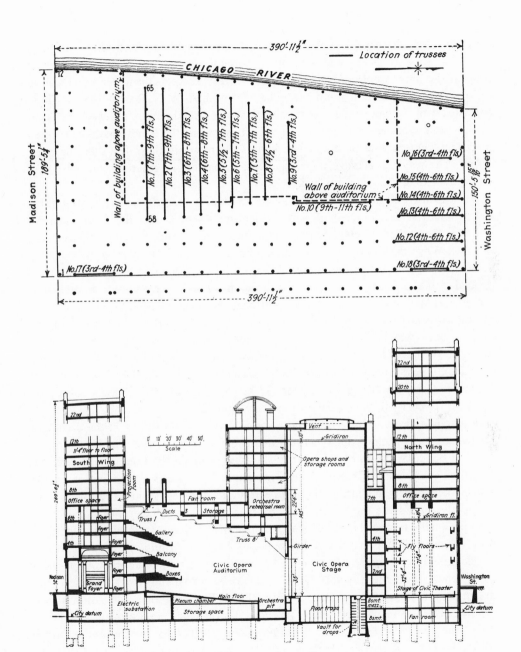

Everything was designed and executed with perfect consistency and unity, and with the surest sense of place, relation, and maximum visual effect. There was not an original idea in the whole marvelous scheme, but if one accepts the underlying assumptions of this architecture it could hardly be improved. As A. N. Rebori wrote, "Those entrusted with the design and execution of this huge structure were never once swayed by the emotion of the creative mind. They followed along the smooth path of accepted precedent, content to achieve a bigger, better, and more striking effect than the other fellow. The result is massive impressiveness, surpassing in grandeur and costliness any work of like character in Chicago."[17]

The expensive elegance and the financial success of the Straus powerfully stimulated the commercial development of South Michigan Avenue, with the result that the building, the land on which it stood, and the surrounding property rapidly appreciated in value. When the Continental Companies bought the structure during the war they acquired a bargain which they proceeded to disfigure. The great banking room was divided into two floors and cut up into little offices and an employees' lounge. The arched windows were replaced by conventional rectangular openings, and the ornamental entrance gave way to an uninviting little rectangular door. The final outrage—capping a twelvefold increase in the company's business—was the addition of a huge electric sign of blue letters at the top of the shaft (CNA, for Continental National America), a now common form of frantic advertisement initiated by the Prudential Insurance Company for its skyscraper on Randolph Street and strongly suggesting a radical insecurity in the Chicago business community.

Rapacity appears to have been more sophisticated, less arriviste, in the decade of the twenties, and nothing demonstrated this better than the genesis and design of the Tribune Building, the third of the new skyscrapers to fill the four prize corners of the Michigan Avenue–Chicago River crossing. The *Tribune* is the oldest of the existing newspapers in Chicago, having been founded in 1847, and its editorials have frequently carried the implication that the paper and the McCormick family have been personally responsible for Chicago's unparalleled growth in wealth and population. The new building that was to house the staff and the printing plant was intended to celebrate the city and its region as well as the prosperity and authority of the newspaper, ends which the directors believed could be served only by an architectural design chosen from an international competition. The need for a new editorial and printing plant was recognized before the end of World War I; the company purchased the property at 431–39 North Michigan Avenue in 1919 (when the connecting bridge was under construction) and built its printing and newsprint storage plant near the rear of the lot in the following year. The celebrated competition for the office tower was announced 10 June 1922, on the day of the paper's seventy-fifth anniversary, and the closing date for the submission of entries was fixed at 1 November of that year, with one month's grace for entries from distant countries. The jury included only one architect and was heavily weighted with business and political figures in addition to directors of the newspaper.[18] The judges reduced the 258 entries received up to the closing date to 12 possible winners by 23 November 1922, but the number was shortly increased to 13 with the late arrival on 29 November of the entry of Eliel Saarinen, which they immediately realized they must include among the designs considered for final decision.

That decision was announced on 3 December 1922. The first prize of $50,000 was awarded to Raymond Hood and John Mead Howells of New York City (fig. 8); the second of $20,000 to Eliel Saarinen of Helsinki (then Helsingfors) and his Chicago associates, Dwight G. Wallace and Bertell Grenman (fig. 11); and the third of $10,000 to Holabird and Roche of Chicago. The balance of $20,000 remaining from the original sum of $100,000 set aside as prize money was distributed equally among the ten architectural firms that were specifically invited to submit designs, a group which included Hood and Howells and Holabird and Roche.[19] A number of architects received honorable mention without any monetary award, but some of these fell into the category of firms paid for submitting invited designs.[20] The 258 contestants whose entries arrived before the deadline represented twenty-three countries, with 143 entries coming, as one might expect, from the United States alone. Among the foreign contestants were men who had already played and were yet to play a major role in the development of modern architecture, such as Gropius, Adolf Meyer, and Bruno and Max Taut in Germany, Adolf Loos in Austria (who was at the time in Paris), and Walter Burley Griffin, the single contestant from Australia. Taken together they represented a complete cross section of architecture as it was practiced in Europe and America in the years between the war and the depression of the thirties. The first-prize design will very likely continue to be a matter of controversy on through the years; one can only say that the jurors could have done far worse in selecting the winner, and that their scorn for the modern style was unfortunately borne out by the undistinguished work that the modernists submitted.[21]

Hood and Howells's final design was based on an exhaustive study of all the formal features that are visible in the tower—the overall silhouette, the proportions of structural, quasi-structural, and external utilitarian elements, the relations of all these elements among themselves, and the strictly ornamental details. Thus the preparation of the working drawings came only after a long evolution of planning that began with siting on the irregularly shaped lot and extended to the coordination of all details, large and small. It was on this basis that the architects wrote an able defense of their design, and it is clear that they regarded their work as a progressive development among the earlier essays at finding a valid form for the skyscraper.

The design is before everything else an expression of The Tribune. The structure is carried to its full height as a square on the Michigan Avenue front only, thus always giving the same impression from wherever seen, and showing the same from all points as The Tribune landmark.

We feel that in this design we have produced a unit. It is not a tower or top, placed on a building—it is all one building.

It climbs into the air naturally, carrying up its main structural lines, and binding them together with a high open parapet. Our disposition of the main structural piers on the exterior has been adopted to give the full utilization of the corner light in the offices, and the view up and down the Avenue.

Our desire has not so much been an archaeological expression of any particular style as to express in the exterior the essentially American problem of skyscraper construction, with its continued vertical lines and its inserted horizontals. It is only carrying forward to a final expression what many of us architects have tried already under more or less hampering conditions in various cities. We have wished to make this landmark the study of a beautiful and vigorous form, not of an extraordinary form. . . .

It is perhaps not necessary to call attention to the fact that the upper part of the building has been designed not only for its own outline and composition, but for the possibilities of illumination and reflected light at night.[22]

Eliel Saarinen's project is unquestionably a distinguished if actually a rather conservative work, although it is free of the more obvious derivative elements, but one may raise the question whether it is far enough removed in appearance from the prize-winning design to justify Sullivan's wildly rhetorical praise of the one and violent condemnation of the other (fig. 11). Saarinen's submission had no immediate influence, but six years after the competition it bore valuable fruit for the development of Chicago building. The third-prize design, submitted by Holabird and Roche, relies on a Gothic provenance, but the base and tower are too high and too heavy for the intermediate shaft. It lacks the scale, the fineness, the rich but thoroughly integrated texture, and the unity of Hood's design. Alfred Granger, the one architect of the jury, suffered no doubts whatever as to the merits of the first choice, and his praise of the building, ironically enough, rests on the unity of truth, morality, and beauty that Sullivan always proclaimed.

Springing from solid foundations which satisfy the eye it soars upward growing lighter and more graceful as it mounts until it flowers at the top with all the grace and beauty of the Gothic spires of the Old World; and yet it is not Gothic, neither is it Romanesque, although the round arch is used wherever the arch is needed. Many have asked me to name its style, but I could not answer because it is not of any of the established styles. Because it has *Style*, it is of our day and our land, a land of aspiration and idealism in spite of the coarse materialism which surrounds us and at times engulfs us. . . . But the main point to be emphasized, the quality which makes it a work of architecture is, as I said, *beauty*. But to be really beautiful it must tell the *truth*, must have beauty of function as well as beauty of line. The men who designed the Tribune Tower did not attempt simply to cover their steel frames with fine material finely cut. They used only stone, but the stone is so handled in scale that it could never be imagined as being self-supporting and independent of the steel behind it. The steel is covered as is the skeleton of the human body, but, while the covering, like the flesh and muscles, satisfies the eye, the frame always makes its presence felt through the covering. The use of lead instead of stone in the spandrels between the windows in the great vertical openings is another refinement which emphasizes the quality of the structure and at the same time adds much to the beauty of the design. There are many of these refinements throughout the building, each adding its note of beauty, its contribution to architecture.[23]

Sullivan, of course, took precisely the opposite view, for he saw the Tribune Building as a total falsity, a kind of sick joke, but at the same time he attached the greatest importance to the competition, which he felt was aimed at satisfying a deep-seated emotional craving that was regularly denied in money-getting America.

The craving for beauty, thus set forth by the TRIBUNE is imbued with romance; with that high Romance which is the essence, the vital impulse, that inheres in all the great works of man in all places and all times, that vibrates in his loftiest thoughts, his heroic deeds, his otherwise inexplicable sacrifices. . . .

If a critique of architecture . . . is to be valid, it must be based upon a reasoned process. It must enter with intelligence into the object or subject at hand, there to seek what signifies, and yet maintain such detachment as to render judgment unconstrained and free. A true critique is not satisfied with the surface of things, it must penetrate that surface to search the animus, the thought; it must go deeply to the roots, it must go to origins, it must seek the elemental, the primitive; it must go to the depths and gauge the status of the work thereby. . . .

Viewed in this light the second and the first prizes stand side by side. One glance of the trained eye, and instant judgment comes; that judgment which flashes from inner experience, in recognition of a masterpiece. The verdict of the Jury of Award is at once reversed, and the second prize is placed first, where it belongs by virtue of its beautifully controlled and virile power. The first prize is demoted to the level of those works evolved of dying ideas, even as it sends forth a frantic cry to escape from the common bondage of those governed by ideas. . . .

Confronted by the limpid eye of analysis, the first prize trembles and falls, self-confessed, crumbling to the ground. Visibly it is not architecture in the sense herein expounded. Its formula is literary: words, words, words. It is an imaginary structure— not imaginative. Starting with false premise, it was doomed to false conclusion, and it is clear enough, moreover, that the conclusion was the real premise, the mental process in reverse of appearance. The predetermination of a huge mass of imaginary masonry at the top very naturally required the presence of huge imaginary masonry piers reaching up from the ground to give imaginary support . . . This is not to say that the individual who made the first-prize design did not *believe* he had a great idea. Certainly he believed it, otherwise he would not have taken himself so seriously. Such seriousness prevented him from seeing the humor of it, from seeing something funny and confiding. If the monster on top with its great long legs reaching far below to the ground could be gently pried loose, the real building would reveal itself as a rather amiable and delicate affair with a certain grace of fancy.[24]

After this outpouring of words—and there was much more in the local press— the building that was eventually completed in the summer of 1925 might have seemed anticlimactic, but this proved not to be the case. If it deserved neither the high-flown praise of Granger nor the bitter denunciation of Sullivan, it has nevertheless compelled serious attention for obvious characteristics of visual and structural form. The site, although somewhat irregular in shape, is in all other respects well suited to a building that must provide facilities for a complex physical process as well as office activities. It extends 100 feet along Michigan Avenue and 136 feet in depth to the west elevation of the six-story printing plant. The newsprint warehouse lies to the east of this struc- ture, immediately adjacent to the river, where newsprint ships can unload their cargo directly into the warehouse. An industrial spur of the North Western Railway lies along the south side of the site, and four relatively uncongested streets surround the property, providing easy access for truck deliveries. The mechanics of producing the newspaper are carried out chiefly on the eight levels that lie below the upper deck of Michigan Avenue, or on the two floors and six basements below the grade of the main thoroughfare. This space, along with the printing structure behind it, constitutes the mechanical heart, the factory, so to speak, and the office structure rises above it. The seven subbasements extend 75 feet below the first basement and hence 41 feet below mean water level in the river; the tower rises to a height of thirty-four stories, or 450 feet, from the grade of the upper street level to the lantern at the top.

The exterior form of this intricately molded and buttressed skyscraper was derived from the southern of the two towers that flank the entrance of Rouen Cathedral.[25]

The main shaft, its steel frame standing on the usual bedrock caissons, rises twenty-five stories with one offset at the fifth floor, where the depth of the building is sharply contracted. At the twenty-fifth floor the main shaft gives way to an octagonal tower which is much smaller than the building below it and which diminishes in diameter in steps at the thirty-third and thirty-fourth floors, terminating in a lantern that serves as a mechanical and electrical penthouse. Chamfered corners, changes in the wall form at the third, fourth, and fifth floors, and the ring of pseudobuttresses around the tower, as well as the setbacks, resulted in extensive deviations from the conventional prismatic form of the high building, which in turn required one of the most elaborate framing systems for an American skyscraper.[26]

The structural frame of the Tribune, the design of which was the work of Frank E. Brown and Henry J. Burt, follows the conventional column-and-girder system up to the twenty-fifth floor, except for offset columns carried on plate girders over the lobby, the ceiling of which lies a little above the third floor level, and for further offsets required by the chamfers and the deviations from the vertical wall planes at the third, fourth, and fifth floors (fig. 10).[27] At the twenty-fifth floor the whole column system changes as the shaft gives way to the tower. Since no columns are continuous above this floor, a dense grillage of girders and beams carries the frame of the octagonal tower and the ring of flying buttresses that rises around it; at the thirty-third floor, where the area again contracts, a similar grillage supports the topmost discontinuities. Near the upper edges of the main roof frame at the twenty-fifth floor are the columns of the flying buttresses, each in the form of an octagonal cage built up out of corner ribs interconnected by latticework strap. The individual column is joined to the tower frame by a single horizontal strut near the top, and the whole assemblage is encased in masonry to simulate the flying buttresses at the top of the Rouen tower. The most remarkable feature of the entire framing system is the presence in the tower of two large trusses designed to carry the interior columns, their depth equal to the floor-to-floor height at the twenty-sixth floor. The wind bracing of the tower is unusually elaborate for several reasons—the proximity of the lake, the exposure of the entire building height to wind loads because of the wide spacing and distances of surrounding buildings, and the turbulence that is common around high structures. The structural engineers accordingly made generous use of knee braces and full diagonal bracing in both horizontal and diagonal planes.[28]

The Tribune Tower is a distinguished work of American building for technical reasons alone: its intricate structural system was dictated by formal considerations, specifically the numerous deviations in the envelope from the pure prismatic shape, the ring of pseudobuttresses that constitutes a transitional device between shaft and tower, and the need to brace the whole complex against wind loads. The building as a whole is undoubtedly overbusy, with its historic stones imbedded in the lower part of the masonry sheathing, its niches and screens and hoods, and its symbolic sculpture drawn from classical and medieval sources; yet this rich detail was not only well executed as ornament, it was ingeniously designed to shed water and hence to prevent damage from cracking of the stonework caused by freezing.

As for the general design, it seems reasonable to conclude after forty-five years of discussion that Granger and Sullivan both overstated the case because they took the building too seriously, the first with his Platonic confusions about truth and beauty, the second for failing to recognize that the tower, the pierlike bands, and the buttresses are elements in a purely aesthetic program that demanded their presence. The tower, of course, was thought of as a separate little enclave of prestigious and high-rent space, but whether an excuse could be found for it or not, it undoubtedly would have been included under any conditions. As a functioning entity, the Tribune Building has worked very well over the years, especially since its pioneer air-conditioning system was installed in 1934. The dominant architectural characteristic of the tower and its two derivative neighbors of the Michigan–Wacker group, standing as they do in their incomparable setting of water, boulevards, and double-level bridge, is that they were designed with consummate skill to maximize sheer visual pleasure, to create bright and vivid forms that are intrinsically restless and yet expertly controlled in their constantly changing visual relations. The whole group constitutes a marvelous—possibly unparalleled—exhibition of pure architectural hedonism.

Derivative and eclectic architecture very nearly reached its end in the Tribune, but the passion for classical and medieval styles was to survive for two more years before finally spending itself. Its end came in an orgiastic fashion with the construction of the Jewelers Building at 35 East Wacker Drive in 1924–26, its design primarily the work of Thielbar and Fugard, the supervising architects, with whom Giaver and Dinkelberg were associated as architects and engineers (fig. 12). This recklessly extravagant work was originally designed for the jewelry trade, but by the end of 1926 its name had been changed to the Pure Oil Building when the oil company became a major tenant and eventually to the North American Life Building following another shift in corporate headquarters. Terra-cotta has never been used more lavishly for strictly ornamental ends: the entire surface of the twenty-four-story main block and the seventeen-story tower above it is covered with molded tile in the thickly encrusted manner of certain kinds of Baroque architecture. At each corner of the lower volume stands a typically classical embellishment in the form of a colonnaded drum surmounted by a little dome, and a fifth, much larger in size, tops the tower. The four smaller of these belvederes conceal water tanks, and that at the top is a mechanical penthouse.

The most interesting internal feature of the Pure Oil was the parking garage that constituted a separate enclosure extending upward from the lower level of Wacker Drive through the twenty-second floor. This was the first garage in Chicago to be built as an integral part of a large office structure and possibly the first in the United States to be completely mechanized. Cars were moved to their locations on a particular floor by three elevators electrically driven and controlled by a key-operated switchboard. These elevators possessed the novel feature of movable floors: when the elevator car reached the designated level the floor tipped forward, allowing the automobile to roll onto a horizontal carrier which conveyed it to its parking berth. The process was reversed when the driver called for his car. This elaborate system, however, proved to be an expensive nuisance: maintenance was awkward and costly, mechanical failures were frequent, and replacement parts were difficult to procure. The system continued to operate for fourteen years, but changes in the size and proportion of cars forced its abandonment in 1940. The openings for the elevator shafts were floored over, and the space was converted to office use.

Classicism in architectural design died a lingering death in the mid-twenties, its last full-blown expression being the Chicago Times Building at 211 West Wacker Drive, designed by the new architectural firm of Holabird and Root in collaboration with the engineer Frank E. Brown, and erected in 1927–28. Meanwhile, a new skyscraper style was in the making, and the same architects were destined to play the chief role in its creation. The transition from the derivative to the purified Sullivanesque, or modern, skyscraper came in stages, and it began during the Tribune competition with the design of the American Furniture Mart at 666 North Lake Shore Drive. This handsome building was erected in two parts, the sixteen-story east end in 1922–24 and the twenty-story west half, surmounted by its ten-story tower, in 1925–26. The architect of the earlier portion was Henry Raeder, who worked with George C. Nimmons and N. Max Dunning as associates; for the extension the architects were Nimmons and Dunning, and the structural engineers for the whole project were Lieberman and Hein. The narrow and extremely long building is trapezoidal in plan because the east elevation parallels Lake Shore Drive, which lies at an angle to the cardinal lines of the ruling gridiron. Although the two parts form a single enclosure, they differ markedly in construction and somewhat in design: the structural system of the east half is a column-and-girder frame of reinforced concrete carried on wood piles, but the higher west portion, with its skyscraper tower, is steel-framed and caisson-supported.[29]

The Mart was specifically and uniquely designed for the merchandising of furniture, or to put it more exactly, for the wholesale buying of furniture before its manufacture, and thus required extensive exhibition and public space as well as office space. The essential problem in planning was threefold: to provide facilities for receiving, unpacking, and distributing to display rooms the large quantities of furniture exhibited during the semiannual shows of June and January; to accomplish these mechanical chores in a short time and with a minimum of confusion, damage, and disturbance to the building's 637 permanent tenants; and finally, to provide adequate space for both the furniture and a maximum crowd of 45,000 buyers and sellers at show time. The heart of the problem was discovering a way to avoid the prohibitive cost of installing elevators and other mechanical and electrical equipment that would lie idle most of the year, while at the same time insuring adequate facilities for the brief periods of peak demand. The solution, beyond providing the necessary balance of office and public display space, was to build a combination elevator system involving three banks of elevators, each group designed for a specific kind of service. The first consists of three large cars used as freight elevators during the installation of a show and as high-speed passenger cars during the display period; the second functions in the same way, but consists of only two cars of smaller floor area; the third is composed of six high-speed conventional passenger elevators.

The exterior treatment of the main masses of the Furniture Mart reveals a mature sense of the visual potential of the high commercial building. The sheathing of the curtain walls is a tan brick with terra-cotta trim, disposed in a vigorously articulated pattern with a vertical emphasis secured through broad continuous piers, narrow recessed spandrels, and paired windows in each bay. The tower is less sure of itself, so to speak. The architects derived its form from the tower of the Parliament Buildings in London: its prismatic volume ends in busy little finials at the corners, then sweeps upward in a steep-sided blue-roofed pyramid surmounted at the apex by a cupolalike object that was originally intended to be a mooring mast for dirigible aircraft. Considered in its totality, however, the Mart is unquestionably a handsome and prophetic building, lively in its articulated pattern, strong in its upward motion, revealing a genuine power in its long clifflike walls with their carefully subordinated ornament.

The interior of the Mart, on the other hand, is virtually an architectural museum. The first floor is given over mainly to the American Exposition Palace and its grand entranceway, known as Whiting Hall, both of which are finished in marble flooring and Caen limestone walls, the whole modeled after King's College Chapel at Cambridge University and decorated with ornamental details supervised by the College of Heralds in London.[30] The mezzanine floor surrounding the Palace provides a monumental access to the rented office space of the second floor. The walls are covered with carved oak panels, very real and costly, designed to express the dedication of the furniture industry to honesty, fine workmanship, and intolerance of fakes. The upper floor space in both the east and west halves is given over to office and display space with its associated service facilities, except for the Erie Street (south) half of the top floor in the 1924 block. This area contains the Furniture Club, a sumptuous and expensive piece of businessmen's social architecture devoted to eating, drinking, smoking, and executive conviviality. The club is entered through the Long Gallery, based in its design on the Long Gallery of Haddon Hall in Derbyshire, England, its floor laid in black and white marble, the walls finished in oak wainscoting, and the ceiling cast plaster in the Elizabethan mode. The lobby between the gallery and the main dining room, the eastward extension of the gallery with its view of the lake, and the women's private dining room are done in the Georgian manner; the lounge contains elements of French chateaux of the sixteenth century; the main dining room is Spanish Renaissance; and the furniture of the club rooms is derived from Elizabethan, Jacobean, Georgian, Spanish and Early American prototypes.

Underlying all this costly surrender to the past was a moral fervor that nicely expressed the spirit of the age. Max Dunning himself explained it in devout yet simple terms. "[The Club] should prove to be a splendid instrument of service in bettering the character and quality of furniture produced in America, and by so doing become an institution of great worth in elevating standards of living, appreciation of the beautiful and a striving for greater refinement in that most fundamental of all influences for good citizenship—the American Home."[31]

A more apparent transition from the Gothic to the modern skyscraper than the Furniture Mart is the Mather Building (now the Lincoln Tower), designed by Herbert H. Riddle in association with the engineers Lieberman and Hein, and erected in 1927–28 at 75 East Wacker Drive (fig. 9). This attenuated steel-framed structure is again divided into a twenty-four-story main shaft and a slender octagonal eighteen-story tower that makes it clearly the most phallic of skyscrapers.[32] The numerous changes in shape and cross-sectional area, the high, narrow proportions, and the expansion of the lower building envelope to the property lines dictated an unusually complex framing system. The main shaft is rectangular in plan and is twice reduced in floor area by setbacks at the rear of the ninth and the sixteenth floors; at the twenty-fourth floor the shaft gives way to the octagonal tower, which is also reduced by several setbacks below the forty-second floor, where the tower terminates in a lantern.[33]

Since the caissons under the long elevations (at right angles to the line of Wacker Drive) stand with their outermost elements at the property lines, the peripheral columns on both sides had to be carried on transverse girders cantilevered for a distance equal to the radius of the caisson drum, or 2 feet 10½ inches. The great height of the building for the small horizontal dimensions exposed the windward side of the shaft to uplifting forces under certain wind loads; as a consequence, the four corner columns had to be anchored deeply in the caissons and further secured by inserting each column between the paired cantilevers and riveting it to both members throughout the depth of the girder web. Four inner columns extending up to the forty-first floor constitute the core of the frame for both the main shaft and the tower, around which eight columns extend without break to the thirty-sixth floor. The shape of the tower required peripheral girders in octagonal rings and offset columns on distributing girders at the thirty-sixth, thirty-ninth, and forty-first floors, and at the roof above the forty-second. The lantern is carried chiefly on eight columns braced by inclined struts rising from the corner columns at the tower roof. The chief problem in framing, as we might expect, arose at the transition from the rectangular to the octagonal prism at the twenty-fourth floor. At this level the peripheral columns of the tower rest on triple sets of I-beams arranged in an octagonal pattern inserted into the circumscribing rectangular floor frame. Wind-resisting elements consist of two parts other than the anchoring of columns into the caissons: first, triangular gussets at all connections between spandrel girders and columns and between all girders and columns in the tower; second, a heavy concrete slab at the twenty-fourth floor designed to distribute wind forces in the tower to the framing of the main shaft. Gothic forms inevitably meant vertical continuity and relatively open bays, so that one readily infers this structural intricacy from the external appearance of the Lincoln Tower.

The decisive step in breaking with the past and reintroducing to Chicago the modern skyscraper that Sullivan had developed years before was effected by Holabird and Roche in 1927, almost at the moment when this highly productive office was transformed into the present Holabird and Root.[34] The process of purification and refinement that produced the new Sullivanesque tower was already well under way in New York, having begun with Arthur Loomis Harmon's Shelton Hotel (1922–23) and Raymond Hood's American Radiator Building (1924–25). The advancing mode that was to sweep everything before it in the last years of the decade reached full development in Ralph Walker's Telephone Building of 1926. The purified style came to Chicago with the aristocratic building known only by its address of 333 North Michigan Avenue, constructed in 1927–28 at the fourth corner of the Michigan–Wacker intersection and designed in collaboration with the engineer Frank E. Brown (fig. 9). A preliminary essay in simplification had appeared a year earlier in the little Tobey Building (1926–27), at 200 North Michigan Avenue, the work of the same architectural and engineering association. The larger building, as John W. Root himself said, was strongly influenced by Eliel Saarinen's project for the Tribune competition. The 333 building, its thirty-five stories constructed with the usual steel frame on rock caissons, is nearly identical to Saarinen's design in height and shows its formal debt most obviously in its narrow north elevation, particularly in the strong vertical movement of the central bays up to the twenty-third floor, the separate windows forming narrow vertical bands in the end bays, the deep setback at the twenty-third floor, and the smaller setbacks above it. This towerlike facade is a little misleading, since the structure is mainly a long narrow slab in which the maximum distance of any interior space from a window is held to thirty feet. Through this emphasis on fundamental geometry and narrow vertical planes the architects not only freed the skyscraper from historical embellishments, but what is of far greater positive value, they gave the form a kinesthetic energy that raised it to the level of a genuine architectural distinction. The slight displacement in the line of Michigan Avenue that makes the Wrigley prominent when seen from the south places the 333 in the same commanding position when viewed from the north. The limestone envelope of the curtain wall is broken only by a frieze at the fifth story that depicts scenes from the pioneer days of Chicago's history. The predominantly uniform rhythm of the long elevations reflects a sober commercial spirit, but the slim, balanced proportions and the graceful lines of the narrow facade make the building very much the proud and soaring thing that Sullivan aimed at.

Once launched in the building boom of the late twenties, the big office of Holabird and Root rapidly produced a series of skyscraper triumphs that were prominent features in the transformation of the city's core. Many of the buildings erected in the fifteen-year period (1910–25) that was split into two phases by World War I were situated on Michigan Avenue, but as the boom reached an explosive level around 1925, the tide of construction moved inland, to LaSalle Street, Market Street (later the Wacker Drive extension), and even Canal Street. The exception is doubly conspicuous: Holabird and Root's Palmolive Building (1928–29) not only clung to a Michigan Avenue site, but at 919 North it was a full mile from the Loop, as far north as one could go short of the Drake Hotel (fig. 13).[35] The Palmolive-Peet Company, as the original owner, chose the site for the prestige conferred by the environment: the sweep of the Lake Shore Drive–Oak Street intersection, the open lakefront at Oak Street beach, the north lakeshore stretching to the horizon (visible, at any rate, above the roof of the Drake Hotel), the broad boulevard lined with only a few widely spaced buildings—all combined to allow the new tower to stand bold and clear, commanding a proud position until it was buried in the shadow of the Hancock

Center. Its formal and functional design, and the structural system by Verne O. McClurg, make it in every respect a skyscraper classic, fully deserving its excellent site.

The steel-framed Palmolive (now the Playboy) stands thirty-seven stories, or 468 feet, in height to the roof, which is surmounted by a 150-foot steel and aluminum mast carrying a 2,000,000,000-candlepower airplane beacon, alleged to be the most powerful in the world.[36] The base of the building is much greater in area than the vertical emphasis of the tower suggests: the base fills out a lot that measures 172 × 231 feet, and the long elevations face north and south, parallel to Walton Street, or at right angles to the line of Michigan Avenue. The swiftly mounting volume above this generous two-story block is characterized by seven clearly marked setbacks, which give the containing envelope the form of an elongated pyramid.[37] Intensifying this play of prismatic volumes is the device of recessing alternate bays in rectangular grooves or channels, which are relatively shallow in the lower masses but deeply indented in the tower that rises above the seventeenth floor. The visual result of both the offsets and the indentations is a rhythmic play of projecting and receding surfaces in the form of broad vertical bands of limestone sheathing, the effect of which is greatly intensified by illumination from floodlights placed on the setback levels. The rising and narrowing blocks suggest mass, but the smooth planes of the curtain walls contradict this by suggesting a volumetric character. The interior design of the public spaces in the Palmolive complements the exterior: rich materials—marble floors and dadoes, Circassian walnut wall paneling, white-metal trim on elevator doors, etched glass lighting fixtures—are disposed in the simple forms of broad planes and long horizontal bands.

This masterpiece of geometric planning was not a matter of arbitrary formalism, nor did it necessitate extensive deviations from straight-line framing. The problem that underlay the architectural and structural design of the Palmolive was one of complying with the zoning requirements that restricted the total volume of the tower and established certain proportions between the volume of the tower, the lot size, and the volume of the lower block. To avoid the New York effect of one ill-proportioned box piled indiscriminately on another, Root decided to use the vertical channels carved in the broad sides of the tower. Because they extend across the bay, they could be made to fit nicely into the planning of office space while at the same time satisfying the zoning restrictions. Both the channels and the setbacks up to the thirty-second floor are deep enough to keep most of the columns in line, and since column loads above that level are relatively low, the necessary distributing girders required no great sacrifice of vertical space. Because of the isolated position of the tower near the lake, the wind bracing of triangular gussets at column-and-girder connections was calculated for horizontal loads well above the code. The highest levels of design and construction went into the Palmolive, and it has enjoyed unbroken prosperity since its opening, with 88.6 percent of its space occupied even in the grim year of 1933.

The dominance of gray limestone in the design of skyscrapers was briefly challenged with the construction of the Union Carbide Building at 230 North Michigan Avenue in 1928–29. A short-lived fashion of the time was the use of a dark sheathing material in association with gold-leaf trim, and the Burnham Brothers brought it to Chicago in a single building which offered the promise of decorative richness that architects have seldom had the courage to explore. In all fundamental formal and working respects—steel frame (designed by the engineer Charles Harkins), rock caissons, forty-story height, setbacks, unbroken vertical lines—the Carbide falls exactly into place for its time. But its most distinguishing visual feature is its color: it was the first skyscraper in Chicago to make extensive use of external color contrasts, and the character of contemporary architecture suggests that except for weathering steel and tinted glass, it may be the only one. The exterior sheathing of the Carbide building is polished black granite over the first four stories, dark green terra-cotta on the remaining thirty-six, and black marble with bronze trim at the entranceway. The fifty-foot mast or campanile at the top and the parapet at the roof level are trimmed in gold leaf. For some reason this combination of dark mass and bright trim came to be regarded as Hollywood bad taste, but for an age that has explored all possible combinations of color in the visual arts, there is no reason why this particular association should have been regarded as any worse than the others.

In the ruling mode of skyscraper design as it was practiced during the frantic two years that preceded the Stock Market crash of October 1929, there is little question that Holabird and Root constituted the front rank. The original Daily News (now Riverside Plaza) Building, constructed in 1928–29 at 400 West Madison Street, was the next to demonstrate their authoritative position, as well as that of their engineering associate, Frank E. Brown (fig. 14). The Daily News was the first building in Chicago to include a public plaza as part of the development and the first to be constructed on air rights over railway trackage. The completion of the new Union Station in 1925, with the associated elevation and improvement of Canal Street, provided the impetus as well as the generous sites, but air-rights development was hindered by the problem of smoke dissipation, since the trains in Chicago, unlike those of New York, continued to be hauled by steam locomotives.[38] The solution to the problem in the case of the Daily News was the hoped-for beginning of overhead construction more extensive than the vast Grand Central development in New York; depression, world war, and the lack of interest in building above tracks in the blighted area south of the Loop, however, have so far limited this promising avenue of civic improvement to a few isolated projects.[39]

The particular site of the Daily News Building offered a number of economic and civic advantages. The "lot" lay above the 250-foot strip of Milwaukee Railroad trackage between Canal Street and the river, which made rail, water, and truck deliveries to the newspaper equally and readily available. On the west side, across Canal, stood the North Western Station; to the east, on the opposite side of the river, the new Civic Opera Building was under construction, its high tower set well back from the water between transverse wings; and two blocks to the south stood the concourse building of Union Station, the intervening space occupied by the handsome monitor sheds of the station tracks, their crowns scarcely above street level.[40] There was space for a grand composition, and the architects took full advantage of it.

The whole complex consists of a twenty-six-story main block in the familiar slablike form, 100 × 389 feet in overall horizontal dimensions, and two eastward projecting entrance wings at the north and south ends which embrace an open plaza along the river. The steel frame of the office block and the wings is sheathed in Indiana limestone, and the shop fronts along Madison in a dark polished granite. The visible external divisions of the building suggest the internal functional arrangements. The massive seven-story base, rising directly from the plaza level, was originally devoted to the editorial and publishing facilities of the newspaper. Setbacks at the seventh floor (fifth floor at the ends) reduce the width of the main structure to sixty feet for the next sixteen stories, the volume being used mainly for the offices of the Chicago and North Western Railway. The upper three floors, separated by minor visual details, are devoted to lounges, the studios of radio station WMAQ, and mechanical equipment. The exterior ornament is minimized, restricted to a few focal points and consisting mainly of panels carved in low relief by the New York sculptor Alvin W. Meyer. The effective composition, as the *Architectural Forum's* correspondent ably described it, rests on

unusual setbacks, upon block-like masses, upon contrasts produced by interesting shadows, and upon a repetition of vertical lines introduced into the wall surfaces. Vertical lines in the buttressed ends are carried out in the treatment of the lower and upper horizontal links of the building,—in the broad base formed by the river and street levels and in the upper floors of the main structure, the vertical effect being again introduced in the topmost set-back section, above a strong horizontal line, with an interesting combination of vertical and horizontal effects at the top of the structure.[41]

There are two entrances to the building, one on Madison Street near the intersection with Canal, the other on the plaza level at the east end of the Madison Street wing. The former opens into the lobby proper, which is finished in marble with white-metal trim (a pewter alloy hardened with antimony and copper); the latter, however, opens directly into a concourse that continues over an enclosed pedestrian bridge across Canal Street and into the main passenger concourse of North Western Station. This convenient passage makes it possible for the pedestrian to walk directly to the track level of the station without climbing stairs or crossing streets; it is used by a high proportion of the railroad's 90,000 daily passengers. The 180-foot long concourse in the Daily News Building, which extends from the second to the fourth floor in height, is paneled in travertine and floored with Tennessee marble, and the flattened vault of the ceiling is covered by an abstract painting done by John W. Norton which represents newspaper publishing operations. The first three floors of the building housed the presses and other mechanical equipment necessary to the production of the paper. The various basements were devoted to the storage of newsprint and repair materials, the shipments of which were received directly at the main basement level by truck, rail, or water. A series of massive piers along the edge of the river support the east half of the plaza and define the openings through which the ships were un-loaded; the structural pattern originally continued a similar array of piers along the Union Station tracks, but these piers were replaced by closely spaced steel columns during the construction of Gateway Center (1963–67).

The peculiar mechanical problem posed by the Daily News Building was that of smoke dissipation, and the solution was the work of Joshua d'Esposito, chief engineer of the Union Station project and consulting engineer to the station company. The locomotive smoke was discharged into a five-foot deep smoke chamber situated immediately below the plaza level and extending over the entire track area within the limits of the overhead structure. The ceiling, or chamber soffit, above the tracks was constructed as a series of longitudinal concrete vaults, each of which contained a slot at the crown line over the center line of the track and at the level of the loco-motive stack. By sloping the sides of the slot inward toward the top, the engineers were able to increase the upward velocity of the smoke and thus prevent it from escaping downward around the stack. From the chamber beneath the plaza the smoke moved upward through two ducts extending the height of the building, the upward motion induced partly by the low density of the gases and partly by low-velocity exhaust fans. The whole system works equally well for the gases discharged by the present diesel-electric locomotives.

The complex of building elements and heavy mechanical equipment had to be carried over the diverging track layout of a busy terminal, where there was insufficient clearance for columns between tracks and between the track system and the river wall. The most awkward difficulty from a construction standpoint was offered by the foundations. The one hundred caissons for the main block were sunk to bedrock 90 feet below the river surface, and the fifty-nine for the plaza and the wings were sunk to hardpan at a depth of 60 feet. This work was carried on between tracks without interruption to rail traffic by performing above-ground operations from platforms high enough to clear locomotives. The foundation system, the footings, the steel frame above them, and the presses had to be insulated from the vibrations caused by passing trains, which are especially severe in this case because of the location of the building near the station throat, with its numerous switches and crossovers. The solution was to place the tracks and platforms on a concrete mat insulated from the columns by asphaltic gaskets, the mat in turn being laid on a clay fill extending down to the tops of the caissons. The underpinning of the presses required even more careful treatment: they were placed on a six-inch reinforced concrete slab that was poured on a thick layer of compressed cork fixed between steel plates, the whole sandwich lying in turn on a ten-inch reinforced concrete slab. Finally, the individual press foundations supporting these insulating layers were separate blocks isolated from the rest of the building.

The problem of construction over an irregular track layout required unusual methods of long-span cantilever and truss framing and suspended construction (fig. 15). The general solution to the problem of framing the south wing was to transmit part of the wing and terrace load through columns to two parallel girder systems under the north and south elevations. Each system is composed of a long-span simple girder and a cantilever, the latter designed to carry one line of columns in the twenty-six-story block. The remainder of the second floor and roof loads are supported by a truss immediately under the roof. At the center of this truss a hanger provides the intermediate support for the second-floor girder. Under the north wing all the spans are nearly double those of the south wing because of the close spacing in the narrower throat area, so that the trusses, hangers, and cantilevers had to be of much greater size. The framing of the plaza, on the other hand, was a relatively simple matter because of the reduced loads. In the columns of the main block there are a large number of offsets arising from the necessity to locate the columns below grade on the curving center lines of the platforms and the clearance lines between adjacent tracks. [42] The whole complex framing system offers a leading example of how structural technology serves an excellent work of architecture and civic art that is thoroughly imbued with the modern spirit. If there is any criticism of the Daily News, or of its successor in name, the Riverside Plaza office building, it is the cold and lifeless character of the plaza, which is a consequence of its being surrounded by railroad stations and business blocks, urban elements that do not generate a continuous and lively movement of pedestrian traffic.

The most impressive of all the skyscrapers erected during the stock market boom, for its cultural institutions and its structural intricacy as much as for its architectural design, is the Civic Opera Building, standing across the river from the Daily News on Wacker Drive (formerly Market Street) between Madison and Washington (fig. 16). Designed by Graham, Anderson, Probst and White in collaboration with the engineer Magnus Gunderson and erected in 1928–29, the office tower with its incorporated theaters was acquired by the Kemper Insurance Company in 1948 and is now officially known by the name of that company. When it was planned in 1927 the building was the first structure in the hoped-for renewal of Market Street, but the depression of 1930 put a sudden stop to further plans to exploit the excellent sites that the old wholesale street offered, with its close proximity to the river, to Union and North Western stations on the west side of the waterway, and eventually to the postwar expressways, which had been proposed in the twenties under the recommendations of the Burnham Plan. But the renewal did not come until the decade of the fifties, when Wacker Drive was extended south to Van Buren Street to carry out another proposal that Burnham had made.

A little more than half of the $23,000,000 original cost of the Civic Opera Building was provided by Samuel Insull through his Midland Utilities Company. The remainder was borne in a unique manner: approximately $10,000,000 was raised by the sale of stock in the building corporation to the 10,000 opera subscribers. In this way the opera company secured a half-interest in the 20 North Wacker property (the present address), which was expected to yield an annual rental of about $2,000,000 from the lease of office space. It would have represented a handsome endowment, but the depression, Insull's possibly fraudulent financial manipulations, and the collapse of his $3,000,000,000 utility and traction empire in 1932 led to the bankruptcy of the brilliant opera company, a cultural loss that left the city without a resident company until the establishment of the present Lyric Opera Company of Chicago in 1954.[43] Thus the larger theater of the two incorporated in the building fabric is once again devoted to the use for which it was originally intended, though on a somewhat reduced scale compared to the spacious days of the twenties.

The great building that towers above the river on the block bounded by Madison, Washington, and Wacker Drive includes a main shaft forty-five stories high to the ridge of its hipped roof, two wings of twenty-two stories that extend transversely between the ends of the tower and the river, and a thirteen-story block housing the larger theater that extends between the wings. The smaller Civic Theater lies largely within the north wing (fig. 17). The overall envelope is not perfectly rectangular in plan because the river deviates slightly from a line parallel to the north-south streets, with the consequence that the wing along Madison is noticeably longer than the one along Washington.[44]

Thorny problems abounded in both the structural design and the construction of the Civic Opera Building. Great open interiors penetrating into conventional floored volumes had to be incorporated into the steel frame of an office skyscraper. Construction had to be carried out within a site lying immediately along the deep rectangular section of a canalized river and in part occupied by the massive concrete footings of earlier buildings. The underpinning of the block-long tower required that all caissons for the main columns be carried to bedrock, the maximum caisson diameter being an unprecedented eleven feet. The expenses and delays of removing old concrete piers on the site were somewhat reduced by the discovery of Gunderson and his staff that some of the piers could be used to support the column loads: in such cases the new footing was built immediately adjacent to the old pier and the column load distributed between the two by means of plate girders. Foundation work had to be carried on inside watertight cofferdams constructed so as to abut against the foundation walls of the Madison and Washington Street bridges.[45] The river wall of the building, in its central area along the opera auditorium, rises in a sheer windowless cliff of lime-stone masonry for ten stories above the water level and as a consequence had to be braced against the impact of badly steered ships by means of reinforced concrete struts that transmit the load imposed on the wall to interior column footings.

The main floor of the Civic Opera is occupied in major part by the lobbies, foyers, auditoriums, and stage areas of the two theaters, so that only a few columns of the office tower along the Wacker Drive elevation can be carried down on straight lines to their footings (fig. 17). This situation is complicated further by the fact that the axis of the larger theater is parallel to the building's long dimension (north-south), whereas the axis of the smaller lies at right angles to this dimension. The outer rows of columns rise along uninterrupted lines to the forty-fourth floor of the tower, where all tower columns give way to the separate framing system of the hipped roof and the mechanical penthouse. The inner column lines, however, break at various levels below the twenty-third floor and extend downward to the transverse trusses that carry both the columns and the stepped ceiling planes of the opera auditorium. These trusses, in turn, are supported at their ends by massive columns that rest on separate footings and caissons (fig. 18). In the south wing there is an additional set of girders that carry overhead columns above the wide foyers located at each of the major seat levels on the first six floors. In the north wing the columns above the Civic Theater are carried on trusses at the fourth-floor level, which forms the flat ceiling of the small single-balcony theater.

Because of the spacious open areas occupied by stages, seating areas, lobbies, and foyers, even though these spaces lie largely to the west of the tower, the loads of five tower columns had to be distributed to five pairs of columns supporting the ends of the bearing trusses, with the consequence that these members are subject to extremely high bending moments and direct loads, the maximum being 7,500,000 pounds transmitted to a single column footing. Many of the loads on the trusses are radically unequal between the two ends of the truss, and in one case (the truss running longitudinally at the side of the stage) five irregularly spaced columns bear on the top chord of the truss. The trusses over the opera auditorium, as one might expect, are the largest structural elements in the building, and by virtue of their number as well as their great size, constitute a framing system unique among American skyscrapers. Adding to its complexity is the system of long cantilever girders that support the mezzanine dress circle and the two balaconies above it. It is to a certain extent the twentieth-century counterpart of Adler and Sullivan's Auditorium, but the precise forerunner in Chicago was the Garrick Theater Building, for which the architects first faced the problem of carrying office floors above the void of a theater. [46]

Beyond offices, stages, seating blocks, restaurants, bars, and other facilities common to buildings that serve the arts as well as commerce, the Civic Opera contains still other working elements and spaces within its immense volume. The stage equipment, designed for the grand spectacles of traditional opera, includes large traps, tilting and sliding floors, and smaller movable areas that are operated by various mechanical devices under electrical control. Thirty-five elevators serve the two theaters, the wings, and the central tower. An unusual feature of the building's internal plan are the fire-escape "courts" that occupy a walled-off space between the auditorium and the river wall, which also provides sound insulation from river and railroad noises. The presence of these narrow volumes without intermediate floors required that the columns in the walls be braced with an array of horizontal struts. Far below all these conspicuous and mostly accessible features, at twenty-eight feet below mean water level in the river, is a connection with the tunnels and tracks of the Chicago Tunnel Company, which were used for a few years to haul coal and ashes to and from the boiler room but now stand empty. The whole intricate complex of spaces, all of it superbly planned for handling great crowds of people concentrated in short periods of time, makes it one of the skyscraper classics of America. Its construction aroused national interest and the particular envy of New Yorkers, who wanted a similar replacement for the old Metropolitan Opera Auditorium but were denied it until the opening of Lincoln Center in 1966.

The architectural design of the opera building might best be described as conservative modern enhanced by decorative principles of the French Renaissance, which was felt to be appropriate to the conservative traditions of the operatic art. The proposal for a Chicago counterpart to the Place de l'Opéra suggested the treatment of the entrances and the principal elevation, facing Market Street: seventeen bays of paired octagonal columns, running the full length of the building, form a broad arcade along the street; at the ends of this arcade there are pedimented porticoes marking the entrances to the Opera House and the Civic Theater. Elsewhere the elevations are characterized by the familiar recessed spandrels and continuous vertical bands, alternating wide and narrow to indicate the column lines and the mid-bay points. The river elevations were treated with the same care as those facing the streets because of the Daily News plaza on the opposite side of the waterway and the long unobstructed view afforded by the depressed train sheds of Union Station. The extensive windowless surface of the river wall is accented by porticolike elements at the center of the wall and at the tops of the transverse wings. The decorative scheme is drawn from the musical arts, in which the chief formal motifs are the lyre, the trumpet, the palm leaf, and the laurel wreath, repeated in circular windows near the top of the main shaft, in balustrades, throughout the Grand Foyer, and on the side-wall panels of the auditorium.

The Civic Opera is the leading example among large commercial buildings in Chicago of great richness of color and surface material disciplined by the geometry of plan and structure. The entire ground floor of the Madison Street (south) wing is given over to the entrance lobby and the Grand Foyer of the opera auditorium. The lobby walls are sheathed in softly polished Roman travertine; the floors are paved with pink and gray Tennessee marble; the entrance doors, the elevator doors, and all trim are bronze; and the ceiling is plaster finished in salmon and gold. In the Grand Foyer, which measures 52 × 84 feet in plan and rises 44 feet in height, these colors and textures are enriched by the fluted marble sheathing of the columns and the gold-leaf covering of their capitals. Color is further heightened by the carpeting that covers the broad stairways leading to the wide mezzanine corridor that extends around three sides of the foyer to provide access to the boxes, the Opera Club, and the women's lounge. All the subsidiary foyers on the second floor through the sixth floor run nearly the full length of the various balcony levels and are unusually wide, probably the most spacious of those in any American theater, where the discomforts of overcrowding are ordinarily most conspicuous.

The auditorium proper is even more colorful than the foyer: the extensive areas of the rectangular wall panels and the flat ceiling planes that step down from the real wall to the stage are finished in vermilion, salmon, and gold. The side walls converge toward the stage, where the ruling color scheme is carried out in the painting on the canvas cover of the steel curtain (35×55 feet) that constitutes the chief protection against the spread of fire. The painting represents a pageant of characters derived from a number of operas, grouped in a hierarchical arrangement and surmounted by a great banner. The author of this work of graphic art and the consultant in charge of the whole decorative scheme was Jules Guerin, who had earlier achieved prominence in Chicago for the water-color renderings that constitute the illustrative plates in the Burnham Plan. The close cooperation between graphic artist and architect set a standard for all subsequent building projects: in the case of the Civic Opera the colors of all carpets, seat fabrics, walls, floors, and curtains were chosen by Guerin and developed for the most harmonious blending of color with color and color with architectural form. These visual harmonies form a counterpart to the acoustical excellence of the opera auditorium, which is second in this respect only to Adler and Sullivan's theater on Michigan Avenue. The consultant for auditory design was Paul E. Sabine of the Riverbank Laboratories in Geneva, Illinois, and the principles he followed were those laid down by Wallace Clement Sabine, who is regarded as the founder of the modern science of architectural acoustics.[47] Talent was used on a lavish scale in the creation of the Civic Opera Building, which stands today a little faded and a little tarnished in places, disfigured by an ugly sign at the tower roof and by the crude housing for air-conditioning equipment at the tops of the wings, but it was the best that the age of Scott Fitzgerald produced. Measured against newer fashions, it is obvious that it has a permanent validity.

The buildings that followed the Civic Opera, before inherent weaknesses brought the economy to total collapse, may seem anticlimactic by comparison, even though they include another triumph by Holabird and Root and a new record for the world's largest commercial structure. The tide of construction continued at full force through 1929, very nearly reaching the unmatched total of 3,000,000 square feet of office space opened in 1927, and except for the Moorish dome and minaret at the top of the Medinah Athletic Club (now the Sheraton Hotel) at 505 North Michigan Avenue, it was clear that the new American modern had won the day.[48] The best of the works that were started shortly before the crash of October 1929 is the Board of Trade Building, opened in 1930 on Jackson Boulevard at the point where the facade can face north into the canyon of LaSalle Street (fig. 19). Steel-framed and forty-five stories high, its location as well as its design make it particularly commanding among the achievements of Holabird and Root, who were associated in this commission with the engineer Verne O. McClurg. The Chicago Board of Trade is the central grain exchange of the United States and by far the largest market of its kind in the world. It was founded in 1848, the year when the city's first railroad began operations, and in its long history it has occupied twelve different quarters, four of which were separate buildings constructed and owned by the board. The present skyscraper stands on the same site as its towered and mansarded predecessor, erected in 1885 after the plans of William W. Boyington. The new building is characterized by the symmetrical and rhythmic setbacks that Holabird and Root handled so expertly in the design of the Palmolive, but the later work possesses a compelling power that comes from the sheer cliff of the central bays, which rise unbroken between the setbacks from the sixth floor level to the base of the pyramid roof. At the top of the roof stands another familiar landmark, the aluminum statue of Ceres, there to remind us that the authority of classical myth extends even into those places where bread is turned to profit for the manipulators of the market.

The great problem in the otherwise straightforward job of designing the steel frame of the Board of Trade arose from the need to carry the tower columns over the void of the central trading hall. The buying and selling of grain is a complex process of many steps, and as a consequence it is carried on in a complex of spaces occupying parts of the fourth, fifth, sixth, and tenth floors in addition to the great hall that covers the front (north) half of the building between the fourth and the ninth floors. It was the position of the trading room, as a matter of fact, that determined the design of at least the lower blocks of the building, those balanced masses that surround the high central tower. The cash grain tables originally needed a northern exposure for a neutral and reasonably uniform light in order for the buyer to assay the grain on the basis of its color; the development of neutral artificial illumination, however, has largely obviated the need for natural light. The internal dimensions of the trading hall are 115×165 feet in plan and 60 feet in height; to maintain this interior space free of columns required a now well-tested solution: the tower columns above the ceiling bear on the top chords of six huge trusses, uniform in their clear span of 115 feet and weight of 227 tons. They are among the largest structural elements of steel so far incorporated in a building, and they typify the heroic size of all parts of the Board of Trade, which easily dominates the relatively small and tightly squeezed buildings of LaSalle Street.

Perhaps the most impressive feature of the building boom of the twenties was the constant expansion in the volume of office construction, passing 3,000,000 square feet of space in 1927 and falling slightly short of the same figure in 1929. The growth

Fig. 19. Board of Trade Building, 141
West Jackson Boulevard, 1929–30.
Holabird and Root, architects.

Fig. 20. Merchandise Mart, 222 West
North Bank, 1928–31. Graham,
Anderson, Probst and White, architects.

Fig. 21. Merchandise Mart. Plan of the
Chicago and North Western Railway
freight station under the building, with
the proposed development of Wolf
Point.

20

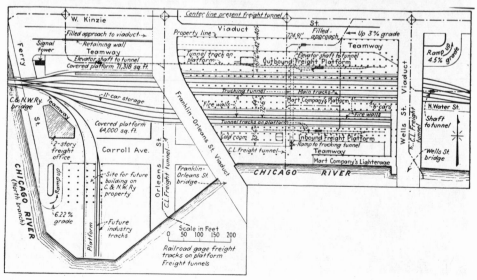

21

Fig. 22. Field Building, 135 South
LaSalle Street, 1931–34. Graham,
Anderson, Probst and White, architects.

of total office area paralleled the steady if irregular increase in the size of individual structures that continued until the still unchallenged record was reached by the Merchandise Mart in 1928–31. The product of another collaboration between Graham, Anderson, Probst and White and the engineer Magnus Gunderson, this mammoth was erected over air rights of the North Western Railway and covers two entire blocks bounded by the river and by Orleans, Wells, and Kinzie streets (fig. 20). Although the main block is only eighteen stories high, its great horizontal dimensions made it the world's largest single building at the time of construction and it remains the largest commercial building to this day.[49] Two separate financial interests lay behind the sponsorship of the huge project. The building was conceived and carried to completion by the chairman and directors of Marshall Field and Company, first, as the new quarters of the company's wholesale division, which was then situated in Richardson's masterpiece at Adams and Wells streets, and second, as a national marketing center for manufacturers of household furnishings and appliances. But since the five-acre site was owned by the North Western Railway and had been used by that company for major operating purposes, it was understandable that the railroad was interested in exploiting it for some of its own facilities. The outcome of this interplay of economic interests was another highly promising air-rights union. The North Western sold its air rights over the level of 23 feet above the water surface together with 450 parcels of land for column footings to Marshall Field and Company, then used the rest of the property for its new in-city less-than-carload freight terminal (fig. 21).[50] But this very sensible marriage of convenience was scarcely consummated. Depression and truck competition robbed the railroad of its merchandise freight, while depression alone was enough to persuade the Field company to abandon its wholesale business. The great Merchandise Mart was sold during the mid-thirties to Joseph P. Kennedy for little more than a third of its cost of $38,000,000 (the 1971 replacement value is about $239,000,000).

Every part of the construction process reached an unprecedented level. The contracting firm, John Griffith and Son, devised a system of belt conveyors for placing concrete that is ordinarily used in the construction of big dams. Rail lines were laid down simultaneously with the sinking of caissons to provide for the rail delivery of materials, which for many months continued at the average rate of twenty cars per day. A maximum of 5,700 men were employed in concrete placement and steel erection. It was an exciting finale to the avalanche of building that roared on seemingly without end, and as construction continued into the depression, it meant the difference for a little while between steady pay and destitution for several thousand men. The finished work, however, is hardly up to the previous level of the Graham office and their engineering collaborators, and certainly well below that of Holabird and Root. The steel skeleton is a straightforward work of column-and-girder framing, and the steady rhythm of the vertical ribbons, perfectly uniform in width above the base, is monotonous over elevations of such length and height.

The last skyscraper that properly belongs to the free-spending twenties carried the process of purification to its logical conclusion and extended the construction of big office buildings well into the depression. The Field Building, erected in 1931–34 at 135 South LaSalle Street (on the site of Jenney's Home Insurance Building and opposite the Adams Street elevation of the Rookery), was planned in 1929, but before its completion it turned out to be the only office structure going up in the United States (fig. 22). It was the last of its kind in Chicago until its post–World War II counterpart, the Prudential Building, was opened in 1955. In the design of the forty-three-story Field Building Graham, Anderson, Probst and White turned their backs once and for all on the past and produced a Sullivanesque skyscraper stripped down to essentials—a dense array of uniform vertical limestone bands topped by a horizontal spandrel that simply marks the outer face of the parapet at the roof. The richness of other days appears only in the sheathing of the lobby walls, which are covered with marbles of various colors, chiefly white, green, and tan, the last two having been imported from Italy; elsewhere there is a sobriety that again borders on monotony, which is perhaps appropriate to the bargain-price construction costs of the early depression. Yet it was thoroughly in the spirit of the time, and like the other works that had grown up around it, seemed to be full of promise for the future development of American architecture. Earl Reed's enthusiastic comment on the designs of Holabird and Root could apply equally well to the whole new city of towers.

During the past five years the Middle West and Chicago, the cradle of metal-skelton construction in the late eighties, have been the scene of the erection of a series of commercial edifices of very unusual architectural interest. Clean and urbane structures of arresting present-day character, usually of stone, have made their appearance in our streets, one close upon another. They are bold in mass, delicate in detail, when it appears at all, and they take their places serenely and assuredly as if by some right inherent in their qualities of useful comeliness. Above all, they are distinguished by a fine regard for relationships of grays, sculptural and chromatic. A dozen or more, all by the young-old firm of Holabird and Root, stand out . . . each as a glorification in architecture of the American commercial spirit at its best. In these buildings the forms of yesterday and today are indiscriminately used with a mastery of proportion and good taste which delights the passer-by. Nothing so truly significant has happened here since the pre–Columbian Exposition days which witnessed the coming to our streets of the epoch-making works of that mighty band which surrounded Louis Sullivan.[51]

Industrial Buildings and Warehouses

The formal tradition of the commercial Chicago school centered largely on its imaginative development of the articulated or cellular wall that is the logical outgrowth of the rectilinear frame, and the characteristic continued a vigorous life in a great number of industrial and warehouse buildings that have thus helped to preserve the continuity between the time of Jenney and our own day. These structures represent architectural refinements of nineteenth-century mill construction, the antecedents of which go back to the earliest factories in New England and their British forerunners of the late eighteenth century. The office and store buildings of the Chicago school are ultimately traceable to the same source. In the twentieth century counterparts of these long-established forms the decorative detail in some cases may have been derived from the forms or techniques of the past, whereas in others the detail may be original or disappear entirely in favor of an elemental geometry growing directly from the underlying structure. Whatever the case, however, these buildings represent an architecture of great structural expressiveness, and they appear to be concentrated to such an extent in Chicago as to constitute another manifestation of the city's special architectural spirit. They are scattered throughout the urban area, but as one might expect, they are concentrated along the main rail lines and the waterways. Construction tends to be uniform in all of them—straight-line, serial column-and-beam framing calculated for high floor loads—and the formal treatment is simple; yet the effect is never monotonous, and the variations secured through different colors of brick, changes in the width of piers and spandrels, and ornamental trim remind us of the great diversity of forms that the original Chicago school was able to develop from equally simple means.[52]

Among the individual industrial enclaves that reveal this architectural distinction the oldest and largest is the Hawthorne Works of the Western Electric Company. The manufacturing division of the various Bell Telephone systems, the organization has been intimately associated with the communications industry of Chicago for more than a century. It was founded in Cleveland in 1869 and its first manufacturing facilities were located in a shop abandoned by the Western Union Telegraph Company. The new firm, known as the Gray and Barton Company after its founders, moved to Chicago later in the same year and acquired the present title of Western Electric

Company in 1872, after its merger with a manufacturing subsidiary of Western Union. The company enjoyed a midwestern monopoly on the manufacture of telegraph equipment for railroads and of electrically operated fire and burglar alarms; the resulting prosperity, having required a steady expansion of the original plant on Kinzie Street, attracted the attention of the railroad financier Jay Gould, who bought a controlling interest in the business but sold it in 1881 to the American Bell Telephone Company.[53] The extraordinary and unexpected growth in the use of the telephone underlay Western Electric's uninterrupted good fortune, which was guaranteed by an agreement of 1882 that gave the company the sole right to manufacture Bell telephones and telegraphic equipment.

The consequent expansion of manufacturing facilities overwhelmed the Kinzie Street site, and so in 1895 Western Electric moved to its present location on a large tract of open land extending south and east of the intersection of 22nd Street and Cicero Avenue, immediately outside the city limits of Chicago in the suburb of Cicero. The original group of factory buildings, some of which are still in use, were a conventional lot of manufacturing enclosures marked by the typical buttressed walls of brick, gabled roofs with central longitudinal light monitors, arcaded wall bays, and internal iron frames. The most striking member of the older group and even today a conspicuous feature of the site is a great square water tower of brick done in the medieval manner with narrow slotlike windows, heavy corbels, and an outward-flaring pyramid roof. It was the new building, however, constructed in 1918–21 from the plans of the company's architectural and engineering staff, that set a new standard of size and dignity for manufacturing structures. The huge volume is rectangular in overall plan but is penetrated by three deep light courts opening to the south, or rear, elevation. It extends thirty-five bays southward along Cicero Avenue and thirty-nine eastward along 22nd Street, for an overall ground area of more than 400,000 square feet. The six-story walls along the streets have the familiar articulated form with buttresslike projections along the column lines and narrow spandrels, these one hundred-foot high palisades sheathed in a dense tawny brown brick which has retained its color surprisingly well for its railroad and manufacturing neighborhood. The main corner, at the intersection of the two thoroughfares, is marked by a heavy tower of square section and emphatic verticality secured through narrow bays and more deeply recessed spandrels and window areas. The steep pyramid roof that tops the tower is a conspicuous landmark along the endlessly dreary commercial strip of Cicero Avenue. The framing system of the immense building is a mixture of steel girders, trusses over wide trucking areas, and heavy concrete floor construction done in the nineteenth-century manner in which the undersurface is cast as a series of little parallel vaults.

Subsequent expansions of the Hawthorne Works followed the mode of the big main building and thus imposed a rare and welcome unity on the sprawling campus. The eastward extensions eventually carried the property across the Belt Railway tracks and hence into the city of Chicago, so that Western Electric offers one of those cases in which a manufacturing complex under single ownership falls in two different municipalities. Perhaps the most unusual feature of the Hawthorne Works, however, is that its central facility continues to exist at all as one of the major producing entities in the American electrical industry, and that it has been retained and extensively modernized since World War II. In an age when the single-story continuous-line factory has become the rule, the old multifloor structure has either disappeared or become increasingly derelict in industrial slums. But in the case of Western Electric the small components of telephonic and telegraphic equipment could be readily moved from floor to floor over routes along which movements could be controlled by electronic switching. The installation of automatic control devices thus proved to be far less costly than the construction of entirely new facilities that would have covered many acres in area, and the big factory was preserved as an efficient manufacturing facility.[54]

Very nearly contemporaneous with Western Electric in the construction of its present plant is the R. R. Donnelley and Sons Company, the founder of the Lakeside Press and the largest printing establishment in Chicago, if not in the entire country. The rebuilding and steady expansion of the company's physical plant provided the largest commission of Howard Van Doren Shaw, an architect of unusual talents whose work deserves more extensive inquiry than it has so far received. The first of Donnelley's Lakeside Press buildings was constructed at 731 South Plymouth Court in 1896–97, but it was eventually superseded by the great complex of buildings stretching along the Illinois Central tracks on both sides of the 23rd Street viaduct. Shaw's association with the Donnelley firm began with the Plymouth Court building and continued throughout the rest of his career, which ended with his death in 1926. This early structure is a seven-story block whose street elevation is marked by a highly original treatment of traditional elements: massive brick piers rising from the third to the top of the sixth story in bold projections form a strong counterpoint to the horizontality of the solid brick planes at the first, second, and seventh floors.

When the company moved to the East Side location Shaw was the architect of the major block, from the initial construction of 1912 through the expansions of 1917 and 1924. After Shaw's death Charles Z. Klauder took over the architectural design, serving until the building was completed in its present form in 1931 (he seems to have been chiefly responsible for the corner tower). The structural engineers, Lord and Hollinger, designed the flat-slab concrete frame.[55] Shaw's architectural treatment is more restrained than it is for the earlier building: the articulation of the street elevations is predominantly rectangular and uniform from the single-story base to the flattened arcade at the top floor; but the broad piers, the corner buttresses of the tower, the finely proportioned composition of spandrels and windows, the white limestone trim of generally Gothic provenance—these give the high dark-brick walls both power and subtlety. Shaw might be classed as a traditionalist in the Chicago spirit, for he used his derivative details with great freedom and imagination.

The Hawthorne and Donnelley plants might be regarded as local forerunners of the industrial park, because of their size, their internal interdependency, and the multiplicity of their buildings, although each remains under single ownership. The American ancestor of all such organized groups is the New England mill town of the nineteenth century, but the immediate progenitor in Chicago was the great manufacturing and residential community that George M. Pullman completed in 1891 on a 3,600-acre site in the region of 114th Street and Cottage Grove Avenue, then well toward the south city limits. The Pullman complex embraced a completely planned town, one of the largest manufacturing groups in the nation, and the supply and maintenance center for the company's vast fleet of sleeping, parlor, and lounge cars, which once numbered nearly ten thousand units. The specific prototype of the multi-industry center is the huge and somewhat amorphous Clearing Industrial District, established in 1898 by the Belt Railway, initially as a classification yard, then expanded around the time of World War I as an organized industrial enclave, with its center roughly at 65th Street and Central Avenue (5600W).

The first true industrial park in Chicago, however, and one that is fully developed in all essential characteristics, is the Central Manufacturing District, extending along Pershing Road (3900S) a little to the west of the mile-square stockyards area (fig. 23). The background to this impressive work of industrial architecture was an ambitious and complicated program of real estate development initiated by the Chicago Junction Railway in 1902.[56] The property of the Union Stock Yards Company, on which the railroad depended for the greater part of its revenue, was fully occupied by 1900, so that any industrial expansion in the area had to take place on vacant land north and west of the yards. In order to provide space and facilities for manufacturing and warehousing, and simultaneously to enjoy a continuing increase in freight traffic, the railroad company began buying land to the north of the yards in 1902 and undertook the essential task of paving streets and installing sewers and utilities in 1908. The total area of developed land reached three hundred acres in 1910, by which date

Fig. 23. Central Manufacturing District, West Pershing Road from Hermitage to Bell Avenue, 1916–20. S. Scott Joy, architect. U.S. Army warehouses and central office building.

23

industry and the federal government had moved into the area and begun to construct factories, warehouses, and rail facilities. By 1920 the number of industrial residents had reached two hundred, with understandably gratifying results for the little railroad company.

The rapid industrial expansion in the north area persuaded the officers of the railroad in 1915 to initiate a unified development in which all manufacturing and storage facilities would be constructed by the railroad according to standard specifications, along with a full complement of industrial community services, and the completed properties then leased to the individual users. The railroad acquired a broad strip of property lying between 39th Street and its own trackage to the south, and extending from the old South Branch of the river to Western Avenue (2400W), and began the process of development in 1916, completing the major part of the program by 1920. Officially designated the Central Manufacturing District, this remarkable development included—in addition to factories, warehouses, utilities, and a freight terminal—a bank, a business club open to district residents, express and telegraph offices, a central telephone switchboard, a medical staff, and a traffic bureau (fig. 23). The district plan constituted a prototype for the industrial parks now often established under urban renewal programs, and its advantages were numerous and compelling: first, the concentration of industrial and related facilities in a small, compact area, with the resulting efficient concentration of transportation; second, a union freight station serving all residents and all railroads operating by trackage rights over the Chicago Junction (one of the chief proposals of the Burnham Plan); and finally, a virtually unlimited labor supply, since at the time of World War I at least one and a quarter million people lived within a radius of four miles of the district.[57]

The buildings erected in the major phase of construction (1916–20) include a Montgomery Ward warehouse combined with the union freight station, three huge supply warehouses for the United States Army, a cold-storage warehouse for the federal government which was the largest in the United States at the time, a number of manufacturing buildings, a central office building with a ten-story clock tower that encloses the water tank for the sprinkler system, a powerhouse, and the Chicago Junction warehouse. All the buildings were designed by the architect S. Scott Joy, who provided standardized structural and planning features and a formal unity that confers harmony without monotony. The trustees of the district demanded the highest architectural standards, to which the various residents agreed on becoming tenants, and all the evidence indicates that the trustees received what they asked for. Joy was given a free rein to design variations on a basic theme which were subject to the owner's or lessee's desire for rich or simpler treatment of formal details. The structural systems of the various buildings fall into two categories: the factories are of timber-framed mill construction with sixteen-foot bays, and the warehouses and freight stations are flat-slab reinforced concrete with twenty-foot bays. The emphasis in the planning of all buildings was to provide generalized space, so that the owner or lessee could locate equipment to suit his own needs. The exterior sheathing is dark-red brick with terra-cotta trim disposed in the familiar articulated walls marked by relatively narrow but strongly projecting piers, grouped windows, and recessed brick spandrels. The exceptions to this program are the army warehouses, which have pigmented concrete spandrels, and the cold-storage warehouse, which is windowless. Formal and planning details are everywhere handled with great skill, providing pleasing and original decorative variations on well-known themes but nowhere sacrificing the overall unity on which so much of the project's construction and maintenance economy rested.[58]

Much of the good industrial architecture of Chicago stands in areas little frequented by the public—most emphatically with the Central Manufacturing District—but one very impressive example occupies a site at a major traffic center of the downtown area. The two tremendous warehouses of the Butler Brothers Company extend along the east side of Canal Street from Washington to Lake, directly opposite the track and platform area of North Western Station (fig. 14). The two identical buildings, designed by D. H. Burnham and Company and the engineer Joachim Giaver, were originally constructed in 1912–13 side by side between Canal Street and the river, but the expansion of the north approach to the new Union Station required the demolition of the east block. It was replaced in 1921–22 to the north of its twin, on the block between Randolph and Lake Street, apparently with Graham, Burnham and Company credited as architects, which means that the plans must have been taken directly from those of the earlier work and prepared before the dissolution of that firm in 1917. The fourteen-story walls of the Butler warehouses, rising from the very edge of the lot line on the west side, face the handsome brick curtain wall at the edge of the North Western station train sheds and thus help to form a major length of the powerful Canal Street corridor. The steel-framed warehouses reveal the familiar articulated walls in their four elevations, but here they are treated in the romantic manner. The dark brick, the broad piers and spandrels, the small windows, and the heavy machicolated parapet give an effect of mass and solidity expressed through simple brick planes. This effect is intensified by the corner bays, which are "strengthened" in the traditional manner whereby windows are reduced to a single vertical row in an uninterrupted brick curtain.

Andrew Rebori placed the warehouses at the top level of work that came from the office of D. H. Burnham and looked upon them as full of promise for a modern urban architecture.

Another distinctive building much simpler and less pretentious is the new Butler Brothers Warehouse occupying an entire block adjoining Randolph Street in Chicago. The success of this massive exterior, built of brick over steel, is striking and un-challenged, and I do not know of a more expressive and enlightened work in its own kind by its author or any other architect. It attains a very noble largeness and simplicity which is due in a measure to the structural emphasis that makes the fronts independent of extraneous ornament. The building relies on means of sup-port that are in this case made visible by the frank and expressive treatment of its long piers. . . . The machicolated cornice that is . . . the crowning feature of the . . . building is excellent in its reconciliation of practical and architectural requirements. Here are plainly enough rows of windows which enable the space they illuminate to be utilized to the utmost; and yet they most effectively accentuate the massive-ness and solidity of the structure itself. In a general way the entire design is handled with like consistency. True, the basement is thickened and the corners strengthened to supply the place of an assumed abutment, but the walls are thickened only to the verge of commercial practicality. It is the vertical lines of the superstructure, however, that thrill me most, for here indeed is a solution of the problem in high design that would be commercially practicable even if this were an office building instead of a warehouse! For this reason alone the architects of tall buildings seeking a modern expression of a modern condition should find the design of the new Butler warehouse worthy of emulation for its structural quality as for its more purely architectural merit.[59]

A later building in the same structural and architectural character as the Butler warehouses, and standing in an even more prominent location, was to inspire a similar comment by an influential critic. The warehouse of Hibbard, Spencer, Bartlett and Company, another fourteen-story steel-framed building, was erected in 1925–26 at 211 East North Water Street after the plans of Graham, Anderson, Probst and White. The address placed it a half-block east of Michigan Avenue between the Tribune Tower and the river, where it stood in clear view until the Equitable Building was completed in 1965. It is another impressive example of the form developed for multi-story industrial buildings: the sharply defined windows are set in smooth red-brick planes, their surfaces and color interrupted only by the slightly projecting piers and belt courses, and by base sheathing, trim, and coping of light terra-cotta. The most interesting elevation is the river wall, where the openings for the unloading of goods from vessels are topped by flattened arches defined by the same terra-cotta sheathing. The Hibbard block eventually became the Mandel-Lear Building, under which name it served as a warehouse for the Mandel Brothers Department Store and as an office building for the Blue Cross program of hospital insurance and for the *Encyclopaedia Britannica*.

Lewis Mumford regarded the Hibbard warehouse and a few other works in its character as standing in absolute contrast to what he considered the fraudulence of eclectic "high design."

Today the best modern buildings in Chicago—if one excludes the gymnasium at Northwestern University, some of Mr. Wright's residences and Mr. Barry Byrne's churches—are within this department: the Butler Brothers' Warehouses, the Pennsylvania Freight Terminal, and the Spencer-Bartlett Warehouse. . . . Unfortunately, these buildings are buried under a great heap of meretricious architecture, built by modern methods, with a highly mechanized modern equipment, but dull in design and feeble in all the apologies for ornamental beauty: office buildings surmounted by Temples of Love or steel towers with lanterns supported by steel buttresses that affect to fly . . . . Today the architecture of Chicago is lost in a deluge of meaningless vulgarity; its vast moving picture theaters, its classic stadium, the dull and merely grammatical Gothic of the University of Chicago buildings—all these things represent a sad falling away from the heyday of energy and originality.[60]

The tradition of utilitarian architecture continued in Chicago into the depression with the construction of the Sanitary District's sewage treatment facilities (pp. 000–00), but among the works sponsored by private investment 1930 was again the cut off point. The last work in the style that Mumford praised is the 1929 extension of the warehouse of John Sexton and Company, the original part of which had been built in 1916.[61] The two parts form a single structure extending along the north side of Illinois Street (500N) for a block west of Orleans (340W). Alfred S. Alschuler was the architect of the original block and the extension, both of which are timber-framed mill construction and thus may have brought this old structural technique to its conclusion, at least in its traditional form. The exterior walls of the long six-story building form a familiar pattern: red-brick sheathing covers the continuous piers, relatively broad and shallow in this case, the narrow spandrels, and the flattened arcade extending across the tops of the bays immediately below the parapet. The white terra-cotta trim, the nonderivative ornament, and the raked horizontal joints in the brickwork suggest the influence of George C. Nimmons and other architects of the Prairie school. The pattern is common but it retains an inherent expressiveness and validity when it comes from the hands of competent architects; compared to the ribbon windows or the endless curtains of glass that emerged in the thirties and that long constituted the ruling mode, the older forms offered a livelier visual character without sacrifice of either utility or contemporary urbanity.

Theaters and Stadia

The design and construction of movie theaters and sports stadia may constitute a minor footnote to the whole city-building process, but for a majority of the city's inhabitants they are a far more conspicuous part of the urban milieu than any other kind of building. This was true for a sizable part of the population in the case of the numerous dramatic and vaudeville theaters of the prewar era, and it proved to be true to an overwhelming degree with respect to the vast and incredibly ornate movie palaces that multiplied in the decade of the twenties. Indeed, to many millions of people the movie theater came to be regarded as the very exemplum of the architectural art: it was what the word *architecture* meant. This feeling is still apparent under the surface of the popular attitude toward modern architecture and in the popular demand for period decor in the interiors of even the most uncomprisingly modern apartment buildings. Chicago had a full complement of stage theaters in the days when the live performance flourished, but except for the Auditorium none of these could claim any architectural distinction until the opening of the two theaters in the Civic Opera Building (pp. 125–29). With the explosive rise in the popularity of movies that followed World War I, however, an entirely new dimension of interior design entered the urban scene. In the movie theater it was a thoroughgoing architecture of make-believe; it was not exactly an architecture of fantasy, since that implies a genuine act of imagination, but rather one of pure illusion representing a wish-fulfillment world put together out of fantastic combinations of historical fragments.

The first of these extravagant palaces in the city's core is the Chicago Theater, built in 1920–21 at 175 North State Street. The architect was George L. Rapp and the builders were Abraham and Barney Balaban and Samuel Katz, whose names soon became synonymous with the whole movie-theater world. The exterior of the Chicago, like that of most big downtown theaters, is scarcely visible because of the densely built streets, the broad overhanging marquee, and the huge sign, but the inside presents a pure shell of plaster ornament done in what might be roughly described as orgiastic Baroque. Rapp himself offered in almost religious terms the philosophy of democratic escape underlying these marvels. "Watch the bright light in the eyes of the tired shop girl who hurries noiselessly over carpets and sighs with satisfaction as she walks amid furnishings that once delighted the hearts of queens. See the toil-worn father whose dreams have never come true, and look inside his heart as he finds strength and rest within the theater. Here is a shrine to democracy where there are no privileged patrons. The wealthy rub elbows with the poor."[62] The condescension, the moral fervor, and the fraudulent therapeutic claims foreshadow the coming world of advertising, in which every human impulse is made to yield a commercial fulfillment.

The Chicago was the first in a series of increasingly astounding essays in illusion. The climax came with John Eberson's design for the Capitol Theater, built in 1924 at 7921 South Halsted Street by the National Theaters Corporation. The theory from which this amazing tour de force sprang may be regarded as a modern counterpart of the illusionistic triumphs of those Baroque muralists who made ceilings or the inner surfaces of domes look as though they rose limitlessly into the heavens. In the Capitol these techniques were carried to the final stage. Determined to escape the monotonous heterogeneity of Greek, Roman, French Baroque, and Georgian theaters which revealed increasingly desperate attempts to establish individuality in decorative splendor, yet equally concerned to give the amusement-craving public the variety and opulence it demanded, Eberson created in the Capitol what he called the "atmospheric theater." His description of how such a design is conceived and carried out is another instructive revelation of the climate of popular culture in the twenties.

[The architect] visualized a magnificent amphitheater set in an Italian garden; in a Persian court; in a Spanish patio, any one of them canopied by a soft, moonlit sky. He borrowed from Classic, ancient and definitely established architecture the shape, form and order of house, garden and loggia with which to convert the theater auditorium into nature's setting. It became necessary to study with utmost care the art of reproducing ancient buildings in form, texture and colors; it was more important to intelligently, appreciatively and artfully use paint, brush and electric light, free ornament, furnishings, lights and shadows to produce a true atmosphere of the outdoors without cheapening the attempted illusion with overdone trickery. The auditorium thus created seemed to please. Despite its vastness and expanse it offered an atmosphere of intimacy,—a highly desirable feature in theaters,—and—most important of all—the atmosphere is always new, fresh and alive.[63]

The means by which this illusion was created represented a veritable museum of the architectural treasures of Italy. The exterior walls are relatively restrained, done in an Italian Renaissance style with ornament of polychrome-glazed terra-cotta and polychrome glass. It is the interior that best reveals the scholarly care with which the architect assembled his effects: details of lobbies and foyers were derived from the Villa Cambiaso in Albaro and from various works of the architect Niccolo Pisano at San Miniato, and the doorheads over the entrance to the theater were drawn from Saint Peter's Church in Rome. All this is, as it should be, mere preparation for the auditorium: here the arch of the proscenium is treated as a Roman triumphal arch; the seating area is set in an Italian garden lying under a moonlit Mediterranean sky complete with stars and gently moving clouds; the stage before the screen continues the garden motif without break. The right side of the auditorium is developed as a terraced roof garden surrounding a temple after the Certosa Monastery at Pavia, and the openings to the boxes are arches corresponding to those in the garden walls. Pilasters from the Academy of the Arts at Verona, caryatids from the Erechtheion, an illusory garden constructed in depth, and festive torches of general classical ancestry complete this tour of established beauties executed in rough-cast plaster with an antique finish.

The whole vision—thrice removed from reality, Plato might have argued—rests on a very real, up-to-date structure. The foundations and the amphitheater for the auditorium seats are reinforced concrete, but most of the remaining structure is a steel frame. The stairs are monolithic reinforced concrete covered with marble treads, and other surfaces subject to wear are finished in marble, faience, tile, bronze, and wrought iron. The unusual structural feature is the massive girder of reinforced concrete, 65 feet long and 12 feet deep, that carries the proscenium arch and the roof above it over the stage in front of the screen. The mechanical equipment included a proto-air-conditioning system: the heating and ventilating plant provided warm washed air in the heating season and, in conjunction with a refrigeration system, cooled washed air in the summer. It was clearly the last word at the time, and if not all these wonders have been preserved over the years, they represented a standard that others felt compelled to emulate at least until the depression.

Another Balaban and Katz extravaganza in the ruling mode of the decade is the Oriental Theater, constructed in 1925–26 on the site of the Iroquois Theater at 20 West Randolph Street, with George Rapp again in charge of the design.[64] The architectural treatment of the Oriental made it the most exotic and possibly the costliest of all the big movie houses. Rapp used Indian and Persian motifs for his interior decor and thus helped to raise the final bill to $3,000,000, or about $12,000,000 at the replacement value of 1971. The glories of the Oriental disappeared in a drastic remodeling program in 1969–70, when the extensive interior volume was converted into two smaller theaters, one set directly above the other.

The Granada, which was built at 6427 North Sheridan Road in the same years as the downtown theater, preserved something of the eastern influence in its Hispanic-Moorish style. The Granada was built by a firm of movie theater entrepreneurs known as the Marks Brothers, whose name can only recall the more traditional spelling of the names of those gifted comedians who created on the screen the modern counterpart of the Aristophanic melodrama.

It was George Rapp himself who broke with the past when the now expanded office of Rapp and Rapp received the commission from Balaban and Katz for the little Gateway Theater, opened in June 1930 at 5216 West Lawrence Avenue (4800N).

The Gateway's facade is an early example of what was once called World's Fair Modern, although it was built at a time when the Century of Progress Exposition was still in the stage of preliminary planning. Above the marquee rise a series of vertical panels of ascending height, symmetrically flanking the overbearing sign, the top of which stands well above the roof. The material of these panels is pigmented precast concrete of a tan color. The same architects revealed the unmistakable influence of the Chicago fair in the Will Rogers Theater, another Balaban and Katz house built in 1936 at 5635 West Belmont Avenue (3200N). A similar arrangement of stepped vertical bands, receding from the frontal plane as their height diminishes, stands on each side of the entrance between swept-back planes of poured concrete. These forms were adaptations of the prismatic volumes and long vertical lines of the skyscraper to the facades of small buildings. Similar forms appeared in the abutment walls, piers, and parapets of bridges built during the thirities.[65]

A bolder step in the direction of modern theater design came with the handsome and innovative Esquire Theater at 58 East Oak Street (1000N). This elegant movie house, once almost next door to the Edith Rockefeller McCormick mansion on the Gold Coast, was designed by William and Hal Pereira and erected in 1937–38 as a rare depression investment that proved to be the last movie theater built in the Chicago area for nearly thirty years. In addition to its modern style the distinctive features of the Esquire is that for the first time in the history of movie theaters the visible external form was derived from the internal divisions of the building. The facade—typically the only elevation that can be seen between party walls—is divided into two radically different parts: one is a slightly projecting rectangular block above the entrance and the marquee; the other and larger is an outward-swelling wall with a kind of convex fluting composed of a series of vertical panels which curve outward like shallow cylindrical segments. The projecting block, finished in polished red-and-green granite, marks the location of the lobby, while the fluted wall of yellow brick constitutes one side wall of the auditorium. In the interior the curving walls of the spacious lobby again correspond to the curving rear wall of the seating area. The interior colors are rich but drawn from a narrow spectrum—orange tan lobby walls, black-striped amber rug, rich red brown walls and curtains in the auditorium—and the emphasis is on broad surfaces of color, a feature of the Century of Progress Exposition that excited the most favorable comment.[66]

There is little architectural and structural similarity between theaters and sports stadia beyond the fact that both belong to the architecture of public recreation. Until the mid-twenties Chicago's only facilities for commercialized spectator sports were the two major league baseball parks, the Cubs' Wrigley Field at Addison (3600N) and Sheffield (1000W) on the North Side, and the White Sox's Comiskey Park at 35th and Shields streets on the South. Built respectively in 1912–13 and 1909–10, they are the conventional steel-framed brick-enclosed structures that were universal for professional baseball until the appearance of the new circular multipurpose stadia such as those in Houston, Saint Louis, San Diego, and Cincinnati. The pioneer example of these later structures, however, is the mammoth Solider Field (originally Grant Park Stadium) that stretches between the separated roadways of South Lake Shore Drive for a thousand feet below 14th Boulevard. Designed by Holabird and Roche as one of the few stadia built in the pure Greek style since classical antiquity, and constructed in 1923–25, the field was planned for civic pageants, meetings, rallies, and exhibitions as well as sports events. The basic structure of reinforced concrete is overlaid and overwhelmed by porticoes, colonnades, and surface details, but once inside the enclosure, one recognizes clearly what it is—an immense U-shaped amphitheater opening to the north and embracing a football field and a quarter-mile running track. A monument at the south end to soldiers killed in World War I is the basis of the present name. The permanent seating was designed for a capacity of 55,000 spectators, but an additional 40,000–45,000 seats can be provided by using the tiers above the theater and across the north end. As many as 100,000 have thus been accommodated for the most popular national events, like the celebrated Jack Dempsey–Gene Tunney fight of 1927.

Holabird and Roche won a citywide competition for the design of the field, and their finished work reflects the requirements laid down by the commissioners of the South Park District. The functional criterion was that the majority of seats should center around a relatively small area for viewing sports other than football, and the formal one was that the architectural treatment should harmonize with the classical Field Museum on the north side of 14th Boulevard.[67] The architects thus considered the museum as the basis of their composition: the axis of the stadium is a continuation of the axis of the building; the seating tiers open to the north for a full view of the museum; the Ionic details of the exhibition halls under the stands and the Doric colonnades above them carry out in part the museum motifs. (The Erechtheion and the Parthenon, as one might expect, are the respective sources of these borrowings.) These formal principles, however, were rendered meaningless by the construction of the Chicago Park District's unified headquarters (1934–35) along the south side of 14th Boulevard, exactly blocking the view of the Field Museum from any point south of the drive. On the functional level the stadium is expertly designed for the circulation of large crowds: a promenade at the esplanade level outside the amphitheater provides access to all tunnels and ramps leading to the lower seats and to all stairways serving the upper tiers; all main aisles lead to the arena, so that spectators, pageants, troops, and others may exit through the open north end or through passages south of the main east and west stands. Under the stands there are extensive column-free areas for industrial, educational, livestock, and dairy exhibitions, and other spaces that can be heated for permanent gymansium, swimming pool, and auditorium installations. In these respects Solider Field was potentially far ahead of its newer counterparts, but the athletic facilities were never built, and the International Amphitheatre proved to be much better adapted to automobile and livestock exhibitions.

The consequence was that the city-owned stadium was seldom used for exhibitions, and although it is well designed, with extensive parking areas to the east and south, its sporting uses declined drastically after the long hiatus of depression and war. By 1960 the vast field was largely derelict, and it now seems strangely anachronistic with its Greek details grossly inflated to preserve the ponderous scale. Proposals have come and gone for replacing it with a sports complex designed for all outdoor athletic activities. But since this would do irreparable harm to the lakefront parks and beaches —already seriously damaged by the construction of high-speed boulevards and the new exposition building—the best solution would be to demolish the stadium and return the area below Grant Park to landscaping and the open-air recreational uses for which the south lakefront was intended by Daniel Burnham.[68]

The size of Solider Field precluded the possibility of roofing any part of the stadium for events that required shelter or for wintertime activities. Yet the need was there, and it was eventually satisfied by private investors through the construction of the roofed Chicago Stadium at 1800 West Madison Street in 1928–29. This strictly utilitarian work was designed by the architectural firm of Hall, Lawrence and Ratcliffe and the structural engineers of the Westcott Engineering Company. Planned as an exhibition hall and a large covered sports arena, the stadium has been used for a variety of purposes, including political rallies, religious revivals, and a jazz festival, but the later addition of provisions for an ice floor converted it to the permanent home of the Chicago hockey team, the Black Hawks, during the appropriate season. In its external appearance the Chicago Stadium is a large volume of limestone curtain walls treated in the style of the new skyscraper, which in this case bears little relation to the steel frame or to the internal functional divisions. The construction of the building involved a now familiar problem, namely, the support of the prismatic vaulted roof over the 266-foot span of the arena and its flanking seating areas. The solution was the orthodox one of truss framing, in this case a transverse series of Pratt trusses with steeply cambered bottom chords. The long clear span suggested the adoption of unusually heavy elements: the bottom chord is composed of a series of built-up box griders, the top chord of I-section members built up of plates and angles, and the web members are H-beams.[69] It had all been done many times before, and until welded connections and rigid framing became common, there was no way in which such systems could be further refined.

Hotels and Apartments

The hotel buildings that were erected in Chicago until depression, war, and oversupply stopped their construction for more than thirty years are noteworthy much more for their size than for their architectural merit, although formal details, functional design, and structural systems always reveal the same sure mastery of the building art that one finds in the office towers. The big urban hotel is the original microcity, a concept which thus has its roots in the nineteenth century and was not invented in the past decade, as many contemporary architects believe. Moreover, in this role it constitutes a remarkably accurate microcosm of American life, the poverty and emptiness of which are represented by the dishwashers, bootblacks, door-holders, and others who perform the menial jobs, and the equally empty extravagance by the free-spending expense-account executives who command the food, liquor, and women.[70] The big hotel thus embraces a great variety of internal spaces and lines of circulation, and such architectural and structural interest as attaches to it arises from the skill with which designers have arranged these various enclosures. The larger the building, the larger will be such public facilities as dining rooms, ballrooms, meeting rooms, and lobbies, with the obvious consequence that the larger and more complex will be the framing system required to carry superimposed floors over those spaces; and this structural complexity will be further increased by the presence of traditional stylistic details that entail deviations from the fundamental rectilinearity of the column-and-girder frame.

The structure that most fully embodied all the characteristics of the large fashionable hotel in the days of the Burnham Plan is the LaSalle, erected in 1908–9 at the northwest corner of LaSalle and Madison streets from the plans of Holabird and Roche and their engineering collaborators, Purdy and Henderson (fig. 24). The twenty-two-story building, rising 260 feet in overall height, fills out a rectangular area 161 × 178 feet in plan (except for a rear light court), and its street elevations reveal the typical three-part arrangement in the base of rusticated stone, the shaft in brick sheathing, and the curving, richly adorned Mansard roof at the top story. The riveted steel frame on bedrock caissons is for the most part the standard form,

Fig. 24. LaSalle Hotel, northwest corner of LaSalle and Madison streets, 1908–9. Holabird and Roche, architects. (Courtesy Chicago Historical Society.)

Fig. 25. LaSalle Hotel. Truss framing of the banquet halls at the nineteenth floor.

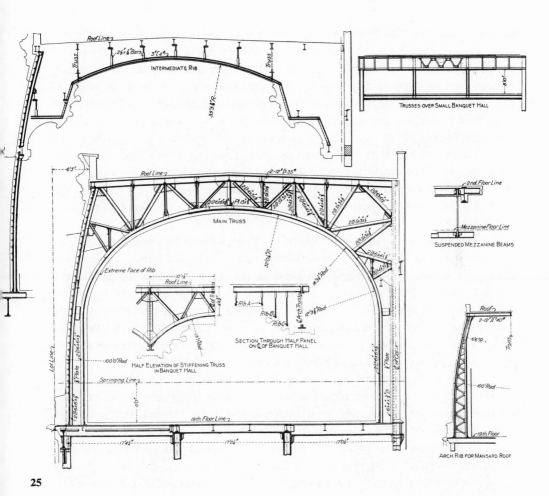

with bay spans varying from 14 to 25 feet, but extensive public areas on the first and the nineteenth floors led to some unusual exhibitions of ingenuity on the part of the structural designers. Over the dining room on the first floor the eighteen-story column lines are supported by built-up plate girders that occupy the entire height of the second floor.[71] Since these girders lie across the second-floor corridor, each web contains a central rectangular opening exactly in the region of maximum bending. The compression of the top flange is transmitted through the missing web by two massive knees, one on either side of the opening, extending from a huge gusset plate under the top flange downward and outward to the bottom flange at the second-floor level. The more extensive lobby area required that the columns rest on a massive Warren truss double the depth of the plate girders and hence extending into the plane of the fourth floor.[72]

The main banqueting hall on the nineteenth floor, which rises through three stories in height and is very nearly equal to the lobby in area, required a framing system more complex in form, although smaller in depth of members since only the roof load is involved (fig. 25). The roof rests on a series of purlins supported in turn by the top chords of six arched trusses. From the bottom chords of these trusses hangs a framework of longitudinal trusses and transverse ribs that carries the metal lath of the heavy, elaborately molded plaster ceiling. The swelling, outward-curving side walls of the Mansard are supported and braced at the corners by open-web ribs that constitute the primary structural members in the framework that underlies this favorite decorative element of neo-Baroque design. The LaSalle Hotel sums up riveted steel construction of the 1910 decade, an assertion that includes the massive riveted-plate construction of its 317-foot smokestack as well as the intricacies of the internal skeleton. The prosperous life of the hotel, which was well located for the financial trade, was disastrously interrupted on 5 June 1946, when a contents fire originating in the cocktail lounge claimed sixty-one lives. Yet the hotel suffered no permanent damage to its reputation and appears to have no trouble in maintaining its position among its numerous competitors.

Two lakefront hotels were the conspicuous additions of the decade following the opening of the LaSalle. The Edgewater Beach, on Sheridan Road at Berwyn Avenue (5300N), stood far removed from the urban clamor when it was built in 1914–16. It was designed by Benjamin Marshall primarily to be a resort hotel, as its Mediterranean style and the yellow stucco finish on its sixteen-story walls were meant to suggest. The prominent steel-framed building stood close to the lake for nearly forty years, until Lincoln Park and Lake Shore Drive were extended north to Hollywood Avenue, and thus enjoyed its own private beach along with its tennis courts, outdoor swimming pool, gardens, and spacious lawns. The Edgewater stood at the very top of the fashionable hotels in the twenties, but changing patterns of travel after the second World War and the conventioners' insistence on being close to the action in the urban core eroded its clientele until bankruptcy forced its closure in 1967. It was eventually demolished to make way for a group of high-rise apartments that fill one of the few remaining openings in the upper Sheridan Road canyon. Well to the south, at Lake Shore Drive and Oak Street (1000N), the continuingly popular Drake Hotel fared much better. Designed by Marshall and Fox and erected in 1918–20, the Drake stands at the elbow of the Gold Coast, its sober classical facade looking out over a scene matched in few cities of the world. Oak Street Beach lies in the immediate foreground; north of it stretch Outer Drive, the shore promenade, and Lincoln Park, while the limitless horizon of the lake encompasses the whole marvelous vista. Not even the avalanche of auto traffic that was to come in later years could threaten the hotel's numerous attractions.

When the Drake was planned, Michigan Avenue above the bridge did not exist, and when the hotel was opened only the Wrigley Building suggested the promise of the future boulevard. Yet the possibilities were obvious, with the proximity of the lake and extensive open land to the east, and in the boom of the twenties the fabric of the inner city was changing rapidly. The Tribune Tower was under construction when the second of the North Michigan hotels began to rise: the Allerton, at Huron Street (700N), was erected in 1923–24, adding a little more than a thousand rooms to the city's transient space. Designed—surprisingly enough for Chicago—by the New York architects Murgatroyd and Ogden, with Fugard and Knapp as their local associates, the building was known as Allerton House, a designation that once suggested a haven for the lonely, who in this case were unmarried men and women. The twenty-five-story steel-framed tower, handsomely clad in rich, dark colors, added another touch of romance through its decorative detail drawn from a medieval north Italian provenance. The original top-floor clubroom was converted to a bar known as the Tip Top Tap, which was long popular for the nocturnal view, but it has been eclipsed by newer, higher, and more expensive drinking establishments.

The rising curve of the boom was perfectly matched by the increasing size of new hotels. A short-lived record came with the latest Palmer House, erected in 1923–25 and extended in 1927 over nearly the whole block bounded by State, Wabash, Monroe, and Adams—very likely the noisiest site in the city, bracketed as it is by the elevated on one side and the shopping traffic on the other. Designed by Holabird and Roche and their engineering associate, Frank E. Brown, twenty-five stories high, embracing a record number of 2,268 rooms and baths, containing every kind of space for gregarious activities serious or convivial, it offered the perfect example of quantitative expansiveness applied to the downtown hotel. It was the fourth hotel to bear the Palmer name, its three predecessors, completed successively in 1865, 1871, and 1875, having all been designed by John M. Van Osdel. The simplified neoclassic design, marked by limestone sheathing at the base and top and by dark-red brick in the intermediate stories, had become standard at the time, for it carried with it the fullest suggestion of dignity and princely magnificence.

Since all the problems had been solved—internal planning, truss and girder framing for wide-span enclosures, sinking caisson foundations to bedrock—there was no reason, if the financial backing existed, why the same team should not repeat the performance on an even larger scale. The result was the Stevens Hotel, constructed on Michigan Avenue between Seventh and Eighth streets in 1925–27, to secure the still-unbroken record of the world's largest hotel. The original sponsors of this 3,000-room behemoth were James W. and Ernest J. Stevens, who sold it to the United States Army in 1941, when it was converted into a short-lived Air Force Radio Technical School. Stephen A. Healy acquired the property in 1943, and Conrad Hilton bought it from him two years later for $7,500,000, or about one-quarter of its original cost and one-fifth of its replacement value at the time. The only permanent change along the way was a reduction in the number of rooms to 2,700 as a result of combining smaller rooms into suites or merging them into public spaces. Included in the hotel's total compass are thirty public meeting rooms, seven ballrooms, and five basements distributed under part of the building area. The vast structure is a city in itself: it can comfortably accommodate 5,000 guests, ordinarily employes 2,000 persons to operate the machinery of comfort, which includes seven heating and hot water boilers, and has frequently handled a daytime traffic of 25,000 persons.

The architectural style of the Hilton is derived from French precedents of the eighteenth century. Like the Palmer House, the whole block is planned as a series of parallel wings extending transversely toward Michigan Avenue and longitudinally toward the streets on the north and south sides. The twenty-five-story height is divided on the street elevations into the familiar three-part system in which the base and top story are sheathed in rusticated limestone and the intermediate stories in dark-red brick. The architects handled the scale with remarkable skill: the great size is apparent but in no way overbearing because the human dimension is everywhere preserved in windows, entranceways, and decorative detail. The chief structural problem in the design of the steel frame was again the need to support overhead column lines above the void of the main ballroom, which lies on the second floor and is three stories in height. The columns above this space bear on four enormous trusses extending in depth from the fifth to the eighth floor and thus constituting near-record dimensions for structural elements to match the bulk of the hotel.[73]

The modern style came to the Chicago hotel with the construction of the Medinah Athletic Club at 505 North Michigan Avenue in 1927–29. Designed by the architect Walter W. Ahlschlager and the engineer Frank A. Randall, the forty-five-story tower conforms more exactly to the simplified pattern of the office block than to any precedent in residential building, as we have already noted (p. 172). The Medinah changed its corporate status successively to the Continental Hotel and the present Sheraton-Chicago, but the Moorish dome and minaret at the top that house penthouse equipment have survived to recall its ancestry under the Shriners. It was the last hotel building to be erected in the inner city for thirty-five years, but after World War II motor hotels sprang up on the periphery of the core and in outlying areas like mushrooms, with about the same architectural interest. The motel has become a synonym for the banality and the poverty of modern building: it is cramped, decoratively empty, pathetic in its fraudulent claim to elegance, minimal in service, and surrounded by the noise and pollution of street traffic; the Stevens, conversely, facing Grant Park and Lake Michigan, represents a standard of material and formal quality that has yet to be approached even in its new inner-city counterparts.

The same assertion may be made with equal justice about the urban apartment building, in those cases where any architectural attention at all has been paid to its form and appointments. Chicago was well on the way to becoming an apartment city at the turn of the century, when the number of apartment units constructed per annum exceeded the number of individual houses by a ratio of three to one.[74] In 1910 the ratio passed 4:1, reached a maximum of 6.8:1 in 1928, and except for the years 1918–21, when large-scale investments were inhibited by war and postwar depression, it seldom fell below the figure that was established at the time of the Burnham Plan. Although the apartment buildings were scattered over many neighborhoods of the city, a high proportion of them were concentrated near the lakeshore, in Hyde Park, along Lincoln Park and Sheridan Road, and on the east-west streets that abutted the shore area of the North Side. The overwhelming majority of individual residential buildings throughout the city were three- and four-story walk-ups erected by contractors from standard plans, or rows of closely spaced detached houses in the various historical and bungalow styles that became popular after 1910.

Few great houses of the wealthy were built in Chicago after the First World War, and most of them were concentrated on the Near North Side above Division Street (1200N) east of Clark, in Kenwood, centered at Woodlawn Avenue and 49th Street on the South Side, in Hyde Park, and on upper Sheridan Road, where only a handful have survived the high-rise onslaught. One has to go to the northern and western suburbs for their newer counterparts. Frank Lloyd Wright's last house in Chicago, for example, was built in 1915 at 7415 Sheridan Road, and he was not to return to the suburban area until 1940. A relatively modest house in the North Shore community of Highland Park that was built as the boom collapsed into depression may well have been the one prophetic work of residential architecture both in its conception and in its realization. When the architect Henry Dubin (the father of the founding partners of Dubin, Dubin, Black and Moutoussamy) built a home for himself in 1929–30 he employed conventional brick and cinder-block masonry for the exterior walls and gypsum block or plaster for the partitions, but he made extensive use of a valuable and possibly original idea for the flooring. The floor structure, which was then known as battledeck from its use in naval vessels, consists of a 3/16-inch steel plate welded to the top flanges of I-beams or channels varying in depth from three to five inches, the form and the dimensions being determined by the span. The finished flooring of cork, slate, or rubber tile was laid in cement grout spread over the steel deck. The architect discovered that the integral system of deck and beams was subject to a deflection under load only slightly more than that of isolated beams twice the depth of those used. This phenomenon suggests a prevision of the orthotropic girders that were to appear in bridge structures after World War II. The technique that seems to have been decisive in suggesting the idea to Dubin was the insulated steel-sandwich wall construction of Pullman cars, and he predicted the day when the mass-production of similar wall components would revolutionize the construction of houses and commercial blocks. The building industry is still waiting for that time to arrive.

Technological innovations such as those of the Dubin house were extremely rare, for the vast bulk of residential building throughout the city was accomplished by methods that had changed little over the previous century. Along the lakeshore, however, especially on the North Side and in the East Fifties on the South, there was a growing concentration of high-rise high-rent luxury apartments on which most of the city's architectural talent was lavished. Among these by far the most elegant, the most expensive, and the most magnificently sited are the buildings of the Gold Coast, the solid strip of luxury that extends along the water's edge from 940 North Lake Shore Drive through 229 to 179 East and up to 1600 North at North Avenue, the odd mixture of house numbers resulting because the drive curves through an east-west segment along its dominant north-south route.

This long eastward extension of the shore at the line of Oak Street (1000N) is a consequence of a curious combination of natural and man-made agencies that remind us how recently Chicago emerged from a frontier culture. The area of the city lying east of Michigan Avenue between the river and Oak Street is largely the product of human activity. In 1833–34, the United States Army Engineers built a groin into the lake at the mouth of the newly straightened river in order to prevent the formation of a bar across the mouth.[75] The deflected shore currents deposited sand in an ever enlarging triangle along the north side of the repeatedly extended groin. Some fifty years after these operations, when a considerable waste of sand and dune grass had grown up, a profane, reckless, hard-drinking, and colorful scoundrel named George Wellington Streeter laid squatter's claim to the area immediately north of the sandy triangle, in the open water of which he had established a home in July 1886. The circumstances of this establishment are perhaps unique in the history of urban building. Streeter had built a vessel which he intended to use in gunrunning for Latin American revolutionists or military adventurers, but a storm grounded the vessel on a bar about 450 feet offshore, a little above the line of Chicago Avenue (the location now would be close to the southeast corner of the Hancock Building). Unable to refloat his schooner, Streeter decided to use it as a house while he waited for higher water, ordinarily a matter of years. Currents and waves deposited sand around the vessel until a stable island had formed, by which time the retired gunrunner had built a causeway of ties and driftwood to connect his home with the shore. The southward-flowing currents that were deflected by the causeway dropped their traction load of sand in sufficient quantities to turn the island into a peninsula, which the resourceful Streeter enlarged by persuading building contractors to dump their rubbish and excavated spoil along the margins. By 1890 he had built up a real estate empire of 186 acres, but the "land" was very likely the most uninviting in and around the urban area, and it was not improved by the owner's substituting a roofed scow for the badly beaten schooner.

Owners of land along Pine Street (the forerunner of Michigan Avenue), finally deciding that this unacceptable squatter would have to be removed, claimed riparian rights along the shore as it existed before the creation of Streeter's sand-and-rubbish estate. The first to demand that he leave was N. K. Fairbanks, who was shot in the foot for his efforts but later enjoyed the distinction of having the short street known as Fairbanks Court (300E) named after him. It was the beginning of thirty years of intermittent warfare between Streeter and his equally flinty wife on the one hand and the Chicago police on the other. The redoubtable Streeter dug in all the harder when he discovered an old map that persuaded him that his land lay outside the State of Illinois, on the basis of which he proclaimed himself governor of a "district," with an alleged patent of right signed by President Cleveland. As the casualties grew the police finally moved in on the outlaw in force and captured him alive. He was tried, found guilty of murder, and sentenced to life imprisonment, but he was released in 1907 on the ground that the original indictment rested on insufficient evidence. By this date the real estate and building interests began to realize that the developmental potential of "Streeterville" might reach millions of dollars—it was eventually to pass the billion-dollar level—and where money was concerned the law soon found a way to make room for the honest businessman. On 10 December 1918 the court ruled that Streeter's patent was a forgery and that all his claims rested on force alone, conveniently overlooking two important facts, namely, that it was his ingenuity that made the land in the first place and that his claim to riparian rights was at least as valid as those of the Pine Street landowners. Beaten by the law of the respectable classes, Streeter retired to a houseboat near Navy Pier and died quietly in 1921, at the age of eighty-four. His second wife survived him by fifteen years, but her own attempts and those of other heirs to recover the property naturally came to nothing.[76]

The creation of the Gold Coast, which extends along the east and north margins of Streeter's land, then northward to Lincoln Park, began shortly before he returned from the state prison at Joliet (fig. 26). The initial step came with the Marshall Apartments, constructed in 1905-6 at 1100 North Lake Shore Drive (Cedar Street). The modest eight-story building was designed by Benjamin H. Marshall, whose career was largely devoted to the planning of Gold Coast apartments. It was the setting, of course, that constituted the prime attraction, and it was probably only the social authority of Prairie Avenue on the South Side that prevented its earlier exploitation. Lake, beach, park, quiet scenic drive, and yet the core of the city only a mile and a half to the south—it was a combination of factors that existed in few other parts of the world, and once the first experiment proved successful, the building of luxury apartments came at an accelerating pace. The second of the Gold Coast group is the nine-story block at 1130 North Lake Shore (1910), which brought the talents of Howard Van Doren Shaw to the scene. Streeterville was invaded in the following year, when the building at 999 was constructed in 1911-12 after the plans of Marshall and Fox (fig. 26). The 999 set the standard for many that followed it not only in its immediate neighborhood but elsewhere in the lakefront areas: ten stories in height, on pile foundations, it stands at the turn from the north-south to the east-west sections of the drive and hence faces the lake in two directions. Its Second Empire decor had invaded the Chicago scene as long ago as the 1880s, but here it emerged in something like its Parisian sophistication: bright red brick spandrels and narrow panels surround each of the broad window groups; rounded and rectangular oriels are symmetrically distributed on the east elevation; white limestone trim fills out this lively play of surface and color.

Fig. 26. Apartment buildings of the middle Gold Coast. *Left to right:* 999 North Lake Shore Drive (1911–12); 229 (1917–18), 219 (1921–22), 209 (1923–24), 199 (1914–15), 181 (1923), 179 (1928–29) East Lake Shore Drive; Drake Hotel, East Lake Shore Drive at Michigan Avenue (1918–20).

Benjamin Marshall repeated the design in the Breakers, erected at 199 East Lake Shore Drive in 1914–15 as the seventh of the Gold Coast group (fig. 26).[77] The building stands one story higher than its predecessor, but the treatment of the elevations is identical except for the elliptical rotunda into which the service drive opens. The geometric form thus carries out the curve of the oriel projections, which are elliptical segments. A more sober eighteenth-century spirit characterizes the limestone facade and separated windows of the Shoreland Apartments, designed by Fugard and Knapp, with Lieberman and Hein as the consulting engineers, and erected in 1917–18 at 229 East Lake Shore. The more restrained form seemed appropriate to the increasing height, and the same architects and engineers twice repeated the design: first in the 219 East Lake Shore building (1921–22), which like the Shoreland is twelve stories high, and again in the 181 East (1922–23), whose nineteen stories are sheathed in brick above the base rather than in the more costly limestone. Expense, however, did not deter Benjamin Marshall from keeping the limestone for the eighteen-story 209 East, erected in 1923–24 as the most sober of all the classical apartment buildings on the Gold Coast.

By this date Chicago had entered an apartment boom that exploded at the end of the postwar depression in 1921, then evaporated just as quickly in 1929. The building industry completed more than 18,000 apartment units in 1922, then expanded the number steadily every year to a high point of nearly 37,000 units in 1927; but the downward slide rapidly shrank the total to fewer than 1,500 in 1930.[78] This immense volume of construction included every type, from Lake Shore skyscrapers of thirty stories to block after block of three-story walk-ups ranging from six to forty-two units, the larger generally disposed in a U-shaped plan around a central court. They lacked the spacious rooms, elevators, doormen, penthouse terraces, swimming pools, and other public facilities of the expensive lakefront buildings, but low rents, dependable steam heat, good kitchen facilities, and safety made them popular, and the long rows filled as fast as they were completed. Between them and the commercial strips lay the endless miles of detached houses. Equally rapid construction along the upper lakeshore produced the high solid cliffs that established the urban character of New York and Chicago as much as their concentrations of office skyscrapers. On the North Side the high-rise apartments present unbroken walls to Lincoln Park and the lake beyond, but the rear elevations are always deeply indented by light courts. On the South Side, especially around East End Avenue in Hyde Park, slender towers once stood far apart in an early though unwitting realization of Le Corbusier's *La ville radieuse*, with its widely spaced skyscrapers in continuous parklike settings.

The building up of the Gold Coast kept pace with the boom as the vacant lots were filled or the great mansions of the millionaires fell before newer fashions. Jarvis Hunt's eighteen-story Lake Shore Club, a residential building as well as a social organization, rose at 850 North in 1923–24 to constitute a kind of southern outpost, although it is now separated from its eclectic neighbors by Mies van der Rohe's four apartment towers at 860, 880, and 900 North. In the next year a new stylistic decor and a new architect emerged with the 1120 North Lake Shore Building, erected in 1924–25 from the designs of Robert S. De Golyer and Walter T. Stockton. The eighteen-story structure has the shape of a slender two-winged tower in plan to provide an outer exposure for all rooms, and all but the rear elevation is sheathed in brick with terra-cotta trim in the Tudor style. Because Lake Shore Drive follows the beach profile and hence does not lie at right angles to the east-west streets, the apartments at 1120 that extend from the short east wing of any one floor into the long west wing presented an awkward problem in planning: the axis through the living and dining rooms makes an angle of seventy-five degrees to the axis joining the centers of the bedrooms, and the triangular space between the two groups of rooms is occupied by a bathroom and a closet of irregular shape. Most of the apartments have six rooms, including two bedrooms and a maid's room, but those at the west end of the long wing are duplex units (divided between two floors) with three bedrooms.

Among the remaining eight apartments that were constructed on the Gold Coast up to 1930, three claim attention for various reasons, social as well as architectural. The narrow sixteen-story building at 1540 North Lake Shore, designed by Huszagh and Hill in association with J. W. McCarthy and erected in 1924–25, enjoys two distinctions: it was the first building to be converted to cooperative ownership, which occurred when it was sold to its tenants in 1947; and it was the first of the Gold Coast group to break the barrier of anti-Semitism, a particularly vulgar form of bigotry from which the ruling class of Chicago has never freed itself. The 1400 North, built in 1926–27 after the plans of Hooper and Janusch and the engineer Frank A. Randall, is a twenty-one-story reinforced concrete structure whose columns are carried on a continuous mat foundation of heavily reinforced concrete that spreads the concentrated loads over a large area and thus reduces the unit load so that the upper level of hardpan clay can easily sustain it. The Drake Tower, constructed at 179 East Lake Shore in 1928–29, was the last from the hand of Benjamin Marshall and the first to be designed in the modern style. The horizontally elongated windows, of which those in the two center bays are divided between fixed and movable sash in the form of the so-called Chicago window, the flat planes of brick, and the absence of any decorative detail all suggest the influence of the International style, which was then beginning to penetrate American architecture through the work of Raymond Hood and William Lescaze in the East and of Richard Neutra in California. The twenty-nine-story height made the Drake the highest of the Gold Coast group, and its date of construction made it second to the last before the depression very nearly brought apartment construction to a complete stop.[79]

The architects and engineers of apartment buildings in the predepression era seldom deviated from well-marked and long-used paths in interior planning, appointments, external design, structure, and mechanical utilities, and there have been many critics who felt that they were far out of touch with the true creative spirit of the time. A restrained but nonetheless telling indictment came from Burchard and Bush-Brown, the ruling historians of American architecture in the decade of the sixties.

The successful American architects, with few exceptions, were simply not full of the spirit of experiment that moved many of the painters, the spirit of compassion or angry repudiation that was common among the novelists and the poets, the spirit of dedication to search that marked the scientists. In such a climate it is not surprising that they ignored or deprecated the important buildings or writings that were appearing in Europe. . . . The admired American buildings were appropriate to an age of complacency. The successful American architects of this day were complacent too.[80]

Yet for all this artistic conservatism, we are forced to the same conclusion about apartment buildings that we reached about hotels: in the matter of spaciousness both of individual rooms and total floor area, soundness of construction, adequacy of insulation, reliability of mechanical equipment, and general appearance, the conservatively designed apartments of the 1920s, with few exceptions, are much superior to their counterparts in the latest of postwar booms. The public did not miss the irony of architects like Mies van der Rohe and Walter Netsch and Bertrand Goldberg living in houses or apartments built a half-century or more before the decade of their greatest activity.

The failure of American architects was their social conservatism: they served a ruling class that was blind to or unwilling to see the realities underlying the Babylon in which they flourished. Chicago contributed its share to the desperate gaiety and the new artistic excitements of the time. Its symphony orchestra and its opera company stood in the front rank of American musical organizations. The literary renaissance under the leadership of Ben Hecht and James T. Farrell still flourished, although the commanding figures of Theodore Dreiser and Sherwood Anderson had departed before World War I. Jazz had migrated from New Orleans to Chicago over the years before and after the war, and by the mid-twenties the northern city had no serious competitor for originality and craftsmanship in the art. The extravagant hedonism of the time flourished among those who could afford the prices, and if the illegal liquor was hard to obtain and sometimes harder to drink, the mob-run speakeasies did their best to satisfy the need. But it was precisely here that one began to see the other side of the coin: the unbelievable idiocy of Prohibition brought organized crime and organized warfare into the streets as the gangs fought each other and the police over control of the liquor traffic. Chicago's long tradition of violence, in which law-enforcement agents contributed more than their share in self-righteous zeal, now reached epidemic proportions. The dichotomy between the architecture of corporate wealth and power on one hand and the residential city on the other reached new extremes as large areas of the human community deteriorated into permanent blight.

This deterioration was nowhere more glaring than in the South Side ghetto, which had been established by 1920 as an ineradicable cancer. The first mass influx of Negroes came with World War I, when industry and the railroads were in desperate need of skilled and unskilled workers. The black emigrés moved into the middle South Side, where the original ghetto nucleus was centered at 40th Street and Saint Lawrence Avenue, and steadily moved outward into areas occupied by Irish, Jewish, and various East European peoples. Angry and abrasive friction at the edges was the natural consequence of white prejudice and its concomitant resistance to black attempts to break out of the social prison. The inevitable explosion came in the summer of 1919. Black and white boys were swimming at a South Side beach when one of the black boys tried to climb on a raft occupied by whites; a stone was thrown, a fight followed, and the black youth either fell or was pushed into the water and drowned. The fast-spreading word was the trigger for the riot that could be the only response of the Negro community to the degradation the white race had forced upon it. Beating, shooting, and savage mutilation led to seven deaths and many injuries, the overwhelming majority suffered by the blacks, and a high proportion of these occurred as the result of deliberate and sadistic malice on the part of the police. The belated call for state troops by Mayor William Hale Thompson prevented what would have been a general massacre of the black community.

It seemed clear to the more thoughtful observers of the city that the building of luxury apartments did not quite reach the heart of the problem. A few philanthropists tried the experiment of building low-cost, low-rent housing as a private investment in the hope that such activity could be shown to be a remunerative business practice. The first to undertake a practical demonstration was Benjamin J. Rosenthal, who founded the Chicago Dwellings Association shortly after the end of the war to carry out his ideas. The organization began its hopeful program with the construction in 1919–21 of the community known as Garden Homes, situated in the 8800-block of

South Wabash Avenue. Designed by a well-known architect, Charles Frost, and considered a business as well as a philanthropic venture, the Homes included 133 detached bungalows and 21 duplex apartments, the individual units set on astonishingly generous lots measuring 30 feet in width and from 162½ to 200 feet in depth. The idea, of course, was to encourage gardening and the landscaping arts, but the individual house and lot were priced at $5,700, a figure high enough at the time to take it well out of the low-income class. As a business venture, however, the project lost money: the neighborhood was too far from the settled area of the city to attract owners, and too far from public transportation to provide access to jobs in the industrial belt stretching south and east of the city. Rosenthal was the first to learn what many have discovered in the succeeding half-century: it is not possible to build housing for the urban poor that is at once decent and profitable, since housing as it is now constructed is simply beyond the means of low-income people.

A more ambitious and successful project was undertaken by the estate of Marshall Field ten years after the abortive Rosenthal scheme. The Marshall Field Garden Apartments, as they were originally known, were built in 1929–30 after the plans of Andrew J. Thomas of New York and Graham, Anderson, Probst and White, with advice on the selection of the site from the Social Research Department of the University of Chicago. Extending the length of the 1400-block on North Sedgewick Street (400W), the location offers the great advantage of being less than two miles from the center of the Loop, within half a mile of two elevated stations, and a mile from North Avenue Beach in Lincoln Park. The ten interconnected buildings were designed as a model community for white tenants in the middle-income range, their garden-city ancestry revealed by the continuous strip of planted space lying between the rear elevations of the two rows of apartments. The entire project consists of 628 dwelling units, a garage for 155 cars, twenty stores, and a central heating plant, all in fireproof construction, with brick bearing walls, concrete floor slabs, and steel columns. Rents, based on operating expenses plus a 5 percent return on the investment, ranged from a minimum of $55 per month for 3½ rooms to a maximum of $97.50 for 6 rooms. The project functioned successfully enough through depression and war until the Hanover Equities Corporation of New York acquired the property in 1961, after it had twice changed hands (1942 and 1955). This corporate and absentee landlord allowed the apartments and public facilities to deteriorate to the point where the tenants, now including blacks as well as whites, were forced to mount a rent strike in 1966–67. An abortive attempt by the nonprofit Community Renewal Foundation to purchase the property for rehabilitation only led to receivership. But the story in this case had a happy ending: eventually rescued by the investment group of McHugh-

Levin Associates and the architectural firm of Dubin, Dubin, Black and Moutoussamy, the apartments were rehabilitated in 1969–70 under section 221(d)3 of the National Housing Act, with the Dubin office acting as architects, and restored as the model middle-income project they were meant to be.[81]

Housing such as that sponsored by Rosenthal and Field was at best a temporary palliative, a bandaging of a wound here and there, a situation that became apparent even to the corporate and political directorate through the lessons of the depression. In Chicago it was no longer possible to hide the fact that there were two cities, one consisting of the skyscraper core and the luxury apartments that stretched along the lakefront, the other its exact opposite—the tangled rail trackage, the deteriorating factories and warehouses, the slums and the spreading ghetto, the miles of gray areas bordering the frantic commercial strips. Just as Chicago's inexhaustible reservoir of architectural and engineering talent created the brilliance of the first city, so the indifference of architects and planners strengthened the hands of the power-holders who preferred to do nothing about the second.

NOTES TO CHAPTER 4

1. See table 1.
2. See tables 2 and 3.
3. Chicago's population in the decade of 1910–20 increased by 23.7%, while that of the metropolitan areas as a whole increased by 27.6% (see table 1).
4. See tables 2 and 3. This decline in housing construction coincided with the great period of Negro migration from the South.
5. Leo J. Sheridan and W. C. Clark, "The Straus Building, Chicago," *Architectural Forum* 42 (April 1925): 225.
6. Leading examples of such buildings around the time of World War I are the following:
   Transportation Building, 608 South Dearborn Street, 1911; Fred V. Prather, architect; height twenty-two stories; a severe and immensely elongated narrow slab, monotonous in the neutrality of its window pattern, standing in a now decaying area of South Dearborn Street near Dearborn Station.
   Mallers Building, 67 East Madison Street–5 South Wabash Avenue, 1910–12; Christian A. Eckstrom, architect; height twenty-one stories; a blocklike mass with strongly articulated walls in the Chicago manner.
   Michigan Boulevard Building, 30 North Michigan Avenue, 1913–14; Jarvis Hunt, architect; height twenty stories. This building differed from the ruling mode in having a strongly vertical accent, intensified by modified Gothic detail, and in its deeply indented U-shaped plan above the two-story base.
7. For City Hall, see pp. 178–82.
8. The site is not as generous as a full-block area would suggest because of the eastward displacement of LaSalle Street at Van Buren required to accommodate the track and platform area of LaSalle Street Station.
9. The total cost of the Rand McNally, including architects' fees, was a little more than

$2,000,000 in 1912, for a unit cost of 23.84 cents per cubic foot. The 1971 equivalent cost would be about $18,750,000.

10. The outbreak of hostilities in Europe was quickly reflected in Chicago building: the volume of completed office space, for example, dropped 83% between 1914 and 1915 (see table 2).

11. The original lighting installation included 214 projectors rated at a total of 103,000 watts and providing 25,000,000 candlepower of illumination, but this has been increased over the years to higher levels of intensity.

12. The original relation of the London Guarantee to the river was altered by the completion of Wacker Drive in 1926, which cleared the foreground and placed the building on a combined boulevard and river site. Its location at 360 North Michigan coincides very nearly with that of Fort Dearborn, the perimeter of which is outlined in bronze strips in the Michigan-Wacker sidewalks.

13. The later and present owner is a large insurance complex, the chief constituents of which are the Continental Assurance and the Continental Casualty Company.

14. The cost of the Straus Building in 1924 was $12,000,000, or about $47,000,000 at the 1971 price level.

15. The Straus tower contained the first office space in Chicago above the old building height limit of 264 feet. This was made possible by the new zoning ordinance of 1922, which allowed the builder to add space above the height limit under the following conditions: the net area in plan of the upper addition could not exceed 25 percent of the lot area; the total volume of the addition could not exceed one-sixth of the total building volume up to the limit; the building envelope had to be set back one foot in ten from all lines of adjacent property.

16. The particular coins chosen and the accuracy of their representation provide excellent examples of the scholarly thoroughness with which the Graham firm executed these projects. The medallions depicted the following five coins: (1) city of Thurii (Thurium), with the head of Athene; (2) common Hellenic tetradrachma, with the head of Heracles; (3) city of Naxos, with the head of a bearded man; (4) city of Syracuse, with Persephone and dolphins; (5) Chalcidian League, with the lyre of Chalcidice.

17. A. N. Rebori, "The Straus Building, Chicago," *Architectural Record* 57 (May 1925): 392.

18. The Tribune Competition jury was composed of the following men: the architect Alfred Granger; Joseph M. Patterson, Robert R. McCormick, Edward S. Beck, and Holmes Onderdonck of the *Tribune*; an advisory committee consisting of Sheldon Clark, Joy Morton, Harry Wheeler, and B. M. Winston of the business community, and the aldermen Dorsey Crowe and E. I. Frankhauser. The contestants were furnished with the following materials: documents indicating the program of the competition, respective duties of the architect and the owner, conditions of the contract between the architect and the owner, nature of the architect's presentation, and the kinds of drawings to be considered; a photograph and a plan of the site; a plan of Michigan Avenue for about half a block on either side of the bridge; an elevation of the present printing plant shown as extending westward to the east column line of the upper-deck viaduct of Michigan Avenue.

19. The firms invited to submit entries were the following: Bliss and Faville, San Francisco; Bertram G. Goodhue, Hood and Howells, Benjamin Wistar Morris, and James Gamble Rogers, all of New York City; Burnham Brothers, Holabird and Roche, Jarvis Hunt, Andrew N. Rebori, and Schmidt, Garden and Martin, all of Chicago.

20. The best-known firms in the category of honorable mention were the following: Fell-heimer and Wagner, the leading architects of railroad stations in the United States after World War I; Claude Bragdon, an early apostle of Louis Sullivan; Burnham Brothers; Bertram Goodhue; Otto Hoffman, leader of the Vienna Secession; Henry Hornbostel; Jarvis Hunt; McKenzie, Voorhees and Gmelin, with Ralph Walker assoc-iated; Andrew Rebori; James Gamble Rogers; Schmidt, Garden and Martin.

21. The distribution of entries by country was as follows: Australia, 1; Austria, 5; Belgium, 2; Canada, 4; Cuba, 2; Denmark, 2; England, 4; Finland, 2; France, 7 (including Loos); Germany, 37; Holland, 11; Hungary, 2; Italy, 9; Luxembourg, 1; Mexico, 1; New Zealand, 1; Norway, 3; Poland, 1; Scotland, 3; Serbia, 1; Spain, 2; Switzerland, 6; United States, 143; anonymous, 8. Total, 258; five more received after the close of the contest, for a grand total of 263. There were 50 designs that might be classified as modern or nonderivative, with 17 coming from the United States, 1 from Australia, and the rest from Europe.

22. John Mead Howells and Raymond Hood, in *The International Competition for a New Administration Building for the Chicago Tribune, MCMXXII* (Chicago: Tribune Com-pany, 1923), page facing plate I.

   The stages in planning that preceded the preparation of working drawings may be roughly outlined as follows: (1) general solution to the problem of siting and planning on the irregularly shaped lot; (2) preliminary studies for the silhouette of the structural mass; (3) alternatives for the design of the tower; (4) alternatives for the relation of the tower to the main shaft, leading to the choice of the flying buttresses as a transitional de-vice; (5) alternatives for the design of the lantern; (6) alternatives for the design of the base; (7) progressive stages in the development of final designs for the base, shaft, tower, lantern, and transitional devices; (8) the coordination of all elements under phase 7; (9) studies for the unification of detail; (10) ultimate solutions for overall form and details and the preparation of working drawings (Leon V. Solon, "The Evolution of an Arch-itectural Design," *Architectural Record* 59 [March 1926]:216–25). In the preparation of the working drawings the mechanical utilities and other details were handled by Holabird and Roche.

23. Alfred Granger, "The Tribune Tower as a Work of Architecture," *Western Architect* 34 (November 1925): 112.

24. Louis Sullivan, "The Chicago Tribune Competition," *Architectural Record* 53 (February 1923): 154–55, 157–58.

25. The right-hand tower at the front of Rouen Cathedral is for some reason called *la tour de beurre*. The date of this celebrated work of Gothic building art is difficult to fix because part of an earlier Romanesque church was incorporated in the fabric of the cathedral: Paul Frankl, a leading authority on Gothic architecture, gives 1150, 1180–90, 1386–87, 1485, and 1509 as the years when the various parts of the structure were built (except for the tower over the crossing, which was reconstructed in cast iron in the nineteenth century). The south tower is square in plan; its four corner and four centered buttresses rise continuously to a "ring" of virtually free-standing buttresses at the top, where they brace and are surmounted by a crownlike lantern. The similarity of the whole structure to the Tribune is unmistakable.

26. The primary changes in dimensions of the Tribune are the following: the depth at the fifth floor is reduced from 136 to 100 feet, making the main shaft in essence a square prism with chamfered corners; the octagonal tower has a diameter of 48 feet to the thirty-third floor, 35 feet to the thirty-fourth, and 16 feet to the top of the lantern.

27. The girders carrying the offset columns over the lobby are much larger than standard framing members of the time: the clear span of each girder is 40 feet, the depth 12 feet, and the weight 39 tons.

28. Each steel column of the pseudobuttress is 76 feet high and 7 feet in diameter, but the overall height from the roof to the top of the masonry cladding is 81 feet 8 inches.

    The individual truss at the twenty-sixth floor has a clear span of 43 feet and a depth of 12 feet 4 inches, the top and bottom chords lying respectively in the floor planes of the twenty-sixth and twenty-seventh stories.

    Wind bracing includes knee braces at all column-and-girder connections, vertical full-panel diagonal bracing in the east and west sides of the elevator shafts, and horizontal diagonal bracing in a number of floor frames. The reinforced concrete floor slabs act as diaphragms in transmitting shearing and bending forces across the frame. All wind stresses are carried to the subbasement level, where earth resistance can absorb the shearing forces. The frame was designed for a wind pressure of thirty pounds per square foot on the entire vertical projected area facing in the two opposite directions.

29. Concrete frames for big multistory buildings were rare up to 1930. The east block of the Furniture Mart was claimed by local enthusiasts to be the largest and highest concrete building in the world at the time, but the first assertion is questionable and the second wholly false. The Marlborough-Blenheim Hotel in Atlantic City (1905–6) probably continued to hold the record for maximum volume until the great expansion in the use of concrete after World War II. As for height, the Ingalls Building in Cincinnati reached sixteen stories in 1903, and the United Brethren Building in Dayton, Ohio, built at the same time as the Furniture Mart, stands twenty-one stories high. The claim that the entire Mart was the largest building of the time was perhaps justified in view of its 2,000,000 square feet of floor area.

30. The hall was named after General Lawrence H. Whiting, chief personnel officer of the American Expeditionary Force in World War I, first president of the American Furniture Mart, and apparently the original author of the profitable idea of having furniture orders in hand before the manufacturer risked a loss on the production of unwanted merchandise.

31. N. Max Dunning, quoted in "The New American Furniture Mart, Chicago," *Western Architect* 34 (April 1925): 38.

32. A literary parallel to the architectural passion for towers, which was an obsession in the nineteenth century, may be found in the symbolic meaning of Solness's tower in Ibsen's *Master Builder*. The intention here is unmistakably phallic.

33. The main dimensions indicate the extent of the changes in section: the height of the main shaft is 265 feet, and of the tower to the top of the lantern, 256 feet, for a total of 521 feet above the upper level of Wacker Drive; the setbacks reduce the area in plan from 65 × 100 feet at the base to 65 × 85 feet at the top of the twenty-fourth floor; the diameter of the tower is 41 feet 10 inches at its lower stories and contracts through successive offsets to 21 feet 10 inches at the forty-second floor; the lantern is 9 feet 6 inches in diameter. The caissons extend to bedrock at 140 feet 6 inches below the upper level of the drive, or 108 feet below mean water level in the river (the Chicago datum).

34. Holabird and Root, who were respectively the sons of William Holabird and John Wellborn Root, established their office shortly after the death of Martin Roche in 1927. They enjoyed immediate success and by 1929 had a staff of two-hundred men, but little time remained to enjoy this prosperity before the collapse of the building industry in the depression of the thirties. John W. Root was in charge of the design of the 333 tower.

35. For the Drake, see p. 155.
36. This famous landmark was originally named the Lindbergh Beacon in honor of Charles A. Lindbergh, who in 1927 made the first solo flight across the Atlantic Ocean, but since he declined to make any public acceptance of the honor, the name was changed to Palmolive Beacon in 1930. The powerful light functions only as a landmark now, since higher buildings, higher flight patterns, and radio signals have rendered it obsolete as a guide to aerial navigation. The beacon gives the structure an overall height of 618 feet, and the caissons extend to bedrock at 132 feet below street grade.
37. The separate volumes terminated by setbacks result in a steady diminution of the individual floor area: first two floors (stores, restaurants, and public space), 15,885 square feet; third to tenth floors, 11,850 square feet; eleventh to sixteenth floors, 10,500 square feet; seventeenth to twenty-first floors, 5,800 square feet; twenty-second to thirty-second floors, 4,100 square feet; thirty-third and thirty-fourth floors, 3,842 square feet; thirty-fifth and thirty-sixth floors, 3,196 square feet; thirty-seventh floor, 2,914 square feet.
38. For the Union Station project, see pp. 264–84.
39. Other air-rights developments in Chicago include the Merchandise Mart (pp. 134–35), the Prudential Building, Gateway Center, and the Illinois Central North Pier Yards.
40. The shape of the Daily News area is somewhat irregular: the frontage along Canal is 394 feet, but the depth varies from 240 feet on Madison to 269 feet on Washington because the river walls and the line of Canal Street are not exactly parallel. The actual depth of the leased area along Canal is 100 feet, the remainder representing an easement to the Union Station Company for tracks and a shipping dock. The Daily News Building must be seen in the context of the other structures in the area: like the Michigan-Wacker enclave they constitute another unique association of water, streets, and buildings in a comprehensive civic design. For North Western Station, see pp. 253–60; for the Civic Opera Building, pp. 125–29.
41. Anne Lee, "Chicago Daily News Building," *Architectural Forum* 52 (January 1930): 26–27.
42. The foregoing description of the Daily News frame is condensed from Carl W. Condit, *American Building Art: The Twentieth Century* (New York: Oxford University Press, 1961), pp. 23–24.
43. The precise extent of Insull's guilt has not been exactly determined, at least in the courts. He was eventually returned to the United States by the Turkish government, having been seized at Istanbul during his flight from self-exile in Greece, tried three times for fraud and embezzlement, but acquitted each time on all the counts in his indictment.
44. The overall height of the Civic Opera to the top of the hipped roof is 560 feet; the length along Wacker Drive is 391 feet, the width along Madison 189 feet 6 inches, and along Washington 150 feet 6 inches. The total area of office space in the tower and the wings is 745,000 square feet. The present capacity of the Civic Opera auditorium is 3,471 seats, and of the Civic Theater 878. The dimensions of the huge opera theater, which is nearly as large as Adler and Sullivan's Auditorium, are as follows: theater proper 122 × 158 feet in plan and 86 feet 9 inches in height to the topmost ceiling plane at the seventh floor level; stage 72 × 120 feet in plan and 157 feet in overall height to the roof of the 13th floor level. The proscenium opening measures 50 feet in width by 36 feet in height at the center. The smaller Civic Theater extends 32 × 70 feet in plan in front of the stage.
45. It is necessary to recall that with the exception of a few expressway bridges, all highway and rail spans in Chicago are movable, either bascule, swing, or vertical-lift in form. In the bascule type foundation walls extend outward some little distance from the shore

wall of the river to support the boxlike concrete enclosure that houses the machinery, trunnions, and shore ends of the rotating spans.

46. Because of high column loads the column bases in the Civic Opera Building are thick circular steel disks, the largest (under the 7,500,000-pound load) being 8 feet 2 inches in diameter, 13½ inches thick, and 14 tons in weight.

All auditorium trusses rest on pin-and-rocker-shoe bearings adopted to avoid the high secondary stresses arising from the deflection of members with fixed riveted ends (fig. 18). Truss spans over the auditorium range from 90 to 120 feet, and the loads from 3,200,000 pounds on truss number 1 to 7,400,000 pounds on number 6 (loads on numbers 7, 8, and 9 fall within this range). The trusses extend through two floors in depth, the maximum being 25 feet 6 inches, and the top chords lie at various levels from the fourth to the eleventh floor. Truss number 10 (running longitudinally) carries the highest and most complex loading, with five irregularly spaced columns bearing on the top chord for a total load of 11,000,000 pounds. The pin at the north end (toward the stage) supports three members under loads of 5,700,000 pounds compression (top chord member), 1,200,000 pounds compression (web members), and 2,300,000 pounds tension (bottom chord member), giving a vertical resultant of 6,300,000 pounds. The truss has a clear span of 73 feet, weighs 235 tons, and has a depth of 24 feet; the bearing pin at the north end is 20 inches in diameter and rests in a steel casting.

Wind bracing was calculated for a direct load of 30 pounds per square foot on the tower and 20 pounds for the lower theater block (the higher figure is equivalent to a wind velocity of 95 miles per hour). The unusual features of the bracing system are the horizontal trusses in the floor frames of the seventh, thirteenth, and twenty-third floors (respectively the top of the opera theater, the top of the stage, and the upper level of column offsets). The diagonals of these trusses are flat bars ½ inch by 8 inches in section. Elsewhere the bracing system consists of diagonal members in the framing of the rear stage wall and triangular knee plates between columns and girders.

The maximum cantilevered length in the balcony frame is 22 feet 10⅛ inches, giving a fulcrum reaction of 162,000 pounds.

47. The principles developed by the elder Sabine are the following: first, the establishment of a proper reverberation period; second, the suppression of echoes; third, the reinforcement of sound for distant seats. The problem, of course, is to adjust the other requirements of interior architecture to those of acoustical excellence so that the optimum balance is achieved. Associated with Paul Sabine as consultants on the Civic Opera project were Dayton C. Miller of the Case School of Applied Science (now Case Western Reserve University), Clifford M. Swan of an acoustical engineering firm in New York City, R. V. Parsons of the Johns-Manville Company, and Wallace Waterfall of the Celotex Corporation.

48. Of the many towers that were completed or under construction in 1929 four are typical of the purified skyscraper with its vertical emphasis. The forty-five story Medinah Club (1928–29) is almost neutral in its simplicity, so subdued is its vertical pattern. The architect was Walter W. Ahlschlager and the structural engineer Frank A. Randall, whose valuable handbook of the history of building construction in Chicago was to be published twenty years later. The Medinah passed through several transformations as owners changed through depression and war: Chicago Towers, Continental Hotel, and finally the Sheraton-Chicago.

The Trustees System Service Building (1929–30), later simply the Trustees and now the Corn Products, was erected at the northeast corner of Wells and Lake streets after the design of the architects Thielbar and Fugard and the engineer James S. Black. The twenty-eight-story building is capped, like the Straus, by a ziggurat and a lantern. A curious structural feature is the presence in the twenty-story main shaft of concrete columns reinforced with solid cast-iron cores and continuous helical bars. The inventor of this composite form was the German engineer Fritz von Emperger, although helical reinforcing had previously been developed by Armand Considère in France. The eight-story tower and ziggurat of the Corn Products Building are framed in steel.

The One North LaSalle Building (1929–30), forty-nine stories in height, was the highest building in Chicago until the completion of the Civic Center in 1965. The slender, flat-topped tower, designed by Vitzhum and Burns, has the most emphatic vertical pattern of all Chicago skyscrapers. The building stands at the northeast corner of LaSalle and Madison, on the site of Holabird and Roche's Tacoma Building and long before that, the supposed site of René Robert de la Salle's camp, which is depicted with other scenes from the life of the explorer in the relief sculpture at the fifth floor over the entrance. The One LaSalle and the Medinah are steel-framed and stand on rock caissons.

The exception to the ruling mode of steel construction is the office building of Montgomery Ward and Company, on the south side of Chicago Avenue (800N) at the North Branch of the river (1929–30), across the street from Richard Schmidt's warehouse of 1908. The office building was designed by the Construction Department of the company under the direction of the architect Frank E. Poschenreiter, who worked in collaboration with the structural engineer S. E. Berkenbilt. The eight-story block, surmounted by a slender four-story tower at the entrance corner, is constructed entirely of reinforced concrete in a column-and-flat-slab frame with the common mushroom capitals and drop panels. What is unusual in this day of costly finishing materials is that the structural concrete constitutes the exposed surfaces of continuous columns and mullions as well as the inner framework and floor slabs. Equally out of the ordinary is the structural system of the pyramid roof over the 60-foot square auditorium on the eighth floor: the roof is carried by rigid-frame bents of 55-foot span in which the top chord has a profile like a central longitudinal section of a hipped roof.

49. The Merchandise Mart is trapezoidal in plan because Orleans Street lies on an angle to the ruling gridiron pattern. The length along the river is 580 feet, along Kinzie Street 724 feet, and the width of 324 feet on the transverse perpendicular is uniform throughout. The total gross floor area is 4,083,400 square feet, of which the net rentable area is 3,100,000 square feet. The building site was partly occupied by tracks of the first railroad line in Chicago (Galena and Chicago Union, 1848) and corresponds roughly to the first unified terminal of the Chicago and North Western.

50. This station (built in 1929–30) was a thoroughly modern facility: it embraced nine tracks (including the two that continue east to Navy Pier; see pp. 240–43), their associated platforms, and berthing space for 224 trucks. The remarkable feature was a system of narrow-gauge tracks connecting the station platforms with elevators descending to the Chicago Tunnel Company's lines under the site. All these facilities were nicely worked into a uniform bay span of 20 feet center-to-center of columns, except in a few places where exigencies required longer spans (the maximum is 41 feet 9 inches over the teamway under the north side of the building). The engineer in charge of the design and construction of the freight station was W. J. Towne, chief engineer of the railroad company.

51. Earl H. Reed, Jr., "Some Recent Work of Holabird and Root, Architects," *Architecture* 61 (January 1930): 1.

52. The Chicago metropolitan area is filled with factories, warehouses, and the shops and

engine terminals of the railroads, and a vast number survive in the city itself in spite of the exodus to other cities and the suburbs that has occurred at an increasing rate since World War II. Most of these structures claim no architectural attention: they range from single buildings with the standard buttressed walls of brick, or their modern counterpart, uninterrupted window walls, to immense manufacturing establishments that reach their maximum size and complexity in the furnaces and mills of the steel industry. The foremost example in Chicago is the South Works of the United States Steel Corporation, built, rebuilt, altered, and expanded since its establishment as the North Chicago Rolling Mills in 1872, and stretching along the south lakeshore from 79th Street to outer Calumet Harbor at 90th. Industrial groups such as this may be regarded as pure manufacturing technology. Another example outside the primary metallurgical industries was the sprawling International Harvester plant, built up over the years since the mid-nineteenth century along the South Branch of the river in the area of 26th Street and California Avenue. All but a fragment is now gone, scattered to other cities in a typical decentralization program.

53. The American Bell Telephone Company was established to manufacture Alexander Graham Bell's invention of 1876. It placed a central switchboard in operation at 18 North LaSalle Street in Chicago on 28 June 1878, but the American District Telegraph Company had anticipated the Bell interests by exactly ten days, having opened its own switchboard at 118 North LaSalle on 18 June. The earlier company was eventually acquired by the Bell system. (I am indebted to Professor Bessie Louis Pierce for the material on the dates of early switchboards in Chicago.)

54. The employees of the Hawthorne Works were the subjects of a celebrated series of experiments carried out in 1927–32 by Elton Mayo and his associates of Harvard University. Their primary aim was to determine the psychological responses of workers to the conditions of factory life. (For various details in the history of the Hawthorne plant I am indebted to Joseph Levinson of the Western Electric Company's Public Relations Department.)

55. The original flat-slab system in the United States was patented in 1908 by Claude A. P. Turner, but the form adopted at the Donnelley plant involved variations later patented by Lord. The frame was calculated for high floor loadings of 250–300 pounds per square foot, required by printing presses and associated facilities. (For these and other structural details I am indebted to Herbert Wolff, plant manager of R. R. Donnelley and Sons.)

56. The Chicago Junction and one of its predecessors (the Chicago and Indiana State Line) provided most of the switching service for the Union Stock Yards. The former was incorporated in 1898 as a consolidation of earlier lines and was leased to the Chicago River and Indiana Railroad in 1922. The Chicago River and Indiana is controlled through stock ownership by the New York Central (now Penn Central).

57. The precise limits of the Central Manufacturing District as it now exists are Pershing Road (39th Street) and the Chicago Junction tracks on the north and south and Hermitage Avenue (1732W) and Bell Avenue (2232W) on the east and west. Half this length lies opposite the attractively landscaped and well maintained McKinley Park. The tributary of the South Branch of the river in this area is a noxious truncated remnant left from the construction of the Sanitary and Ship Canal and known locally as Bubbly Creek because the gaseous products of chemical reactions in the water keep the surface constantly agitated. The Chicago Junction performed a public service in 1916 by placing most of the length of this disgusting stream in a sewer, but a short stretch is still exposed (1970).

The transportation efficiency of the district is a consequence less of density (which may result in traffic congestion) than it is of trackage density combined with the railroad's mode of operation. Since every building has its own spur track and all rail transportation is controlled by the district, rail shipments require no transshipment to street vehicles for direct delivery. In handling tonnage the railroad devised a clockwork system under which each twenty-four-hour period was regarded as a unit, with all deliveries and switching activities beginning and ending within the period. In this way all yard and switch tracks except those used for the servicing of railroad equipment were cleared once a day.

Financial arrangements between the district and its residents include three types of agreement: in the first the district sells the land outright and erects the buildings; in the second the district leases the land and the building, the tenant paying the cost in the form of an annual rent; under the third the district leases the land and the building, the tenant paying 25 percent of the construction cost on occupancy and the balance as an annual rent over a period of ten to fifteen years.

58. The Central Manufacturing District is so important in the history of the planned industrial district that certain technical features are worth pursuing in detail. Economy resulted not only from the unity of design but equally from the large scale of the project, the concentrated plan, and the rapidity with which individual buildings were erected. In this last respect, the construction of the military warehouses set extraordinary records: for example, the one designated Warehouse C, Quartermaster Department, was placed under construction on 10 April 1919 and completed on 31 December of the same year, although work was suspended during the strike of construction workers that extended from 17 July to 21 September 1919. Feats of this kind were accomplished by a carefully prepared method: the architect provided preliminary plans for the contractor's estimates; excavation began the following day and continued while correctly detailed excavation and foundation plans were prepared, usually in complete form by the fourth day; building plans were completed during the foundation work, sometimes within ten days. It must be added, however, that life was simpler in 1920: in spite of wartime inflation, building costs were little more than one-fifth of what they became in 1971; low wages and extensive unskilled work in the building process allowed contractors to hire hundreds of men who would be retained throughout the period of construction.

The structural systems embodied in the district buildings provided a good basis for comparing the relative merits of the new flat-slab concrete frame and the traditional mill construction, which was extensively used for warehouses up to six stories in height until the 1930s. At the time of World War I and the immediate postwar period the respective costs of the mill and the flat-slab systems were nearly identical, although this was not so with column-and-girder concrete frames because of the more elaborate formwork and reinforcing. The flat-slab system, however, offered great advantages—chiefly deeper penetration and more uniform distribution of light through the absence of beams and girders; lower story-to-story height for the same reason; greater vertical headroom, thus facilitating the location of pipes, conduits, ducts, and shafting with less sacrifice of vertical space; maximum height under floor slabs for storage; lower insurance costs for concrete than for timber.

59. A. N. Rebori, "The Work of Burnham and Root, D. H. Burnham, D. H. Burnham and Co., and Graham, Burnham and Co.," *Architectural Record* 38 (July 1915): 165–66. Rebori's advice, as we have seen in the case of the office tower, was followed with fidelity.

60. Lewis Mumford, "New York vs. Chicago in Architecture," *Architecture* 56 (November 1927): 244. For a discussion of the Pennsylvania Railroad Freight Station, see pp. 267–68.

The three unnamed structures to which Mumford alludes are the London Guarantee (p. 100), the Tribune (pp. 108–14), and Soldier Field (pp. 149–50). The gymnasium at Northwestern University was designed by George W. Maher.

61. I am indebted to the Distribution Department office of John Sexton and Company for the information on dates of construction.

62. Quoted in "Gilded Palaces of the Silver Screen," *Chicago Sun-Times Midwest*, 8 December 1968, pp. 16–17.

63. John Eberson, "A Description of the Capitol Theater, Chicago," *Architectural Forum* 42 (June 1925): 373.

64. For the Iroquois Theater fire and its cause, see p. 25.

65. I am indebted for information on the dates of the Gateway and the Will Rogers theaters to the Real Estate Department of the ABC–Great States Theater Company, the successor to Balaban and Katz.

66. The Esquire Theater twice changed hands: the Balaban Brothers sold it to Paramount Pictures, from which the Walter Reade–Continental Company, the present owners, acquired it. I am indebted to the Public Information Office of Harry and Elmer Balaban for information on the ownership of the Esquire.

67. The details of the Field Museum are dervied from the Ionic order; for a complete discussion of the building, see pp. 187–94.

68. Solider Field gained at least a temporary reprieve in 1971 when the Park District leased it to the Chicago Bears football team for their home games.

69. Because of the prismatic roof the trusses of Chicago Stadium have a polygonal profile. The clear span is 266 feet, the depth at the center 28 feet, the depth at the ends 15 feet, and the rise of the bottom chord 21 feet 6 inches. The members were calculated for the following loadings: dead load of roof and structure, 42 pounds per square foot; live load, 25 pounds; wind load on side of building, 20 pounds.

By the time Chicago Stadium was opened Wrigley Field had been twice expanded in size (1922–23, 1926–27) to raise its capacity from the original 14,000 spectators to 36,000. The improvement in the bleachers stands in 1937 brought the park to its present capacity of 36,667. Given the number and size of stadia, arenas, fields, and parks available for sporting events, it is difficult to defend the argument that Chicago has any need for additional facilities of this kind.

70. The hotel as a cross section of urban life is revealed, for example, by the symbolic as well as descriptive use that Theodore Dreiser made of the fictitious Green-Davidson Hotel in *An American Tragedy*.   .

71. The open area of the dining room measures 48 × 76 feet in plan, but the full length of the transverse girders is 53 feet and their overall depth 11 feet 9 inches. The total load on any one girder is 18,720,000 pounds.

72. This truss, with web members reduced to diagonals alone, is 77 feet 6 inches long end-to-end, 23 feet deep, and weighs 110 tons. The lobby measures 76 × 90 feet in plan.

73. The area of the Stevens ballroom is 84 × 175 feet; the trusses, spaced 35 feet center to center, have an end-to-end length of 86 feet and a depth of 31 feet. They are comparable in size to the trusses of the Civic Opera and the Board of Trade buildings.

74. See table 3.

75. The river in the area of what became the Michigan Avenue–Wacker Drive intersection originally flowed through a sharp S-curve and into the lake a little south of the Art Institute site. Without the groin to deflect the sand-laden shore currents, the bar would

have reformed and diverted the river to its old course, which was an obvious nuisance to shipping.

76. The story of "Captain" Streeter has been told many times in print. My own account is condensed from M. W. Newman, "A Ghost at Big John," *Chicago Daily News*, 15 February 1969, pp. 3–4. The U-shaped street at the foot of Navy Pier was named Streeter Drive and the plaza of the Hancock Center Streeterville Place after this lively whiskey-drinking tough. The decision to preserve the name shows a far better sense of historical values than the official city hall practice of naming major traffic arteries—to cite two examples—after time-serving politicians (Ryan Expressway) or visiting fascist aviators (Balbo Drive).

77. Every year saw a new apartment go up: Marshall was again the architect for the twelve-story building at 1200 North Lake Shore (1911–12); William Ernest Walker designed the two at 936 and 942, both ten-story structures on concrete piling (representing possibly its first use in Chicago), respectively erected in 1912–13 and 1914–15.

78. See table 3.

79. At the time the 1400 North Lake Shore and the Drake Tower were opened the following buildings were constructed on the Gold Coast: 1448 North (1926–27), Childs and Smith, architects; 1430 North (1927–28), Robert S. De Golyer, architect, and Smith and Brown, engineers; 1242 North (1928–29), same architect and engineers; 1420 North (1928–29), Hooper and Janusch, architects. The last of the original group came after the crash: the 1500 North was built in 1930–31, with McNally and Quinn as architects in charge, Rosario Candela as associated architect, and Smith and Brown as engineers. The 1500 building attracted attention because it contained the twenty-two-room duplex apartment of William Wrigley.

For information on the history of the 1540 building I am indebted to Sidney Fields.

80. John Burchard and Albert Bush-Brown, *The Architecture of America*; *A Social and Cultural History* (Boston: Little, Brown and Company, 1961; copyright held by American Institute of Architects), p. 331.

81. Parts of the foregoing description are derived from a history of the Garden Apartments prepared by the office of Dubin, Dubin, Black and Moutoussamy. I am indebted to Arthur Dubin for making this material available to me.

5. Public Buildings and Parks

Parks, Museums, and Cultural Institutions

The public recreational space and the public institutions that Chicago established in the two decades following the adoption of the Burnham Plan represent the greatest and most valuable civic achievement of any American city. Nothing like it in extent or quality has been attempted or even imagined in the urban world of the later twentieth century, and certainly Chicago itself gives no indication of ever being able to repeat this extraordinary performance. The major part of the program was born of the impetus provided by the plan, and those elements associated with the lakefront development were consciously designed to conform to its requirements. Chicago experienced two particularly concentrated periods of civic renewal, the first falling within a few years around 1895, when the Art Institute, the Field Museum, the great libraries, and the University of Chicago were established or given their present homes, and the second following in the late years of the twenties, shortly before depression, war, militarism, and the decline of the urban economy placed all such activity in seemingly permanent eclipse. The establishment of those institutions that belong to the second phase is so inextricably bound up with the creation of the present lakefront parks and drives that it is very nearly impossible as well as artificial to try to disentangle the two aspects of civic construction. It would be a mistake, however, to suppose that the great civic works are exclusively concentrated along the lake, since a sizable volume of the public building and landscaping that was produced at a steady pace year after year lay in inner areas of the city.

The first great civic work to follow the Burnham Plan is the present City Hall and County Building, which fills to the very edge of the sidewalk the entire block bounded by Clark, LaSalle, Washington, and Randolph streets (fig. 27). Its immediate predecessors stood on the same site, the County Building having been built in 1881–82 from the designs of James J. Egan and Alex Kirkland, and the City Hall in 1884–85, with the indefatigable John M. Van Osdel as the architect. The Public Library occupied the entire fourth floor of the City Hall until the new library building was opened in 1897.[1] The City-County Building that took the place of these relatively youthful structures was designed by Holabird and Roche and erected in 1909–11, following close upon the demolition of the older group. The thirteen-story block is nearly square in overall plan, measuring 320 × 374 feet in horizontal dimensions, but its two governmental functions are internally separated into east (county) and west (municipal) halves, each volume having been constructed around its own central light court (fig. 28). The structural system combines an internal steel frame with external granite columns of overpowering size. Although the huge enclosure is far below the skyscraper in number of stories, the high column and wall loads required caissons extending down to bedrock at a minimum depth of 120 feet below grade.[2]

The monumental classicism of the City Hall and Court House is carried out throughout the exterior elevations on an immense scale but with remarkable fidelity to the appropriate forms and proportions. Above a four-story base of smooth granite ashlar stand the long rows of Corinthian columns that rise through the next six stories, and these are surmounted in turn by the entablature and cornice covering the top three floors. The interior steel frame supports a superbly planned arrangment of central lobbies, long transverse corridors, and individual enclosures ranging in size from offices through courtrooms and council chambers to the Municipal Reference Library. The broad lobbies are particularly impressive, distinguished by their generous area and their ceilings of flattened groin vaults covered with marble and glazed tile. The whole internal volume is characterized by great spaciousness, secured through extensive horizontal dimensions and lofty ceilings, and by a thoroughly functional planning in which reason and tradition were combined to produce the grand axial simplicity. The only defect to later eyes is that the external treatment of the massive building bears no relation to the arrangement and the relative importance of the internal divisions. A contemporary critic described the excellence and the difficulty very ably.

What is asserted is that the division denoted by the great columns is superior in importance to the lower divisions from which the order is omitted, and this is distinctly "not so." The real inequalities are suppressed, and inequalities which do not exist are asserted. Of course, this is the contradiction which we always encounter in modern examples of monumental classic, and, of course, having once noted them, we have to ignore them and admit that it makes all the difference how they are done. . . . In "scale" the order exceeds anything west of Albany. . . . This would, of itself, make a building noteworthy anywhere, but it is also to be said that it has been well and faithfully studied in mass, in scale, and in detail. It is not only much the most impressive thing of its own kind that Chicago has to show, but one of the most impressive in the United States, and in the interior . . . there is not only a faithful study of style, but features which show an escape from the style into vigor of individual invention, and a richness which has even elements of novelty in decorative effect.[3]

The structural requirements of the City Hall–Court House block offered the common problem of framing for large interior voids because of the presence of the two-story Council Chamber, which measures 65 × 96 feet in plan and rises from the

180

Fig. 27. Chicago City Hall and Cook County Court House, LaSalle, Randolph, Clark, and Washington streets, 1909–11. Holabird and Roche, architects. (Courtesy Chicago Historical Society.)

27

Fig. 28. City Hall and Court House.
Plan of the main floor (the west elevation
is at the top).

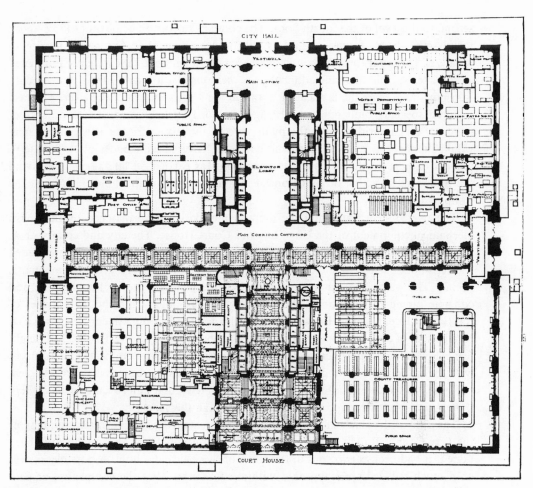

second to the level of the fourth floor. The columns for the nine floors of offices above the chamber bear on massive girders with a clear span of 65 feet and a maximum weight of forty-four tons. Although these are built-up girders, they were not fabricated at the site, so that the chief difficulty in their installation arose from the need to transport them from the fabricating plant on the North Branch of the river. The task required specially built multiwheel wagons hauled by ten teams of two horses per team. Of all the bridges over the main stem of the river only the Rush Street span would support the load, but the deck had to be covered with tracks of steel plate to prevent damage to the paving. The operation was carried on late at night to avoid the prolonged blocking of traffic on all the major north-south thoroughfares of the Loop.

The riveted steel frame and the monumental design were matched by the lavish mechanical equipment of the City Hall and Court House. The city and county areas together were served by a total of 28 elevators, and internal communications included 750 telephones at the time of construction and a complete installation of pneumatic tubing. The water and waste circulation systems included special kinds of tile and concrete piping to carry acids and other corrosive liquids from the laboratories of the Health Department. Hot water and steam for the heating system were provided by a battery of coal-fired boilers located in a subbasement with the floor at thirty-eight feet below grade, from which coal- and ash-handling conveyors connected the furnaces with the tracks of the Illinois Tunnel Company. It was the best that the mechanical technology of building afforded at the time, and regular improvements have kept the physical plant in sound working order through the years.

The skill with which Holabird and Roche treated the monumental grandeur of the City-County Building may well lead to the question how this might have been done if it had been carried out in the spirit of the Chicago school. A possible answer on a much reduced scale appeared within a few years after the completion of City Hall, although it is about 500 miles from Chicago. The Woodbury County Court House at Sioux City, Iowa, represents the only governmental building designed by architects of the Prairie school, as the second generation of the Chicago group is now generally called. The building was authorized in 1914, when the voters of the county approved the necessary bond issue, and the commission for its design was offered in the following year to a local architect, William L. Steele, who won a closed competition for the prize. Steele, whose office was too small for the project, secured the collaboration of the architectural firm of Purcell and Elmslie, the structural engineer Paul D. Cook, and the sculptor Alfonso Ianelli, who together created the unique work that was constructed in 1916–18 on a most ordinary site in a midwestern town (figs. 29–32).

The building consists of two separate and not particularly well unified parts. The lower is a large 2½-story block exactly square in plan, supported by a reinforced concrete frame, and the upper, which rises above the central area of this square, is a tower equivalent to another six stories in height. The tower differs from the main volume not only in appearance, having a marked horizontal emphasis as opposed to the dominant verticalism of the lower portion, but also in its structural system of steel framing. The external sheathing throughout is so rich in color and texture as to have a powerfully sensuous character: the base and coping are granite, the piers and wall areas are covered with tawny brown Roman brick, and the trim and sculpture are glazed polychrome terra-cotta. The ruling motif in the composition of the exterior elevations is the close vertical pattern bounded at top and bottom by strong bands that is the distinguishing characteristic of most of the work that has come to be designated as that of the Prairie school.

The interior finishings of the courthouse are even more colorful than the exterior: the Roman brick is retained for piers and walls, the floors are quartzite tile, the stair treads are marble, plastered surfaces are colored by brilliant mural paintings, and the trim is cream terra-cotta with inlays of glass mosaic. The chief interior feature is a great stained-glass dome that lies directly under the tower and is naturally lighted by the ingenious device of carrying the first tower floor over the dome at a height sufficient to allow the daylight to enter unobstructed through the broad ribbon-like windows in the sides of the high enclosure. As busy and inharmonious as it is, the Court House at Sioux City is an exuberant statement of the Prairie idiom beside which both the older classicism and its modern counterpart of mass concrete seem depressingly sober.

The first group of civic and cultural institutions in Chicago was completed with the opening of Orchestra Hall in 1904. A relatively quiet decade followed before a second powerful upsurge of civic renewal reached its culmination in the great public buildings of the lakefront parks. The new period of construction was inaugurated by the nearly simultaneous extension of the Art Institute and building of the Field Museum. The location of the former posed a peculiar problem when the need arose for an expansion of the institute's exhibition space. The building is flanked on the north and south sides by landscaped areas of Grant Park which include fountains with sculptural groups, and immediately to the rear lie the depressed tracks of the Illinois Central Railroad. The difficulty was compounded by the fact that the court

184

Fig. 29. Woodbury County Court House, Sioux City, Iowa, 1916–18. William L. Steele, Purcell and Elmslie, associated architects.

Fig. 30. Woodbury County Court House. Rotunda at the second-floor level.

29

30

Fig. 31. Woodbury County Court House. Typical courtroom.

Fig. 32. Woodbury County Court House. Dome above the rotunda.

31

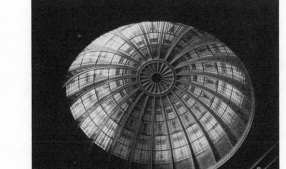

32

rulings in the so-called Montgomery Ward cases prohibited the building of any structure standing above grade in the park.[4] The trustees of the Art Institute thus had only one choice that did not involve either the disturbance of park features or the usurpation of land, namely, the building of an elevated wing eastward over the Illinois Central tracks. The decision to carry out this plan was made in 1913 and construction began the following year, but more than three years passed before the facility was opened. The architects who designed this novelty among museums were Coolidge and Hodgdon, and the structural engineer was Julius Floto, who worked in collaboration with the railroad's engineering department.

The rail line for some distance north and south of the Art Institute consists of the multitrack approach to the suburban terminal and the narrow Congress Street Yard, which for many years was the arrival and departure point of merchandise freight trains. In order to span the tracks and to provide sufficient exhibition space the wing had to be designed as a two-level truss bridge with an overall length of 230 feet and a width of 58 feet. This enclosure was treated as a two-span simple structure with each pair of trusses extending between the walls enclosing the railroad line at their outer ends and a median pier at the inner. The bottom chords of these trusses were put in place in 1914, then allowed to remain isolated for two years until the wing was erected in 1916–17. The longitudinal trusses that support the two floors and the roof have a Pratt web system; they are joined at the bottom and the midline by the conventional deck frame of girders and beams and at the top by transverse trusses with arched bottom chords and sloping top chords matching the profile of the gable roof. These gable trusses also serve to support part of the second-floor load by means of hangers suspended from their bottom chords. The exterior curtain wall of this enclosed bridge is limestone, and the interior partitions are tile, with special wall surfaces suitable for hanging pictures. As every visitor to the Art Institute quickly discovers, no provision was made to insulate the wing from the vibration of passing trains, which has never damaged any part of either the building or the collection but which is readily transmitted through the central pier and the framework, especially when it arises from the impact of coupling freight cars.[5]

The two additions to the Art Institute's facilities in the next decade took the now celebrated museum well beyond its traditional role of exhibition and education in the visual arts. In 1924, the McKinlock Garden was added in a depressed area enclosed by walls built up east of the Illinois Central tracks. The sunken garden, again designed by Coolidge and Hodgdon, is an attractive oasis for its very simplicity: a paved terrace, part of which serves as a little outdoor cafe, and a landscaped border surround a square pool. It is pleasing to bird-watchers because many of the less common types of birds find their way into its protected space during the migratory periods. The second expansion involved the addition of the Goodman Art Theater, as it was originally known, again situated east of the rail line and toward the north side of the Art Institute property, along Monroe Street. Designed by Howard Van Doren Shaw and erected in 1924–26, the Goodman is a curiosity because only the structure enclosing its shallow entrance lobby stands recognizably above grade, a characteristic dictated by the requirement of conforming to the Montgomery Ward decisions. The auditorium, stage, main lobby, and associated facilities are well below the surrounding grade, the various roof levels being hidden behind a low wall. Although Shaw's little entrance building is scrupulously done in the Doric order, the Goodman suffers from a poverty-stricken setting: the sunken theater is backed against the railroad line, and the entrance opens onto a parking lot that lies between it and Columbus Drive to the east. There has never been any attempt to landscape the area, so that the isolated block attached to its low wall suggests something that remained in an arrested stage after the rest of the structure sank into the ground. The Goodman Theater was built as the home of the Art Institute's drama department, but in 1969 student productions were abandoned in favor of those of a resident professional company.

As the Art Institute was being expanded eastward over its railroad barrier, the South Park District was engaged in constructing the new home of the Field Museum of Natural History, which was soon destined to become one of the foremost institutions of its kind in the world. The preliminary planning for this most prominent of all Chicago's public buildings, the choice and preparation of the site, and the process of construction together constitute one of those intricate narratives of plot and subplot that usually characterize the undertaking of large and expensive public enterprises. The chief problem in the location of the Field Museum arose from the conflict between the proposal in the Burnham Plan that it be placed at the focal point of Grant Park and the Montgomery Ward decisions prohibiting any such construction in the park, the consequence of which was a considerable waste of time and money before the South Park Commissioners reached a decision satisfactory to all concerned. Two parallel phases of Chicago's development thus converged in the creation of a monumental work of such size that it required a good eight acres of land for a proper setting. One was the founding and growth of the museum itself, and the other was the city's vast program of lakefront reclamation.

The Field Columbian Museum, as the institution was first called, was established in the Fine Arts Building of the Columbian Exposition at the conclusion of the fair in 1893, although the official opening did not occur until 2 June of the following year.

The structure was a temporary one, and by 1897 it had deteriorated to the point where the leaking roof threatened permanent damage to various exhibits. Marshall Field, who had given the museum $1,000,000 in 1894 to expand its collection, offered to leave the institution at least $4,000,000 more for a new building if a satisfactory site could be found within six years of his death. This melancholy event occurred in 1906, but the lamentations at the museum must have quickly turned to rejoicing when it was learned that the generous entrepreneur had in fact bequeathed twice the promised sum, of which half was to be used for the building and half for endowment. Various other individuals expanded the total by another $500,000 before 1910, and the South Park District agreed to bear the expected maintenance costs of $100,000 per annum by means of tax revenues. Seldom have the richest empires treated institutions of learning and the arts with such generosity.[6] Meanwhile, plans for the new building were taking shape: the first discussions involving Field, Burnham, Ernest Graham, and Henry Dibble had begun around the turn of the century; Burnham ordered preliminary plans from his office in 1902, since it was obvious that the commission was to be his, and completed working plans in 1906. Although the Chicago Plan was still in the formative stage, Burnham had reached the point where his scheme for the downtown lakefront was well enough advanced so that the museum trustees and the South Park Commissioners could enter into a contract for the Grant Park site on 31 January 1907.

Most of the present area of the park between Randolph and Roosevelt drives had been reclaimed by 1910; landscaping with trees had begun in 1907, but many of the nearly two thousand elms died on the exposed shoreline site, so that three years later the park district began a less costly program of simple lawn seeding. The next phase of expansion began in 1911, and by 1914 the area between Roosevelt Road and 14th Boulevard had been filled. While this operation was under way the commissioners made a brilliant and far-sighted move in 1912, when they secured riparian rights to the entire lakefront between Grant Park and Jackson Park on the South Side—an accomplishment impressive to any age, but especially to one that sees the steady attrition of park acreage and the deterioration of what remains. Although there was plenty of space, the Grant area was an unprepossessing sight in the decade following the Burnham Plan, when the Field Museum was built. There was a meadow-like strip of grass between Michigan Avenue and the Illinois Central line, with a few shrubs and small trees scattered below Congress Street, but the space east of the tracks was mostly raw fill, parts of which were depressed below the finished grade level and hence became muddy land-locked ponds during rainy weather. It was all to be magnificently transformed, as we have seen, in Burnham's brave vision: the new museum was to be situated at the intersection of the two axes formed by Congress Parkway and the shore drive, the west elevation to face a fountain and the vista of the widened Congress Boulevard, the east to look upon a grand stairway descending gently to the yacht basin at the inner edge of Chicago Harbor.

With plans completed, a princely endowment in hand, and a contract for the site properly executed, Burnham should have seen construction under way before his death in 1912, but in the previous year a number of concerned parties, hitherto silent, remembered the Ward decisions. Opposition mushroomed quickly; threatened litigation raised the possibility of wasting precious income and the very evident likelihood that the courts would uphold the Michigan Avenue property owners, with the result that the museum trustees quickly voted to shift the site to Jackson Park. Burnham's dream for the Grant Park focus was suddenly shattered, but his staff made the necessary revisions in the plans, a contract for construction was let to the Thompson-Starrett Company, steel began to be stockpiled at the site, and the quarrying of marble began. Yet there were many who could not abandon the dream, among whom were the South Park commissioners, and in 1914, two years after Burnham's death and after the site had been prepared in Jackson Park, they offered ground on the newly extended fill between Roosevelt Road and 14th Boulevard. In the following two years the fill was raised to the elevation of thirty feet above park-grade level that Burnham's scheme called for, and with the site thus under final preparation, Thompson-Starrett began construction on 26 July 1915. It was five years before the great work was completed, a construction period that was long enough for the inevitable revisions of the plans to be handled first by Graham, Burnham and Company, and then by Graham, Anderson, Probst and White, both of whose offices worked in collaboration with the structural engineer Joachim Giaver (figs. 33, 34).

The erection of the museum building began with the driving of piles under the footing areas and the pouring of the concrete foundations, a process that consumed about a year and a half through 1916 and 1917. The piling was driven to refusal on a hardpan stratum at a depth of 60 to 65 feet below lake level, and the space between the tops of the piles and the undersurface of the basement floor was filled with sand, on which the concrete slab was poured. The structural system of the building is a combination of masonry wall piers, inner concrete piers, and an internal steel frame of girders, trusses, and arched ribs.[7] The walls, the interior framework, and the floors were constructed in 1917–18. The exterior load-bearing wall panels between the marble Ionic columns are as antique in structural character as they are in form: their 21-inch thickness is divided between 15 inches of brick and 6 inches of marble facing, which is thick enough to indicate that Burnham conceived of the marble as a

190

Fig. 33. Field Museum of Natural History, Grant Park at East 14th Boulevard, 1911, 1915–20. D. H. Burnham and Company and Graham, Burnham and Company, successively, architects.

33

Fig. 34. Field Museum. *Top:* Basement
plan. *Bottom:* Main-floor plan.

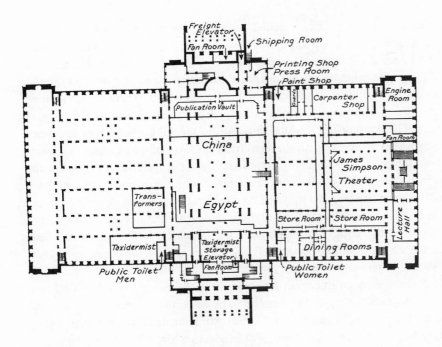

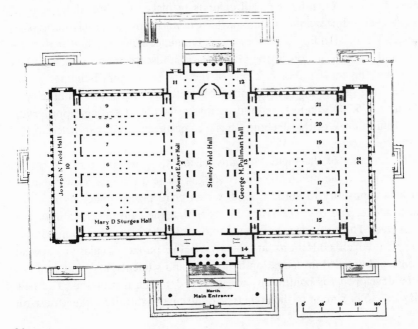

bearing material as well as a rich external covering. The remainder of the internal structure is a combination of traditional masonry techniques and modern steel framing: the floors are reinforced concrete finished in tile and supported on steel girders and joists; the gabled roofs of the transverse wings are carried on steel rafters; and the second-floor galleries are covered by hollow-tile vaults. There are no interior columns, the girders and ribs of the wide-span galleries being carried on the massive concrete piers. The flooring and the retaining walls of the public and service entrances are partly supported by brackets cantilevered from the faces of the external wall piers.

The whole fabric was substantially completed by the summer of 1918, when the War Department temporarily took over the immense volume as a hospital for military casualties. The property was relinquished to the museum trustees shortly after the armistice of 11 November, but the installation of internal fixtures required another year, so that the public could not be admitted until June 1920. The cost at the time of construction was $7,000,000, but the 1971 replacement value would be more than $35,000,000. The immense task of moving the thousands of exhibits and other specimens from Jackson Park to Roosevelt Road began at the end of the war in 1918 and required two and one-half years to complete. The proximity of the Illinois Central line, at the west edge of both Jackson and Grant parks, made it possible to transport the collection by rail as well as by street: 400 freight cars and 1,000 trucks were used in the process. The final opening, with all exhibits in place, was thus delayed until 4 May 1921. The vast edifice in its shining marble dress was an immensely impressive sight to its first visitors, standing as it does on an eminence markedly higher than its surroundings, and the completion of the Grant Park landscaping and parkways has enhanced its visual impact (fig. 33). It is one of the largest museum buildings in the world—706 feet long on the main elevations, 450 feet deep, originally embracing a total floor area of 775,000 square feet—and its formal lakefront setting, appropriate to the elegant Ionic Greek of the structure, has a majestic sweep unparalleled in the contemporary urban scene.

The interior planning of the Field Museum reflects the changing concept of the museum that emerged in the twentieth century (fig. 34). The traditional view regarded the museum as a repository of static objects which were placed under its roof for protection and safekeeping over the years, in order that the cultural or natural past might be preserved. The new idea, however, holds that the institution is an active, working entity in which collections are preserved for public circulation, special demonstrations, and detailed investigation by experts and students, and that facilities must hence be developed for continuous research and public instruction. The new museum thus came to be similar to the archetype of all such institutions, the Mouseion founded at Alexandria in 290 B.C. by Ptolemy I Soter, which itself was an ancient counterpart of the university research programs of our own day. Burnham, accordingly, designed the Field Museum as a highly organized complex of lecture halls, classrooms, libraries, laboratories, preparation rooms, cafeterias, and storage space, as well as a traditional arrangement of exhibition halls and public service facilities. The great majority of visitors, of course, see only the public space, in the design of which the architect faces a special threefold problem: he must provide an adequate floor area for visitors, work out a satisfactory visual relation between spectators and objects exhibited, and guide the spectators along some organized sequence of spaces. All the special facilities of the Field Museum were expertly planned; it is in the design of the exhibition areas that we are compelled to raise questions.

The main floor is divided into a huge central hall extending along the longitudinal axis of the building and flanked by seven pairs of galleries that terminate in wide halls running along the east and west elevations and hence parallel to the main axis (fig. 34).[8] The galleries are reduced to four on either side of the nave above the second floor, where they are separated by narrow light courts. The entire plan above the basement level is perfectly symmetrical, so that the arrangement and the relationship of the various parts are readily apparent. The defect in this classical axiality is that one must first study the directory and the plan made available to the visitor in order to determine where to go and what the logical sequence of spaces might be. But the visitor is still cast adrift: lines of movement are unmarked, and there are no signs to indicate directions or suggested routes. The difficulty arises in part from the classical plan in which the two systems of hallways lie at right angles to each other and are perfectly balanced to the right and left of the central nave. To make the situation worse, the area of a single floor is measurable in acres, and the individual spaces seem endless in the dim overhead light. Casual Sunday visitors may be forgiven if they feel discouraged, but the feeling has not prevented their coming in steadily increasing numbers through the years.

The overall form and the decorative details of the museum are handled with the authority that marks the work of the Burnham office, although the sheer size of the structure, the inflated scale, and the uniform marble finish make it a little chilling in its effect. The main motifs were all derived from the Erechtheion (421–405 B.C.), most prominently the Ionic order, the caryatids, and the device of bringing cornices together at different levels. The placing of the building on its site must also have had the authority of the Acropolis behind it: the entire perimeter is surrounded by a terrace fifty feet wide and six feet high, which is exactly defined by a continuous retaining wall and a balustrade that is broken only by monumental stairways at the north and south entrances, all constructed of the same white Georgian marble as the walls and columns of the building. An equally generous treatment of space and a similar exactitude of detail characterize the interior, especially the central hall and the large theater in the basement, which is surrounded on three sides by a Doric colonnade that marks off a continuous lobby around the seating area. [9] The mechanical equipment includes chiefly the steam boilers for the heating system, fans for ventilating the basement and the theater, elevators, and pumps to maintain pressure in the fire hydrants; it is all perfectly sound but falls short of what is needed to provide the complete environmental control that is now regarded as essential in museums and libraries.

The Field Museum is a national institution with a worldwide reputation. If it seems forbidding to the visitor in its size, it is none too big for the enormous collection it houses or the multifarious activities it carries on. By the date of its seventy-fifth anniversary in 1968 the museum's various departments owned at least 9,500,000 specimens representing the works of man and the living and extinct forms of animals and plants. Of the total number, except for 50,000 specimens on loan to institutions throughout the world, 2 percent of the collection is exhibited at any one time and 98 percent is kept in storage. The number of visitors reached almost 2,000,000 in 1969, a total nearly double that of a decade ago.[10] But the years that brought the museum's enviable endowment and its prestige also brought the inevitable deterioration of the building and steadily rising costs. Except for the introduction of fountains into the central hall in 1966—a renovation expertly handled by the office of Harry Weese Associates—the building has remained unchanged since its official opening in 1921; yet the need for extensive improvements in electrical and mechanical equipment, environmental control, structural features, and visitors' facilities has in some cases reached the level of urgency. The museum's current income, which is derived from invested endowment and Park District tax revenue, falls discouragingly short of meeting current expenses, and must be supplemented by the annual gifts of patrons and guarantors, as is the case with the symphony orchestra and the opera company. The Field Museum is thus a prize example of a fundamental irony in the American economy: as the affluent society grows in material wealth, it becomes increasingly unable to support those civic institutions that serve recreation and the life of the human spirit.[11]

The effort and the resources poured into the construction of the Field Museum and the necessity of extending the lakefront fill south and east of the museum building led to a hiatus of nearly a decade in the further implementation of Burnham's proposals for cultural institutions in the Grant Park–Chicago Harbor area. The one work that was executed in the mid-twenties is a piece of pure civic art rather than a civic institution, and although it was not specified in the Burnham Plan, its installation was closely related to his scheme for the main area of the park. The Clarence Bucking-ham Fountain was erected at the east end of Congress Parkway in 1926–27, having been given to the people of Chicago by Kate Buckingham as a memorial to her brother. Three different talents were involved in the creation of this aqueous monument: the architects were Bennett, Parsons and Frost of Chicago; the sculptor of its dolphin motif and its baroque decorative elements was Jacques Lambert of Paris; and the engineers of its hydraulic system were drawn from the engineering staff of the city's Water Department. Providing a delightful example of fluid and transitory architecture, shaped by aerial and hydrodynamic processes, Buckingham is one of the largest fountains built in the twentieth century, with 133 subsidiary jets surrounding the central column of water that can be forced to a height of 200 feet, and it is extremely popular among natives and visitors alike on summer evenings, especially those on which the outdoor symphony concerts are scheduled. The fountain stands at the focal point of the park as Burnham conceived it, where the longitudinal axis lying midway between the Illinois Central tracks and the lake intersects the axis of Congress Parkway, and where he planned to locate the natural history museum. But the decision had been made, as we have seen, to place the museum and its sister institutions along the southern flank of Chicago Harbor.

Having secured riparian rights to the entire length of the shoreline between Grant and Jackson Park, the South Park District was now in a position to begin the heroic undertaking aimed at creating the south closure of the harbor and at providing the equivalent of Lincoln Park along the city's south shore. The ultimate program as it was drawn up in the Burnham Plan required extensive negotiations with the Illinois Central Railroad, which culminated in the Lake Front Ordinance of 1919. Another extraordinary example of civic foresight, this act of the city council spelled out in detail the respective responsibilities of the railroad and the park district in the develop-ment of the shore below Grant Park, including the agreement on the part of the railroad to build a new station at 12th Street and to electrify its operations (only the latter, restricted to suburban service, was accomplished; see pp. 285–86).

Filling south of 14th Boulevard, in the form of a continuous park lying east of the Illinois Central line, was begun in 1917 and was carried out in stages that have no clear lines of demarcation, either spatial or temporal. The operation reached approximately the line of 23rd Street in 1924, continued over the two miles from 23rd to 39th Street in 1924–26, and rounded out its first phase by covering the remaining distance to Jackson Park at 57th Street in the succeeding four years. The method of filling represented a refinement of the highly economical process that had been developed years before for the creation of Grant Park. The first step was the construction roughly parallel to the shore of a continuous cofferdam of massive stone blocks set in concrete. Behind this seawall spoil accumulated from excavations for buildings, canals, tunnels, and railroad facilities was deposited by trucks and shovels from the shore outward, while at the same time wet sand dredged from the lake bed was pumped into the outer area of the fill behind the cofferdam. This technique of hydraulic filling, which was developed by the Chicago engineer J. R. Sensibar, had the two merits of being inexpensive and of providing rapid compaction of the material because the sand was saturated. The construction of South Lake Shore Drive followed in the wake of the reclamation operations (see pp. 250–51).

Burnham's program, as we have noted, called for a chain of narrow islands and peninsulas at the outer edge of the fill to form a series of protected harbors between the outer lake and the shore park. By the time the South Park District turned to this aspect of the work little time was left before the depression of 1930 put a stop to all these grand schemes; yet even this limited accomplishment is of such magnitude as to place it in the front rank of civic works. As the south fill was nearing completion at Jackson Park, the commissioners of the district in 1928 turned their attention to creating, first, the peninsula that was to bound Chicago Harbor on the south and, second, the northernmost of the so-called islands that were to parallel the shore, both of which were completed about three years later. From a rounded anchor end immediately east of the Field Museum the fill was steadily pushed eastward and southward into the configuration that now marks the Northerly Island–Burnham Harbor area (see fig. 6 for a map of how Burnham conceived this part of the shore development). Space was thus provided for a new yacht harbor, a beach, the eastward drive—named Achsah Bond Drive after the wife of Illinois' first governor—and two new buildings that fill out the impressive row extending along the line of Roosevelt Road for a distance of more than 4,000 feet from the original shore.

No setting for a major civic building could compare to this, and when Graham, Anderson, Probst and White received the commission in 1928 for the aquarium that John G. Shedd had endowed, though the final dimensions of its site were yet to take shape, they rose fully to its magnificent promise (figs. 35, 36). Working in collaboration with the engineer Magnus Gunderson, they designed a building whose orthodox classical shape was dictated by the most carefully studied functional plan. The white marble structure that was opened in the fall of 1929 may be regarded either as a blunt-armed Greek cross measuring 300 feet end-to-end across the wings, in which the corners are filled in with triangular enclosures, or as an octagon with extremely short wings extending along the lines of the cardinal directions. The central area, or crossing of the arms, is surmounted by a pyramidal skylight roof that is octagonal in outline and constructed of thick translucent glass set in a steel armature. The primary structural system is a steel frame designed for the extremely heavy load imposed by the water-filled concrete tanks, but the steelwork, except in the working areas, is wholly hidden under the white Georgia marble of the exterior walls, the interior plaster vaulting, and the green marble and tile of the interior partitions. The foundations of the frame, as in the Field Museum, rest on wood piling driven to a stratum of hardpan clay. The decorative scheme of the interior, like the colors themselves, is derived from wave forms and aquatic fauna, while that of the exterior is composed of Doric details nicely subordinated to the smooth-walled enclosure. Structure, equipment, and finishing materials meant that the final cost was high—$3,250,000 in 1929, or about $15,600,000 in 1971, for a little less than 75,000 square feet of main-floor area.

The entrance of the aquarium, facing west toward Lake Shore Drive, opens into a broad lobby that occupies one of the four main wings (fig. 36). The rotunda at the intersection of these wings, under the pyramidal skylight, formerly embraced a circular pool that surrounded a mass of stratified rock planted in vines and ferns, but this was replaced by a coral reef in 1971. The six main exhibition galleries are arranged by parallel pairs in the other three wings that radiate from the central rotunda, and the exhibition tanks lie in a linear series along the outer edges of the galleries. The exhibition and working facilities ordinarily contain a population of about ten thousand individual specimens, but this number is far from constant because of changes in the collection and the necessity in this corrosive and aqueous world of constant maintenance and repair work.[12] The galleries are covered by vaulted ceilings of plaster on metal lath fixed to thin steel ribs. Above the exhibition tanks and the work space behind them there are sawtooth skylight monitors carried on continuous beams that correspond in their linear shape to the profile of the monitor section. The natural and artificial lighting systems are ingeniously designed to keep the gallery floors relatively dark while providing uniform overhead illumination for the tanks.

The most elaborate part of the mechanical installation of Shedd Aquarium is the water storage and circulation system. Immediately behind the exhibition tanks, each with its continuous inflow of oxygen, are the ninety-five reserve tanks designed to hold reserve stock and the exhibit specimens when the public tanks are cleaned. The total capacity of all tanks is 450,000 gallons, a volume of water maintained at an approximately constant quantity by means of four storage reservoirs in the basement with a combined capacity of 2,000,000 gallons, divided between salt and fresh water.

198   Fig. 35. John G. Shedd Aquarium,
Grant Park at East Roosevelt Road,
1928–29. Graham, Anderson, Probst
and White, architects.

35

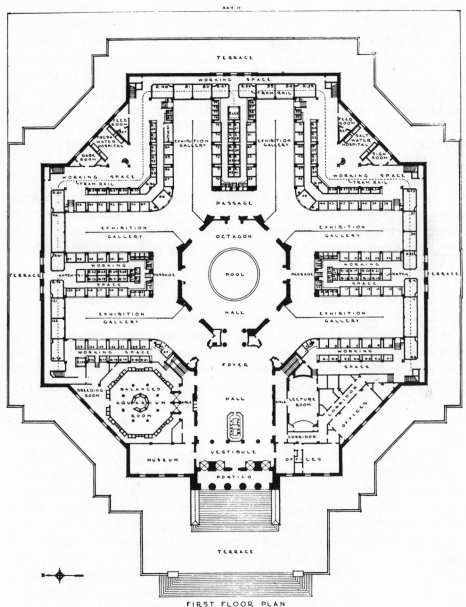

The fresh water is pumped from the lake through an intake on the east side of the building, but the salt water, of prime Gulf Stream quality, is brought by tank car and truck from Key West. To keep a great variety of fish, however, necessitates a wide range of water conditions, and as a consequence the tanks are divided into the following five groups according to the salinity and the temperature of the water: heated salt, chilled salt, heated fresh, chilled fresh, and natural fresh. Each group has its own reservoir, with the exception of that for heated fresh water, which is auxiliary to the natural fresh supply. Each storage reservoir is further divided into two tanks, one for idle water and one for the working quantity. The supply of water and its heating or cooling are maintained by a circulation system that differs from the standard building supply system in that it operates as a closed and continuous circuit with heating, cooling, and aerating elements at focal points along the way.[13] All new specimens are transported to the aquarium in a railroad car specially built by the Pullman Company as a unique traveling variation on the fixed structure.

In every functional and aesthetic respect the Shedd Aquarium must be judged a highly successful design; yet in spite of an income derived from endowments and admission fees as well as the tax revenues of the Park District, rising costs have taken their toll in the form of reduced maintenance and a shrinking collection. The building and its exhibits are owned by the society that founded the institution and are thus relatively immune to the ravages that have followed the growing irresponsibility of the Park District, but in the deterioration of the cities that accompanied the new militarism that began in 1950 the aquarium declined visibly in the quality of its fabric. The Shedd Aquarium, which took the place of an earlier structure in Lincoln Park (see p. 208), was the most popular of all the city's cultural institutions even in the depression years, although it eventually dropped to fourth place in annual attendance.

The third and last of the celebrated row of public buildings at the south end of Grant Park occupies the most commanding site of all, at the end of the narrow peninsula that constitutes the harbor's south boundary, from which one can see the whole panorama of the city's shore spread out in immense perspective. The institution is the Max Adler Planetarium, named for the donor who provided the building and its associated astronomical museum and planetarium projector, the latter the first such instrument to be installed in the United States (fig. 37). Erected in 1929–30, the structure was designed by Ernest Grunsfeld, Jr., and the engineers Lieberman and Hein— the former a new name in Chicago architecture and a fresh talent that offered an entirely new approach to the design of public buildings. In this overpowering setting dignity and simplicity had to be the ruling principles, and Grunsfeld, acting with rare courage and self-restraint, created what was immediately recognized as a classic in the modern idiom. The American Institute of Architects awarded him its gold medal in 1930 for this lake-set jewel of geometry.

The external walls of the building form three concentric, similar, dodecagonal prisms that rise in receding tiers to the base of a hemispherical dome. The two geometric elements, prismatic and spherical, reflect the internal functions of the building, which embraces an astronomical museum with its associated library as well as the planetarium instrument in its domed circular enclosure. The feature peculiar to such a structure is the hemispherical surface on which the images of the sun, moon, planets, and stars can be projected from the planetarium. Grunsfeld's solution is admirable for its geometric purity, its symbolic character, and its functional interior arrangements. The twelve-sided nested figures have a maximum inscribed diameter (that is, the diameter of the circle inscribed within the largest prism) of 151 feet and a circumscribed diameter of 160 feet. The architect chose the dodecagonal form to stand for the twelve months of the year and their associated zodiacal signs, which are represented in low-relief sculpture by Alfonso Ianelli at the upper corners of the main prism. The size of the outermost block was dictated by the need to house the working spaces of the museum; the setbacks, on the other hand, were required in order to secure an easy transition to the hemispherical dome above the planetarium chamber. The lower part of this enclosure is a cylindrical auditorium that contracts slightly at the top of the wall into the surface of the inner hemisphere.[14]

The extreme simplicity of the planetarium building is relieved by narrow bands of fluting running vertically at the corners of the lowest prism and horizontally at its upper edge and by the zodiacal signs at the upper corners. Although the exterior walls are reduced to smooth planes, they have a richly sensuous character because they are sheathed in a softly polished rainbow granite marked by dark-green veins in a reddish ground. The entrance doors are sheathed in bronze, and the roof of the dome is covered with copper sheets. The entrance opens into a small lobby, on the rear wall of which is a large dedicatory panel of green brown Tennessee marble decorated with white-metal symbols of the planets cast in low relief. In other areas the simplicity of the interior matches that of the outer surfaces: the plaster walls are a uniform dark cinnamon color, and the ceilings of the exhibition area are gold. The building stands on a grass-covered terrace raised about five feet above the ring drive that surrounds it, a traditional device that brings out to the full the restrained monumentality of this superb design.

The simplicity and the purity of the Adler Planetarium are in one respect deceptive, since they hide a complex internal structure. The foundations rest on composite piles

Fig. 37. Max Adler Planetarium, Grant Park at east end of Achsah Bond Drive, 1929–30. Ernest Grunsfeld, Jr., architect.

Fig. 38. Chicago's cultural center. *From left to right under the arrows:* Adler Planetarium (1930); Shedd Aquarium (1929); Field Museum of Natural History (1920); Orchestra Shell (1931); Auditorium (1889); Orchestra Hall (1904); Art Institute (1893); Public Library (1897).

37

38

Fig. 39. Museum of Science and Industry, Jackson Park at 57th Street, 1893, 1933 et seq. D. H. Burnham and Company, architects.

39

of wood and concrete that were driven through the fill and into the original lake bed to a depth of 44 feet below the bed level. The structural system is also composite: the walls of the prismatic volumes are supported by a concrete frame, whereas the floor, roof, and dome frames are steel. The horizontal slabs are carried by standard girders and joists, but the double dome required more elaborate curvilinear forms. The primary members in the frame of the outer dome are twenty-four meridional open-web ribs built up of steel plates, angles, and straps and curving on an outside radius of 40 feet 7 inches. Alternate ribs spring from twelve steel columns disposed in a ring around the planetarium chamber, and the intermediate ribs between them from I-beams joining successive pairs of columns, the entire group of twenty-four bearing on a steel compression ring at their upper ends. This ring, which is 10 feet in diameter, also serves as an opening for the smokestack. The ribs are stiffened laterally by circumferential struts, and the whole assembly is braced by double diagonals in all but the topmost ring of the spherical trapezoids formed by the primary framing members. The steelwork of the dome is covered by one-inch-thick cement tiles caulked with elastic cement, and these in turn are covered by copper sheathing. The inner dome is a lightweight duplication of the outer and its crown and spring line stand seven feet lower than those of the external covering. The inner ribs and rings, formed of steel angles, are suspended by steel hangers from a light horizontal framework fixed to the outer built-up ribs. Wooden ribs attached to their steel counter-parts once formed the nailing base of the stretched and treated cotton fabric that originally constituted the planetarium screen, but this flimsy material was later re-placed by anodized aluminum.

Adler Planetarium was sturdily constructed and braced against the shore winds, and its exposed location far from the built-up streets has kept it safe from the worst concentrations of atmospheric pollution. The problems of the institution thus arose less from physical deterioration than from unimaginative administration; the exhibits of the museum remained unaltered over the years, unrelieved by special displays or new acquisitions, and the planetarium displays formed a cycle as unchanging as the celestial bodies themselves. Much ill will was generated among the members of the star-gazing community when the staff several times refused to open the roof areas, which were consciously designed as observation terraces, during various natural and artificial celestial events. In 1969 the Park District planned an ambitious program aimed at increasing the popularity of the planetarium and extending the range of its activities. The major and most expensive part was the addition of a restaurant and space theater, to be constructed underground in order to leave the splendid site in its original condition. The theater was to be designed to give the spectator the illusion of seeing the stars and the bodies of the solar system from a point far removed from the planetary orbits. Within the existing structure the planetarium projector was to be replaced by a new Zeiss instrument, and two-thirds of the present seats were to be replaced by a new variety with reclining backs. The only trouble with these laudable aims was that the major part of the necessary funds was far from assured at the time the program was adopted.

The last of the cultural institutions to round out the Grant Park group is the orchestra shell, constructed near the south end of the original park area in 1931 for outdoor summer concerts. Its cost of $15,000 made it by far the cheapest of all civic improvements, and for the short season in which it is regularly used it is probably the most popular. The opening of the shell completed the great ring of buildings bordering Grant Park that house eight of Chicago's twelve public institutions devoted to the intellectual and aesthetic life. Only the Civic Opera House, west of the Loop on Wacker Drive, the Historical Society and the Academy of Sciences in Lincoln Park, and the Museum of Science and Industry in Jackson Park stand outside the central group. The buildings that constitute this primary complex were completed at varying intervals over a period of forty-two years—in chronological order, the Auditorium (1889), the Art Institute (1893), the Public Library (1897), Orchestra Hall (1904), the Field Museum (1920), Shedd Aquarium (1929), Adler Planetarium (1930), the orchestra shell (1931)—and together they compose the largest, oldest, architecturally richest and most diversified cultural center of all American cities (fig. 38).

If the spectacular works of building art and civil engineering were taking shape under the jurisdiction of the South Park District, other plans were simultaneously bearing fruit in the parks to the north and south of these showplaces and in the inland areas of the city. It was the landscape art that flourished in the western corridor. The appointment of Bernard A. Eckhart as chairman of the West Park Commission in 1905 led, as we have seen, to the elevation of Jens Jensen in the following year to the position of chief landscape architect for the district. For fourteen years Jensen's talented hands were free enough to create the masterpieces of the western park chain in their present form—Garfield, Douglas, Humboldt, Columbus, and Eckhart—of which the last two were wholly new works rather than improvements of those already in existence. Under the irresponsible maintenance, however, that increasingly characterized both the old separate districts and the unified one that took their place, these parks have deteriorated steadily, and only Humboldt retains the character of the Jensen legacy. The entire history of the western system is filled with the ugly ironies of American municipal politics. Eckhart appointed Jensen in part to reform the corrupt system, and backed him in the increasingly unequal struggle, but the municipal corruption that deepened and spread under the last term of Mayor Carter Harrison (1911–15) and the first two terms of his successor, William Hale Thompson (1915-23), eventually made Jensen's position untenable. He faced an impossible situation for a man of his integrity: rather than see his work undone by staffs of incompetent and dishonest political appointees, he resigned in 1920, never to work again in Chicago. Thompson, popularly known as Big Bill, was a loud-mouthed oaf who kept public attention focused on himself by conducting a campaign of anti-British propaganda in which he vowed, with unspeakable vulgarity, that he would punch King George in the nose; yet he served still another term (1927–31), and his name is on the bronze plaques that identify some of the greatest works of civic art in America.

Two small neighborhood parks on the South and West sides provided sites for recreational buildings each unique in its way but representing at the same time the innovative Chicago spirit in architecture. The general recreational building and gymnasium in Fuller Park, at 45th and Princeton streets, were erected in 1914–15 from the design of Edward H. Bennett. The two structures are disposed so as to form a quadrangle around an open protected court and are connected by covered walkways extending from the rear corners of the main block. Their distinctive characteristic is that they are constructed entirely of concrete, something of a novelty in itself but here made more remarkable by the use of the material for striking wall patterns cast as an integral part of the structural mass. For the main building Bennett created an original design from highly personal variations on classical motifs: three huge arched windows in each of the long elevations are topped by small gables; these openings are bounded at the sides by vertically fluted panels reminiscent of pilasters whose grooves continue downward over massive consoles that support thick projecting slabs at the sills; and the broad windowless side panels of both the side and the end elevations are covered with a kind of incised diaper pattern like the *opus reticulatum* of Roman masonry. The widely overhanging gable roof that tops the whole mass strongly suggests the Prairie idiom.

A straightforward example of the late Prairie style is the recreation building constructed in two parts (1916–17 and 1928) for the little Shedd Park that fills the truncated block bounded by Millard (3632W) and Lawndale (3700W) avenues, 23rd Street, and the embankment of the Burlington Railroad line. The whole enclosure is L-shaped in plan: the long wing, designed by William E. Drummond, contains the auditorium and club rooms, and the shorter, added eleven years later from the design of Michaelson and Rognstad, houses the gymnasium. The two-story brick building under a low-pitched gable roof is easily identified as the product of the late

Chicago school, chiefly in the long rows of grouped windows and the dense vertical pattern of wooden posts in the gable ends, both bound by strong horizontal lines or by the sloping ends of the roof with its wide-flaring eaves. The heavy end piers of brick contain stairs and dressing rooms, a currently fashionable device long ago anticipated by Wright and his Chicago contemporaries. The best interior feature in this admirable little work of recreational architecture is the ceiling of the auditorium, which is simply the highly varnished, natural-colored framework of paired rafters carrying the diagonal tongue-and-groove sheathing of the roof.

The improvements and additions to Lincoln Park very nearly matched the magnitude of the South Park District's vast program of lakeshore reclamation and development. By means of the same technique of spoil and hydraulic filling behind permanent seawalls, Lincoln was steadily pushed northward at its present width during the period from the beginning of the world war to the early depression years, the older beaches above Fullerton Avenue (2400N) being largely obliterated along the way. The present area of the park, with much of its landscaping, was largely completed from Fullerton up to Diversey Avenue (2800N) by the early twenties. The extension from Diversey to Montrose (4400N) was accomplished in 1925–29, adding not only a mile and a half to the length of the park, but the great oval basin of Belmont Yacht Harbor at the same time. In 1929, before the Montrose fill was completed, the park district began the next northward extension and carried it by 1933 to Foster Avenue (5200N), which was to remain the north limit of the park for more than twenty years. This final extension under the Burnham program included subsidiary shore works that in themselves constitute an unparalleled civic achievement. Foremost of these was the creation of the Montrose-Wilson Beach, a sand fill placed in eighteen to twenty feet of water along a length of one-half mile and over an area of twenty-six acres, making it the largest man-made bathing beach in the world. In addition to the beach the district constructed a bathhouse and the Montrose Yacht Harbor to provide still more recreational facilities in another mile-and-a-half extension of the park's length. Long before they were opened to use, however, the depression had reduced the city to bankruptcy, and as a consequence the State of Illinois and the federal government, through the immense public works programs of the New Deal, had to come to the rescue in order to complete the lakefront plan. As we shall see, it marked the end of grand civic enterprises such as these.

The institutions and subsidiary structures of Lincoln Park multiplied as the park area expanded. A small field house was built near North Avenue (1600N) in 1922, and another much larger, with a gymnasium and full recreational equipment, was added east of Waveland Avenue (3700N) in 1931, both designed by the architect

Edwin H. Clark. The administration building of the Lincoln Park District came along the way, having been built in 1926–27. Meanwhile the Lincoln Park Zoological Garden, the best known and the most popular of the park's institutions, shared in these ambitious programs. Dwight Perkins's Lion House of 1912 brought its author the gold meal of the American Institute of Architects. A simple brick structure under a gable roof, the building was planned to provide generous, well-lighted space for both animals and human spectators by the device of placing only a single row of cages along the south wall of the enclosure and reserving the rest of the space for broad hall-like areas for circulation and viewing. An aquarium for freshwater fish was added in 1922–23 and the second Monkey House in 1926. Since Shedd Aquarium provided far more extensive facilities for exhibiting fish, the Lincoln Park building was transformed in 1936 into the present Reptile House, but the hydraulic system was retained for aquatic reptiles, seals, and various amphibia. The handsomest and possibly unique feature of the zoo is the Zoo Rookery, which was constructed in the same year. An uncovered outdoor exhibition space for aquatic birds, the enclosure is densely landscaped around a pool with shrubs and trees, and its walkways, stairways, and retaining walls are built up of broad flat-faced limestone slabs that form a kind of masonry appropriate to the naturalistic setting. At the edge of the pond stands a little pavilion in the form of an open timber framework whose design places it exactly in the Wrightian-Prairie mode. The Rookery was designed by the landscape architect's staff of the Chicago Park District but was built by the federal Works Progress Administration as part of a general improvement of zoo property.

By the time of the depression the zoo had reached its present area of twenty-five acres and its collection of over 2,500 specimens, but it is small, generally unattractive, and many of its buildings belong to the nineteenth century not only in their time of construction, but equally in their cramped, dark, and badly designed spaces. Deterioration from age, inadequate maintenance, and overuse, as much as from insensitivity and irresponsibility on the part of the Park District administration, took a heavy toll, and in spite of a few post–World War II additions, the zoo eventually reached the desperate stage where only drastic reconstruction could rescue it from oblivion.

The last of the Lincoln Park buildings to be planned before the depression ended municipal improvements is the present home of the Chicago Historical Society, which faces Clark Street a little above North Avenue. Designed by Graham, Anderson, Probst and White, in collaboration with Magnus Gunderson as engineer, the structure was planned as early as 1928 and erected in 1931–32 as the fourth of the society's quarters. The previous three were built successively on the northwest corner of Dear-

born and Ontario streets, where the last of them, a massive Romanesque work of
stone masonry, still stands. The present building is thoroughly conventional in design
and construction but at least has the merit of being derived from antecedents closer
to the American heritage: the three-story structure is built of red brick in the Georgian
style, with a central portico and long flanking wings. Its site is doubly appropriate
because the park has not only been intimately bound up with the history of Chicago
since the end of the Civil War, but is also filled with sculpture that memorializes the
the national heritage of the different peoples who have composed the population of
the city. Scattered through the lawns and gardens of Lincoln Park are statues of
Beethoven, Goethe, Schiller, Hans Christian Andersen, Linnaeus, Shakespeare,
Eugene Field, and Benjamin Franklin, all of them providing eloquent testimony to
ethnic and cultural communities that have lost the spirit which once placed the images
of composers, poets, and scientists at the focal points of a great public park.

Jackson Park had seen no activity beyond landscaping and beach improvements
since its completion at the turn of the century, and with the opening of the Field
Museum in 1920, the former quarters of the natural history museum, originally
constructed as the Fine Arts Building of the Columbian Exposition, stood empty and
highly vulnerable to deterioration. In the civic and commercial boom of the twenties,
however, the vast edifice was soon to be transformed into what eventually became
Chicago's most popular museum. The Fine Arts Building had been designed by
Charles B. Atwood of D. H. Burnham's office as an impressive example of Greco-
Roman forms expertly adapted to the huge size required for major exhibition space
at a world's fair.[15] The structural system formed a mixture of the permanent and the
temporary which was reasonably fire-resistant, but both the exterior and interior
elements included a considerable volume of combustible material. The roof and floor
loads were divided between stone columns and brick bearing walls covered inside and
out with a kind of gypsum plaster known as staff. Some exterior columns were built-up
box members of wood with two sides of plate and two of latticework lathing. The
interior columns, stairways, and armatures of the roof skylights were cast iron. It
served the Field Museum well enough for twenty-six years, but when the collection
was removed to Grant Park the inevitable deterioration that occurs even under
maintenance was greatly accelerated. By the mid-twenties the building had reached
a disgraceful condition, although there had been a number of proposals for preserving
and using it.

The plan that bore lasting fruit, because it was backed by adequate resources,
proposed that the building be suitably restored for use as a museum of science and
technology. The idea met with immediate popular and philanthropic enthusiasm:

in 1925 the voters of the South Park District authorized a bond issue of $5,000,000 to restore the exterior of the building and to reconstruct the interior in such ways as might be necessary for the kind of museum intended; in the following year the newly organized Museum of Science and Industry received its charter from the state, and Julius Rosenwald, the president of Sears, Roebuck and Company, gave the trustees $3,000,000 to establish the institution as a working entity. Rosenwald appears to have been the original author of the idea, which came to him during a visit to the Deutsches Museum in Munich, easily the first scientific and technical museum in the world. He was sufficiently enthusiastic about providing Chicago with an American equivalent that he soon offered an additional $4,500,000 to cover the remaining costs of reconstructing the building and installing the initial exhibits. The unique feature of the Deutsches Museum, and the one that Rosenwald particularly wanted to recreate in Chicago, is the exhibition of moving models that can be operated by the spectators. Thus to the tasks of rebuilding an old temporary structure in permanent form and assembling the exhibits there was added the problem of finding craftsmen who could be trained to make the intricate scientific, mathematical, and technological models. It was a slow, costly process; the physical aspects did not begin until 1929, and the completion of the various parts of the museum came in stages: the North and South courts and the rotunda were opened in 1933, the West Pavilion in 1937, and the Central Pavilion in 1940.

The architectural design of the renovated structure was the work of two large Chicago offices, Graham, Anderson, Probst and White, and Shaw, Naess and Murphy (fig. 39). Since the plan of the old Fine Arts Building lent itself with little alteration to the purposes of a scientific museum, the reconstruction was largely a matter of substituting permanent and durable materials for the staff and wood of the original fabric. The badly deteriorated plasterwork on the exterior was replaced by limestone and on the interior by marble except in areas where wall hangings might be located. The interior columns were rebuilt in stone, and the skylights with their iron armatures were replaced by domes covered with copper sheathing and tile, or by gable roofs sheathed in copper. Some stainless steel and other metals were used to cover the columns in the rotunda under the central dome in order to provide an appearance more consonant with the modern spirit, but all the carefully executed classical details were preserved on the exterior. Floor framing was introduced to increase loading to 250 pounds per square foot on the main floor, 200 pounds on the first balcony, and 100 pounds on the second. When the task was finally completed in 1940 the program of reconstruction had opened 400,000 square feet of floor area for exhibits and 200,000 square feet for offices, auditorium, lecture hall, cafeteria, and the numerous museum services.

There is no question about the extraordinary popularity of the Museum of Science and Industry, since it is second in attendance only to the Smithsonian Institution's Museum of History and Technology, but its status as an exhibition and educational establishment is a matter of considerable controversy. Over the years since its full opening the exhibits have changed drastically in character, away from an emphasis on science, mathematics, and technology considered historically and analytically, and in the direction of industrial processes and products. The deliberate policy of the museum administration lay behind this shift in focus: the carefully prepared exhibits designed to show the interrelations of science and industrial technology gave way to a program aimed increasingly at showing the interrelations of industrial products and a consumer economy, in which 10 percent of the exhibition material is changed every year. The chief reason the museum has seldom lacked funds is that a high proportion of the most costly exhibits are designed, paid for, and installed by manufacturers, who thus use the institution as an advertising and public-relations medium; and this mode of operation is readily apparent in the garish and sensational character of many of the presentations. Eventually only three halls came to be devoted to mathematics and the physical and biological sciences; the remainder of the extensive space is given over to exhibits in which color, light, legends, models, and architectural settings, developed into complex pictorial, auditory, and kinesthetic images, are combined to produce simultaneous multiple-sensation impacts. Many models can be operated by the spectator with push button, lever, or crank; others are life-size or overscaled to such a degree that the visitor may participate in the action of the object represented. Many of the museum's exhibits are nonverbal, nondiscursive, nonhistorical, and highly kinetic, so that the institution runs perilously close to becoming what Rosenwald feared, a Coney Island of industrial and technological gimmicks. The proponents, on the other hand, argue that it offers a new kind of exhibition technique imbued with the spirit of modern visual art that achieves the relevant psychological response in hitherto unexplored ways. Whatever the case, the museum reaches a large and ever expanding audience, by 1970 well past 3,000,000 per annum.[16]

Outside the city limits the most valuable public achievement for the entire metropolitan area was the successful establishment of the Forest Preserve District after the abortive attempts that marked the years before the Burnham period. The Chicago City Council passed an ordinance asking the state for new legislation to enable the city and county to establish the district, and the general assembly complied by passing an act in June 1913 that authorized the creation of the Forest Preserve District of Cook County. Under its terms the commissioners were granted the power "to acquire and hold lands containing natural forests, or lands connecting such forests for the purpose of protecting and preserving the flora, fauna and scenic beauties and to restore, restock, protect and preserve the natural forests and said lands, together with their flora and fauna, as nearly as may be, in their natural state and condition, for the purpose of the education, pleasure and recreation of the public."[17] The commissioners began to carry out the program in 1915, when they purchased 500 acres of land under the recommendation of Dwight Perkins, who designated the areas for the initial purchase program of 13,000 acres. Down through the years the commissioners have shown unswerving devotion to the principles laid down in the enabling legislation: by the end of World War II the district had acquired 36,000 acres of forest and meadow land, and by 1969 it had expanded the total to 59,500 acres. Private and public bodies of every description have tried to secure Forest Preserve land for special purposes, but only in rare cases of eminent domain or in the face of the ruthless demands of the military establishment in the decades of the fifties and sixties has the district given up any of its holdings. In view of the extraordinary area of these holdings, the land-protection policy of the district, as it has been steadily refined and enlarged over the years, forms a model for all public recreational bodies and is worth presenting in full.

The Forest Preserve Commissioners . . . reaffirm . . . their long-standing policy to the effect that Forest Preserve lands were acquired for one purpose only, that under the law no power is granted the District to divest itself of title to such lands, that the said properties are increasing constantly in value, for the purpose for which they were acquired, and that the continuous acquisition of lands in the Comprehensive Plan will be jeopardized by any severance from the present holdings. . . . No severance of such lands shall be made for other municipal, school, park and similar public uses for which such public bodies have power to finance and acquire needed lands. . . . Where the rare exception may arise under which a public agency persists in condemnation of Forest Preserve property, the Board of Forest Preserve Commissioners may ask for an exhaustive analysis and report on the matter by the Advisory Committee. In general, the Forest Preserve District shall resist rather than accede to such action, in Court, and shall place in evidence such exhaustive survey and report, together with the current appraised value of the full, fair market value of the land, the forest and of any improvements. . . . For essential highway needs, for essential sewer, water, or other public utility, underground, surface, or overhead improvements required in the interests of all the public, the District may accede to such grants, in Court, or otherwise, on the basis of the full, fair market value of the property acquired.[18]

It was this last exception that made possible the destruction or spoilation of forest land resulting from constructing the Tri-State Toll Road on a long skew alignment through the bottom lands of the Des Plaines River in Des Plaines, from the erection by the Commonwealth Edison Company of a transmission line through Linné Woods in Morton Grove, and from the establishment of a military radar base in the preserve known as Skokie Lagoons. Otherwise the steady expansion of Forest Preserve lands has constituted the one happy feature in the otherwise deteriorating character of recreational properties in Chicago and its contiguous area. As a matter of fact, it is only because of the activities of the district that the recreational lands of the metropolitan area remain reasonably close to the standard of one acre of land for every one hundred inhabitants.

The largest of all the individual public institutions that were established during the Burnham period is directly associated with the development of the Forest Preserve program. The second and much more extensive of Chicago's zoos required so much land to realize the aims of its founders that it had to be located in the suburban community of Brookfield, fourteen miles west-southwest of the Loop, on the streetcar (later bus) line of the Chicago and West Towns Railroad and the main line of the Burlington Route. The Chicago Zoological Society, which built and stocked the new park, was founded in 1921 and was incorporated under state law two years later. The date of the society's establishment was unquestionably determined by the availability of an appropriate area of land: in 1921 Edith Rockefeller McCormick gave the Forest Preserve District 83 acres along Salt Creek under the stipulation that it be used exclusively for a zoo; the district added 113 acres purchased for the same purpose through its acquisition program, to bring the total to 196 acres, or nearly eight times the area of Lincoln Park Zoo. With land available and the initial costs underwritten in good part by a bond issue passed in the referendum of 1926, the trustees began construction of the new park in the same year and brought it to completion in 1934. The balance of the costs of constructing the zoo were borne by a variety of sources—the endowment raised by the society, the operating revenues of the Forest Preserve District, which has always held title to the property, and grants from the Works Progress Administration and the Federal Art Project of the first New Deal administration. The architect in charge of site planning, landscaping, and the design of buildings was Edwin H. Clark, but he enjoyed the assistance of celebrated consultants in the creation and operation of zoological parks: William T. Hornaday, director of the Bronx Zoo in New York City, and Carl and Lorenz Hagenbeck, the founders of the Tiergarten in Hamburg, Germany, the first and still the finest open-air zoo.

The flat prairie setting and the influence of the Burnham Plan together suggested the classical character of Clark's site plan: it is an axial and symmetrical scheme in which the various animal enclosures are disposed along two broad malls extending at right angles to one another and bordered by the main walkways that connect the chief zoological areas. At the intersection of the mall axes stands the inevitable memorial to President Theodore Roosevelt in the form of a great circular pool with a fountain at its center and pedestals carrying gilded skulls of animals on the circumference. (The skulls make an appropriate irony, since Roosevelt spent more time in shooting animals than he did in keeping them alive.) The buildings and outdoor spaces, arranged along the sides and at the west end of the rectangular area, include animal houses, outdoor bird cages, numerous expertly designed pools, broad fenced outdoor enclosures for ungulates, barless and moated enclosures for fissipeds, and various utility structures, among them an animal hospital. The architectural style of the buildings is derived from Italian farmhouses of the fifteenth century, which might be characterized as an Italian vernacular of the late Middle Ages. The informal nature of these structures allowed Clark to use asymmetrical and irregular plans that could be readily adapted to the requirements of a modern zoo, but the tile roofs and the white-painted brick walls with their studied "antique texture" indicate the architect's fidelity to his sources. The various fountains, the animal statuary in stone, and the carved wooden guideposts were added in 1933–34 under the sponsorship of the Federal Art Project.

The most impressive features of Brookfield Zoo, however, are the outdoor barless enclosures invented by the Hagenbecks for the Hamburg garden and developed to their present standard by the Swiss architect Ursus Eggenschwiler (fig. 40). The individual compound is bounded on the viewing or spectator's side by a deep empty or water-filled moat too broad for leaping over and too steep-walled to climb out of, and on the rear side by connecting tunnels to the indoor cages and by synthetic rockwork walls again too steep and too high for scaling or leaping. These rock walls are built up of mortar or sand plaster from small-scale models that constitute a guide for the masons. The first step in the process is the construction of a framework of steel rods with a maximum diameter of ¾ inch. The rods are wired together in a pattern of 12-inch squares, covered with metal lath, and coated with a light layer of mortar applied by hand troweling. This forms the basis of the heavy mortar coat that is sprayed on by a pneumatic tube to a thickness of one inch on all exposed sides. Before it sets the material is sculptured by hand and colored by a fresco technique to a reasonable simulation of the natural outcropping of columnar basalt (fig. 40). Among the buildings housing indoor cages—and these bear no visual relation to the naturalistic outdoor compounds—the most interesting is the Pachyderm House, built in 1931–32. The walls are conventional brick bearing elements, but the flat roof and part of the clerestory above the animal enclosures are carried by transverse beams supported in turn by short posts that extend downward to the haunches of seven parabolic arches

215 Fig. 40. Chicago Zoological Park, Brookfield, Illinois, 1926–34. Edwin H. Clark, architect. The Pachyderm Compound.

Fig. 41. Chicago Zoological Park. Interior of the Pachyderm House.

40

41

in the form of steel ribs covered with concrete (fig. 41). The structure measures 110 ×
259 feet in plan; the arch span out-to-out is 80 feet, and the single row of animal stalls
extends 30 feet beyond the south springing points of the arches. The number of
specimens exhibited at Brookfield is about the same as at Lincoln Park Zoo, but since
the area is nearly eight times greater, it is obvious that the emphasis at the suburban
park is on open space for both animals and spectators.

In the thirty-five years that followed the completion of all its facilities Brookfield
Zoo lived through successive periods of depression, war, and uncontrolled inflation.
The physical deterioration caused by time, weather, hard usage, and an inadequate
maintenance income reached a progressively accelerating stage, like a terminal illness,
by 1960; unfortunately, this crisis state coincided with a four-year period of irresponsible management and steeply rising costs, which persisted while attendance and income
remained static. The zoo has always been guided by able directors, but between the
resignation of Robert Bean in 1964 and the appointment in 1968 of W. Peter Crowcroft,
former curator of mammals in the British Museum, the institution was administered
by an incompetent, indifferent, and useless committee of trustees who were chiefly
responsible for the rapid intensification of its troubles. This disgraceful state of
affairs is neither a temporary phenomenon nor peculiar to Brookfield Zoo: it is a
characteristic of all the public institutions of Chicago, for reasons not at all obscure,
which the more enlightened newspapers finally publicized. Brookfield, wrote one
reporter, is "afflicted with a board of trustees picked from the same groups that
stagnate so many other civic cultural institutions. The trustees are wealthy, busy,
WASP . . . and their inner circles are tightly closed, allowing no new money or fresh
enthusiasm"—and he might have added, ideas, whether new or old.[19] The result at
Brookfield was that by 1969 the zoo needed new capital to the extent of $15,000,000
and had no way of raising it except through a bond issue, for which the necessary
enabling legislation was passed by the general assembly in the fall of that year. But
this sum had to be supplemented by increasing revenues from the Forest Preserve
District and from potential donors to an enlarged endowment if the park was to
retain its front-rank status.

Schools and Universities

The great impetus toward civic improvement generated by the Burnham Plan affected
the board of education, as it did all the other departments, agencies, and districts of

the municipal and county governments. School construction continued at a steadily accelerating pace, reaching a high point in the decade of the twenties that the city was again never to regain. The school-building program, along with all aspects of the national life and economy, was seriously retarded by the First World War: in the decade of 1911–20 the board placed sixty-one new schools in service, of which forty-five were added up to 1916, but only sixteen in the following four years.[20] If the earlier pace had been maintained throughout the decade, the total by the end of 1920 would have been seventy-five schools. The board made a valiant effort to recoup the loss, however, for during the boom that came in the next decade it opened the record number of eighty-eight schools, which represented not only the second highest total for any census period but also the greatest number of high schools, and which coincided with the record number of sixty additions to existing schools. If the overall design of individual buildings fell below the level established by Dwight Perkins in his brief tenure as architect to the board of education (1905–10), there was a reasonable attempt on the part of his successors to maintain his functional standards and to exploit what few technological innovations were applied to this stepchild of the building industry. Lighting, fireproofing, special-purpose rooms such as gymnasiums and laboratories, details of classrooms, furnishings, and planning were steadily improved, while exterior details were derived about equally from classical and Gothic antecedents.

The first large high school to be built after the dismissal of Perkins is Nicholas Senn, erected at 5900 North Glenwood Avenue (1400W) in 1911–12 after the plans of Arthur F. Hussander, who replaced Perkins as chief architect to the board and who held the position until 1921. The original building was a solid rectangle in plan, its overall dimensions about 260 × 360 feet, but this was greatly enlarged in 1930–31 by the addition at the ends of two long transverse wings that gave the resulting U-shaped plan a length of 584 feet and a width from the rear elevation to the ends of the forward-projecting wings of about 440 feet. The 1912 block is three stories in height and is supported by a combination of internal steel framing and brick and concrete piers in the exterior walls, which are characterized by grouped windows between pilasters, columns flanking the entranceway, and a full complement of other classical details. The first floor is reserved chiefly for large special-purpose enclosures—gymnasiums, swimming pool, assembly hall, Reserve Officers Training Corps drill hall—together with administrative offices, a few classrooms, and two laboratories. The second and third floors, which embrace narrow interior light courts, are given over mainly to classrooms, counseling rooms, laboratories, and library, and the low tower over the entrance that provides a small fourth floor is used for band and orchestra practice. It was a serviceable design on the whole and if it showed no great imagination in planning and formal details, it satisfied the board's requirements well enough to be retained for another decade.

The shift to an elongated open plan came with a change of architects. In 1921 Hussander was replaced by John C. Christensen, who was to continue as chief architect for thirty years, and who most strikingly indicated the presence of a new hand in the design of Calumet High School, erected in 1924–26 at 8131 South May Street (1132W). The building was constructed in an unusual form which may have been unique at the time, although Christensen very nearly duplicated it in Fenger High School, opened in the same year at 11220 South Wallace Street (600W). The four attenuated wings of Calumet are disposed in a G-shaped plan, or in an open rectangle with a 132-foot break between the rear wing and the end of the transverse wing lying along the south side of the figure. The overall dimensions are about 376 × 573 feet, but much of the area enclosed is given over to an extremely generous interior court. Christensen repeatedly used the G-plan or its simpler variation, the U-type, but the most distinguished of his numerous buildings is Theodore Roosevelt High School, constructed at 3436 West Wilson Avenue (4600N) in 1926–27 (fig. 42). The largest of the Chicago public schools up to the time, it represented a collaborative work between the board of education architect and Edgar Martin, who held the short-lived position of supervisory architect from 1924 to 1926. Martin had been associated with Richard Schmidt for many years and was at the time a partner of Irving and Allen Pond.

Roosevelt is a three-story building that spreads out over the first-floor level in a broken rectangle with overall dimensions of 378 feet in width by 589 feet 6 inches in length, or a full east-west block from end to end. The structural system is composed primarily of reinforced concrete—footings and foundations, floor slabs, frame, and roof—but this is supplemented by steel members in areas of long spans and high loads. The roof areas over the assembly hall, gymnasium, lunchroom, and swimming pool are carried on steel Warren trusses, with the longest clear span being the 94-foot internal width of the gymnasium, but elsewhere roof slabs rest on steel I-beams. Steel H-columns encased in a heavy cladding of concrete support the ends of roof girders and trusses in the assembly hall and gymnasium wings and in the heating plant. The main block along Wilson Avenue and the deep wings are elongated narrow enclosures widely separated from each other so that all internal areas have a generous exposure to natural light. The first floor contains large special-purpose areas such as the assembly hall, swimming pool, the shops and laboratories of the industrial arts program, and the boiler room, as well as the administrative offices and a few

Fig. 42. Theodore Roosevelt High
School, 3436 West Wilson Avenue,
1926–27. John C. Cristensen, architect.

classrooms. The second and third floors, which do not extend over the rear wing but form instead the common U-shaped plan, house the classrooms, science laboratories, and art rooms, along with various other specialized enclosures. A distinctive feature of the interior finishing is the use of tawny orange glazed brick for a wainscoting that extends to a height of about six feet above the floor. The external curtain walls of brick are highly articulated in the Gothic mode: continuous stepped buttresses along the column lines define the bays, which on the front elevation and on all inner elevations are opened into closely grouped windows, three to a bay, separated by narrow mullions; in the side and rear elevations, however, continuous brick mullions rise between the buttresses to intensify the already marked verticalism of the wall areas. The upward movement terminates in a parapet whose terra-cotta coping forms a series of flattened cusps. The finely proportioned and rhythmic walls are composed of dark-red brick and tawny gold terra-cotta trim that together give the long elevations a richness of color unmatched even among the colorful school buildings of modern design.

Roosevelt was Christensen's best design, and he retained its essential features in most of the schools planned before the depression curtailed the lavish building program of the twenties. A modernized or simplified variation on the Roosevelt theme, with lighter colors, was used in the smaller but equally handsome Frederick W. von Steuben High School, constructed a little north of its predecessor at 5039 North Kimball Avenue (3400W) in 1928–30. As good as these two designs are, however, they are eclipsed by the last of Dwight Perkins's commissions executed before illness forced his retirement from active practice. In spite of the loss of his board of education position on charges of insubordination and incompetence, there were few who questioned the fact that Perkins was the leading architect of schools, and the partnership that he formed with William K. Fellows and John L. Hamilton in 1911 enjoyed continuous prosperity until its dissolution in 1927. Their foremost work is unquestionably the original building of Evanston Township High School, erected in 1923–24 along Dodge Avenue immediately below Church Street in the suburb from which the township takes its name.

The site is as generous as a wealthy and education-conscious community could afford: it extends 1,495 feet along Dodge and 1,620 feet in depth along Church and Lake streets, the area embracing both the building complex and the contiguous athletic fields. Perkins's initial design called for a two-winged plan in the shape of a T, but this was later expanded to an H-plan in which the gymnasium, auditorium, classrooms, and study halls are in the wings, and the lecture rooms, laboratories, and offices are in the central block extending along Dodge Street. The structural

Fig. 43. University of Chicago, 59th Street from Woodlawn to Ellis Avenue, 1892 et seq. *Left and center:* The Quadrangles. *Right:* Rockefeller Memorial Chapel.

Fig. 44. University of Chicago. South Quadrangle, with William Rainey Harper Memorial Library in the foreground.

43

44

system is steel framing throughout, with Pratt trusses supporting the roofs over the auditorium and gymnasium. The curtain walls of light-red brick and cream terra-cotta trim stand recognizably in the Chicago tradition: the strong articulation of continuous projecting piers and broad open bays is overlaid by a fine vertical pattern of thin continuous mullions. The decorative details—window moldings, coping, finials at the corners of the low tower over the entrance—are a simplified Gothic in character but are carefully subordinated to the primary wall rhythms and the main volumes of the building. Unfortunately, this handsome composition is nearly buried under the numerous additions of the 1960s designed by Perkins and Will, the architectural firm that was founded by Dwight Perkins's son Lawrence.[21]

Among all the educational and cultural institutions that were multiplying and expanding in the confident age that Burnham ushered in, none flourished more vigorously than the University of Chicago. The spectacular rate of growth that was established in the first eighteen years of its existence was maintained through the two decades that ended with the depression of 1930. The university's construction program added thirty-five buildings to the thirty-two that had been opened by 1910; the total enrollment on the Midway campus and in the newly opened downtown facilities multiplied nearly twenty times between 1892 and 1929, from 742 to 14,433 students of all categories, full- and part-time, while the full-time faculty increased in somewhat smaller proportion, from 120 to 789. The famous Quadrangles continued to be filled out to their ultimate rectangular form, but the need for all-university buildings and for the institutions appropriate to a medical school required that the original campus area of seventeen acres be greatly expanded, west to Cottage Grove Avenue (800E), east to Blackstone (1500E), and south to the other side of the Midway along 60th Street, for a new total of 105 acres (figs. 43, 44).[22] In the formal character of all these buildings the architects with rare self-effacement steadfastly followed the Tudor principles laid down by Henry Ives Cobb in 1892, with the consequence that an equally rare unity of design came to match the geometric harmony of the quadrangular site plan. If this passion for medievalism might have seemed obsessive at times, it was nevertheless essential in order to preserve the visual and functional qualities of campus and setting that place the institution in the front rank of university planning.

The centerpiece of the South Quadrangle, conspicuously situated in the side that faces the Midway, is William Rainey Harper Memorial Library, erected in 1911–12 at 1156 East 59th Street as one of the many buildings on the campus designed by the Boston firm of Shepley, Rutan and Coolidge (fig. 44). Steel-framed and sheathed in the blue Bedford limestone of the quadrangular groups, its Tudor forms follow with little variation the formal themes established under Cobb's architectural tenure. The three-story building, 262 feet long on the main axis, was constructed at a cost of $1,250,000 (more than $13,500,000 at the 1971 levels), but the insatiable demand of all major universities for library space long ago required that Harper be supplemented by numerous departmental collections. Typical of the classroom and laboratory buildings is Julius Rosenwald Hall, built in 1914–15 at the inner corner of the southeast Quadrangle to house the university's departments of geology and geography. The celebrated philanthropist met the $306,000 cost of construction through a gift offered on the occasion of his fiftieth birthday, and Holabird and Roche were commissioned to follow Cobb's principles in their design of the steel-framed, limestone-clad structure. Rosenwald was expertly planned to house a great variety of highly specialized enclosures in addition to the usual classrooms and offices—mineralogical laboratories equipped for work under high pressures and temperatures, rooms for preparing topographical and geological maps, a seismographic instrument founded on a separate concrete caisson four feet in diameter and extending to bedrock at 62 feet 6 inches below the footing plane, a machine shop with special cutting and polishing equipment for sectioning mineral specimens, libraries, conference rooms, and a museum, all of which served the requirements of research and instruction very well until progress in the earth sciences eventually compelled the construction of the new Henry Hinds Laboratory for the Geophysical Sciences that was opened in 1969.

Perhaps the most conspicuous feature of Rosenwald's decorative scheme is the continuation in secular twentieth-century terms of the medieval tradition of memorial, symbolic, and allegorical sculpture. The building is almost overloaded with a profusion of such elements. At the main entrance stands a carved wooden screen covered with bas-relief sculpture of famous geologists, which constitutes a background for Lorado Taft's bust of Thomas Chrowder Chamberlin, head of the department of geology for many years and coauthor with Rollin D. Salisbury of a classic text in the science (1909). The panel above the main entrance depicts the hammer and theodolite of the geologist beside capped and gowned students who support a shield below which extends a frieze of roses, an allusion to the donor's name (*rosen-wald*, or forest of roses). To the left of the entranceway an old man throws away a world scarred by geological agents, while on the right a child molds a new world out of the surrounding chaos. Pendants at the first-floor level bear floral emblems suggestive of the various nations of the world, and to the right and left of the central bay lie reliefs of the eastern and western hemispheres. The cornice of the facade carries sculptured portraits of famous geographers, geologists, and paleontologists, among them Leopold von Buch, Georges Cuvier, James Hall, William Logan, and Karl Ritter; and the west cornice offers Leonardo da Vinci as the first inquirer to understand the nature of fossils and the east honors Marco Polo for his geographical explorations in Asia.[23]

At the top of the square tower on the east side of the building are gargoyles in the shape of a bison, a bull, an elephant, and a lion, respectively representing the fauna and hence the continents of North America, Europe, Asia, and Africa (a hexagonal form would have allowed the inclusion of animals for South America and Australia). The octagonal meteorological tower provides space for eight gargoyles, all of them allegorical figures, four of them standing for the winds, and four birds (duck, eagle, albatross, and condor) serving as emblems of the air. The inevitable inscription—"Dig and Discover" in this case—appears on a shield near the tower entrance, surmounting the geologist's collecting bag and hammers. Decorative art of this kind came to seem affected and fraudulent, and the tradition that produced it is now dead, but since nothing has arisen to take its place we are forced to admit that we are the poorer for it. Abstract sculpture and so-called pure architectural forms cut themselves off from the allegorical and symbolic traditions of western culture, and so they cannot speak for the life of the mind that we have all inherited.

Among the buildings outside the quadrangle groups two command attention for architectural distinctions. Ida B. Noyes Hall, erected in 1915–16 at 1212 East 59th Street, was designed by Shepley, Rutan and Coolidge to fit squarely into the Cobb tradition. Housing a variety of recreational facilities for women, it was carefully planned as a sumptuous Tudor manor, with paneled ceilings and wainscoting in oak, flooring in Spanish tile, and heavy pierlike columns sheathed in Champsville marble. Allegorical art is again a prominent feature: mural paintings on the walls of the theater, executed by Jessie Arms Botke, represent the spirit of youth, but in this case they also commemorate a masque performed by students at the dedication of the hall. The Quadrangle Club on 57th Street (1920–21), although vaguely Tudor in its provenance, is informed by Howard Van Doren Shaw's innovative spirit. Built of red brick, it is more intimate, less monumental in character, and strongly marked by a kind of free sculptural effect. Heavy nonstructural buttresses standing in groups of three at the end and side elevations terminate in sloping slate-covered caps at the middle of the second story, well below the steeply pitched roof with its rows of gabled windows. The window groups are not fixed in dimension but vary with seeming irregularity in size and proportion. The most arresting feature is the chimney near the northwest corner: the base is a massive alcovelike embayment, above which the solid brick volume diminishes as it rises in a series of pitched slate-covered steps like those at the tops of the buttresses.

Beside Noyes and the Quadrangles, the numerous buildings of the Medical School that Coolidge and Hodgdon designed and the Oriental Institute of Mayer, Murray and Phillip seem comparatively sober in their restrained medieval dress. The university's own medical and hospital program was established in 1925, following a collaborative arrangement with Rush Medical College that had been inaugurated in 1902, and the various buildings of the initial plan were opened at intervals between 1927 and 1936 in the area between Ellis and Maryland avenues.[24] The Oriental Institute was constructed in 1929–31 at 1155 East 58th Street, a little east of the Quadrangles and a short block west of the Robie House. Beyond its academic facilities the structure includes the celebrated museum of Egyptian and Mesopotamian antiquities that stands as a great working memorial to James Henry Breasted, who played a major role in the establishment of preclassical archaeology in the United States.

The building constructed expressly for academic convocations and ceremonies was originally known simply as the University Memorial Chapel, but when John D. Rockefeller died in 1937 it was given his name as a conspicuous and expensive acknowledgement of the millions that the Rockefeller family had lavished on the institution (fig. 43). It was erected in 1925–28 at 1156 East 59th Street, where it stands as the most prominent building on the Midway. Designed by Bertram G. Goodhue Associates and erected at a cost of $1,500,000 (about $7,200,000 at the 1971 level), the chapel grew out of that innovative Gothic spirit by means of which Goodhue sought to adapt the medieval style to modern function and structure. The building is of considerable intrinsic size, having a capacity of 1,889 seated spectators, but it gives the impression of embracing a much larger interior volume because of its great unobstructed breadth and height.[25] It is a structural tour de force in load-bearing masonry, tile vaulting, concrete slabs, and steel framing, the combination of which expresses what the architects thought of as the contemporary equivalent of Gothic construction and brings the three materials together in ways that allowed each to work in the manner most appropriate to its physical properties.

The piers and buttresses of the nave walls and the tower, where they reach a maximum thickness of 8 feet, rest on fifty-six concrete caissons carried to bedrock at a depth of 80 feet below floor level, or something under 70 feet below street grade. Since the long side walls are opened to broad windows and since the architects had elected to retain full masonry construction below the roof, it was necessary to introduce massive arches over the windows to carry the load of the nave vaulting and the spandrel areas to the buttresses, which sustain both the gravitational load of the superincumbent masonry and the overturning thrust of the vault. The entire working fabric is composed of solid vitrified-brick masonry faced with the blue Bedford limestone that remained the campus standard throughout the age of Cobb. Above and within the walls, however, the structural system gives way radically to twentieth-century techniques. The groin-vaulted ceiling of the nave is a rigid shell of thin tiles constructed according to the Guastavino system and equally loaded in all directions, the ribs, as a consequence, having no bearing function but serving only to mark the groin lines.[26] An indication of the thinness of the tile shell is that the ceiling weighs only 300 tons for an area of more than 60,000 square feet. The ventilating system represents another step in the direction of air conditioning: the air, drawn in by fans at the northwest corner, is neither cooled nor dehumidified, but it is washed and heated before being circulated through the floor under the pews.

Rockefeller Chapel may claim some kind of record for the sheer quantity of emblematic and allegorical sculpture; the stone figures were executed by Lee Lawrie and Ulric Ellerhasen of New York, and the wood screen was designed in the architect's office and carved by Alois Lang of Oberammergau, Germany. The major figures on the south turrets and gable, all of them life-size, represent the history of Christianity and its Old Testament antecedents from Abraham to the Reformation—prophets, saints, teachers, theologians—and high on the buttresses framing the big south window are Matthew with the angel, Mark with the lion, Luke with the ox, and John with the eagle. Elsewhere on the exterior are a great number of allegorical and representational figures, heraldic emblems, and symbolic devices. The statues include representations of secular human types such as the Philosopher and the Scientist, allegorical figures of Faith, Love, Learning, and others, and depictions of specific persons, among them Theodore Roosevelt and Woodrow Wilson, with the arms of their respective universities, Harvard and Princeton. The arms of other universities cover a considerable area: those of ten state institutions adorn the walls at various places around the west windows, and those of ten foreign universities appear in similar locations around the east windows. At the level of the tower belfry are sixteen stone shields with emblems of the life and death of Christ, surmounted, twelve feet higher, by the allegorical figures of Faith and Love and the arms of eight more state universities. On the interior the chief features are the thirty-five-foot high stonework reredos and the panels and medallions on the ceiling of the apse illustrating Saint Francis's *Canticle of the Sun*, the latter executed by Hildreth Meiere of New York. Even a partial catalog of statuary and relief-work suggests that architecture here is overloaded by sculpture and other carvings, but such is not the case, simply because Goodhue and his designers had studied Gothic building well enough to know how to make decorative detail serve rather than obscure the forms of structural and enclosing elements.

Because of the University of Chicago's lavish investments in physical plant, Northwestern's building program might seem modest by comparison, but in truth the older institution created a wholly new campus close to the city's core during the great upsurge of civic expansion in the twenties. Although as a consequence it plunged deeply into the urban milieu, the continuing separation of the activities as well as the locations of the Evanston and Chicago campuses did little to break down the suburban insularity of both the undergraduate and graduate schools. Northwestern University had actually established professional schools in Chicago long before the great expansion of the twenties produced a unified campus group. The schools of medicine and law have existed very nearly since the university received its charter in 1851, both having been established in 1859; the dental school came in 1891, and the business school in 1908, but the evening division waited for the creation of more generous physical facilities. The possibility of uniting these scattered institutions into a new lakefront campus along East Chicago Avenue (800N) reached the promise of realization in 1923, when gifts of money and land (much of the latter provided by the McCormick family) allowed the trustees to inaugurate the construction program. The enviable architectural commission went to James Gamble Rogers in 1924, after his preliminary plans had been reviewed and recommended by two juries, and Rogers in turn selected Childs and Smith as his Chicago associates. The result, after seven years of construction, is the university's Alexander McKinlock Campus, which originally extended in a long narrow block lying between Chicago Avenue and Superior Street from Fairbanks Court (300E) to Lake Shore Drive (434E at Superior). Later additions of two hospitals, a dormitory, and an enlarged heating plant pushed the campus boundaries west of Fairbanks and south to Huron Street.

The original group forms a linear series of four distinct buildings on a site that offered several pleasing advantages: the narrow strip was long enough so that a considerable open area could be preserved along the east-west line; the termination at Lake Shore Drive gave one end of the campus a lakefront setting; and the presence of a large recreation field of the Park District on the north side of Chicago Avenue provided a broad sweep of open space up to Pearson Street (850N). The high steel-framed buildings, designed externally in Rogers's adaptation of collegiate Gothic to skyscraper requirements, thus enjoyed a more spacious setting than a downtown campus could ordinarily command, and the extensive grounds were once handsomely landscaped in the formal manner, although the post–World War II expansions have largely filled these with a succession of remarkably uninspired and inharmonious buildings. The first and largest of the McKinlock group is Montgomery Ward Memorial Hall, its fourteen stories surmounted by a five-story tower, which was built in 1925–26 primarily to house the medical and dental schools. Following it in order of construction are the eight-story Wieboldt Hall of Commerce, also opened in 1926, the four-story Levy Mayer Law School and Gary Law Library, 1927, and George R.

Thorne Hall, serving mainly as a law school auditorium, 1932. The structural engineers of these conventional works of pile-supported steel framing were F. William Seidensticker for Ward and Thorne halls, and Lieberman and Hein for Wieboldt and the law buildings. The anchoring and unifying element of the group, beyond the similarities of a simplified Gothic verticalism, is the nineteen-story Ward tower, which is conspicuous from the city sides of the area.

The fundamental motif in the design of all the buildings might conveniently be described as the Gothic of Rogers's Harkness Memorial at Yale University, but reduced in the case of the McKinlock group to continuous piers and buttresses, grouped windows opening the whole bay, and ornamental detail confined largely to the parapet level. The one distinctive element in the general plan is the arrangement of the law school and the law library in an asymmetrical U enclosing a handsome little quadrangle that still survives, though it is completely hidden from the street by later buildings. An unusual feature of interior construction and its architectural treatment was the original central heating plant and associated smokestack in Wieboldt Hall. The library and the classrooms of the School of Business Administration were situated above the boiler room, and the huge stack, with an internal diameter of 11 feet 3 inches, was set in a surrounding structure of stairways, elevator shafts, and toilet rooms, the entire enclosure continuing above the roof in a stepped and buttressed tower. The various buildings of the campus can hardly be said to constitute a distinguished architecture, but the original site plan and the individual designs give them some merit as civic art. The irregular limestone ashlar that serves as an exterior sheathing strengthens the unity imposed by the architectural style, and the arrangement of the whole group shows a progressive rise in irregular steps from the low auditorium of the law school group on the east to the buttresses and finials of the Ward tower on the west.

Before Northwestern's Chicago campus was completed in 1932 Rogers was awarded the commission for the showpiece of the long-established Evanston campus, where he was offered a site that architects of the urban milieu can seldom command. This most conspicuous work in the Rogers canon is Deering Library, planned in 1929 and constructed in 1930–32 at the inner edge of a spacious meadow that separates the two wooded halves of the James Wilson Campus, as the university's original Evanston area is known. The architectural design of the library was derived, with the candor that architects were proud to exhibit in the last days of eclecticism, from King's College Chapel of Cambridge University, a masterpiece of English collegiate Gothic that was completed in 1515. If one needed a model he could hardly have done better, but, unfortunately, in translating this work of medieval building art to the requirements of a modern steel-framed university library Rogers softened and thickened its chief working elements to the point where he sacrificed completely the tense and dynamic equilibrium of its attenuated forms. In spite of such defects as locating the circulation center on the floor above the main entrance and sacrificing stack area for lobbies and secondary reading areas, Deering was designed well enough to satisfy the needs of the university in 1930, when the library collection totaled 500,000 volumes. Keeping pace with enlarging demands, however, became an increasingly desperate struggle, and when the holdings reached nearly 1,000,000 volumes in 1967 the construction of a new library was obviously overdue.

Deering was meant to be impressive in its own right and to play the role of centerpiece in the old university plan. The Wilson Campus extends over a broad fourthousand-foot-long strip between Sheridan Road and the lake in east central Evanston. At the time the library was planned the campus group—including John M. Van Osdel's Old College (1855), the charming Gothic-Revival University Hall (1869), and two buildings by George W. Maher—had spread out irregularly in the form of a roughly balanced arc that centers on Deering Meadow and opens toward Sheridan Road. What the majority of buildings lack in architectural distinction is offset by excellent landscaping in the informal and heavily planted manner of the romantic tradition, in which the various structures are partly hidden by densely grown areas of trees and shrubs that extend north and south of the meadow. The library itself thus forms the crown piece of the arc, and the great stretch of grass in front of it constitutes a naturalistic contrast to the wooded areas. This nicely scaled and informal harmony survives throughout much of the Wilson Campus, but the subsequent construction of the Technological Institute (1941) and Kresge Centennial Hall (1956) introduced a geometric rigidity out of keeping with the idea of a lakeshore woodland, and the destruction of Maher's gymnasium in 1940 was simply an act of vandalism.

Among the scores of ecclesiastical buildings erected in Chicago during the years of the Burnham legacy, three command serious attention for architectural or structural features. The Fourth Presbyterian Church, built in 1911–12 at 126 East Chestnut Street, provided the city with a leading work from the hand of America's foremost apostle of medievalism, Ralph Adams Cram, and the associated parish house, opened in 1925, offers still another example of the unorthodox traditionalism of Howard Van Doren Shaw. The architectural character of the church, of course, is impeccable Gothic, which is faithfully carried out in the stained-glass windows of Charles Connick. Standing in ironic contrast to this Protestant monument is the Catholic School and Church of Saint Thomas the Apostle, at 5472 South Kimbark Avenue, constructed in 1921–22 as Barry Byrne's Chicago swan song. The solid planes of tawny brick are typical of Byrne's unique and largely unstudied talent, but the terra-cotta ornament of the jagged parapet, the pinnacles, and the panels above the doors, all of it the work of the sculptor A. Faggi, gives the complex a restlessness that suggests an unsure hand.

A structural masterpiece that irritates the sophisticated as much as it pleases the layman is the monumental Baha'i House of Worship that dominates a superb site in Wilmette, at the point where Sheridan Road curves downward from the Ridge Avenue spit and crosses the North Shore Canal. Many years and many talents went into the composition of this tour de force in reinforced concrete: the irregular flow of funds from a small but well-endowed sect meant that building was an intermittent process carried on mainly in the periods 1920–21, 1930–43, and 1947–52; the architect in charge of the design was Louis Bourgeois, and his associate was Alfred P. Shaw; the structural engineer was Allen B. McDaniel, with whom Henry J. Burt, F. H. Newell, and Benjamin B. Shapiro were associated; and the sculptor of the ornamental panels was John J. Earley. The finished work is essentially a lofty dome and drum standing on a two-tiered enclosure, the dome being divided by ribs into nine segments, and the drum and tabernacle having the form of nine-sided polygonal prisms. The dome rises to an overall height at the crown of 191 feet above the basement floor, which is identical with the average elevation of the sloping grade, or 165 feet above the high circular platform that constitutes the visible base. The dome is actually a double shell composed of panels of marvelously intricate filigree work in precast concrete. The nine ribs of the outer dome are carried on the columns situated at the corners of the drum and the upper tier of the tabernacle, but these columns are offset by half of a single central angle and thus fall on the bisectors of the lower-tier sides, where they are supported by peripheral beams spanning between the inner ends of massive radial girders. The columns of the inner dome are wholly independent of the outer framing system and are carried by their own bedrock caissons, which are separated in turn from those of the main tabernacle piers. It represents an ingenious modern variation on the double and triple domes constructed in masonry by Renaissance and Baroque builders, but if one looks for a decorative precedent he is more likely to find it in an orientalized Art Nouveau than in any of the older styles.

NOTES TO CHAPTER 5

1. Certain structural features of these now forgotten buildings deserve to be recorded: the County Building was possibly the first in Chicago for which column footings were supported on short wood piles, which were apparently used as a means of consolidating the soil under the footings; the City Hall stood on a concrete mat foundation, undoubtedly the first of its kind.

2. Internal column caissons for the City Hall and County building range from 4 to 8 feet in diameter, but those under the huge wall columns had to be expanded to a 10-foot diameter. The caisson wells, which were sheeted with 3-inch maple lagging, were dug by hand at a pace that set another one of those astonishing records of the days before the First World War: the entire operation was completed in eighty-six working days, between 5 January and 1 April 1909, with the crews working three eight-hour shifts a day, six days a week.

3. Franz Winkler, "Some Chicago Buildings Represented by the Work of Holabird and Roche," *Architectural Record* 31 (April 1912): 370. Some half-century after City Hall was opened its giant Corinthian order was to be one factor in determining the proportions of the openings between columns at the base of the new Civic Center (1963–65).

4. The decisions in question were handed down by the Illinois Supreme Court in four cases heard at intervals between 1890 and 1911 and arising from suits brought by Aaron Montgomery Ward against various organizations with plans to erect buildings in Grant Park. As a major property-holder on Michigan Avenue, Ward recognized that the value of the property was considerably enhanced by the presence of the open parkland and the lake east of the street. The rulings held specifically that before an above-grade structure may be built the builder must secure the consent of all the property owners on the Grant Park length of Michigan Avenue. This proved to be one of the rare cases in which permanent civic benefit flowed from private financial interests.

5. The trusses of the Art Institute wing are of a size that one might encounter in bridge construction. Each pair of parallel trusses spans 101 feet 3½ inches between bearings and stands 27 feet 3 inches deep, and the two trusses are spaced 53 feet 7 inches on centers. The bottom chords, which were made heavy enough to obviate the use of falsework during construction, are built-up box girders 48 inches deep. The frame and flooring were calculated for a floor load of 300 pounds per square foot on the lower level, so that sculpture could be exhibited, and 100 pounds on the upper.

6. The bequests of the Field family eventually reached a total of $20,000,000. The establishment of the museum's initial endowment and Field's role in it form an instructive chapter in the history of American philanthropy. This endowment, totaling $500,000, was made up of Edward E. Ayer's anthropological collection, valued at $100,000, and cash gifts distributed as follows: George M. Pullman, $100,000; Harlow N. Higginbotham, $100,000; James Ellsworth, Carter H. Harrison, A. C. McClurg, and Martin Ryerson, diverse sums together equaling $200,000. It required considerable eloquence on the part of Ayer to persuade Field to add his original $1,000,000; after that the department-store magnate's own enthusiasm was a sufficient motive.

7. The footings for the main wall piers standing between the vertical window groups rest on twenty-two piles each, and the secondary piers, which carry the steelwork of the main-floor frame, are supported by twelve piles each. The 60-foot piles of Georgian pine were cut off at a level 2 feet 6 inches below the surface level of the lake. The material of the fill on which the Field Museum appears to stand is largely sand placed by hydraulic filling (see pp. 195–96). The piers carrying the frame are monolithic concrete and stand 30 feet high above the footing plane.

8. The central portion of this nave was named Stanley Field Hall in honor of the man who held the museum's presidency for fifty-eight years (1906–64) and who was one of its major benefactors. The overall dimensions of the entire central area are 68 × 299 feet in plan and 75 feet in height to the ridge of the gable roof.

9. The James Simpson Theater, as it is designated, seats 953 persons and measures 95 × 100

feet in plan. The model for its peripheral lobby and colonnade of squared shafts must have been the bouleuterion, or council hall, of the Hellenistic cities. The particular work that formed the antecedent was probably the Bouleuterion at Priene (200 B.C.).

10. The chief departments of the Field Museum are those of zoology, paleontology, botany, archaeology, and anthropology. The distribution of the specimens in the collection is as follows: 3,000,000 plants; 2,000,000 insects and other arthropods; 1,000,000 fossil forms; 3,000,000 birds; 100,000 mammals; 200,000 reptiles and amphibia; 400,000 marine fauna; 50,000 archaeological and anthropological specimens; 170,000 volumes in the library. The collection of primitive art is considered the finest in the United States. The number of visitors in 1968 was 1,829,616, including 398,000 students from 6,800 school groups.

11. In 1968 the total income of the Field Museum was $2,825,000, 85 percent of which came from endowment income and 15 percent from the tax revenues of the Park District. This sum failed to meet the year's expenses by $400,000. The precise improvements needed to bring the building up to contemporary standards were broken down by the director, E. Leland Webber, as follows: renovation of wiring and electrical equipment, $1,500,000; air conditioning for the preservation of specimens as well as the comfort of visitors and staff, $3,000,000; covering and flooring light courts to increase space, $2,000,000; installation of escalators, renovation of exhibition halls (many have the drab, ill-lighted character of the traditional museum), cafeteria, and exhibits, sum unestimated; raising and stabilizing the ground floor, sinking on inadequately compacted hydraulic fill, $1,000,000. The last improvement must be completed before the expansion of the floor area can be undertaken. (E. Leland Webber, quoted in "Let's Go to the Field Museum," *Chicago Daily News Panorama*, 29 March 1969, p. 5.)

12. The individual gallery measures 30 × 90 feet in plan, the six together providing space for 132 tanks of different sizes, ranging from a minimum of 3 feet 6 inches by 3 feet 6 inches by 5 feet in depth (capacity 445 gallons) to a maximum of 10 feet by 30 feet by 6 feet in depth (capacity 13,500 gallons).

13. The water circulating system constitutes an unusual form of internal hydraulic technology so complex that only a brief outline must suffice for a description. Incoming water flows by gravity into a sump in the basement floor, from which it is pumped to a pressure tank near the roof, thence flowing by gravity to the reservoirs and the exhibition and reserve tanks. The supply is cleaned by drawing the water from the tanks to the reservoirs through filters that remove organic debris. At four points in this primary circuit the water is aerated by means of a subsidiary parallel circuit in which air compressors maintain a pressure of five pounds per square inch above atmospheric pressure. Heating of water is confined to the months of winter, late fall, and early spring and is accomplished by steam coils in the compartments of the gravity tank. In the same way chilling is effected by coils connected to refrigeration machines. All water pipes are an antimony-lead alloy that minimizes corrosion, an extremely important consideration in an aquarium with a closed circulation system. All pumps and refrigeration machinery are electrically operated.

14. The outer diameter of the planetarium chamber is 72 feet. The inner hemispherical dome, which constitutes the projection screen for the planetarium, has an inner diameter of 68 feet and a spring line situated 9 feet 10 inches above the floor of the chamber. The capacity of this enclosure is six-hundred spectators. The outside diameter of the outer dome is 82 feet.

15. The sheer size of the Fine Arts Building, associated with the multiplicity and exactitude of its classical details, may give it some kind of unique status. It extends 1,145 feet in

overall length, stands 120 feet in height from the elevated first floor to the crown of the central dome, and embraces 263,000 square feet in area of plan, for a total floor area of 600,000 square feet. The colonnades include 276 free-standing and engaged stone columns varying in weight from five to fifty tons each. Yet the derivative ornamental details are precise copies of the originals: the metope panels of the portico and the friezes of the connecting wings are reproduced at actual size from the entablature of the Parthenon; the caryatids are copied at an enlarged scale from the portico of the Erechtheion at Athens, each of the transplanted and expanded Athenian maidens standing thirteen feet high and weighing six tons.

16. If we measure the value of the museums in terms of the audience reached, there is no question of the civic importance of Chicago's cultural institutions. The attendance at the various museums in 1968 was as follows:

Museum of Science and Industry	3,166,429
Field Museum of Natural History	1,829,616
Art Institute	1,819,264
Shedd Aquarium	1,130,000
Adler Planetarium	571,264
Chicago Historical Society	233,230

Together they accommodated a total of 8,749,803 visitors, and the number grows year by year.

17. Forest Preserve District, *Land Policy* (River Forest, Ill.: Forest Preserve District of Cook County, 1950), p. 12.

18. Proceedings of the meeting of the Commissioners of the Forest Preserve District, 11 June 1946; quoted ibid., pp. 12–13. For the locations of Forest Preserve land, see pp. 000–00 and fig. 2.

19. Norman Mark, "Brookfield Zoo . . . ," *Chicago Daily News Panorama*, 10 May 1969, p. 5.

20. See table 5.

21. The attendance at Evanston Township High School was 1,700 at the time of the initial construction, but this was expected to rise to 3,000 by 1935; the postwar increase in suburban population, however, eventually brought the enrollment to more than 6,000.

22. The chief buildings constructed at the University of Chicago from 1910 to 1930, with their architects, are the following:
    South Quadrangle
        William Rainey Harper Memorial Library (1912); Shepley, Rutan and Coolidge
        Classics (1915); Shepley, Rutan and Coolidge
        Rosenwald (1915); Holabird and Roche
        Swift (1926); Coolidge and Hodgdon
        Bond Chapel (1926); Coolidge and Hodgdon
        Wieboldt (1928); Coolidge and Hodgdon
        Social Science Research (1929); Coolidge and Hodgdon
    North Quadrangle
        Ryerson Annex (1913); Shepley, Rutan and Coolidge
        Jones Laboratory (1929); Coolidge and Hodgdon
        Eckhart (1930); Charles Z. Klauder
    Outside the Quadrangles
        Noyes (1916); Shepley, Rutan and Coolidge
        Quadrangle Club (1921); Howard Van Doren Shaw

School of Medicine group (1927–31); chiefly Coolidge and Hodgdon
Rockefeller Chapel (1928); Bertram G. Goodhue Associates
Sunny Gymnasium (1929); Armstrong, Furst and Tilton
Chicago Lying-in Hospital (1931); Schmidt, Garden and Erickson
Oriental Institute (1931); Mayer, Murray and Phillip (the Goodhue Associates)
International House (1931); Holabird and Root

23. The architects, sculptors, and their academic advisors could have established their data a little more exactly in the matter of memorial sculpture. There were two geologists named James Hall, the earlier a Scotsman and an associate of James Hutton, the latter an American, and both are equally deserving of honor. As for Leonardo, one can make a good case for including his portrait, but not as the first to understand the meaning of fossils. The first to interpret them correctly was Xenophanes of Colophon (fifth century B.C.), but the medieval and Renaissance knowledge of fossils was derived chiefly from Aristotle, Strabo, and Avicenna.

24. The medical group included the following: Albert Merritt Billings Hospital, 1925–27; Roberts Memorial Hospital for Children, 1930; Chicago Lying-in Hospital, 1931; Home and Hospital for Destitute Crippled Children, 1931; William G. Zoller Memorial Dental Clinic, 1936. They are all steel-framed structures with limestone curtain walls.

25. The main dimensions of Rockefeller Chapel are the following: overall length, 265 feet; width at the transept, 120 feet; exterior height to the ridge, 102 feet; maximum interior height, 79 feet; overall height of tower, 207 feet.

26. The Guastavino system of rigid tile-shell construction was introduced in Chicago with the construction of North Western Station; for a discussion of the technique, see under the section on that rail terminal, pp. 258, 293.

6. The Structures and Arteries of Transportation

Street Railways, Rapid Transit, and Interurban Lines

The basic pattern of Chicago's widely ramifying and yet rigidly orthogonal street railway system had been substantially laid down by the time the Burnham Plan was officially launched. The numerous separate companies were progressively reduced in number and finally merged into the single corporation of the Chicago Surface Lines in 1913. It was the largest street railway system in the world, embracing nearly a thousand miles of line, and its already immense traffic increased steadily at an average rate of nearly 21,000,000 passengers per annum, from 482,000,000 in 1910, past 634,000,000 in 1913, to the high point of just under 900,000,000 in 1929.[1] The new system had no competitor at grade level until 1917, when the Chicago Motor Coach Company was established as a subsidiary of the Fifth Avenue Company in New York City to operate buses chiefly on Sheridan Road, Michigan Avenue, and North Lake Shore Drive, where there were, of course, no car lines. The comfortable double-deck buses and the attractive shoreline drive produced an astonishingly rapid expansion of traffic, the total volume multiplying twenty-three times between the first year of operation and 1929; moreover, the smaller decline of the depression and the greater increase of the years during and immediately following World War II indicated that the bus company enjoyed a much more stable traffic reservoir than the car lines, chiefly because its location allowed it to draw on a higher income group less disastrously affected by the depression.

It may be claimed that a street railway system capable of carrying nearly a billion passengers in a single year serves its city very well, and no vitally damaging charges of mismanagement and misoperation could be brought against the Chicago Surface Lines beyond the usual financial chicanery of the corporations. Yet the company suffered from handicaps that were common enough, and a city with the wealth and the planning tradition of Chicago deserved better than it received. The streetcar itself was an unwanted stepchild of technological development: it remained slow and clumsy, retaining its dangerous hand-operated doors and its power controller without the deadman control feature until a brief new order came around 1945, shortly before the street railway disappeared entirely. There was no fully developed integration of surface and elevated lines, in spite of the numerous transit plans that came and went in steady succession, and the concentration of streetcar lines and elevated structures at or above grade level in the Loop frequently led to chaos and congestion that nearly immobilized the urban core. The downtown tunnel system of Boston and Philadelphia gave them a much superior circulation in the central district, and the improved streetcar designs that appeared in Cincinnati and Saint Louis in the the twenties offered safer and more comfortable rides.[2] The beginnings of an underground system in Chicago came with the construction of the LaSalle and Washington Street tunnels under the Chicago River, but that was as far as this desperately needed improvement was destined to go.

The rapid transit system, on the other hand, was for the two decades of 1910–30 a reasonably efficient model of the elevated variety. A fair proportion of the wooden cars were progressively replaced by heavier steel types in 1913, 1923, and 1924; the separate companies that had multiplied and expanded since 1890 were merged into the single Chicago Rapid Transit Company in 1924, and a citywide system of transfers was gradually developed over the years. At the time of its greatest extent, which coincided with the opening of the Westchester branch in 1926, the company embraced 227.49 miles of track in a radial network of two-, three-, and four-track lines, carried an average of 627,157 passengers per weekday, and operated 5,306 scheduled trains in the same time period. The average speed of all express trains was a modest 18.5 miles per hour (24 in the case of the Evanston rush-hour express), but it was at least better than one could possibly achieve by driving a car over any combination of streets and boulevards. Under unusual circumstances the Chicago elevated was capable of extraordinary feats of mass transportation, the most impressive of which came on 24 June 1926, on the occasion of the International Eucharistic Congress held at Mundelein, Illinois, at the end of a branch line of the North Shore Railway. The Chicago Rapid Transit operated 320 special trains from its South Side terminals at Englewood and Jackson Park through the Loop to the Howard Street connection with the North Shore at the north city limits and carried 930,327 passengers in the twenty-four-hour period. This was accomplished without accidents, injuries, or serious delays, but it required a year of planning to bring it off. The highest annual total of passengers came in 1927, but the relatively slow decline thereafter, which included a modest recovery during the years of the Second World War, revealed that even a conventional rapid transit system was less vulnerable to automobile competition than the crawling surface cars.

The Chicago elevated, at the same time, suffered from serious defects, some of which still remain uncorrected. In the first place, the lines themselves fell substantially short of reaching the limits of the major industrial, commercial, and residential quarters of the city. The north, northwestern, and western areas were adequately served, but the South Side lines terminated at 63rd Street, far short of the extreme south city limit at 138th, and the southwestern neighborhoods had and continue to have no service whatsoever. Extensive areas within these large urban regions were well served by the suburban trains of the Rock Island and Illinois Central railroads, but a fully developed system required the coordinated operation of all three forms of public transportation. More serious from the standpoint of safety have been the continuing absence of automatic block signals on tangent track and the former operation of the heavy, high-speed cars of the North Shore and Aurora lines over the same tracks used by the lighter elevated rolling stock. Both practices were an invitation to disaster, and the wonder is that it was so long in coming.[3] As with many urban rail systems, however, the skill and the esprit de corps of operating personnel stood at a far higher level in the twenties than they were ever to reach in later years.

If the service offered by the various mass-transit companies was not always in the front rank, the riders may have derived some comfort from the fact that Chicago was the richest city in the world in the production of transit plans. The first came with the publication of the Burnham Plan in 1909 and was succeeded by six others of varying scope and detail. The second in the series was the most comprehensive: it rested on the most thorough analysis of public transit and offered the most ambitious proposal for its expansion and improvement. Under an ordinance of 31 January 1916 the city council appointed the Chicago Traction and Subway Commission and charged it to prepare a comprehensive report on the development of a unified system of surface, elevated, and subway lines. The voluminous document that emerged from the commission's investigations was produced in ten months, having been submitted to the council on 15 December of the same year. The chairman of the commission was William Barclay Parsons, a leading subway engineer and some twenty years later the author of a pioneer work in the history of technology, *Engineers and Engineering in the Renaissance* (1939). The enormously detailed report that was produced under his guidance included probably the most extensive study ever made of the operations of mass-transportation systems, street railway, motor coach, rapid transit, and railroad, and the interrelations of these operations with the populations, employment, residential distribution, and commercial and industrial regions of the city.

On this carefully prepared basis the commission offered its proposals, the chief features of which for the downtown area were the rearrangement and extension of the elevated Loop, the construction of two long north-south subways and a subway loop somewhat outside the elevated structure, and the construction of a streetcar loop within the bounds of the elevated equivalent. The vast program was to be divided into two phases, the first extending over the period of 1917–26 and estimated to cost $98,273,000, and the second covering more than twenty years, 1927–49, its cost running to a staggering $277,566,000. If these amounts were based on 1916 building costs, the equivalents for 1971 would be respectively about $900,000,000 and $2,540,000,000—enormous sums, but not unexpected in a city that created a lakefront recreational area with a 1971 replacement value of well over a billion and a half dollars. The essential validity of the Parsons plan with respect to subway lines is attested by the facts that the subway system which Chicago eventually built was in good part based on the report's proposal and that the subway loop system which reached the planning stage in 1970 closely parallels that of the report. The program for streetcar lines lost its meaning with the eventual abandonment of street railways in favor of buses.

The transit plans that followed the 1916 document proved to be anticlimactic, for they offered little that had not been covered more thoroughly in the earlier work. The third, prepared under the direction of R. F. Kelker, Jr., appeared in 1923 in response to the request of the council's Committee on Local Transportation. The fourth was submitted to the council on 22 October of the following year; its author-in-chief was Henry A. Blair, then president of the newly organized Chicago Surface Lines. The report included a proposal for a subway under State Street that was very nearly exactly followed in the construction of the present north-south underground line. The fifth plan, presented in 1927, was also prepared under the direction of Henry Blair, and the sixth consisted of an ordinance of 1930 that embodied various recommendations of the plans of 1916, 1923, and 1927. The depression reduced still further the likelihood of realizing any of these proposals, at least until President Roosevelt had launched the Public Works Administration, but the zeal for producing new plans remained as strong as ever. The council's Committee on Local Transportation directed its engineering staff on 15 December 1936 to undertake a study of the various transit systems and to prepare plans for their unification, expansion, and modernization. The resulting document, submitted on 22 November of the following year under the authorship of Philip Harrington, R. F. Kelker, Jr., and Charles E. De Leuw, was the first to be predicated on the two most obvious facts of contemporary urban life— first, the absolute decline of the city's population, and second, the rapidly increasing automotive traffic in the face of steadily declining transit patronage. The 1937 plan proposed chiefly the unification of all surface and rapid transit lines into a single company operated under the regulation of a transit commission, the transformation of existing lines into high-speed routes protected by automatic block signals, the progressive substitution of buses for streetcars, the construction of four subway lines, and the revival of suburban service on the Baltimore and Ohio Chicago Terminal and the Grand Trunk railroads. The program was partly realized in subsequent years through the construction of the two subway lines and the establishment of the Chicago Transit Authority, but the long-hoped-for improvement in service was much diluted by the self-defeating financial arrangements under which the authority was required to operate.

Over the main intercity routes within a radius of about eighty-five miles the electric interurban railways played a dominant role in the movement of passengers until the automobile began to eclipse all of its competitors in the mid-twenties. For the industry as a whole the high point of traffic came in the years 1915–19, but the three leading Chicago lines enjoyed a rapid and continuing increase in business through the early twenties because of the negotiation of trackage rights over the rapid transit lines and the Illinois Central Railroad. The North Shore Line gained the leading position in the extent and the quality of its service when it built a new double-track line between Howard Street at the Chicago city limit and North Chicago Junction in 1924–26 to provide high-speed through service between Chicago and Milwaukee. The generous financial resources for this venture came from Samuel Insull's Midland Utilities Company. The combination of hundred-pound rail, deep rock ballast, automatic color-light block signals, and heavy rolling stock which included dining and parlor-observation cars, guaranteed a quality of service that probably had no equal between 1926 and the beginning of the Second World War. The company was awarded the industry's Charles A. Coffin medal "for distinguished contribution to the development of electric transportation" at the convention of the American Electric Railway Association in October 1923. The great test of the North Shore's capacity to handle traffic again came on the final day of the International Eucharistic Congress at Mundelein, 20–24 June 1926, when the line safely transported 465,000 round-trip passengers between Chicago, Lake Bluff, and Mundelein (930,000 total for both directions). Speed combined with reliability and safety of daily service brought the North Shore national and eventually international recognition. In 1933 the industry's journal, *Electric Traction*, granted the company a permanent award of its Annual Speed Trophy after the railroad won it for three consecutive years. Two years later the British *Railway Gazette* commented that "the timings of the hourly trains between leaving the Milwaukee suburban area and entering that of Chicago make the whole service the fastest of its kind in the world."[4] Depression-born deterioration, heavy wartime traffic generated chiefly by the Great Lakes Naval Training Station, the impossibility of replacing worn equipment, and automobile competition ultimately drove the company beyond the point of salvation, but in its heyday it stood in the front rank.

The equivalent line south and east of the city was the former Chicago, Lake Shore and South Bend Railroad, which was reorganized as the Chicago, South Shore and

South Bend in 1925 and again substantially rebuilt and reequipped with Insull capital. The South Shore has been unique among interurban carriers in that it enjoys a heavy freight tonnage as a line-haul carrier which interchanges traffic with ten trunk and four belt lines, and this profitable business has enabled it to retain passenger service long after the latter became a deficit operation. The eventual control of the property by the Chesapeake and Ohio Railway brought a ready source of capital, but there have been few signs that the larger company plans to make any of it available. The Chicago, Aurora and Elgin, serving the western metropolitan territory, followed a similar history of massive upgrading of line and rolling stock by the Midland firm in the profitable decade of the twenties. This was succeeded by the wild swings of the economic pendulum—near collapse during the depression followed by the sudden revival of traffic in the brief period of gasoline rationing that was imposed during the wartime years. The coming of the postwar expressway found the Aurora line particularly vulnerable, and it was blasted out of existence as thoroughly and nearly as quickly as though it had been struck by a natural cataclysm. Besides the three Insull companies, filling the interstices of the metropolitan hinterland, so to speak, there was a network of single-car interurban lines that flourished for about a decade and a half after 1910, but only two of these, the Chicago and Joliet Electric Railway and the Chicago and Southern Traction Company, touched the city limits. They lived a precarious existence at best, and like the underground system of the Chicago Tunnel Company, which transported as much as 650,000 tons of freight in 1920 (fig. 59), they were destroyed in an incredibly short time by the competition of automotive transport. The few vestiges that remain are as completely hidden as the artifacts of ancient cultures.

Waterways and Boulevards

Burnham's proposal for harbor facilities at the "mouth" of the Chicago River (fig. 6), designed to form the north side of the grand waterfront scheme that centered on Grant Park, was predicated on the assumption of continued growth in the volume of miscellaneous waterborne cargo and passenger traffic. It was expected that both the lake and the river would share in this commerce, with the larger body of water taking the major portion, and since this proved true at least up to 1920, the city undertook to carry out this phase of the Burnham program two years after the plan was accepted. The result was a multipurpose harbor structure that was built immediately north of the river in 1913–16 under the authority of the Chicago Harbor and Subway Com-

Fig. 45. Municipal (now Navy) Pier,
foot of Grand Street, 1913–16.
Chicago Harbor and Subway
Commission engineering staff,
engineers. (Courtesy Chicago Historical
Society.)

mission, of which Edward C. Shankland was the chief engineer and William Artingstall the harbor engineer (fig. 45). Long known as Municipal Pier, this prominent feature of the Chicago shoreline is more modest in its dimensions than Burnham intended but still very impressive in total size, with a length of 3,000 feet and an out-to-out width of 292 feet. The major part of this length (2,335 feet) is given over to dock and shed space in the form of two parallel double-level buildings separated by a central 80-foot driveway containing the double-track rail line that constitutes the Harbor Branch of the North Western Railway. The remaining length of the pier was originally devoted to office space at the shore end and to areas designed for recreation and public ceremonies at the outer end. This public space was served by car lines carried on elevated bridges at the inner edge of the dock buildings, a service that was included because of Burnham's insistence on public access to the recreational areas of the lakeshore. It was this association of facilities built for commerce and pleasure that gave the pier its unique character.

The structure consists of a series of brick-faced, steel-framed enclosures carried by a concrete foundation in turn resting on extensive timber piling driven in depths ranging at the time from 20 to 27 feet. The first step in the construction process was the driving of three rows of piles into the lake bed on each side of the pier area, piling which then formed the support for the dock walls of massive concrete. Outside the wall line, timber sheet piling was driven around the entire periphery of the walled area to retain a protective fill of sand, clay, and rock which was placed by means of scows and hydraulic dredges. The piling is held in place by two devices, one a system of lateral steel tie rods extending under the concrete walls, and the other a rock fill on the outside face low enough to clear the bottoms of laden vessels. The steel columns of the various pier buildings are supported by footings resting on independent pile clusters. The office space, freight and passenger sheds, and recreational areas are for the most part framed in a conventional column-and-girder system, but the roofs of the sheds and the big public hall at the outer end are supported by three-hinged arched trusses that represent the most extensive installation of this form in American building. The hall is particularly distinctive: designed to seat four thousand spectators for concerts, entertainments, public ceremonies, and festivals, it measures 140 × 150 feet in plan and is covered by a skylighted vault carried on three-hinged arches with a span of 136 feet 8 inches and a rise of 74 feet 4 inches. The domed roof over the semi-circular end of the building is supported by radial trusses in the form of half-arches.[5]

Municipal Pier flourished as a dock and recreational facility throughout the decade of the twenties, but the steady decline of passenger and general cargo traffic and the economic attrition of the thirties left it largely deserted by the time of the Second

World War. Since American cities seldom sponsor public festivals and pageants, or enjoy a ceremonial life, the spacious recreational areas of the pier stood empty. The United States Navy used it as a training center for the crews of aircarft carriers in the wartime years of 1942–45, and the city leased it to the University of Illinois in 1946 to provide a campus for a two-year college, which survived in its watery setting until the university's own facilities were opened in 1965. The immense structure, with its floor area of more than a million square feet, redesignated Navy Pier after the war, was eventually converted to a cargo dock for ocean vessels, but on a much reduced scale beside its earlier status.[6]

If the traffic for which Municipal Pier was designed steadily approached extinction, the riverborne tonnage that reached the city over the Illinois Waterway held steady for the thirty years from 1900 to 1930, then suddenly doubled during the next decade following completion of the first five dams in the Illinois River that provided a guaranteed pool stage.[7] But the construction of the supplementary waterways in the Chicago area that eventually came to share this traffic with the existing Sanitary and Ship Canal was carried out by the Metropolitan Sanitary District in connection with the establishment of sewage treatment facilities for the area it served. All the phases of urban technology in Chicago having to do with natural and artificial waterways form a unified pattern that developed out of the problem of sanitation, even though the subsequent enlargement of these waterways was carried out in the interests of commerce. Thus the chronological succession of events and the interrelations among the various aspects of city building require that the focus shift to the operations of the Sanitary District.

Sewage disposal in the first thirty years of the district's history was accomplished by discharging raw sewage directly into the canal and eventually into the Des Plaines and Illinois rivers, where dilution and natural bacterial action in the flowing streams was expected to provide sufficient dissolved oxygen to oxidize the organic matter. The act of 1889 establishing the district fixed a minimum quantity of 3.3 cubic feet per second of diluting water per 1,000 persons, a volume that would necessitate a flow of 10,000 cubic feet per second in the canal by 1920 in order to serve the expected population of 3,000,000. But the maximum flow that could then be diverted from the lake was 8,500 cubic feet per second, and this was to be drastically cut to 1,500 cubic feet by the Supreme Court decision of 1930. Moreover, the problem was rendered acute because the oxidation potential of the various waterways was much reduced by industrial wastes and the effluent discharged into the canal from the Stockyards. The smell of the canal alone was sufficient to make it clear to the district trustees as early as 1910 that sewage treatment would be imperative no more than a decade later, and they initiated the necessary action before the year had ended by appointing a commission to investigate the hydroelectric potential of the canal and the methods of sewage disposal other than natural dilution and oxidation.

After a year's study of the entire problem and its possible solutions the commission issued a report that made two fundamental recommendations of profound importance for the urban ecology. The first proposed the construction of combined sanitary and storm sewers so that the natural runoff of rainwater would aid the discharge of effluent and so that the district might realize what seemed at the time to be the economy of building one system of sewers in place of two parallel systems. In a region of moderate rainfall (33.18 inches per annum at Chicago) such a system may work satisfactorily enough, but during heavy summer storms and periods of rapid snow melting the runoff may be so great that the treatment plants, if they exist, cannot handle the volume and must discharge raw sewage into the waterways. The second recommendation may be said to constitute the beginning of practical large-scale sewage treatment in the United States.[8] The essential feature of the proposal was the filtration and sprinkling of incoming sewage, followed by sedimentation in settling tanks called Emscher or Imhoff tanks after the initial user, the Emscher River Authority in Germany, or the inventor, Karl Imhoff, who was the chief engineer of the authority. The purpose of this process is twofold: first, to remove suspended solids before discharging the liquid into the waterway, and second, to allow partial oxidation in the settling tanks, further oxidation then being accomplished by means of sprinkling filters associated with secondary settling vessels. The commission finally made specific proposals for the construction of treatment facilities in the form of sixteen settling basins along the rivers and the canal, three secondary treatment plants with sprinkling or trickling filters, and four pumping stations on the north, near south, and far south sides.

The immense disposal system that the commission proposed was unprecedented in its scope and far-reaching in its potential for creating a healthy urban environment. Before any of its various phases were placed under construction, however, new discoveries in the treatment of sewage offered the possibility of substantially increased efficiency in the whole sanitation process. Investigators in England had tried as early as 1882 to purify waste water by blowing air through it under elevated pressure as a subsitutute for the expensive process of mixing dilute acids with the effluent, but systematic studies of the effects of forced aeration were not undertaken until 1893. Progress in understanding these effects seems to have been slow for an age characterized by a rapidly expanding knowledge of bacteriology and by the growth of a new symbiotic union between science and technology. The crucial discovery did not come until 1912, when investigators at the Manchester Sewage Works in England found that by holding back a certain proportion of flocculent organic solids and introducing them into the incoming sewer discharge, the time of oxidation by pressure aeration was contantly decreased as the quantity of retained solids increased. The cause of this phenomenon, now known as the activated-sludge principle, is that the bacteria necessary to the oxidation process multiplied in the accumulating organic matter. The next step, after the results of these experiments were published by E. Arden and W. T. Lockett in 1914, was to adapt the process to a continuous-flow operation on an adequate scale. The first successful plant to embody the new discovery was built at Withington, England, in 1917, and the first in the United States at Houston, Texas, in the same year.

These valuable developments came early enough to be incorporated in the Chicago program, and they constituted the chief ground for the realization by Sanitary District engineers that the numerous settling basins to be constructed along the waterways would be unnecessary. The implementation of the commission's plan involved a three-fold construction program in addition to the steady extension of the primary sewer system that had been put in place by 1907.[9] The first step was the construction of a subsidiary network of sixty-foot canals to carry effluent from the proposed treatment plants, to equalize the flow of water in the Sanitary and Ship Canal, and to reverse the flow of the Calumet River. The first of these waterways is the 8-mile-long North Shore Channel, completed in 1911, and the second is the 16.2-mile Calumet-Sag Channel, whose construction dragged on from 1911 to 1922 because of piecemeal congressional appropriations. The two subsidiary channels, the main canal, and the natural streams give the city a total of 71 miles of navigable waterways (fig. 1). Paralleling the expansion of surface waterways has been the construction of seventeen pumping plants scattered over the metropolitan area to supplement the inadequate gravity flow of combined waste water and surface runoff.[10] The first two phases of the Sanitary District's program had been nearly completed before the initial treatment plant was placed under construction in 1921. The four plants that constitute the core of the Chicago metropolitan system were opened to service between 1922 and 1939, one on the far South Side of the city proper and three in suburbs north and southwest of the city limits.[11] The architectural design of the various buildings provides another excellent example of what we have called the Chicago industrial style. The simple blocklike masses, done in dark-red brick with limestone trim, are strongly articulated by means of heavy continuous piers at the column lines, recessed spandrels, and deep window reveals.

The method of purification at the Chicago stations, as we have seen, was not originated by the district's engineers and scientists, and it falls discouragingly short of providing adequate treatment for the population (from 5 to 10 percent of the sewage ordinarily goes untreated); but since the system is easily the largest in the world, the techniques that have been refined over the years are of major importance in sanitation technology. The activated-sludge process under normal rainfall can provide secondary treatment for 95 percent of the sewage, but this proportion drops under heavy storm runoff. The incoming waste material in its aqueous vehicle enters the plant through bar screens equipped with automatic cleaners for removing large solid pieces, which are then ground in hammer mills and sluiced back into the stream of incoming sewage. The milled solids and water are pumped into the preliminary settling tanks, where any single gallon of the mixture remains for about thirty minutes (the capacity of the individual tank is 855,000 gallons). The settled sludge is drawn off the bottom of these vessels into aeration chambers in which filtered air is pumped through the highly liquid mixture by blowers driven by steam turbines. The waste in the oxygenating tank is "seeded" with a small quantity of bacteria-laden sludge drawn from the batch that had previously been partly oxidized—the activated-sludge process that may be said to constitute the heart of the operation. If the volumes of organic material, air, and water are properly proportioned, the essential bacteria multiply at a rate sufficient to oxidize the wastes during the three-to-four-hour period that the mixture is held in the aeration tanks.

After oxidation the wastes flow into the settling tanks, circular in outline and with conical bottoms, from which the settled sludge is drawn off and conveyed by underground pipes to the sludge control building, while the liquid is pumped into any one of the district's three canals, whence it eventually flows into the Illinois Waterway.[12] Inside the control building the sludge remains in concentration tanks for four and one-half hours, during which it is treated with ferric chloride to speed the coagulation process and hence the spearation of the solid from the liquid, which is returned to the incoming sewage.[13] The highly concentrated sludge-water mixture left as a residue from this separation flows to drum-shaped vacuum filters, from which the relatively dry "cake" (82 percent moisture, as against 98 percent for raw incoming sewage) is conveyed to a pug mill where it is mixed with dry sludge to bring the solid-liquid ratio to 60:40. The sludge then passes by gravity into flash-drying units where the remaining moisture is rapidly evaporated, the source of heat being a mixture of standard combustion gas and inflammable sludge vapor. The dry product, having a maximum moisture content of 5 percent, is a commercial fertilizer that can be produced for sale at the rate of five hundred tons a day at the district's largest plant. What is not sold presents a disposal problem that has yet to be finally solved. This vast and intricate system works well enough except during periods of heavy rainfall, when the combined storm and sanitary sewers convey so much water to the treatment plants that it is impossible for oxidation to take place in the aeration tanks. The result is that the mixture of runoff and raw sewage is discharged into the canal system, and if the rainfall is heavy enough to threaten flooding, the flow in the main canal may be reversed, thus discharging untreated sewage into the lake.

The subsidiary waterways of the Chicago system were designed initially to carry effluent from the treatment plants into the Illinois River, but it was quickly discovered that 60-foot canals with a depth sufficient for barges and shallow-draft river tugs are prime commercial arteries. The result was that the North Shore Channel soon began to carry a bulk-cargo traffic chiefly to the warehouses and building-materials yards scattered along its length. The Calumet-Sag Channel, ideally located to carry barge tows from the main canal across the south city limit to the Calumet industrial district, experienced a sudden upsurge of traffic after the completion of the last two dams in the Illinois River in 1939. The Corps of Engineers estimated its capacity at 1,000,000 tons per annum at the close of World War II, but the waterway carried more than 2,000,000 tons in 1948 and about 6,500,000 tons ten years later, a volume which proved to be the limit of its capacity. The corps had estimated that this could be increased to 18,000,000 tons per year if the waterway were widened to 225 feet, a long-overdue operation that the engineers finally initiated in 1955.

Two further improvements were necessary to continue the program that would maximize the efficiency of Chicago's extensive system of natural and manmade waterways. The earlier of the two was the straightening of the Chicago River that Burnham had recommended in the plan of 1909. Along a length extending roughly from Congress Street (500S) to 18th Street the river swung in a wide arc to the east, resulting in tight reverse curves in the stream itself and an awkward layout for the yards and main lines of various railroads, especially the approach of the Baltimore and Ohio Chicago Terminal to Grand Central Station. The replacement of this curve by the present walled and straightened course of the river, accomplished in 1928–30, not only improved the stream as a commercial waterway, but also made it possible to disentangle the huge rail ganglion in the area of Canal and 15th Street (p. 286). The second improvement was the construction of the controlling lock at the "mouth" of the river by the Corps of Engineers and the Sanitary District in 1936–38. The installation was necessary, first, to maintain a uniform flow of water in the river in spite of changes in the lake level arising from precipitation, wind action, and barometric variations and, second, to limit the diversion of water to the 1,500 cubic feet per second fixed by the decision of the United State Supreme Court in 1930. The cost of this project, totaling $58,630,000, was borne by a grant initially made by the Federal Emergency Administration of Public Works, later designated simply as the Public Works Administration.

The expansion of waterways and sanitation facilities in the Burnham period was paralleled by a continuing enlargement of the city's water supply system. What we might designate as the middle phase in this development extends intermittently from 1910 to the time of World War II, when the first of the filtration plants was nearing completion. Three intake cribs were added to the original group—the Edward F. Dunne, 2 miles off the foot of 68th Street (1910–11); the Wilson Avenue, 2.1 miles off the foot of that artery (1917–18); and the William E. Dever, 2.65 miles off the shore end of Chicago Avenue (1934–35). The Wilson Avenue installation was subsequently put on a standby status; only the Dunne and the Dever now remain regularly in use, and they are supplemented by the shore intakes of the South District and Central District Filtration plants.[14] The rapid growth of the built-up areas and of the metropolitan population required a constant extension of the water tunnel system and a multiplication of the associated pumping plants. From 1910 to 1930 a total of 24.92 miles of reinforced concrete tunnels was placed in service and four pumping stations were constructed.[15]

The intake structures are unique works built to withstand the severe and at times highly destructive forces of hydrostatic pressure, wave action, currents, and ice. The Dunne crib of 1911 represents a mixture of traditional and modern forms of building in timber, masonry, concrete, and steel. The entire enclosure is circular in plan and rises from a foundation composed of a timber grillage that rests on a compact layer of lake-bed sand at a depth of 32 feet below the mean level of the water surface. The lower portion of the crib wall, of timber construction 26 feet thick, extends from the top of the grillage to about 8 feet below the water surface, at which point it gives way to a reinforced concrete wall faced with stone to provide protection against the ice. This cylindrical structure is the crib proper; above it stands a masonry-walled house with a conical roof supported by radial ribs and trusses of steel. The water-intake system consists essentially of two steel-shell shafts that extend into bedrock at 146 feet below the water surface. Eight ports spaced at equal intervals around the crib wall near the bed of the lake admit water through gates and fish screens to the intake shafts, through which the water descends by gravity to the supply tunnel now serving, in this case, the South District Filtration Plant. Until this plant was placed in service in 1947, however, no Chicago drinking water was filtered, because under ordinary conditions—if they could ever be said to exist—the lake water was clear enough to make it unnecessary; but natural turbidity, the pollution from shipping, and the threats of massive pollution attendant upon flooding of the Calumet River led the commission on sewage disposal to recommend in 1910 the early filtration of the water. The cribs that followed the Dunne differ from it in construction chiefly by substituting steel and concrete for the timberwork of the older structure. In the Dever, for example, the foundation is a steel grillage and the walls are built up of masonry-faced concrete.[16]

If the boulevard system that grew out of the Burnham Plan had no necessary physical or technological connection with the waterways of Chicago, it was nevertheless closely associated with the lake and the main river in a visual and a formal sense. Burnham, of course, saw the streets and the boulevards as devoted mainly to wagon and carriage traffic, but the number of automobiles was increasing at a rate sufficient to multiply the total more than ten times between 1910 and 1920, and on the through drives the automobile traffic exceeded the horse-drawn at the very beginning of the decade.[17] The generous width of the major arteries proposed in the plan suggests that the authors foresaw quite accurately the traffic to be expected in the coming years. The most valuable step in carrying out the arterial program, which began with the construction of the Roosevelt Road viaduct and the widening of that street (completed in 1912), was the erection of the Michigan Avenue bridge—the original "Link Bridge" in Chicago—in 1919–21. The engineer in charge of the design for this project was Thomas G. Pihlfeldt, the city's engineer of bridges, and the architect was Edward H. Bennett, coauthor of the Chicago Plan and staff architect of the Plan Commission. The first double-level bascule span in the city, its lower level was originally planned for commercial vehicles serving the river docks, but the opening of Wacker Drive and the decline of river track converted the lower deck to part of the northward extension of the new drive between Wacker and Grand Avenue (530N). The completion of this structure opened the way to the intensive commercial development of the Near North Side, in which the Wrigley Building led the way (pp. 98–99), and also compelled the abandonment of the Rush Street bridge, since its retention would have transformed the rush-hour traffic congestion on the south side of the river from intolerable to hopeless.

The widening of Ogden Avenue as the major southwest artery in the plan's double-diagonal system was carried on by stages from 1921 to 1924. This thoroughfare extends from Clark Street, along the west edge of Lincoln Park near Armitage Avenue (2000N), southwestward to the west city limit (4800W, 2500S), but the widened portion terminates at Sacramento Boulevard (3000W) in Douglas Park. The lower half of this length is a modestly landscaped boulevard characterized by the separation of through and local traffic that Olmsted had inaugurated for the South Park systems in 1869. The numerous railroad overpasses across Ogden are massive concrete structures whose attractive texture was obtained by sandblasting the surfaces to expose the dark flinty aggregate. A more impressive accomplishment than may be found in any of the interior arteries, however, was the construction of Wacker Drive along the south bank of the river in 1925–27, the first step in Burnham's hoped-for transformation of that stream into Chicago's equivalent of the Seine. The new artery took the place of West South Water Street, which was the first residential street in the city, once having been lined with the cabins of the original settlers, and for many years thereafter was the public produce market of Chicago. This colorful, lively, and unbelievably chaotic institution served the expanding city well enough until 1925, when the construction of the boulevard compelled the removal of the market and its many small entrepreneurs to the newly constructed steel-framed buildings that fill the two blocks extending from Morgan (1000W) to Racine (1200W) between 14th and 15th streets. This was the initial example of the forcible relocation of business establishments under the Burnham Plan and serves to remind us that the bulldozer technique of urban renewal was one of Baron Haussmann's legacies in Paris. Wacker Drive was the first two-level boulevard in the world, but the absence of the promenades that were originally planned and the presence of a heterogeneous mixture of buildings and parking lots along the western portion prevent it from being the work of civic art that Burnham envisioned. From the structural standpoint, however, Wacker is impressive: it is the most massive work of flat-slab concrete framing other than railroad viaducts and freight terminals, and its river side forms a handsome work of bridge design in the tradition of monumental classicism, with massive piers clothed in rusticated masonry and a sturdy balustrade topping the narrow horizontal bands that mark the edges of the upper deck.[18]

The most celebrated of all the vehicular arteries to grow out of the Chicago Plan is Lake Shore Drive, although it must be said at the outset that Burnham conceived it as a connected series of scenic park drives rather than as the high-speed overloaded traffic artery it became. Since such a system of winding pleasure drives had been laid out in Lincoln Park long before the adoption of the plan, the city first concentrated its attention on the South Side portion of the new boulevard, that part which was to extend from the river southward to Jackson Park. Grant Park had long been established, and the filling to the south of it for Burnham Park and what was for some time called Leif Ericson Drive was under way by 1917 (pp. 195–96). The construction of the drive and the associated connecting viaducts over the adjacent Illinois Central tracks very nearly kept pace with the reclamation process: the inner drive through Grant Park (later designated Columbus) from Monroe Street to Roosevelt Road was completed in 1923; the construction of the 23rd Street viaduct came in 1923–24, to provide a connection with the city street system at the temporary south end of the outer drive, which was opened from Randolph to 23rd Street in 1926. Construction of this parkway southward from 23rd followed soon after the raw hydraulic fill had settled sufficiently to take the traffic load: the length extending from 23rd to 39th streets, with the connecting viaducts at 31st and 39th, was built between 1925 and 1929, and the remaining portion, extending to 57th Street at the north side of Jackson Park, with the cross-viaduct at 47th Street, was laid down in 1927–32. Thus the whole vast complex of parks, drives, museums, yacht harbors, and beaches lying south of Grant Park was created out of the open water itself in an interval of only eighteen years, a schedule that allowed it all to be opened shortly before Chicago launched its second world's fair, the Century of Progress Exposition, in 1933. The subsequent construction of an expressway interchange, airport, exposition hall, and parking lots has done irreparable damage to the lakefront, but it has not yet eclipsed the grandeur of this mighty vision.

The comparable work on the north side—that is, the construction of a multilane high-speed boulevard and the bridge that joins the two systems—was delayed until the depression years of the thirties, so that the state and the federal government had to undertake what the bankrupt city could no longer even contemplate. The reclamation work in the Lincoln Park area and the associated building of the park drives represented a continuous process carried out over the years from 1911 to 1933, but the great expansions that filled out the present configuration of parkland and beaches was largely an accomplishment of the extravagant twenties.[19] The only interruption to this program came in November 1913, when a lake storm carried away 300,000 cubic yards of new fill between Diversey (2800N) and Cornelia Avenue (3500N). The inner boulevards of the park, such as Cannon and Stockton, which went back in their origins to the nineteenth century, were narrow two-lane pleasure drives, but those segments of the older Lake Shore that lay between Ohio Street (600N) and Cornelia were laid out chiefly between 1910 and 1930 on a more generous 45-foot width.

Simultaneously with the spectacular lakefront activity, the municipal government was carrying out other Burnham proposals in inner areas of the city. The chief elements in this program were the construction of the Roosevelt Road viaduct, the widening of Roosevelt, LaSalle (together with the now-unused streetcar tunnels under the river and Wacker Drive), Ogden, Ashland (1600W), Damen (2000W), Western (2400W), Kimball (3400W), Cermak (2200S), and Archer (the second of the long southwest diagonals), the conversion of portions of Western Avenue to boulevard links in the West Parks system, and the northward extension of Kimball Avenue as McCormick Boulevard, mostly a county project, since the major length of the drive lies adjacent to the North Shore Channel through Skokie and Evanston. The widening and elevation of Canal Street from Randolph to Roosevelt Road was carried out in conjunction with the construction of Union Station (1916–25) and was intended to be the first step in the planned conversion of that thoroughfare into a monumental double-level boulevard, but this part of the great scheme was never realized, although the railroads spared neither expense nor talent in their share of the work.

The impetus behind this unparalleled program of civic improvement was not to spend itself until the depression, but disturbing signs of trouble ahead appeared as early as 1925. Charles H. Wacker, chairman of the Plan Commission and the most energetic apostle of the Burnham scheme, was forced to conclude that further realization of the plan was approaching an impasse from lack of capital, an ironic difficulty that arose not from any shortage of money in Chicago but from the municipal debt limitation imposed by the outmoded constitution of Illinois.[20] The per capita debt of Chicago stood at $46.35 in 1925, well below the level of any other major American city, and at the time there was every reason to believe that it could be increased several times without jeopardizing the financial soundness of the city.

Wacker saw the continuing realization of the plan as something of the greatest value to the business community as well as to the citizens who enjoyed the beaches and the parks and their children whose education was enhanced by the museums and the zoos. He saw the enormous benefits the plan had already conferred in balanced terms, and he spoke from what seemed to him to be an unassailable position when early in 1925 he publicly urged the Association of Commerce to use its authority and prestige as a lobby to work for an immediate increase in the debt limit arbitrarily imposed on the city. His emphasis on planning as a business proposition was echoed with exaggerated zeal by Robert Craik McLean, the editor of *Western Architect*. "Mr. Wacker appeals to the Association of Commerce," he wrote, "because he believes the business men of Chicago must provide a suitable plant in which the city's business —their business—may be operated. He looks upon the city in the light of an industrial plant, the efficiency of which may be greatly increased by proper planning, but the capital for expansion of which is withheld by a legal limitation."[21] Unfortunately, the later ascendency of the viewpoint that the city is a business seeking to maximize its tax revenue, combined with the Neanderthal mentality of a rural-dominated legislature, eventually assured the destruction of a genuine community-oriented planning in spite of the billions poured into public works.

Steam Railroads and Railroad Stations

The sheer immensity of the railroad plant of Chicago and the steady expansion though rapidly changing pattern of its traffic make it readily understandable that the resources devoted to rail improvements during the Burnham period very nearly matched those that went into parks and civic institutions. The largest facilities placed in service during the expansive years before the depression, and the most apparent to the traveling public in their character and value, were the two Canal Street stations, North Western and Union, but their construction was accompanied by extensive improvements in line, signaling, and operations undertaken by all the big passenger carriers in Chicago. Many of these changes, such as the replacement of mechanical interlockings by the electropneumatic variety, could be recognized only by an expert in railroad technology, whereas others, like the electrification of the Illinois Central suburban service, were of such obvious and immediate benefit that the whole city rejoiced; all of them, however, played varying though important roles in the steady increase in the speed of trains and in the safety and efficiency of their operation. The improvements were planned primarily to meet the challenge of constantly expanding rail traffic in the early years of the automobile, but as it turned out many of them proved to be of greatest value in making it possible for the railroads to handle the flood of traffic that came with the war years of 1941–45.

The project that inaugurated this climactic age of railroad reconstruction was the building of the new terminal of the Chicago and North Western Railway at Canal and Madison streets. The company's first unified station had been completed in 1881 at Kinzie and Wells (later the site of the Merchandise Mart), but in spite of the fact that the subsequent addition of an annex along the south side increased the number of tracks from eight to fifteen, the rapid growth of both through and suburban traffic compelled the company to think in terms of a new and much expanded facility shortly after the turn of the century. The Canal Street site having been selected, the railroad awarded the commission for the design of the station building in 1906 to the architects Alfred Hoyt Granger and Charles S. Frost—both of whom were related by marriage to Marvin Hughitt, the North Western president—and to the structural engineers Edward C. and Ralph M. Shankland. The design and construction of the track layout, approach, control devices, and associated bridges were carried out under the authority of the company's engineering departments. The clearance of the densely built site between Canal and Clinton streets and the excavation for the foundation work delayed the erection of the building proper until 1908, and the finished complex was opened to the public in the late spring of 1911. Among the great metropolitan terminals that

Fig. 46. Chicago and North Western
Railway Station, West Madison Street
from Canal to Clinton, 1906–11. Frost
and Granger, architects. (Courtesy
Chicago Historical Society).

Fig. 47. Chicago and North Western
Station. *Left:* Plan of the second floor
and the track-platform layout. *Right:*
Plan at the street level.

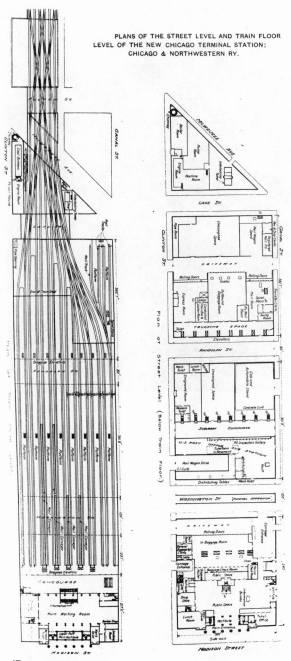

PLANS OF THE STREET LEVEL AND TRAIN FLOOR
LEVEL OF THE NEW CHICAGO TERMINAL STATION;
CHICAGO & NORTHWESTERN RY.

Fig. 48. Chicago and North Western
Station. Approach tracks, as they
appeared during a typical morning rush
hour in 1949, when the steam
locomotive was still dominant.

48

were built between 1900 and 1930, works that brought the art of their design to its highest level, the North Western is a leading example of maximum traffic-handling capacity obtained through the highly efficient use of the available space. Planned and opened at a time when the number of rail passengers was increasing at such a rate that the total more than doubled during the first two decades of the new century, the station was carefully designed to accommodate large moving crowds concentrated in short intervals of time (figs. 46, 47).

Although the station building embodies several structurally notable features, the erection process involved no unusual difficulties except for the foundation work. The presence of large quantities of water in the heterogeneous stratum of glacial till immediately above bedrock made it impossible to reach the bearing stratum by the customary method of open caissons. The contractor was forced to excavate each caisson well through the water-bearing material within a closed chamber whose interior was placed under sufficient pneumatic pressure to prevent the water from flowing into the caisson enclosure. The opening was lined with the usual tongue-and-groove sheeting and the concrete was poured into the lowermost portion of the cylindrical volume immediately on removal of the steel lock that roofed the pressure chamber. This costly and time-consuming process had to be repeated for all the 176 caissons that support the footings of the station headhouse.[22] The overall dimensions of the station complex that rises above these extensive foundations are 320 feet in width by 1,112 feet in length from the Madison Street entrance to the outer limits of the train shed. The station building (or headhouse, as it is traditionally called) extends 218 feet on the north-south line, but the sixteen-track train shed is divided into a shorter length of 741 feet covering seven tracks and a longer of 894 feet covering the remaining nine. The total area of station and approach is forty-three acres, of which approximately thirteen may be said to comprehend the station building and its appurtenant structures and thirty the approach system. It is the combination of these generous dimensions with expert planning that gives the station its extraordinary capacity.

The station forms a double-level system in which the elevated track-and-platform area is carried on a bridge structure over the mail-handling facilities and the east-west streets that occupy the space below it. The four-story headhouse is sheathed in masonry done in a rusticated Renaissance style that reaches an overpoweringly monumental character at the main entrance on Madison Street, where the entablature of the portico is carried on six huge granite columns 61 feet in height (fig. 46). This entrance is supplemented by two others, one at the side along Canal Street, and another on the interior, reached from the automobile rotunda that opens off Washington

Street, but with the completion of the Daily News Building in 1929 a second-floor access way was built in the form of a covered pedestrian bridge spanning Canal Street between the two buildings. In this way suburban passengers could enter the south entrance of the Daily News and walk directly to the concourse level of the station. On the interior of the headhouse the first floor, situated at the grade level of the surrounding streets, was given over mainly to service facilities such as ticket offices, automobile entrances, telephone and telegraph enclosures, stairs, elevator lobbies, and a special waiting room for immigrants equipped with baths and a medical center; but because of the virtual disappearance of the railroad's through traffic, the public areas on the ground floor and the main entrance were eventually closed, restricting all pedestrian movement to the Canal and Washington street entrances. The second floor has always been the active heart of the station, for it is here that the main waiting rooms, dining rooms, concourses, track and platform area, and suburban ticket offices are located (fig. 47).

The supporting structure of the first two floors is for the most part a straightforward column-and-beam system made up of rolled sections, but the long spans in various places and a number of offsets in the column lines required built-up plate girders ranging from 20 to 55 inches in depth, the deepest being restricted to girders carrying offset columns at the ends of short cantilevers. The outer ends of all peripheral girders rest on cast-iron plates inserted in the brick piers of the outer wall. The one exception to the consistent use of steel-framed concrete flooring throughout the building constitutes one of the two most impressive architectonic features of the station, but unfortunately it is now hidden within the area of the closed first floor. The entire waiting room floor and a 50 × 100-foot area east of it are carried on the most extensive installation of the time of Guastavino thin-tile vaulting in the United States, covering an area of more than 25,000 square feet.[23] The floor loads above this space are sustained by a system of tile domes springing from elliptical arches that form the four sides of the rectangular bays, each measuring 18 feet 4 inches by 27 feet 6 inches. The tile arches, however, are supplemented by 18-inch steel girders imbedded in the concrete infilling that brings the space above the extrados of the domes up to the level plane of the second floor.

The third floor, which is now little used but originally contained special rooms for invalids and women with small children, forms a U-shaped enclosure around the 175 × 202-foot void of the waiting room and concourse and is framed in a conventional column-and-beam system. The fourth floor, disposed in an open rectangle around the same internal space, is framed in a similar way except for the long clear spans over the concourse, where the members under the concrete roof slab are six Pratt trusses with a span of 62 feet 6 inches between columns.[24] The main waiting room, which rises in height far above the roof level of the headhouse, forms the grandest spatial, formal, and structural feature of the station. This great enclosure, measuring 102 × 202 feet in plan, is covered by an elliptical vault that stands 84 feet above the floor at the crown. The inner surface is finished in buff terra-cotta tile laid in a herringbone pattern and supported by steel purlins that are joined to the lower chords of seven arched Pratt trusses with a clear span of 90 feet 4 inches and a rise of 31 feet.[25]

The train shed, lying entirely north of the headhouse, is the Bush type, in which a series of low parallel vaults of concrete are carried on steel arch ribs spanning between rows of columns situated along the center lines of the eight platforms. Rectangular skylights are set directly in the concrete slab in a linear series along either side of the narrow smoke slots that are centered above the tracks. The shed was raised two feet in 1954 to clear dome cars and the double-deck, or gallery, cars used in suburban service, but the essential structure, with its long parallel lines and its rhythmic accents of columns, ribs, and girders, has remained unchanged. Outside the limits of the station complex stand the usual appurtenant structures of a big terminal: interlocking towers, steam generating plant, housing for various kinds of electrical equipment, signals, and switch machines, all of them seemingly discrete elements but actually bound together in the intricate web of a huge megastructure.

The overall efficiency of North Western Station as a working entity rests in good part on the generous provisions for the operation of trains. The approach line extends from the station throat to the junction of the Galena Division with the joint line of the Milwaukee and Wisconsin divisions (approximately on the latitude of Kinzie Street) and consists of six main tracks, over which trains can be moved in either direction (fig. 48). All switches, movable frogs, and signals are controlled by an electro-pneumatic interlocking, the central machine of which is located in the tower at Lake Street. Train movements north of the station throat are governed entirely by three-position upper-quadrant semaphores placed on overhead gantry bridges, while those through the approach and within the platform area are governed by dwarf signals, each consisting of a white circular disk bearing a red semaphore band and two lenses, respectively red and yellow, for night indications. The entire installation of signals, interlocking, and switch machines has remained unchanged since it was completed in 1911, and as a consequence North Western Station is one of only two metropolitan terminals in the United States in which light signals have not replaced the older motorized or semaphore variety. From the standpoint of the movement of trains, however, this has made little difference, since the railroad long ago adopted high-intensity signal lights like those used in color- or position-light systems.[26]

The headhouse was designed to accommodate 250,000 passengers per day, and although the terminal has seldom handled more than half this number, there is no reason to doubt that it could comfortably do so. Moreover, the construction of the pedestrian overpass across Canal Street in 1929 freed the surrounding thoroughfares from enough traffic for the busy facility to be easily integrated into the urban circulation system. In the second full year after the station was opened the number of passengers had grown to 49,394 per weekday, divided between 32,583 commuters and 16,811 through passengers, at the time the highest number of through passengers for any Chicago station.[27] The total traffic rose steadily to the time of the depression, dropped drastically, then slowly and irregularly increased to the level of 90,000 passengers per day in 1970, but by this date the through traffic had virtually disappeared, whereas the suburban volume reached new records.

If the number of passengers was to be expanded to the full quarter-million, however, the obvious question would be whether the track layout could accommodate the necessary number of trains, and in this respect no guiding principles have ever been developed, so that train-handling capacity has to be determined from an empirical investigation of operating practices in the United States. The most striking conclusions to emerge from such an inquiry are that only two terminal stations (South Station, Boston, and Broad Street, Philadelphia) have been regularly used to their full capacity and that all the others built since 1900 have reserve capacities sufficient to sweep most urban expressway systems clear of traffic. In more precise terms, any station designed according to the standards of the leading metropolitan terminals that followed the Boston facility can comfortably and safely handle at least thirty trains per track per day.[28] It is obvious that the North Western Railway could operate five hundred trains per day on its sixteen tracks, and given the usual average of commutation systems of five hundred passengers per train, the station could at last be used on the scale for which it was intended.

The construction of North Western Station and the simultaneous preparation of Burnham's Chicago Plan enormously stimulated interest in the fascinating, perplexing, and never-to-be-answered question of the unification of railroad terminals in Chicago. Various official and unofficial bodies in the city produced more proposals on the subject than any other kind of public document: the first was submitted by the architect and planner Frederick A. Delano in 1906; the majority were concentrated in the three years following the acceptance of the Burnham Plan (1910–13), but these, like all that came after them, proved to be abortive. There were good reasons for interest in the question and for the ultimate failure of this concern to produce any tangible results. First and most obvious was the sheer magnitude of the problem—the tangled miles of railroad trackage, the extensive areas of prime urban land preempted by rail facilities, the inefficiency of the system, the multiplicity of stations and rights of way; yet it was the very extent of the problem that revealed the civic benefits that would follow from its solution. Although these matters were well understood by all who gave them serious attention, there were obstacles that always led to frustration. Foremost, perhaps, was the narrow corporate and competitive viewpoint of the railroad companies: they all saw advantages in what they had, and with investments in station properties substantially amortized, they resisted all changes that appeared to involve sacrifices. In addition there was the changing pattern of rail traffic, the total volume of which expanded steadily up to 1920, then just as steadily and somewhat more rapidly entered into its long decline.[29] Finally, there was a persistent tendency on the part of both planners and railroad engineering staffs to exaggerate the scope of the problem: the approximately 1,500 trains per day operated at the Chicago terminals during the twenties could have been accommodated in a single double-level station of fifty loading tracks, well below the sixty-six-track total of Grand Central Terminal; but by the middle of the decade there was an even simpler solution than that, one that lay ready to hand, as we shall see.

Yet the difficulties, real and imagined, only stimulated the theorists to greater efforts, and they offered seventeen plans, in addition to the Delano and Burnham proposals, up to 1913. Several railroad companies submitted plans of their own, but these understandably favored existing arrangements and were drawn up with little consultation among the other carriers. The Chicago and Western Indiana (the proprietary company of Dearborn Station) proposed a three-terminal system with two terminals on Roosevelt Road between State Street and Stewart Avenue (400W) and the third to be the North Western's new facility. The Union Station Company and the Illinois Central offered a simpler scheme involving two terminals to be constructed, of course, on the sites of the existing Union and Illinois Central stations. The Chicago Plan Commission's program was very nearly a combination of the railroad plans: there were to be four stations, the North Western, a new Illinois Central, and two new facilities on Roosevelt Road flanking the river (the latter two to be built with loop tracks). The most imaginative schemes but not always the most practical came from various architects. Jarvis Hunt proposed a single tremendous union terminal with a track system arranged in such a way that all station tracks at the ends opposite the approach would merge into a single loop surrounding the headhouse. This vast complex was to occupy a site bounded by Roosevelt and 16th Street on the north and south and by State Street and the river on the east and west, an area of twenty blocks. Irving and Allen Pond, favoring a multiplicity of small facilities, suggested five stations, the North Western, a new Illinois Central, and three extending in a linear series along Canal Street from Monroe to 16th. The tracks of the different stations would not run through on tangents but would form a series of loops to be joined at the north and south ends by a huge 270-degree loop that would encompass the whole group. The scheme was fantastic and revealed more than anything else that these imaginative architects had little understanding of the operation of a railroad terminal. Guenzel and Drummond proposed a similar tandem arrangement of even greater size, extending from Lake Street to 17th Street along Canal, and of equal impracticality. Various engineers offered assorted plans in which the number of stations ranged from six facing a great public square extending along Canal Street between Madison and Jackson (Josiah Gibson) to a single double-level station with entires by reverse movements as at Saint Louis and New Orleans (Henry A. Goetz).[30]

The one engineer and planner in this field who could speak with authority was Bion J. Arnold, and in 1913 he submitted four alternative proposals that were equally feasible and revealed a more careful study of the situation than any of the numerous forerunners. The first of these Arnold designated a "unit station," although it was in fact a linear series of four stub-end stations which were to include the new North Western terminal and to extend between Canal Street and the river from Madison to Maxwell Street (1330S). The three below Madison were to be connected by continuous passing tracks which would serve as an approach, the whole constituting a rather awkward scheme that could have been much simplified and thus much improved by adopting the principle of two stub-end track systems incorporated in a single terminal that was later embodied in Union Station. The other three plans that Arnold submitted involved two, three, and four stations, one of which was North Western and the remainder new structures on the sites of Union, the Illinois Central, and the area centering on Roosevelt Road and Franklin Street.

Two years after the publication of the Arnold plans the architect William Drummond offered a novel proposal that appears to have been suggested by Grand Central Terminal in New York (1903–13) and the Michigan Central Station in Detroit (1912–14), since it involved a program of air rights construction to be carried on simultaneously with the building of rail facilities. The central feature was a linear series of through stations situated in a two hundred-foot depressed right-of-way lying immediately adjacent to a double-deck river boulevard, apparently in the Canal Street area, although this is not specified. Above each station, which was to present a triple-arch entrance to the drive, was to rise an office skyscraper, the whole group forming a long row of widely spaced towers closely related visually and in plan to the railroad facilities.[31] All the railroads entering the city were to use this rail "highway," as Drummond called it, which he conceived as a kind of rapid transit operation expanded to the magnitude of the steam railroad. The scheme was full of valuable civic possibilities, as the belated air-rights development of the Union Station property eventually revealed, but it was also full of probably insurmountable difficulties. The great defect in all these proposals for stations arranged in linear series, especially if they were to be situated in a relatively narrow right-of-way, as Drummond suggested, arises from the problems of operating empty trains to and from coach yards, locating such yards, and operating loaded trains through or past one station on their way to another. Plans of this kind have consequently never been adopted, however promising they seem in their concentration of rail facilities in a minimum area, although Drummond was confident that his program would work for a city five times the size of Chicago.

The war and the postwar depression brought a brief hiatus in merger plans, but this ended in 1921, when John F. Wallace, chairman of the Chicago Railway Terminal Commission, submitted a report on terminal unification to Mayor Thompson and the city council. Wallace's proposal proved to be more valuable for its summary of legislation affecting railroad and lakefront developments in Chicago than for the unimaginative unification program, which involved three electrified passenger stations on existing sites, North Western, Union, and Central, and a consolidation of inner-city freight-handling facilities. The next group to join the procession of station planners was the Committee on Coordination of Chicago Terminals, an organization that again revealed greater capacity for gathering useful statistics than for creating feasible unification plans. The committee's report of 1927 is marked by a thorough and possibly unique analysis of the handling of railroad freight in the Chicago Terminal District during the four years from 1923 to 1927, along with the now familiar proposal to consolidate passenger facilities into three large terminals.

Undismayed by the failure of the railroads and appropriate public bodies to act on any of these plans, the city council appointed still another Committee on Railway Terminals and was pleased to accept the report prepared in 1933 under its direction by the consulting engineer Edward J. Noonan. It proved to be the last until depression, war, and the drastic decline of rail passenger traffic required and made possible an entirely new approach to the question. Noonan proposed, once again, a three-terminal scheme embracing the existing North Western and Union stations and a new lakefront station to be situated on the east side of Michigan Avenue between Randolph and East Wacker Drive, thus breaking for the first time with the tradition of Roosevelt

Road sites that Burnham and all the other planners had followed. This alteration in the customary arrangement arose from the committee's belated recognition that the city's central business district had expanded north of the Loop rather than south, as Bennett and Burnham had hoped as well as expected. The Randolph-Wacker terminal, embracing twenty tracks, was to provide facilities for all the roads using Central, Dearborn, LaSalle, and Grand Central stations, and its adjacent coach yard, occupying the site of the Illinois Central freight yards, was to be covered by a spacious plaza, which in itself would have been an immense improvement over the disreputable tracks and parking lot that continue to disfigure this area. Under the plan of the Noonan committee the extensive suburban service of the Illinois Central was to continue to be housed in the narrow terminal at Randolph, squeezed between Michigan Avenue and the new station tracks, and this service was to be supplemented by a new rapid transit subway that eventually was to replace all of the remaining commutation service offered by other railroads. It was a bold scheme with considerable merit, but the state of the economy in 1933 made it seem downright chimerical.

While this rage for creating paper diagrams was approaching its climax, a group of West Side railroad lines was taking the first steps in executing the vast Union Station project, a great railroad and civic complex that embraces much more than a single passenger terminal and that remains the largest unified work of public construction undertaken in Chicago outside of the lakefront development. It was not quite the grand scheme that Burnham proposed; yet the irony of it all is that if the engineers of railroad stations had ever paused long enough to make a careful analysis of potential terminal capacity in 1915, they would have learned that the two post-1910 facilities in Chicago could easily have been designed to solve Chicago's seemingly baffling problem at two strokes. The initial phase in the reconstruction of the dense mass of railroad trackage lying along Canal Street was the building in 1912–14 of the Wisconsin Central Railway's freight station on the south side of Roosevelt Road between Canal and Clinton streets.[32] The concrete-framed, brick-clad headhouse represents a nice adaptation of classical pilaster and entablature to the requirements of industrial and transportation buildings, but the element of greatest structural interest is the elevated track and platform layout that extends southward along Canal Street. Constructed as a continuous slab on mushroom columns and covering an area of more than 800,000 square feet, it represents one of the largest examples in the United States of the Turner flat-slab system adapted to rail loadings. Various hands were involved in the design of this handsome freight terminal, among whom the primary author was C. N. Kalk, chief engineer of the railroad company.[33]

The next step and properly the first to be conceived as an organic part of the Union

Fig. 49. Pennsylvania Railroad Freight House, 323 West Polk Street, 1915–18. Price and McLanahan, architects.

Fig. 50. Pennsylvania Railroad Freight House. The main street elevation and the tower.

49

50

Station program was a more ambitious and impressive work that must be examined in terms of the plan as a whole. The Pennsylvania Railroad Freight Terminal, constructed in 1915–18 over the entire block extending from Polk Street to Taylor Street between the south approach of Union Station and the river, is an overlooked masterpiece of Chicago architecture that took form only after a long controversy such as often accompanies great urban projects (figs. 49, 50). By 1913 the popular demand for a new and genuine union station as proposed in the Burnham Plan had reached the level where it was politically expedient for the municipality and the railroads to take positive action in response to it, and as a consequence the new Union Station Company was organized on 3 July to undertake the construction of new freight and passenger stations and to coordinate this work with the associated civic projects required for the full realization of the Burnham Plan. The ownership of the new company followed that of the old Union Station of 1880 in being divided equally among the Pittsburgh, Fort Wayne and Chicago, the Pittsburgh, Cincinnati, Chicago and Saint Louis (the two roads constituted the bulk of the Pennsylvania Lines West of Pittsburgh), the Chicago, Burlington and Quincy, and the Chicago, Milwaukee and Saint Paul railroads, while the Chicago and Alton remained a tenant. The railroad companies and the city faced a formidable task: in addition to building a new passenger terminal and relocating the associated streets, which together were to cost $75,000,000, the Pennsylvania, Burlington, and Alton planned to build new freight stations at a further cost of $8,000,000 at 1913 prices, or $24,000,000 by the time they were completed, and all parties were to be involved in real estate transactions totaling $45,000,000.[34] Beyond these activities the federal government was to undertake the construction of an associated metropolitan railway mail terminal, the first in the United States, and a new central post office to serve the city of Chicago.

Since the headhouse, passenger concourse, and train concourses of the proposed station would cover all the land extending between Canal Street and the river from Washington Street (100N) to Harrison (600S), the existing freight terminals in the area, which were approaching the limits of their capacity in 1910, had to be relocated and expanded. The arrangement adopted for the location of the Alton and the Burlington facilities was to place the Alton on the east side of the new station approach, between Congress Street and Harrison Street, and the Burlington on the west side, immediately below Harrison, and they were eventually built on these sites during construction of the passenger facilities. It was the much larger station of the Pennsylvania Lines that became the occasion of controversy. Planning for this structure had been undertaken as early as 1911, when it became obvious that the scattered freight-handling facilities of the Fort Wayne company needed to be expanded, unified, and much improved in efficiency. The road's original plan, adopted by the time the station company was established in 1913, was to build a unified terminal in the two-block area bounded by Van Buren and Polk streets on the north and south and by Jefferson and Des Plaines streets on the east and west, a block to the west of the Canal Street properties. The proposal met with the unanimous opposition of the city council and the Plan Commission—an incredible assertion of public interest to a later day—because the station would lie directly athwart the Congress Street axis that was to join Grant Park and the Civic Center. But the rich and powerful Pennsylvania Railroad was not easily dissuaded from the aims of its subsidiaries. The city council accordingly engaged the engineer John F. Wallace, and the City Club of Chicago the engineer and planner Bion J. Arnold, to review the railroad's plans in the fall of 1913 and to recommend a solution acceptable to all the parties. Unfortunately, this traditional approach to public controversy only made matters worse, because Wallace largely accepted the railroad plan while Arnold offered an alternative scheme, which was to locate the freight terminal on the east side of the station approach at Polk Street (800S), three blocks south of Congress.

The whole matter was thus brought to an impasse that lasted for nearly six months and was not finally broken until the city agreed to accept the railroad plan for the passenger station, with the provision that Congress remain a through street by locating it on a viaduct over the south approach, and the Pennsylvania Lines accepted the Arnold plan for establishing the freight station below Polk between the approach tracks and the river.[35] The unhappy consequence of all these negotiations was that the construction of both the freight station and the passenger station was postponed until after the beginning of the war in Europe, with the result that the entire project was subject to delays, rapidly increasing costs, and labor difficulties that compelled a long suspension in the construction of the passenger terminal. The city council passed the ordinance authorizing the construction of Union Station and its associated facilities on 23 March 1914, but the autumnal equinox passed before the ponderously moving railroad bureaucracies accepted it on 23 September.[36] The building of the Pennsylvania freight station was initiated in 1915 and completed in 1918, but the passenger terminal was put off until 1916 and was then repeatedly frustrated by what the economists might call the unsettled state of the world.

The plans for all the working elements in the freight-handling facilities—structure, tracks, platforms, elevators, other electrical and mechanical utilities—were designed by the engineering staff of the Pennsylvania Lines West of Pittsburgh under the direction of Thomas Rodd, chief engineer of the company, leaving only the exterior treatment of the brick curtain walls as the work of the architects, Price and McLanahan. The excellence of their achievement is still apparent, even after the increasingly careless maintenance and the atmospheric corrosion of more than half a century (fig. 49). Restricted to the handling of nontransfer less-than-carload freight, the huge steel-framed building contains more than 1,500,000 square feet of floor area on its five levels, making it perhaps the most generously scaled structure of its kind.[37] The tracks lie at the original grade level, which was reserved exclusively for rail lines in the Union Station project, and for this reason all streets were elevated sufficiently above grade to clear passing trains, necessitating in the case of the freight terminal the construction of cross viaducts for Harrison, Polk, and Taylor streets. In spite of the increased operating costs and the inefficiency of handling and moving cargo arising from dependence on elevators, the multistory plan was adopted because of the high price of land in the Canal Street corridor and because of the limited width of the land available under the plan that the railroad agreed to accept, which restricted it to the narrow zone between the approach tracks and the river.

The rectangular volume of the station building encloses five transverse light courts under skylights with sawtooth profiles in section. Grouped in banks between adjacent courts are thirty-two elevators, most of them reserved for transporting cargo between the warehousing and the loading-unloading floors, but a few providing access to the subterranean tracks of the Chicago Tunnel Company for the disposal of ashes and rubbish. The long silhouette of the whole mass is repeatedly interrupted by slightly projecting wings and by low upward-swelling curves near the end bays, but the feature that dominates the surrounding area is the octagonal clock tower rising 190 feet above the street level at the north end of the building (fig. 50). The visible manifestation and the emblem of the metropolitan rail terminal throughout much of its history, the tower in this case also provides space for two utilitarian functions: the first three floors serve for the storage of records, and the next two stories embrace a 50,000-gallon water tank to maintain supply and pressure for fire protection. The remaining three are given over to the clock mechanism, which no longer functions, and apparently empty space topped by a pyramid roof. The interior construction of the main volume is distinguished chiefly by the massive concrete floor slabs common to railroad freight stations and warehouses, the maximum loading factor being 300 pounds per square foot and the associated slab thickness 11 inches.[38] The huge red-brick enclosure, punctuated by a few small windows, is marked by a bold massing that is a little restless in the numerous projecting bays, in the shallow piers, buttresses, and corbels, and in the deep massive arches at the end bays, but it possesses a monumentality that adds powerful rhythmic accents to the long rectilinear vistas of its rail and river setting.

The freight terminal at Polk Street formed a fitting overture to the immense Union

Station project that extends for nearly two miles from Lake Street to 14th in the area squeezed between Canal and the river. The complexity of the railroad facilities themselves, the long negotiations with the Chicago Plan Commission and the city council, the elevation of Canal Street for much of this length, the construction of viaducts to carry east-west arteries over the station approach tracks, changes in plans and in the architectural and engineering designers, the need to maintain an old station while building the new around it, war and postwar depression—these along with the usual delays and frustrations attendant upon great civic works stretched out the period of construction to nine years, from 1916 to 1925. When it was completed everyone could readily understand that it was one of the grandest railroad developments in the world; yet no one, apparently, has appreciated the staggering irony of the whole thing: with minor changes in design and track arrangement, and in conjunction with the newly opened North Western Station on Madison Street and the Illinois Central suburban terminal at Randolph Street, which was then in process of electrification, Union Station could have handled all of Chicago's rail passenger traffic even at the level that existed in 1925. The architects of this masterpiece of planning were originally Graham, Burnham and Company, who were replaced on the dissolution of that firm in 1917 by Graham, Anderson, Probst and White. The structural engineer was William Braeger, and the chief engineer Thomas Rodd until his death in 1919, when his place was taken by Joshua d'Esposito.

Following the establishment of the Union Station Company in 1913, the engineering staff of the organization worked out the main features of the overall program, so that Graham, Burnham and Company were able to complete their preliminary plans shortly after construction was authorized in March of the following year. A number of major characteristics were to make this complex scheme unique among railroad terminals and their appurtenant structures. The big headhouse, embracing the usual collection of waiting rooms, restaurants, unloading areas, barber shops, toilets, and other facilities, was to occupy the entire block on the west side of Canal Street between Adams and Jackson, and to serve as the lower portion of a projected twenty-story office building. The concourse building, a wholly separate entity above the street grade, was to stand on the east side of Canal, where the area of the building, the train concourses, and an access drive along the east side would entirely fill the space between the street and the river. Abutting the concourse building on the north and south sides were two groups of stub tracks with their associated platforms, or two stub-end terminals, originally to consist of fourteen tracks each and two passing tracks along the river but later reduced to ten tracks on the north side and fourteen on the south. An extremely broad connecting passage, as wide as the main concourse itself, was to extend under the street, thus uniting the two buildings while providing space at the same time for ticket offices, baggage checking facilities, a small shopping area, a subsidiary waiting space, and telephone and telegraph centers. Under the tracks and the concourse floor and incorporated into the track-platform areas the designers planned an intricate system for the handling of mail, express, and baggage which has never been improved in other terminals of any type, including airports, where its equivalent devices remain grossly inferior. A separate mail and express terminal was to stand on the east side of the south throat and a new central post office was eventually to rise over the south terminal tracks between Van Buren and Harrison streets, although this later element was not included in the original plans. A broad vehicular drive opening into cab stands was included in the rear area of the headhouse building, the passage arranged so that one could drive in a continuous line from the entrance at Clinton and Adams streets to the exit at Clinton and Jackson.

All these features were embodied in the Union Station complex as built, except that the office building was never raised to a height above eight stories, but the architects' original design for the headhouse (1914) was considerably modified before construction began in 1916 (fig. 51). In the initial plan the building was to be surmounted by a longitudinal clerestory under a gable roof, from each side of which three subsidiary gables were to extend transversely, each of them ending in a broad arched window. The immediate ancestor of this design must have been Pennsylvania Station in New York (1903–10), since there were obvious similarities between the two. The original plan was superior to the one later executed by Graham, Burnham and Company and their successors by virtue of its openness and the play of its clerestory volumes, and the change in favor of the present heavily monumental building with its immense colonnade along Canal Street appears to have been dictated primarily by the decision to incorporate the headhouse into an office building. The retention of all the essential features of the plan, however, gave the great terminal its unique character of being divided physically and visually into distinct but firmly unified elements. Union Station has remained the only double stub-end station with two separate track systems and a division into two distinct buildings, the only one in which baggage, mail, and express are handled on platforms isolated from those used by passengers, and the only one in which interior drives and loading-unloading zones are generous enough to eliminate vehicular curb space along the surrounding streets.

It was on this basis that the station company and the city placed the whole project under construction in 1916. The elevation of Canal Street to a level sufficient to clear trains on the two westernmost tracks, the raising of the Chicago Rapid Transit Company's elevated line over the street and the south tracks, and the replacement of the

Fig. 51. Union Station, Canal Street
between Adams and Jackson. The
original design by Graham, Burnham
and Company, 1914. The two renderings
differ in minor details.

51

272

52

Fig. 53. Union Station. *Top:* Plan at the street level. *Bottom:* Plan at the track and concourse level.

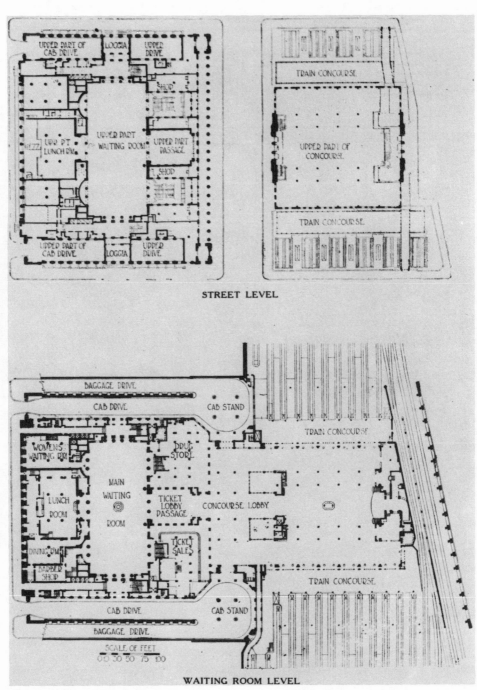

STREET LEVEL

WAITING ROOM LEVEL

Fig. 54. Union Station. *Top:* Section along the east-west axis of the station building and the concourse. *Bottom:* Interior of the passenger concourse, looking west, toward Canal Street.

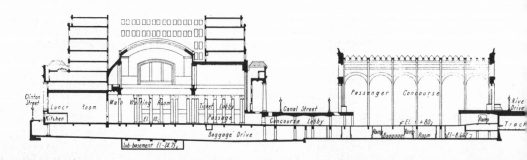

Fig. 55. Union Station. Interior of the passenger concourse. (Courtesy Chicago Historical Society).

55

Fig. 56. Union Station. Cross section of the train shed showing the framing over a platform.

Fig. 57. Union Station. The south approach, showing the interlocking tower at the left, a dwarf signal in the foreground, and overhead signals on street viaducts in the background.

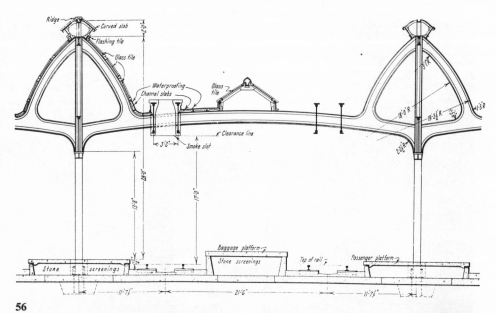

56

57

old bridge structure by a new truss span were accomplished by the end of 1917. The construction of street overpasses, approach tracks, subsidiary buildings, and the foundations for the main station buildings was undertaken in the same year, but delays arising from wartime exigencies meant that little of this phase other than the caissons for the column footings was accomplished before 1919. The postwar depression inhibited further activity for two years: the resumption of work was marked by the erection of the six-story mail terminal on a narrow strip over the south track layout in 1921–22, and by the initiation of construction of the headhouse and concourse buildings in 1922.[39] It was this phase of the long and tedious process that brought exasperating frustrations to the traveler as the old station building and its thousand-foot train sheds were progressively demolished in 1923–24 while construction preceded on the new terminal.[40] The earlier structure had disappeared entirely before the end of the latter year, but the official opening day for the new work was delayed until 15 May 1925.

Before the air-rights constructions of later years the concourse building stood isolated beside the river at the center of a five-block area where only the tops of the train shed light monitors were visible above the street grade, so that in any overall view the big headhouse surmounted by its office floors easily dominated the whole group (fig. 52). This eight-story structure, measuring 319 feet 10 inches by 372 feet in plan and occupying a full city block, was designed on the exterior as a conventional limestone-sheathed office block in which the only features suggesting a railroad terminal are the massive colonnade along Canal Street and the two generous entrances strongly marked off from the smaller doorways along Adams Street and Jackson Boulevard that provide access to the office floors. Each of the public entrances opens into a spacious lobby measuring 40 × 85 feet in area and enclosing a broad stairway that descends to the central waiting room. The headhouse enclosure is penetrated from the rear, or Clinton Street elevation, by subsidiary pedestrain entrances opening to corridors running the width of the building and by the vehicular drives that form a continuous U-shaped passage immediately inside the north, south, and west walls (fig. 53, bottom; the connecting drive along the west wall is not shown because it is below the waiting room and concourse level). All avenues of movement form a symmetrical pattern expertly planned to converge on the main waiting room. This rectangular space is almost overpowering in its monumental scale: it lies under a vaulted skylight of glass set in steel ribs that stands 112 feet above the floor at the crown, and its periphery is defined by twenty enormous Corinthian columns that rise to the springing level of the vault. The columns, of course, are steel enclosed in plaster, but the wall sheathing of the waiting room and entrance lobbies and the stair treads are Roman travertine. The lunchroom and the elegant walnut-paneled dining room (one unit in the Fred Harvey chain) lie to the west of the main enclosure, and the toilets, barber shop, and beauty shop extend beyond the northwest and southwest corners. The allegorical figures of Night and Day occupying two free-standing columns were executed by the New York sculptor Henry Hering, and the interior color scheme, like that of the Civic Opera House, was designed in consultation with Jules Guerin.

The concourse building between Canal Street and the river—demolished in 1969 for the third Gateway Center building—was much smaller than the headhouse both in horizontal dimensions and in visible external height above the street grade, but its interior represented the most distinguished architectural feature of the whole complex (figs. 54, 55). It was a simple blocklike mass with few windows in the walls, the interior light coming chiefly from the ridge-and-furrow skylight in the gable roof and the continuous openings in the sides of the low vaulted enclosures covering the train concourses that flanked the main mass. The primary entrances, situated in the narrow end elevations, were recessed behind two Doric columns in antis and led to broad stairways that descended to the concourse floor (details of windows, entrances, and skylights are best illustrated in fig. 52). A novel and ingenious feature of the circulation system was the presence of subsidiary entrances on Adams Street and Jackson Boulevard opening into steeply sloping ramps that terminated at the floor level underneath the landing of the divided east stairway. These passages were provided for commuters, who came by foot almost entirely from the Loop area over the two east-west thoroughfares. The undivided interior of the concourse building was the finest spatial and architectonic feature of the entire station complex, and it was the only enclosed space that rivaled the grand concourse of Pennsylvania Station in New York, on which its design was in part based (figs. 54, bottom, and 55). The roof consisted of three parallel longitudinal vaults of glass and tile carried on a superbly articulated yet fluent system of steel arch ribs supported on slender built-up columns of steel angles and latticework strap. The central vault spanned 84 feet center-to-center of columns and rose 90 feet clear to the crown. Flanking the main concourse on each side was the broad, relatively low train concourse that lay immediately outside the train gates and provided access to all the tracks on either side of the terminal.

The concourse was connected to the waiting room and other facilities in the headhouse by a broad passage designated the concourse lobby, which passes under Canal Street and hence lies under a low flattened vault over its central passage (figs. 53, bottom, and 54, top). Baggage and parcel checkrooms flank the main passage on both sides, while the numerous ticket offices occupy much of the remaining area along the south side. This lobby thus transforms the two separate parts of the terminal at street grade into a single unified space at track level. The most obviously unique characteristic of Union Station, however, was that the great concourse (and the new concourse designed to take its place) formed a central space that served two stub-end terminals placed back to back. The smaller of the two, abutting on the north side of the concourse, consists of ten tracks serving the Milwaukee railroad; the larger, on the south side, embraces fourteen tracks, since it serves three companies, the Pennsylvania (now Penn Central), the Burlington, and the Chicago and Alton (now Gulf, Mobile and Ohio).[41] Lying along the east sides of the two track systems are two passing tracks and one through track, which is served by the easternmost platforms of each side and is hence useful for accommodating extremely long trains, or passenger trains with an unusual number of mail and express cars. The two groups of tracks converge respectively into a six-track approach on the south side and a four-track approach on the north. The east edges of the train sheds, over the outermost passing track, and the access drive at the east end of the concourse building were supported by a series of massive concrete piers carrying flattened segmental arches, whose surfaces were everywhere covered with rusticated masonry, but much of this system has been replaced by the conventional steel columns of the Gateway Center group. This long arcade, standing directly on the low river wall, formed the most powerful of the structural features that are visible through the station's external masonry cladding (fig. 52).

The baggage-handling facilities of the concourse building constituted another ingenious element of this intricate plan—indeed, it may be argued that they represented the most efficient solution so far developed to this still perplexing problem. What we might call the baggage-circulation system centers on a large open area extending under the entire floor of the passenger concourse (fig. 54, top). A 400-foot-long platform along one side of this area was connected throughout much of its length to special station platforms by sloping ramps and at its inner end to the elevators that served the baggage checkrooms on the floor above. The baggage platforms, which are raised sufficiently to discourage the passengers from trying to use them, also serve for the handling of mail and express, but most of this nonhuman cargo is loaded and unloaded either in the mail terminal southeast of the station or on a special island platform lying along the inner passing track in the south terminal.

The whole vast system of tracks, concourses, platforms, ramps, stairs, entrances, vehicular drives, ticket offices, waiting rooms, dining rooms, and all the subsidiary facilities constitutes a planning masterpiece that has few serious competitors among the stations, piers, and airports of the United States. For all its intricacy, the working fabric of Union Station has a simple and logical character that arises primarily from the device of placing all those elements regularly used by the passenger on the same level, on which the waiting room with its customary appurtenances stands at one end, the train concourses and tracks at the other, and the ticket offices and baggage rooms between them. The only characteristic that prevented the achievement of the nearly perfect unidirectional movement of Grand Central Terminal is the presence of numerous entranceways, four in each of the two station buildings, which compel the passenger entering the east side of the concourse building or passing through its special commuters' entrances to traverse the entire length of the main concourse and part of the concourse lobby to reach the ticket offices, whence he must then retrace his steps to the train gate. But since the fundamental idea was to locate the offices midway between the two major public enclosures, it was impossible to provide every passenger with the shortest possible distance between the points of entrance and embarkation. The vehicular passages, on the other hand, were the first to make adequate provision for traffic in the automobile age, and they were designed with such foresight and intelligence that they have functioned over the years with a congestion well below that of any other metropolitan terminal or port. As a work of classical design, Union Station attracted an enthusiastic response from the architectural critics, among whom Rexford Newcomb, later dean of the College of Arts and Architecture at the University of Illinois, offered the most balanced judgment.

Externally the structure is treated in a monumental, if somewhat severe, denticulated Roman Doric. The great plan area, the division into two masses, and the adjacent street traffic make it impossible to comprehend a view of the entire structure near at hand. . . . It bespeaks, on the whole, a triumphal entry into the city and, while perhaps not so unified in outline or distinguished in detail as some other American stations of its class, it holds a high place in that class.

Internally the architectural treatment, while simple, is . . . far more interesting than the exterior. The Waiting Room is monumental in scale (100 ft. by 269 ft.) and distinguished in detail. Some delightful studies in Roman Corinthian—and in real Italian travertine—are afforded by the various vistas and angles of the Waiting Room, while the adjacent public rooms, like the Dining Room, are excellently handled in grammatical Classic of less formal character. . . .

The most interesting feature of the Station . . . is the interior handling of the Concourse (192 ft. by 203 ft.) where the modern material of which the structure is fabricated—steel—is allowed a full and frank expression. These weblike, aspiring, lattice columns rise from the floor in a sheer and stalwart fashion to bear aloft a beautifully graceful segmental roof. Only enough of the Classic architecture is introduced to indicate the character of that exterior. This is indeed the high point, the achievement of the Station, artistically speaking. Those of us who admired the aspiring beauty of the Pennsylvania Freight Terminal had hoped for a passenger station in some similar vein. This wonderfully light, graceful and airy interior is therefore a joy to those who see in modern materials and constructive methods the basis for a vital modern architecture. [42]

Partly because of the dominant architectural treatment, the structural details and the operating processes other than the movement of trains are mostly hidden from or inaccessible to passengers. The columns of the steel frame rest on conventional reinforced concrete footings carried in turn by caissons extending to hardpan clay lying a little more than 70 feet below the track grade. The caissons under the headhouse were tested under a total load of 1,200 tons each to determine whether they would support a twenty-story building, but although the settlement was only 1⅛ inches, the need for office space has never required more than the eight stories that were constructed. The structural system of the headhouse around the skylighted waiting room is a standard column-and-girder frame, but the presence of Canal Street above the concourse lobby required a heavy viaduct framework of massive built-up girders and posts. The great vault over the main concourse rests on a system of transverse and longitudinal arched trusses springing from parallel rows of columns that divide the enclosure into six bays along the east-west axis and five symmetrically arranged aisles of varying height along the north-south line (fig. 54). [43]

The train sheds, both in form and in supporting structure, constitute another unique element in the station complex. They represent a variation on the Bush shed in which the low vaults with their smoke slots alternate with high light monitors developed into an ogival section like a Gothic arch. The vaults over the tracks and the crowns of the monitors are covered with cement tile, while the flanks of the monitors are built up of prefabricated glass-and-concrete panels made by dipping the glass tile in hot asphalt and imbedding it in the concrete frame while the latter was still in a plastic state. The builders sought several ends in the adoption of this relatively costly construction: first, to obtain complete protection of tracks and platforms with maximum light over the latter and exactly the headroom over the tracks necessary for all locomotive smoke to be dissipated through the smoke slots; and second, to provide a form of reasonably attractive appearance when seen from the street. At those locations where one of the raised baggage platforms lies between adjacent tracks the maximum transverse span of the roof is 44 feet 9 inches center to center of columns. The double necessity of avoiding extremely deep girders at these spans and of keeping the tops of the sheds at the street level led to the unique framing system of the entire shed structure (fig. 56). The main supporting member is a slightly arched girder that rises from the column to a height sufficient to provide a clearance of 17 feet between the top of the rail and the underside of the smoke slot. At points above the edges of the platform this girder is rigidly connected to two curving, upward-extending legs that meet at the top of the column in the form of an inverted heart-shaped truss whose outer profile matches the transverse section of the monitor. This truss, the equivalent of a pair of brackets, makes possible a marked shortening of the clear span and hence a reduction in the depth of the girder. Between the primary frames the roof rests on a system of purlins carried in turn by arched girders spanning between the smoke-slot frames at one end and the ridge beam of the monitor at the other.[44]

The big metropolitan terminal is a widely ramifying megastructure, often far larger and more complex than the later buildings that gave the word its fashionable currency, and the train shed provides a visual as well as a functional transition from the building and its human occupants to the tracks with their locomotives and cars. In Union Station, before air-rights construction covered much of its property, the sheds marked the outer limits of the platform area, where the tracks converge into the approach system. On the north side this approach is a four-track line reduced to double track through and beyond the sharp curve at the Canal Street crossing, but outward from this point the station approach tracks are supplemented by the two main tracks of the Pittsburgh, Cincinnati, Chicago and Saint Louis Railroad as far as the crossing of the North Western Railway at Western Avenue (2400W). Trains are operated on right-hand tracks in accordance with standard wayside or overhead block signals of the position-light type, which had been introduced by the Pennsylvania Railroad for its Philadelphia suburban electrification in 1915.[45]

The south approach is considerably more impressive, matching the station layout as a sophisticated work of railroad planning (fig. 57). All intersecting streets are carried on overhead viaducts crossing the six main tracks that lie on a tangent to the junction with the Burlington at 14th Street, and the major coach yards flank the approach tracks on either side, the Pennsylvania's on the east between Taylor Street and Roosevelt Road, the Burlington's on the west, between Roosevelt and 14th Street. It is a superb artery for mass transportation, and even the difficulties led to novel solutions in signaling. The viaducts of Polk and Taylor streets cross the approach tracks not far below the south throat (now lying mainly under the Central Post Office), and since the elevation of these structures and their close spacing are such as to obscure any overhead signals set between them, the engineers adopted the expedient of placing the signals on frameworks fixed to the concrete bridge girders. The spacing of the signals was thus dictated by the location of streets, but this proved useful in the operation of suburban trains, for which a close headway of numerous short trains makes possible a uniform and uninterrupted movement at high traffic density.

The capacity of the approach was further increased by the provision of reverse-direction signaling on all six tracks—that is, signals facing in both directions on any one track, thus allowing the operation of both inbound and outbound trains on each of the tracks. The peculiarity of these signals is that because of low clearance under the street viaducts, all lights necessary for showing two positions at one time had to be located in a single group.[46] All switches and signals at Union Station are controlled by an electropneumatic interlocking system, and all train movements over station tracks and through either throat are governed by dwarf signals with three or four lights showing horizontal, diagonal, or vertical positions in pairs.

At the time of its opening the four constituent railroads of Union Station operated an average of about 390 trains per weekday in and out of the terminal, with a high proportion of these concentrated in the morning and evening rush hours because of the heavy volume of suburban and overnight sleeping-car traffic.[47] The number remained constant throughout the remainder of the decade, having fallen in 1929 to about 365 trains, a volume based on a total of 332 scheduled trains listed in the public timetables. The number declined rapidly during the depression, then suddenly and drastically turned upward under the enormous demands of the Second World War. The high point of wartime rail travel came in 1944, but it is doubtful whether traffic at Union Station ever exceeded 400 trains daily. The division between north and south halves of the station resulted in a somewhat greater density of traffic on the Milwaukee's side than on that of the other three roads during the early years of operation, but changing patterns of travel ultimately led to a close balance between the two halves. The great irony in the operation of Union Station, however, is that the spacious facility has seldom been used to more than half its capacity. The track system of the north half can easily and safely accommodate 300 trains per day, and that of the south half 420, while the concourses, waiting room, and entrance and exit ways provide sufficient area for the comfortable movement of 400,000 passengers a day. As incredible as it seems after years devoted to the formulation of merger plans, Union, North Western, and the Illinois Central's newly electrified suburban station were all that Chicago railroads needed to handle the city's maximum total of 1,600 daily trains. In the case of the Canal Street terminals, this enlarged traffic would have required the expansion of coach yard facilities and the rearrangement of connecting tracks, but these would have been simple tasks for a city that had built up the largest metropolitan rail system in the world. It is one of the curiosities of urban technology that city planners and the designers of railroad facilities never recognized the immense reserve capacity available in the big metropolitan terminals that were completed during the years from 1899 to 1933 (South Station, Boston, to Cincinnati Union Terminal). That this capacity might some day—even in the late twentieth century—prove essential eventually impressed itself on a few transportation planners.

The ultimate fulfillment of the vast Union Station plan included the construction of the freight stations of the Alton and the Burlington on either side of the south terminal throat, the coach yards of the Pennsylvania and the Burlington on the east side of the south approach in the vicinity of Roosevelt Road (the Burlington yard was later shifted to the west side), and the Central Post Office. This structure, built in 1930–32 on air rights over the south terminal tracks between Harrison Street and Van Buren Street, was the last public building planned in the halcyon days of the twenties and very nearly the last from the hand of a now celebrated team, the architects Graham, Anderson, Probst and White and the engineer Magnus Gunderson. The twelve-story structure is in every way an immediately recognizable product of its time: steel-framed and standing on rock caissons, it reveals in its exterior treatment the stripped pattern of vertical bands that had everywhere become the distinguishing feature of the new skyscraper. The location of the Central Post Office over the tracks was adopted to provide for the mechanized handling of mail on a direct path from trains to sorting areas, and hence necessitated the same system of smoke dissipation that had previously been installed in the Daily News Building. Another factor in the building's location led to a unique structural feature: since it stood athwart the Congress Street axis that Burnham had proposed, the frame was designed to leave an opening of sufficient size to clear the thoroughfare; it was eventually used in this way when Congress Expressway was constructed on the line of the former street. [48]

The realization of the Union Station project coincided with the midportion of an extensive program devoted to the renewal, expansion, and improvement of rail properties in the Chicago area. This widely ramifying activity was largely initiated and completed in what we have called the Burnham period, or the twenty years preceding the depression of 1930, and it provided the city with a thoroughly modernized railroad plant that proved essential in handling the burdens imposed by a second wartime mobilization. The first step was the construction in 1910–11 of an entirely new railroad line, the Des Plaines Cutoff of the North Western, which was laid out on a direct route to unite the company's Proviso Yard with the main freight line of the Milwaukee Division in Northfield and to provide trackage rights to the Milwaukee railroad for the operation of freight trains between the Milwaukee's yard at Bensenville and its main line north of Glenview. What followed was an accelerating succession of projects that were heavily concentrated in the decade of 1915–25—new lines, line elevations, grade separations, the replacement and expansion of freight yards, the addition of new freight and suburban stations, the modernization of existing passenger stations, the replacement of the traditional right-hand semaphore signals by color lights and reverse-direction signaling, additions to standard train control methods such as automatic stop and centralized traffic control, a great increase in the number of electrical interlockings, and the electrification of suburban service—all of them together forming so intricate a pattern of overlapping works as to make detailed descriptions of the individual projects unmanageable.[49] Certain of them, however, not only are typical but are of such magnitude as to require extended comment in a history of urban technology.

Among the signaling installations the most extensive and the most representative of the contemporary technological innovations is the system put in place by the Burlington Route on its three-track main line between Western Avenue in Chicago and the Aurora station, a distance of thirty-six miles. The bulk of this work was accomplished in 1925–26, but that portion associated with the junction of the Omaha and Minneapolis lines at Aurora was not completed until 1935. The Burlington operates only a single main line in the Chicago metropolitan area and possesses no belt and transfer tracks, with the consequence that the main artery is called upon to carry an extremely heavy mixed traffic consisting of through passenger trains, local and express suburban trains, through freight west of Hawthorne Yard, and freight transfer and switching runs. Because of the diversity and volume of through traffic, which alone required a three-track line, a minimum of additional investment was necessary to accommodate suburban trains, in contrast to the North Western Railway, for example, where a multitrack system was necessary because of passenger density alone, the freight service being relegated to separate lines. The Burlington trains had previously been governed by lower-quadrant semaphore signals arranged for straight right-hand operation. These were progressively replaced by color-light signals of the reverse-direction, four-aspect type, which allow train movements in either direction on all three tracks and which show four positive indications by means of a flashing yellow light in addition to the three standard colors.[50]

The most ambitious program of rail improvements was that undertaken by the Illinois Central Railroad under the terms of the so-called Lake Front Ordinance of 1919 and was thus the only project precisely designed to implement Burnham's plan for the reconstruction of Chicago rail lines. According to the 1919 ordinance the railroad agreed to replace its station at Michigan Avenue and Roosevelt Road and to carry out over a period of years the electrification of its operations within the city of Chicago. The new station was never built, and only the company's suburban service was electrified, but even this partial realization of the plan was to benefit a substantial proportion of the urban population. Operating factors peculiar to the Illinois Central as well as the road's lakefront location dictated both the form and the extent of this program. First was the fact that the main line north of 115th Street carried the greatest volume and the greatest diversity of traffic among the Chicago railroads—a heterogeneous mixture of through freight and passenger trains, suburban trains, switching and transfer runs, and the interurban trains of the South Shore, all of them together once reaching a total of at least eight hundred movements per day. The density and the diversity of this volume required a line of six to ten main tracks, the various parts of which were wholly separated by character of traffic into three corridors, reserved for through freight, through passenger, and suburban trains. The electrification program that was carried out in 1924–26 accordingly could be confined to the suburban line and terminal alone, and it proved to be the only electrified operation that was introduced by the steam railroads of Chicago, for the depression and diesel-electric motive power put an end to all further plans. The Illinois Central project embodied the overhead-wire or catenary system of power transmission in which the electrical lines are carried on steel gantry bridges that also support the signals. The 280 cars, divided equally between motor units and trailers, provided a sufficient body of rolling stock for the maximum of 542 trains per day that was reached in 1929. The construction of the new Randolph Street suburban terminal in 1930–31 completed that part of the lakefront agreement that the railroad was prepared to execute.

Among grade separation projects the largest and most intricate provided the classic illustration of the tangled interweavings of Chicago's railroad lines. In the region of Canal and 15th Street an immense rail ganglion had grown up over the years, like some morbid area of the vascular system. Here the main lines, wyes, junctions, and coach-yard leads of the Alton, Burlington, and Pennsylvania railroads crossed the east-west tracks of the Baltimore and Ohio Chicago Terminal and the Saint Charles Air Line in a snarl through which ten separate companies operated seven hundred trains and engine movements per day.[51] The primitive character of this track pattern, with all its inherent delays and risks, was retained down through the years: all switches were the individual hand-thrown type, and all train movements were governed by the manual signals of a corps of switchmen. The situation was further complicated by the presence of the Canal Street–Burlington Railroad grade crossing 550 feet west of the rail crossing's center point and of the Burlington coach yard between the Union Station approach and the river. The substitution of a rational and much simplified layout for the old tangle was made possible by the removal of the eastward-swinging curve in the Chicago River in 1928–30 (p. 247).

The straightforward plan of reconstruction, designed and carried out under the direction of G. A. Wiegel and L. W. Skov, required the vertical interweaving of the various arteries at three levels: the Baltimore and Ohio Chicago Terminal and the Air Line were lifted entirely above the whole complex of street and ground-level rail lines on parallel jackknife bridges over the new river channel and on slightly diverging concrete viaducts that extended west to the appropriate connecting points with their existing tracks; Canal Street was placed on another viaduct that dipped down to pass below the two east-west railroad bridges, then climbed sharply upward to clear the diverging main and wye tracks of the Burlington. The problem of yard leads was solved by removing the Burlington coach yard from the east side of the Union Station approach and rebuilding it on the west side, on which the main tracks diverged from the approach. Light signals and an electropneumatic interlocking replaced the manual signals and the hand-thrown switches of a more leisurely day.

An immense rail terminal like Union Station, with its associated approach tracks and its traffic-control techniques, is more than a device designed simply for the movement of people; it is at the same time a thoroughly urbanistic element that constitutes an essential visual and working part of the urban fabric, a great structural fact of the city core that was a conspicuous feature of public life in the days of rail ascendency. Indeed, the railroad was the most intensely urbanistic of all the forms of transportation: the station and its trains could be made to penetrate conveniently and harmoniously into the business center of the city, playing an active role in the pattern of buildings, streets, spaces, and life in the core area. Between the commuter rush hours of morning and evening, still a major feature of the big city's rhythm, a steady stream of people, rising and falling with the arrival and departure times of trains, passed through the station concourses bent on vacation adventures, holiday fun, business, politics, homecoming, reunion, family and public ritual, or on shopping, dining, sight-seeing, and theater-going in the city. A microcosm of urban life was concentrated within the station itself, from the swirl of taxis, cars, and people at its entrances and exits to the movement of crowds in the terminal's open spaces and in its shops, restaurants, bars, ticket offices, telephone and telegraph centers, and in a few instances, theaters. The rich, diverse life of the urban core was intensified and enlarged by the drama that went on in the station, even to the lonely derelicts or the cheerful drunks in the gray predawn of the milk runs.

The trains themselves enhanced this heightened sense of the city's promise: during the busy hours of Pullman traffic, concentrated in the morning and spread out in the afternoon and early evening, they stood in long rows, their crews on the alert at car doors and engine cabs, men and vehicles alike suggesting the paradoxical sense of calmness and expectancy that the heavy-breathing locomotives evoked with an almost poignant intensity (fig. 58). The Pullman train was itself a microcity, and those that survive make us realize how closely it can be identified with this new concept in urban form. On the train one carried on most of the activities of public and private life in the narrow compass of cars, vestibules, berths, and rooms—sleeping in a genuine bed, observing the rituals of dressing, undressing, and preparing oneself in the morning for a public world; eating at an elegantly set table in a dining room served by experts who brought excellent food and wine from a kitchen organized like a tiny inferno; drinking as ceremony, social stimulant, or private debauchery; reading or enjoying conviviality in a clublike setting, with everything quickened by the restless visual experience of the passing scene. All these activities went on in their appropriate enclosures, which made it necessary to walk from place to place in a moving vehicle, accompanied by the sounds of motion and power, subdued in the curtained aisle, bursting forth like an explosion in the forbidding passage from car to car.

The decline of the intercity passenger train and its terminal home brought with it the loss of a potent, exciting, irreplaceable dimension to the urban experience. Indeed, the fatal attrition that was interrupted only by the demands of war in the early forties foretold the melancholy decline of the city itself. The Christmas travelers who filled Union Station in the days when its marble gleamed in sunlight still unfiltered by dirt coincided with the high point of Chicago's history in its material achievement and its community life. The housing industry constructed nearly 43,000 dwelling units in each of the years 1926 and 1927 within the corporate limits of the city alone, and they ranged in sale price or rent through a wide spectrum of income levels, from lower middle to the topmost brackets. Commercial builders placed 3,000,000 square feet of office space in use in 1927, and came very close to repeating the achievement in 1929.[52] The various agencies of the municipal government, acting under the impetus and guidance of the Burnham Plan, created thousands of acres of shoreline parks, beaches, drives, and athletic facilities in a burst of creative civic activity that has no parallel in American urban history. Wealthy philanthropists and park planners acted together in founding, constructing, maintaining, and enlarging museums and cultural institutions that remain among the finest of their kind. The public schools and universities of the city expanded their numbers, campuses, faculties, and courses of instruction at rates that kept pace with the surrounding tide of material and intellectual progress. The metropolitan area enjoyed a balanced multilayered transportation network of streets and boulevards, street railway lines, elevated rapid transit, underground freight-handling lines, electric interurbans, and steam railroads, each providing a special kind of service in its appropriate place, the whole forming an integrated hierarchical

Fig. 58. The heyday of Pullman travel. Five sections of the New York Central's Twentieth Century Limited stand in the snow at LaSalle Street Station awaiting the departure signal, Christmas holidays, 1922.

Fig. 59. The freight-handling tunnel system of the Chicago Tunnel Company, 1901–9.

58

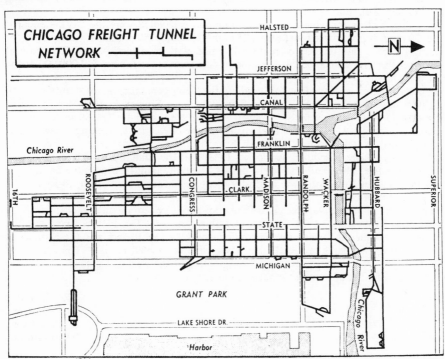

CHICAGO FREIGHT TUNNEL NETWORK

HALSTED
JEFFERSON
CANAL
FRANKLIN

Chicago River

ROOSEVELT
CONGRESS
CLARK
MADISON
RANDOLPH
WACKER
HUBBARD
SUPERIOR

16TH
CLARK
STATE
MICHIGAN

GRANT PARK

LAKE SHORE DR.

Chicago River

Harbor

59

system (figs. 3, 4, 5, 59). It was an extraordinary climax to the history of the new industrial city; yet panic and depression suddenly brought the whole vital motion to a standstill. Years of economic paralysis, war, militarism, racism, and civic bankruptcy took a frightful toll, and the city never regained either its stature or its once unassailable confidence in the future.

NOTES TO CHAPTER 6

1. See table 7. This figure was exceeded in 1946, the first full year following World War II and the year in which wartime restrictions on the use of gasoline were removed. The Chicago Street Railway was the nearly universal single-trolley direct-current system in which the running rails were used as return conductors.
2. The presence of major car-building companies in Cincinnati and Saint Louis obviously helped to stimulate the demand for new rolling stock in these cities.
3. The abandonment of the interurban lines, the construction of the subways, the laying of new track in the expressway medians, and the establishment of the Chicago Transit Authority brought about extensive changes in operation and equipment.
4. Quoted in William R. Middleton, *The Interurban Era* (Milwaukee: Kalmbach Publishing Co., 1961), p. 226.
5. The loading factors for which the steel frame was calculated were the city's standard: wind, 30 pounds per square foot; snow, 25 pounds; floors, 250 pounds for cargo, 200 for passenger areas, and 100 for recreational, office, and promenade areas. The cost of Municipal Pier was $4,000,000 at the time of construction, or about $42,000,000 at the 1971 price level.
6. The reconstruction of Navy Pier for handling the heavy general cargo of standard ocean freighters followed the opening of the Saint Lawrence Seaway in 1959. Chicago had become a port for ocean vessels, however, long before that date. The steamer *Anna* of the Norwegian Fjell Line made a trial voyage to the city in 1931, docking at the Montgomery Ward Warehouse on the North Branch of the Chicago River. The company established regularly scheduled service in 1933, and the Dutch Oranje Line followed shortly thereafter. The small size of the canals originally built to bypass the Saint Lawrence rapids limited these ships to a 258-foot length, 43-foot 6-inch beam, 14-foot draft, and 1,200 tons of cargo.
7. The name Illinois Waterway designates the continuous system of waterways formed by the Chicago River, the Chicago Sanitary and Ship Canal, the Des Plaines River, and the Illinois River, which is formed by the confluence of the Des Plaines and the Kankakee. The remaining two dams in the Illinois River were completed in 1939. The growth of total lake and river tonnage reaching or originating at the Port of Chicago is indicated by the following list of annual tonnage at ten-year intervals:

1891	9,281,516 tons
1911	10,633,572 tons
1921	8,848,332 tons
1931	9,990,120 tons

1941	22,465,260 tons
1951	34,337,461 tons
1961	36,623,446 tons
1969	46,154,966 tons

(Source: U.S. Army, Corps of Engineers, *Waterborne Commerce of the United States*, annual reports; quoted to 1961 in Irving Cutler, *The Chicago-Milwaukee Corridor* [Evanston: Northwestern Universities Studies in Geography, no. 9, 1965], p. 174.)

8. The history of sewage treatment and water purification has yet to be written, and what I offer herewith constitutes only the beginning of an inquiry.

9. By the time of the Burnham Plan the Metropolitan Sanitary District served all the city and the northern suburbs up to and including Northbrook and Glencoe. Subsequent annexations (1913, 1917, 1919, 1921, 1927, 1939, 1945, 1947, 1949, 1951, 1953, 1955, 1956, 1961, 1963, 1964, 1965) added all the remaining built-up areas of Cook County as they existed in 1966. The 250 miles of concrete interceptor sewers range in diameter from 6 to 27 feet.

10. The Sanitary District pumping stations stand at the following locations, in clockwise order: Elmwood Avenue near Lake, Evanston; Lawrence Avenue (4800N) at the North Branch; Wellington Avenue (3000N) at the North Branch; Racine Avenue (1200W) at Pershing Road (3900S); 95th Street at the Calumet River; Little Calumet River near 130th Street; in the suburbs of Harvey, Glenwood, Tinley Park, Chicago Ridge–Oak Lawn, Palos Hills, McCook, Western Springs, Westchester, River Forest, Arlington Heights–Mount Prospect, and Palatine–Rolling Meadows.

11. The treatment plants of the Metropolitan Sanitary District are the following: Calumet, Little Calumet River at 130th Street, 1921–22, 1935, 1938–39; North Side, McCormick Boulevard between Howard and Oakton Street, Skokie, 1927–28, 1937; West Side, 59th Avenue at 43rd Street, Stickney, 1930–31; Southwest, same address, 1937–39. The last two were later combined into a single working unit which is claimed to be the largest single sewage treatment plant in the world. The major part of the treatment facilities and the interceptor system constructed after 1935 was built by the federal Public Works Administration under grants totaling nearly $60,000,000. As of 1962 the total capacity of the four treatment plants, serving an area with a population of 5,500,000, was 1,300,000,000 gallons per day; the investment in treatment facilities alone was $175,000,000; and the total investment in all facilities was carried on the books at about $525,000,000.

12. This clear and odorless liquid is water containing a high concentration of dissolved carbon dioxide. Before the introduction of biodegradable detergents in the decade of the sixties it was covered with white detergent suds that could be seen at the foot of every dam down the length of the Illinois River.

13. Before the development of the activated-sludge process such treatment as was practiced in England and Germany was entirely chemical and inorganic in character: the waste was treated with lime (CaO) as a disinfectant and ferric chloride ($FeCl_3$) as a coagulant.

14. These plants were opened in 1947 and 1964, respectively.

15. The expansion in the physical plant of the water supply system, 1910–30, comprehended the following elements, divided by type of facility, with dates of completion:
   I. Water tunnels
      1. Southwest Lake and Land, 1911. Length 9.65 miles; interior diameter 9, 12, and 14 feet (indicates height to crown of horseshoe section).

2. 68th Street connection to Southwest, 1916. Length 0.63 mile; interior diameter 6 feet and 8 feet.

3. Wilson Avenue, 1918. Length 8.62 miles; interior diameter 8, 12, and 13 feet.

4. Western Avenue, 1927. Length 6.02 miles; interior diameter 10 and 12 feet.

The supply tunnels carrying water directly from the intake stations are so located and pitched as to provide a gravity flow of water from the intake to the pumping plant and a flow by siphon action into the pump chamber.

II. Pumping stations

1. Roseland, 351 W. 104th Street, 1911. Five steam-driven reciprocating pumps; capacity 305 mgd.

2. Mayfair, 4850 W. Wilson Ave., 1918. Six steam-driven reciprocating pumps; capacity 400 mgd.

3. Western Avenue, 4925 S. Western Ave., 1927. Four steam-driven reciprocating pumps; capacity 320 mgd.

4. Thomas Jefferson, 2250 W. Eastwood Ave., 1928. Four electrically driven centrifugal pumps; capacity 160 mgd.

All the pumping stations are steel-framed and classical in design, except for Roseland, which exhibits the articulated pier-and-spandrel curtain wall of red brick that is characteristic of Chicago industrial architecture.

16. The size of the intake cribs and their associated intake shafts may be inferred from the following dimensions of the Dunne crib: outside diameter 112 feet; inside diameter 60 feet 6 inches; foundation thickness five feet; timber wall thickness 26 feet extending through a height from −27 feet (surface = 0) to −8 feet; concrete wall height, from −8 to +16 feet; masonry facing from +8 to +16 feet; intake shafts, outside diameter 14 feet, inside 12 feet; ports 7 × 7 feet in dimensions of opening, center line located at −25 feet. In the Dever crib the diameter of the outer wall ranges from 90 feet at the bottom to 75 feet at the top; the thickness of the concrete wall is 25 feet; the intake ports are circular, with a diameter of 8 feet; the single intake shaft is 16 feet in diameter and extends to a depth of 190 feet below mean water level (the pressure at this depth is 11,874.24 pounds per square foot on the projected bottom area of the shaft).

17. A survey made on 13 March 1911, for example, at the intersection of Grand Boulevard and 38th Street produced the following totals of vehicular traffic for the twenty-four-hour period:

Automobiles	3,467
Horse-drawn vehicles	341
Motorcycles and bicycles	294

The greatest hourly concentration of automobile traffic came at 5 P.M. to 6 P.M., when the total was 260, whereas the maximum number of horse-drawn vehicles, 50 in one hour, came at 2 P.M. to 3 P.M., the two figures indicating that cars and boulevards were used for transportation to and from work, whereas wagons and carriages were used for pleasure driving, visiting, and deliveries. The ratio of motor-driven to horse-drawn vehicles would probably have been reversed in core and industrial areas with a heavy vehicular traffic. (For motor vehicle registration in Chicago, see table 7; the above table is taken from Linn White, "Park Drives and Boulevards," *Municipal Engineering* 44 [February 1919]: 89.)

18. Flat-slab framing with mushroom capitals and drop slabs was required because the prox-

imity of the river made it impossible to lower the bottom level sufficiently to introduce the deep girders necessary to support the upper deck.

19. For the filling of the Lincoln Park area, see p. 207.
20. The convention to rewrite this antique document was authorized by the voters in November 1968 and assembled in the following year.
21. "The Chicago Plan after Fifteen Years" (editorial), *Western Architect* 35 (January 1926):1.
22. The soil in the area of North Western Station is typical of the material along the South Branch of the river: the upper portion is an unstable mixture of spoil left from the fire of 1871 and wet sand; below this lie layers of clay increasing in stiffness to a dense hardpan at a maximum depth of −75 feet and with a maximum thickness of 20 feet; under the clay the till of sand, gravel, and boulders extends downward to levels ranging from −106 to −116 feet.

The diameter of the caissons under the station ranges from 4 feet 6 inches to 8 feet. The total volume of excavation for foundations and subgrade space was 15,000 cubic yards.
23. The Guastavino system of domed and vaulted construction in thin tiles was invented in Spain about 1880 by Rafael Guastavino y Moreno and brought to the United States by himself and his son, R. Guastavino y Esposito, in 1881, when the two obtained a United States patent and established a contracting business that flourished until the latter's death in 1950. The principle of self-supporting vaults and domes built of thin masonry shells was derived from medieval Catalonian techniques that were influenced in turn by Islamic and Byzantine precedents. In the Guastavino system two or more layers of thin rectangular terra-cotta tiles are laid in a herringbone pattern in such a way as to stagger the joints and orient the tiles in one layer at a 90-degree angle to those below and above it. By using enough strong mortar to constitute 50 percent of the total mass, Guastavino was able to obtain a load-carrying capacity well above that of conventional masonry vaulting (up to 300 pounds per square foot) with a marked reduction in weight. Moreover, the thick beds of mortar give the whole mass a plasticity that allows it to shape itself in response to the loads upon it, thus tending to limit it to rigid membrane action alone. An additional advantage derived from the pattern of the tile is that vaults can be erected without formwork.
24. These trusses are unusual: although the bottom chord is horizontal, the top chord slopes at an angle conforming to the pitch of the roof; the depth thus varies from 5 feet 6 inches at one end to 7 feet 6 inches at the other.
25. The arched trusses are matched in size only by the bridge structure that carries the track and platform area: their depth varies from 10 feet 3 inches at the crown to 14 feet at the springing points; the individual members are 12-inch H-beams.
26. If it cannot literally be argued that the electrically operated pneumatic interlocking system made the big terminal possible, it can certainly be claimed that such a system made it economically feasible. The first designed for the scale of the metropolitan terminal was installed at the Pennsylvania Station in Jersey City (1888–92). The North Western Railway had introduced electrical interlocking into the Wells Street Station by 1907, and the installation at the Madison Street complex, along with those built for the new stations in New York and Washington, constitutes one of the earliest group incorporated in the high-capacity terminals of the twentieth century. In the electropneumatic interlocking, all switches, signals, and locking devices are controlled by a single electrically operated machine, and all movable elements are electrically operated except for switches,

which are moved by compressed-air pistons actuated by electric relays. The prime advantage of the system is that it assures positive automatic control over all elements and thus renders it impossible for the towerman to align switches into conflicting routes and to set signals in conflicting aspects (the older mechanical interlocking accomplishes the same result but in a less positive, less reliable, and more cumbersome form). With full control in this way effectively established, other valuable operating features follow: train movements may be carried out at predetermined and uniform speeds through approaches and throat tracks, regardless of the route; trains may follow a predetermined and uniform reduction in speed as they approach the terminal tracks; trains may be admitted to terminal tracks at the speed and frequency for which the track system was designed; all these factors insure maximum frequency of train movements, or in other words, minimum headway consistent with safety and continuous movement, and the simultaneous movement of trains on parallel or diverging tracks.

The practice of governing train movements between approach and terminal tracks by little independent signals set close to the ground—dwarf signals, in the railroad argot—goes back to the invention of the individual switch lamp, which still survives for spurs, yard tracks, and sidings. (Dwarf signals are customarily used to govern train movements against the normal current of traffic on unidirectional main tracks.)

27. This large and steadily growing volume of through traffic arose from the unusually high number of 250- to 500-mile runs on the North Western system (e.g., Chicago to Green Bay, Ishpeming, Marquette, Ashland, Duluth, Minneapolis–Saint Paul, Rochester, Sioux City, and Omaha), which meant a high volume of overnight coach and Pullman traffic that would be concentrated at Chicago during the morning and evening rush hours.

28. The evidence for this assertion rests on the daily average of scheduled trains in the 13 largest stations in the United States throughout the year 1911, as shown in the accompanying table.

Daily Average of Scheduled Trains

Station	Number of Tracks[a]	Number of Trains per Day
Boston (North Station)	23	607
Boston (South Station)	28	786
Chicago (Chicago and North Western)	16	300
Chicago (LaSalle Street)	11	210 (est.)
Chicago (old Union)	9	270[b]
Hoboken (Delaware, Lackawanna and Western)	14	263
Jersey City (Pennsylvania)	12	334
Kansas City (Union)	16	313 (est.)
New York (Grand Central)	66	479
New York (Pennsylvania)	21	392
Philadelphia (Broad Street)	16	574
Saint Louis (Union)	32	322
Washington (Union)	26	244

[a]Number of tracks used for loading and unloading; excludes loop and storage tracks.

[b]The figure for old Union Station in Chicago is misleading because the facility was actually operated as two stub-end terminals with a continuous track system.

The high averages for the group are 35.9 trains per track per day at Broad Street Station and 28.1 at South Station. But even the traffic at the Philadelphia terminal fell short of that at Gare St. Lazare in Paris: for years this station handled 250,000 passengers per day and 1,200 trains on 31 tracks, for an average of 38.7 trains per track.

There are other, more dramatic figures that might prove instructive to urban planners. By 1915 the average number of daily trains at South Station had risen to 817, with a maximum of 90 scheduled movements in one hour, and the staff had already been well prepared for even further increases: on 8 June 1912, during the Boston streetcar strike, traffic rose to 1,001 trains and 208,380 passengers. That the Chicago terminals had an equal reserve capacity was demonstrated during the city's own streetcar strike: over the four days of 13–16 June 1915, the railroads handled an average of 625,000 suburban and 75,000 through passengers per day. The Illinois Central reached the high point when it operated 611 trains for 252,650 passengers on 15 June 1915. (The Illinois Central had previously broken all the records on 9 October 1893, when it transported 541,312 passengers in the twenty-four-hour period.)

29. For the volume of rail passenger traffic at ten-year intervals, see chap. 2, note 24. The changes in the pattern of traffic were complex in the decade preceding the depression and consequently not readily predictable: in a rapidly expanding metropolitan area like that of Chicago, commutation traffic increased rapidly (e.g., Burlington, 1920–29, 33.5%; Rock Island, 35.0%; Illinois Central, 89.5%), and Pullman business on the major long-distance lines also increased substantially; but local and short-haul traffic, extremely vulnerable to automobile competition, suffered a drastic decline that eventually resulted in its disappearance.

30. Other engineers submitting proposals were the following: Gustave E. Lemmerich, for two stations with loop tracks; Carl A. Bessey, for refinements on the existing arrangement; R. C. Sattley, for two stations, one through and one suburban (a device likely to yield maximum confusion); George E. Sanford, for the most expensive and pointless of all, the diversion of the North Branch of the river to the Des Plaines and the construction of the station on the exposed bed.

31. The similarity of the individual station–office building complex to the Michigan Central Station and office building in Detroit is so striking that there can be little question that Drummond was influenced by their design. Both the Grand Central and Michigan Central projects were the work of the same architects, Reed and Stem and Warren and Wetmore.

32. The Wisconsin Central was later merged with the Minneapolis, Saint Paul and Sault Sainte Marie Railway (Soo Line). The company's new freight station was not planned as a part of the Union Station program, but its proximity to the various freight and passenger facilities lying along the station's south approach and the deliberate intention to design the structure in accordance with the Burnham principles place it in close relation to the later Canal Street developments.

33. The elevation of the track and loading areas at the Wisconsin Central station makes it in effect a bridge structure measuring 325 × 2,475 feet in overall dimensions of the area that extends to the outer limits of the platforms. The slab has a uniform thickness of 18 inches except over the mushroom capitals, where the drop or shear slabs add another 16 inches in depth.

34. It would be difficult to translate these figures to the 1971 price level because of the rapid rise in prices during the ten-year period of construction (1915–25). A conservative estimate would place the equivalent cost of the passenger terminal and street relocations at

$750,000,000 and of the freight stations (the cost estimate of which was based on 1913 prices) at $80,000,000.

35. Congress Street was never built as planned in the station area: it was blocked by construction of the Central Post Office and was not made a through artery until the opening of Congress Expressway forty-four years after all these deliberations.

36. The provisions of the 1914 ordinance as affecting the rights and obligations of the municipality and the railroad companies make it an archetype of its kind and worth summarizing in detail.

   I. Rights and other provisions granted to the Union Station Company.

   1. Creation of a district bounded by the Chicago River on the east, Canal Street on the west, Kinzie Street (400N) on the north, and Roosevelt Road (1200S) on the south, within which the participating railroads have the right to arrange passenger and freight terminals in any manner not in conflict with the ordinance. (The area of this district is about 112 acres, of which 100 were used for terminals, approaches, coach yards, and appurtenant structures.)

   2. Vacating of all streets and alleys within this district, and the vacating of all streets and alleys in an additional area bounded by the river, Canal Street, Roosevelt Road, and 16th Street, within which the railroads have the right to rebuild and rearrange all freight facilities. (The tracks in this area, given over chiefly to the Burlington coach yard, eventually had to be drastically rearranged to clear a nearly impassable tangle of intersecting lines [see p. 286].)

   3. Granting the railroads the right to occupy the entire area under the new viaducts which are to be built for all intersecting east-west streets between the east line of Canal Street and the river.

   4. Granting the railroads the right to remove from the areas described above all sewers and other municipal improvements in order to allow themselves full and free use of these properties without interference.

   II. Obligations of the proprietary railroad companies of the Chicago Union Station Company.

   1. Payment of an agreed-on sum of money to the city for the vacating of streets and other grants (this sum eventually came to $2,686,558.92).

   2. Reconstruction at the railroad's own expense of all viaducts in the defined areas in a form acceptable to the city, and the perpetual maintenance of such viaducts.

   3. Reconstruction of the sewer system outside the defined areas in such a manner as to provide a drainage equivalent to that provided by the sewers removed from the defined areas.

   4. Widening, elevation, and reconstruction of Canal Street at a uniform grade from Washington to Roosevelt Road, at the railroads' own expense, except for compensation from the city for a twenty-foot strip of air rights required for widening the street.

   5. Construction of two bridges over the North and South branches of the Chicago River at Kinzie Street and Monroe Street, the cost of such bridges to be deducted from the sum due the city for vacating streets.

37. The dimensions of the Pennsylvania Freight Station, center-to-center of the outermost columns, are 745 feet 4 inches × 419 feet 8 inches, giving a ground area of 312,802 square feet. The loading and unloading area includes nineteen tracks and eighteen platforms with a capacity of 375 cars. Associated with Rodd in the supervision of design and construction was Robert Trimble, chief engineer, maintenance of way, Pennsylvania Lines West of Pittsburgh.

38. The structural system of the Pennsylvania facility is a straightforward work of heavy steel framing supporting reinforced concrete floor slabs. The piers and footings of the foundation rest on 18,000 piles driven 40–50 feet below grade to a hardpan stratum. The floor and roof slabs were designed for the following loadings: first floor (loading and unloading), 300 pounds per square foot; second floor (warehousing), 250 pounds; third and fourth floors (warehousing), 200 pounds; office floors throughout, 125 pounds; roof, 30 pounds. The columns are built-up members of H-section, and the floor framing system is for the most part composed of plate girders ranging from 30 to 34 inches in depth and 24-inch I-beams. The slabs range in thickness from 11 inches for the first floor and 8¾ to 10 inches for the warehousing and office floors, to 5½ to 6 inches for the roof.

39. The mail terminal, mostly a conventional work of steel framing with curtain walls composed chiefly of baywide areas of glass in factory sash, includes what was thought to be the largest steel truss ever used in a building. Dictated by the necessity of carrying six-story column lines over a group of station tracks, the truss measures 149 feet 4½ inches in length, 28 feet 6 inches in depth, and weighs 365 tons.

40. At the very time that the original Union Station was falling before the demolition crew it was destined to achieve a literary immortality. A poignant and evocative passage in Fitzgerald's *The Great Gatsby*, in which Nick Carraway recalls the Christmas reunions of his college days, will undoubtedly preserve it for generations who could never even have heard of the old red-brick, iron-framed structure.

    One of my most vivid memories is coming back West from prep school and later College at Christmas time. Those who went further than Chicago would gather in the old dim Union Station at six o'clock of a December evening, with a few Chicago friends, already caught up into their holiday gayeties, to bid them a hasty good-by. I remember the fur coats of the girls returning from Miss This-or-That's and the chatter of frozen breath and the hands waving overhead as we caught sight of old acquaintances, and the matching of invitations: "Are you going to the Ordways'? The Herseys'? The Schultzes'?" and the long green tickets clasped tight in our gloved hands. And last the murky yellow cars of the Chicago, Milwaukee & St. Paul railroad looking cheerful as Christmas itself on the tracks beside the gate. [F. Scott Fitzgerald, *The Great Gatsby* (New York: Charles Scribner's Sons, 1925, 1953), p. 133].

    One who insisted on absolute fidelity to visual detail might argue that the Milwaukee railroad cars were actually painted a dark orange color rather than a "murky yellow."

41. When the station opened in the spring of 1925 the ratio of total numbers of scheduled trains between the north and south sides (160:194) exceeded the ratio of numbers of tracks (10:14), with the consequence that the traffic density in trains per track per day was somewhat higher in the Milwaukee terminal than in the three-road south terminal (16 on the north as opposed to 13.86 on the south). The imbalance was even greater with respect to traffic density on the approaches (see pp. 282–83).

42. Rexford Newcomb, "The New Chicago Union Station," *Western Architect* 35 (January 1926): 6–7. Newcomb's dimensions for the main concourse are open to question: as I read the plans, the dimensions of the concourse proper (exclusive of the low flanking wings or aisles) are 124 feet in width by 204 feet in length; if the aisles are included, the overall width is 260 feet.

43. The six longitudinal bays span 34 feet each center-to-center of columns, and of the five transverse divisions, the center spans 84 feet, those flanking it 20 feet each, and the outermost, which lie under flat roofs and appear as low wings in the exterior view (fig. 52), 68 feet each. The north and south train concourses, outside the train gates, are covered by low, greatly flattened vaults also carried on steel arch ribs.

44. The foregoing account of the train shed structure is derived largely from Carl W. Condit, *American Building: The Twentieth Century* (New York: Oxford University Press, 1961), pp. 61–62. As of 1971, the Union Station train sheds have survived only in the short block between Jackson and Van Buren Street.
45. Position-light signals give indications by means of rows of amber lights, three to a row, which duplicate the standard positions of upper-quadrant semaphores: vertical for clear, diagonal for approach, and horizontal for stop; the more elaborate indications of home signals are given by two rows of lights, one above the other (fig. 57).
46. This curiosity requires further explanation, following note 45. Home signals are designed to govern train movements through junctions, crossings, and terminal throat tracks as well as to give block indications and hence must show two or three colors, or two or three positions, at one time. This is ordinarily accomplished by placing two or three light groups or semaphores one above the other on the mast, but low clearances and obstructions to a clear view made this impossible from the practical standpoint of operations at Union Station. The full benefits of reverse-direction signaling can be obtained only by double ladder tracks such as those provided at the Chicago terminal. Ladder tracks extend diagonally over and switch into all approach tracks; a double system thus makes it possible to move two trains simultaneously into or out of the station from any approach track to any station track. All these characteristics of signaling and track layout, working together, make possible the extraordinary efficiency and compactness of the large high-density metropolitan terminal.
47. The number of scheduled trains operated at Union Station in May 1925 was 354, divided among the various railroads as in the accompanying table.

Number of Scheduled Trains at Union Station

Railroad	Through	Suburban	Total
Chicago and Alton	20	2	22
Chicago, Burlington and Quincy	28	90	118
Pennsylvania Lines	48	6	54
Total south terminal	96	98	194
Chicago, Milwaukee and Saint Paul	74	86	160
Total combined terminals	170	184	354

The number must be increased by about 10 percent to include additional mail and express trains not shown in the public timetables, special trains, and extra sections of regularly scheduled trains, which would add another 35 trains, for a final total of 389.
48. For the Daily News Building, see pp. 121–25.
49. The chief railroad additions and improvements, other than the North Western and Union Station projects, in chronological order, 1910–30, were the following:
    Chicago and North Western, new freight lines, 1910–11.
    Illinois Central, Lake Shore and Michigan Southern (later New York Central), Grand Crossing grade separation, first phase, 1909–12.
    Wisconsin Central: new freight station, 1912–14 (see text, p. 264).
    Dearborn Station: annex station, 1914; reconstruction of office building following fire, 1922; expansion of mail-handling facilities, 1924–25.
    Belt Railway of Chicago: expansion and modernization of Clearing Yard, 1914–15.

Chicago, Rock Island and Pacific: track elevation, 1914–16; color-light signals, 1917; reverse-direction signals, Blue Island–Joliet, 1926.

New York, Chicago and Saint Louis (Nickel Plate Road): track elevation and Grand Crossing grade separation, second phase, 1915–16.

Chicago and Western Indiana: track elevation, 1916.

Chicago and Alton: new freight station, 1919–20 (part of Union Station project).

New York Central: color-light signals and automatic stop, 1923 et seq.

Illinois Central: electrification of suburban service, terminal improvements, color-light signals, 1923–26 (see text, below).

Chicago and North Western: color-light signals, Wisconsin Division, 1924–25.

Chicago, North Shore and Milwaukee: new Skokie Valley main line, 1924–26.

Chicago, Burlington and Quincy: color-light reverse-direction signals, Chicago–Aurora, 1925–26, 1935 (see text, below).

Dearborn Station: expansion of mail terminal, 1930.

Baltimore and Ohio Chicago Terminal, Chicago, Burlington and Quincy, Saint Charles Air Line, Union Station Company: Canal–15th Street grade separation, 1930–31 (see text, below).

Illinois Central: Randolph Street suburban terminal, 1930–31.

50. The full advantage of double-direction operation on main lines (as opposed to right- or left-hand operation) can be realized only by means of closely spaced crossovers over which trains can be switched from one track to another, the faster train thus bypassing the slower in front of it. All such crossovers must be under the control of a single interlocking system that places the entire line, in effect, under centralized traffic control.

The Burlington began a revolution in rail motive power and rolling stock in April 1934, when it placed in operation a lightweight stainless-steel train pulled by a 600-horsepower diesel-electric locomotive, cars and engine respectively manufactured by the R. G. Budd Manufacturing Company of Philadelphia and the Electro-Motive Division of General Motors Corporation at La Grange, Illinois. Known as the Pioneer Zephyr, the little three-car train was initially tested on main-line track on 9 April 1934, then dispatched on an exhibition tour on 18 April that ended with a celebrated run from Denver to Chicago on 26 May that broke all records for the long-distance operation of trains. The Zephyr covered the distance of 1,015 miles in 13 hours 5 minutes, for an average speed of 77.6 miles per hour and a top speed of 112.5 miles per hour. It led to the establishment of new high-speed schedules on the western roads, which would have been impossible without the new forms of signaling, while the new motive power marked the beginning of the end for the steam locomotive.

51. In addition to the three Union Station companies operating on the north-south and diverging tracks, the intersecting lines carried the passenger trains of the Baltimore and Ohio, Chicago Great Western, Pere Marquette, and Soo Line (Baltimore and Ohio Chicago Terminal) and the freight transfer runs of the Burlington, Illinois Central, North Western, and Michigan Central (Saint Charles Air Line). The whole tangle was claimed to be the world's busiest crossing. (For the history of the transfer company and the origin of the name, see p. 57).

52. See tables 2 and 3.

Tables

TABLE 1

POPULATION, AREA, AND DENSITY OF CHICAGO

Year	Population of City	Population of Metropolitan Area[a]	Area of City in Square Miles	Density per Square Mile
1830	ca. 100		0.417	240
1840	4,470		10.186	439
1850	29,963		9.311	3,218
1860	109,260		17.492	6,246
1870	298,977		35.152	8,505
1880	505,185		35.152	14,371
1890	1,099,850		178.052	6,177
1900	1,698,575		189.517	8,963
1910	2,185,283	2,805,869	190.204	11,489
1920	2,701,705	3,575,209	198.270	13,626
1930	3,376,438	4,733,777	207.204	15,862
1940	3,396,808	4,890,674	212.863	15,958
1950	3,620,962	5,586,096	212.863	17,011
1960	3,550,404	6,794,453	212.863	16,679
1970	3,366,951	6,892,509	227.251	14,816

SOURCES: United States Census; Frank A. Randall, *History of the Development of Building Construction in Chicago* (Urbana: University of Illinois Press, 1949), p. 4; Municipal Reference Library of Chicago.
a The Standard Metropolitan Area of Chicago includes Cook, Du Page, Kane, Lake, and Will counties in Illinois, and Lake and Porter counties in Indiana.

TABLE 2

OFFICE SPACE CONSTRUCTED IN THE CENTRAL BUSINESS DISTRICT
OF CHICAGO, 1872 TO THE PRESENT

Year	Net Area in Square Feet (area added less demolished space)	Continuing Total	Year	Net Area in Square Feet (area added less demolished space)	Continuing Total
1872	322,007	322,007	1912	1,884,780	12,605,638
1873	—a	—	1913	1,280,265	13,885,903
1874	—	—	1914	1,278,914	15,164,817
1875	49,550	371,557	1915	211,020	15,375,837
1876	—	—	1916	293,479	15,669,316
1877	—	—	1917	171,053	15,840,369
1878	—	—	1918	73,651	15,914,020
1879	—	—	1919	150,916	16,064,936
1880	—	—	1920	233,471	16,298,407
1881	—	—	1921	—	—
1882	88,430	459,987	1922	151,687	16,450,094
1883	—	—	1923	2,018,792	18,468,886
1884	92,266	552,253	1924	1,110,345	19,579,231
1885	319,560	871,813	1925	447,510	20,026,741
1886	418,480	1,290,293	1926	1,044,953	21,071,694
1887	17,953	1,308,246	1927	3,017,778	24,089,472
1888	303,703	1,611,949	1928	2,072,474	26,161,946
1889	45,901	1,657,850	1929	2,890,594	29,052,540
1890	335,046	1,992,896	1930	1,674,555	30,727,095
1891	189,923	2,182,819	1931	−119,177	30,607,918
1892	957,615	3,140,434	1932	78,853	30,686,771
1893	730,046	3,870,480	1933	49,392	30,736,163
1894	288,270	4,158,750	1934	383,868	31,120,031
1895	499,037	4,657,787	1935	13,569	31,133,600
1896	216,776	4,874,563	1936	—	—
1897	125,250	4,999,813	1937	—	—
1898	89,025	5,088,838	1938	−17,953	31,115,647
1899	22,664	5,111,502	1939	−193,724	30,921,923
1900	334,039	5,445,541	1940	−33,678	30,888,245
1901	—	—	1941	−157,643	30,730,602
1902	359,323	5,804,864	1942	—	—
1903	463,319	6,273,183	1943	—	—
1904	513,739	6,786,922	1944	—	—
1905	480,388	7,267,310	1945	—	—
1906	431,365	7,698,675	1946	517,709	31,248,311
1907	591,646	8,290,321	1947	523,205	31,771,516
1908	211,523	8,501,844	1948	—	—
1909	—	—	1949	940,000	32,711,516
1910	1,208,614	9,710,458	1950	526,052	33,237,568
1911	1,010,400	10,720,858	1951	296,287	33,533,855

SOURCE: Building Managers Association of Chicago.
a A dash indicates that no figures were available.

TABLE 2—*Continued*

Year	Net Area in Square Feet (area added less demolished space)	Continuing Total	Year	Net Area in Square Feet (area added less demolished space)	Continuing Total
1952	14,000	33,547,855	1962	187,369	38,045,782
1953	—	—	1963	1,034,000	39,079,782
1954	202,500	33,750,355	1964	150,000	39,229,782
1955	45,766	33,796,121	1965	2,227,066	41,456,848
1956	665,734	34,461,855	1966	280,000	41,736,848
1957	888,085	35,349,940	1967	1,269,093	43,005,941
1958	1,029,186	36,379,126	1968	1,056,207	44,062,148
1959	−78,782	36,300,344	1969	890,206	44,952,354
1960	492,986	36,793,330	1970	2,385,412	47,337,766
1961	1,065,083	37,858,413			

TABLE 3

DWELLING UNITS CONSTRUCTED ANNUALLY, CITY OF CHICAGO AND
CHICAGO METROPOLITAN AREA, 1904 TO 1970

	City of Chicago			Chicago Metropolitan Area[a]		
Year	Homes	Apartment Units	Total Residential Units	Homes	Apartment Units	Total Residential Units
1904			13,185			
1905	3,609	12,437	16,046			
1906	3,905	11,205	15,110			
1907	3,605	11,276	14,881			
1908	3,271	15,894	19,165			
1909	3,261	16,801	20,062			
1910	3,387	14,131	17,518			
1911						
1912	3,827					
1913	3,745	15,105	18,850			
1914	3,846	16,577	20,423			
1915	3,995	19,925	23,920			
1916	3,887	20,525	24,412			
1917	2,033	5,491	7,524			
1918	916	1,030	1,946			
1919	4,222	4,758	8,980			
1920	1,826	1,091	2,917			
1921	4,608	6,708	11,316			
1922	6,390	18,125	24,515			
1923	7,851	25,918	33,769			
1924	8,579	28,503	37,082			
1925	9,412	32,107	41,519			
1926	7,564	35,368	42,932			
1927	5,762	36,875	42,637			
1928	4,381	29,945	34,326			
1929	2,973	13,146	16,119			
1930	1,088	1,487	2,575			
1931	603	372	975			
1932	178	44	222			
1933	116	21	137			
1934	136	63	199			
1935	332	1,118	1,450			
1936	810	1,463	2,273			
1937	975	109	1,084			
1938	1,366	472	1,838			
1939	2,282	2,515	4,797			
1940	3,123	255	3,378	10,684		
1941	4,431	514	4,945	15,873		

SOURCES: Randall, *History of the Development of Building Construction in Chicago*, p. 298; Bell Savings and Loan Association, *Bell Survey of New Building in the Chicago Region, Annual Review*.
[a] Chicago Metropolitan Area (outside of Chicago) as used here excludes Porter County, Indiana, up to 1966.

TABLE 3—*Continued*

Year	City of Chicago			Chicago Metropolitan Area		
	Homes	Apartment Units	Total Residential Units	Homes	Apartment Units	Total Residential Units
1942	1,870	2,649	4,519	7,810		
1943	1,276	3,158	4,434	4,342		
1944	2,610	2,480	5,090	6,087	2,557	8,644
1945	3,672	1,687	5,359	8,940	2,190	11,130
1946	4,283	1,532	5,815	16,068	1,980	18,048
1947	3,986	1,982	5,968	18,431	6,313	24,744
1948	4,425	1,654	6,079	19,929	2,727	22,656
1949	4,944	4,869	9,813	21,532	6,244	27,776
1950	8,498	9,109	17,607	32,656	10,697	43,353
1951	6,640	4,698	11,338	27,378	5,560	32,938
1952	6,552	4,181	10,733	28,932	5,115	34,047
1953	8,682	3,165	11,847	36,486	4,096	40,582
1954	8,201	4,819	13,020	41,430	5,749	47,179
1955	9,278	6,797	16,075	44,529	8,341	52,870
1956	6,971	6,654	13,625	39,919	8,713	48,632
1957	4,937	5,632	10,569	30,884	8,694	39,578
1958	4,117	4,675	8,792	31,135	9,452	40,587
1959	5,237	4,616	9,853	35,432	12,177	47,609
1960	4,016	10,344	14,360	26,113	17,760	43,873
1961	3,430	10,829	14,259	24,415	20,549	44,964
1962	3,110	9,394	12,504	22,037	20,765	42,802
1963	2,663	6,308	8,971	19,737	19,777	39,514
1964	2,438	7,588	10,026	18,866	18,620	37,486
1965	2,620	7,071	9,691	20,897	19,405	40,302
1966	2,063	9,083	11,146	16,332	11,076	27,408
1967	1,714	9,966	11,680	20,165	16,371	36,536
1968	1,546	14,194	15,740	22,133	20,331	42,464
1969	869	10,245	11,114	17,527	22,790	40,317
1970	1,188	6,677	7,865	13,282	17,055	30,337

TABLE 4

ANNUAL AMOUNT OF NEW CONSTRUCTION IN CHICAGO, 1854 TO 1970

Year	Amount	Cost Index (1913 = 100)	Adjusted Amount (millions) (1913 = 100)	Population Ratio
1854	$ 2,438,910	62	$ 3.9	2.80
1855	3,735,254	53	7.0	3.40
1856	5,708,624	54	10.6	3.57
1857	6,423,518	58	11.1	3.72
1858	3,246,400	53	6.1	3.82
1859	2,044,000	54	3.8	3.95
1860	1,188,300	57	2.1	4.64
1861	797,800	58	1.4	5.10
1862	525,000	61	0.9	5.87
1863	2,500,000	75	3.3	6.37
1864	4,700,000	86	5.5	7.19
1865	6,950,000	92	7.6	7.58
1866	11,000,000	95	11.6	8.57
1867	8,500,000	96	8.9	9.56
1868	14,000,000	96	14.6	10.71
1869	11,000,000	96	11.5	11.89
1870	20,000,000	89	22.5	12.70
1871–72[a]	40,133,600	92	43.6	15.60
1873	25,500,000	92	27.7	16.14
1874	5,785,541	87	6.7	16.79
1875	9,778,080	77	12.7	17.01
1876	8,270,300	76	10.9	17.31
1877	9,071,050	70	13.0	18.26
1878	7,419,100	67	11.1	18.55
1879	6,745,000	64	10.5	20.88
1880	9,071,850	68	13.3	21.37
1881	8,832,305	71	12.4	22.93
1882	16,286,700	77	21.2	23.81
1883	22,162,000	75	29.5	24.63
1884	20,857,300	68	30.7	26.75
1885	19,624,100	68	28.9	28.24
1886	21,324,400	71	30.0	29.89
1887	19,778,100	71	27.9	32.28
1888	20,350,800	70	29.1	34.09
1889	25,065,500	69	36.3	39.71
1890	47,322,100	68	69.6	46.71
1891	54,001,800	66	81.8	48.79
1892	63,463,400	66	96.2	50.95
1893	28,517,700	65	43.9	53.22

SOURCES: Randall, *History of the Development of Building Construction in Chicago*, pp. 294–95; Bell Savings and Loan Association, *Survey of New Building in Chicago, Annual Review;* American Appraisal Company and *Engineering News-Record* (cost index); United States Census; Standard Rate and Data Service, Incorporated (population ratio).
a Period of 9 October 1871 to 9 October 1872.

TABLE 4—*Continued*

Year	Amount	Cost Index (1913 = 100)	Adjusted Amount (millions) (1913 = 100)	Population Ratio
1894	33,805,565	65	52.0	55.58
1895	34,920,643	64	54.6	58.05
1896	22,711,115	63	36.0	60.63
1897	21,690,030	61	35.6	63.32
1898	21,294,325	62	34.3	66.13
1899	20,857,570	68	30.7	69.07
1900	19,100,050	74	25.8	72.14
1901	34,911,755	77	45.3	74.21
1902	48,070,390	80	60.1	76.27
1903	33,645,025	82	41.0	77.92
1904	44,724,790	84	53.2	80.41
1905	63,455,020	87	72.9	82.47
1906	64,298,330	95	67.7	84.54
1907	54,093,080	96	56.3	86.61
1908	68,204,080	91	74.9	88.67
1909	90,558,580	94	96.3	90.74
1910	96,932,700	96	101.0	92.81
1911	105,269,700	97	108.5	95.53
1912	88,786,960	99	89.7	97.77
1913	89,668,427	100	89.7	100.00
1914	83,261,710	97	85.8	102.39
1915	97,291,480	100	97.3	104.66
1916	112,835,150	116	97.3	106.91
1917	64,244,450	141	45.6	109.14
1918	34,792,200	170	20.5	111.37
1919	104,198,850	224	46.5	113.61
1920	79,102,650	294	26.9	114.75
1921	125,004,510	226	55.3	120.28
1922	227,742,010	202	112.7	123.06
1923	329,604,312	228	144.6	125.91
1924	296,893,990	225	132.0	128.74
1925	360,794,250	224	161.1	131.51
1926	366,586,400	219	167.4	134.30
1927	352,936,400	222	159.0	137.14
1928	315,800,000	222	142.3	139.94
1929	202,286,800	222	91.1	142.71
1930	79,613,400	205	38.8	143.40
1931	46,440,130	185	25.1	143.47
1932	3,824,500	162	2.4	143.55
1933	3,683,960	156	2.4	143.63
1934	7,898,435	166	4.8	143.72
1935	17,120,947	169	10.1	143.81
1936	25,031,933	179	14.0	143.89
1937	28,806,443	204	14.1	143.98
1938	21,258,299	205	10.4	144.06
1939	41,597,282	205	20.3	144.15

TABLE 4—*Continued*

Year	Amount	Cost Index (1913 = 100)	Adjusted Amount (millions) (1913 = 100)	Population Ratio
1940	39,928,096	207	19.3	144.27
1941	49,151,997	216	22.8	144.40
1942	37,647,648	235	16.0	144.50
1943	15,607,975	244	6.4	144.59
1944	31,648,547	250	12.7	144.67
1945	61,495,655	260	23.7	152.68
1946	116,382,777	303	38.4	152.90
1947	113,431,800	404	28.1	153.32
1948	147,942,400	456	32.4	154.96
1949	141,872,200	452	31.4	155.60
1950	245,665,500	467	52.6	153.79
1951	205,062,583	503	40.8	153.48
1952	166,490,900	525	31.7	154.87
1953	226,548,200	539	42.0	156.58
1954	237,136,480	550	43.1	158.29
1955	285,365,302	569	50.2	160.96
1956	329,637,404	595	55.4	162.50
1957	346,129,984	614	56.4	164.21
1958	373,633,769	626	59.7	162.26
1959	287,413,202	643	44.7	164.17
1960	424,930,631	658	64.6	150.79
1961	409,365,008	671	61.0	150.86
1962	316,984,982	684	46.3	151.07
1963	338,360,257	709	47.7	150.56
1964	373,590,787	726	51.1	150.33
1965	294,225,216	747	39.4	150.56
1966	506,826,336	765	66.3	149.05[b]
1967	299,354,275	785	38.1	147.54[b]
1968	523,688,216	813	64.4	146.03[b]
1969	560,434,015	852	65.8	144.52[b]
1970	395,062,294	946	41.9	142.99[b]

[b] Estimated by extrapolation.

TABLE 5

SCHOOLS BUILT BY THE CHICAGO BOARD OF EDUCATION,
1872 TO 1970, BY DISTRICT

I. Schools Built before 1900

District 1 (Far Northwest)
None
District 2 (Far North)
Field, 1890
District 3 (Upper North)
McPherson, 1888
Blaine, 1893
Greeley, 1893
Nettelhorst, 1893
Ravenswood, 1893
Audubon, 1894
Burley, 1896
Morris, 1896
Lakeview High School, 1898
District 4 (Far Northwest)
Byford, 1892
Howe, 1896
Nash, 1896
District 5 (Middle Northwest)
Brentano, 1893
Avondale, 1895
Linne, 1895
Funston, 1896
Nixon, 1896
District 6 (Near Northwest)
Otis, 1879
Von Humboldt, 1885
Prosser, Logan Branch, 1889
Mitchell, 1892
Anderson, 1893
Drummond, 1893
Lafayette, 1893
Chase, 1894
Motley, 1894
Goethe, 1895
Peabody, 1895
Talcott, 1895
Yates, 1896
Burr, 1897
Schley, 1899
District 7 (Middle North)
Schiller, first, 1873
Headley, 1875
Sexton, 1883
Headley, Thomas Branch, 1890

Mulligan, 1890
Lincoln, 1894
Franklin, 1896
Schneider, 1896
District 8 (Middle West)
Calhoun South, 1881
Sumner, 1894
Marshall Upper Grade, 1895
District 9 (Near West)
King, 1873
Gladstone, 1884
Irving, 1884
Jefferson, 1884
McKinley, Emerson Branch, 1884
Brainard, 1885
McLaren, 1886
Jackson, 1894
Medill Intermediate, 1895
Smyth, 1897
Jirka, 1899
District 10 (Middle Far West)
Bryant, 1894
Farragut High School, 1894
District 11 (Near South)
Ward, 1874
Doolittle Intermediate and Upper, 1881
Haven, 1885
Haines, 1886
Douglas, 1889
Abbott, 1890
District 12 (Near Southwest)
Longfellow, 1881
Everett, 1892
Burroughs, 1893
Greene, 1895
District 13 (Middle South)
Vincennes Upper Grade, 1884
Farren, 1898
Willard, 1898
District 14 (Middle South Hyde Park)
Ray, 1894
Scott, 1896
Kozminski, 1897
District 15 (Far Southwest)
Fulton, 1895
Earle, 1896

SOURCE: Chicago Board of Education, Office of Operation Services. The table shows schools in existence in 1968 and those added up to 1970, other than mobile and portable units.

TABLE 5—*Continued*

District 16 (Far South)
　Westcott, 1880
　Gresham, 1895
　Burnside, 1898
District 17 (Far South Shore)
　Sheridan, Phil, 1888
　Thorp, 1893
　Gallistel, 1898
District 18 (Far South)
　Esmond, 1891
　Van Vlissingen, 1893
　West Pullman, 1894
　Scanlan, 1897
District 19 (Middle West Southwest)
　Harrison High School, Froebel Branch, 1885
　Cooper Primary and Intermediate, 1885
　Walsh, 1886
　Komensky, 1891
　Howland, 1893
　Whittier, 1893
　Lawson, 1896
　Pickard, 1896
　Spry Primary and Intermediate, 1899
District 20 (Middle Far South)
　Wentworth, 1890
　Kershaw, 1893
　Bass, 1895
　Parker Elementary, 1899
District 21 (Middle South)
　Englewood High School, 1887
　Beale Upper Grade, 1892
　Ross, 1894
　McCosh Intermediate and Upper, 1895
District 22 (South Shore)
　Bradwell, 1895
District 23 (Near South)
　Forrestville Upper Grade, 1892
　Shakespeare, 1893
District 24 (Far North)
　None
District 25 (West)
　Beidler, 1881
　Ryerson, 1891
　Lowell, 1894
　Tennyson Upper Grade, 1896
　Cameron, 1897
District 26 (Near Southwest)
　McClellan, 1881
　Sheridan, Mark, 1881
　Flower Vocational High School, Richards
　　Branch, 1885

　Holden, 1893
　Seward, 1894
　Hamline, 1898
District 27 (South)
　Cornell, 1896
Total built up to 1900 and retained　117
Total built and razed　52
Grand Total　169

II. Schools Built 1900-1910
District 1
　Chicago Parental, 1902
　Henry, 1904
　Cleveland, 1910
District 2
　None
District 3
　Coonley, 1902
　Hamilton, 1903
　Budlong, 1907
　Jahn, 1908
District 4
　Spencer, 1904
　May, 1905
　Key, 1907
District 5
　Darwin, 1900
　Belding, 1901
　Stowe, 1903
　Beaubien, 1905
　Monroe, 1905
　Lloyd, 1907
　Schurz High School, 1910
District 6
　Kosciuszko, 1906
　Moos, 1907
District 7
　Prescott, 1900
　Waller High School, 1901
　Cooley Vocational High School, 1908
　Jenner, 1908
District 8
　Marshall High School, 1902
District 9
　Crane High School, 1903
　McKinley Upper Grade, 1904
　Garfield, 1910
District 10
　Burns, 1903
　Whitney, 1905
　Penn, 1907

TABLE 5—*Continued*

Magellan, 1909
District 11
    Drake, 1900
    Oakland, 1903
    Phillips High School, 1904
District 12
    Sawyer, 1901
    Shields, 1902
    Davis, 1905
    Hedges, 1906
District 13
    None
District 14
    Fiske, 1905
District 15
    Libby, 1902
    Altgeld, 1905
    Copernicus, 1905
    Eberhart, 1906
    Raster, 1910
District 16
    Fernwood, 1901
    Oglesby, 1907
District 17
    Warren, 1907
    Bowen High School, 1910
    Marsh, 1910
District 18
    Poe, 1905
    Fenger High School, Curtis Branch, 1906
    Pullman, 1907
District 19
    Jungman, 1903
    Plamondon, 1903
    McCormick, 1905
    Washburne, 1909
District 20
    Harvard, 1905
District 21
    Goethals, 1902
District 22
    Sullivan, 1902
    Bryn Mawr, 1903
District 23
    Felsenthal, 1901
District 24
    Hayt, 1906
    Stewart, 1906
    Trumbull, 1909
District 25
    Morse, 1904

Tilton, 1909
    Nobel, 1910
District 26
    Dewey, 1900
    Armour, 1901
    Graham, 1905
    Tilden High School, 1905
District 27
    Revere, 1903
Total built 1900–1910   72

III. Schools Built 1911-20
District 1
    Haugan, 1911
    Hibbard, 1916
    Norwood Park, 1916
District 2
    Armstrong, 1912
District 3
    Waters, 1911
    Bell, 1916
    Le Moyne, 1916
District 4
    Emmet, 1913
    Thorp, 1918
District 5
    Gray, 1911
    Irving Park, 1911
    Mozart, 1911
    Reilly, 1914
    Portage Park, 1915
    Kelvyn Park High School, 1918
    Prosser Vocational High School, 1918
    Falconer, 1919
District 6
    Columbus, 1911
    Sabin, 1915
    Chopin Primary and Intermediate, 1917
    Tuley High School, 1918
District 7
    Agassiz, 1912
District 8
    Roentgen Educational and Vocational Guid-
      ance Center, 1913
District 9
    McLaren, 1911
    Birney, 1915
    Cregier Vocational High School, 1915
    Riis, 1915
District 10
    Corkery, 1911

TABLE 5—*Continued*

District 10 Continued
  Gary, 1911
  Herzl, 1916
District 11
  None
District 12
  Gage Park High School, Maplewood Avenue
    Branch, 1917
District 13
  Parkman, 1911
  Burke, 1912
District 14
  Hyde Park High School, 1911
  Kenwood High School, 1912
  Wadsworth Primary and Intermediate, 1920
District 15
  Harper High School, 1911
  Lindblom Technical High School, 1919
District 16
  Ryder, 1913
  Perry, 1920
District 17
  Clay, 1917
District 18
  Kohn, 1911
  Vanderpoel, 1912
  Morgan Park High School, 1914
District 19
  Hammond, 1912
  Harrison High School, 1912
  Shepard, 1914
  Pope, 1918
District 20
  Guggenheim, 1912
District 21
  Carter, 1913
  Sexton, 1915
  Lewis-Champlin, 1916
District 22
  Parkside, 1917
District 23
  None
District 24
  Senn High School, 1912
  Swift, 1914
  Peirce, 1915
District 25
  Delano, 1913
  Madison-Kildare Upper Grade Center, 1917
  Orr High School, 1919

District 26
  None
District 27
  Park Manor, 1913
  Avalon Park, 1917
Total Built 1911–20   61

IV. Schools Built 1921-30
District 1
  Bateman, 1921
  Farnsworth, 1925
  Peterson, 1925
  Hitch, 1926
  Ebinger, 1927
  Roosevelt High School, 1927
  Onahan, 1928
  Von Steuben High School, 1930
District 2
  Gale, 1922
  Clinton, 1926
  Sullivan High School, 1926
  Boone, 1928
District 3
  Amundsen High School, 1930
  Hawthorne, 1930
District 4
  Hay, 1921
  Young, 1924
  Bridge, 1926
  Lewis, 1926
  Lyon, 1926
  Key, Clark Branch, 1927
  Locke, 1927
  Lovett, 1927
  Burbank, 1929
  Austin High School, 1930
  Sayre, 1930
District 5
  Murphy, 1924
  Palmer, 1926
  Scammon, 1926
  Barry, 1927
  Prussing, 1927
  Foreman High School, 1928
  Reinberg, 1928
  Schubert, 1930
District 6
  None
District 7
  None

TABLE 5—*Continued*

District 8
 Gregory, 1923
 West Garfield Park Upper Grade, 1926
 Manley Primary and Intermediate, 1928
District 9
 Grant, 1925
 Spalding High School, 1928
District 10
 Mason Upper Grade, 1922
District 11
 None
District 12
 Gunsaulus, 1924
 Edwards, 1925
 Nightingale, 1926
 Peck, 1926
 Christopher, 1927
 Pasteur, 1927
 Twain, 1927
 Kelly High School, 1928
 Tonti, 1928
District 13
 Colman, 1922
 Horner, 1922
District 14
 None
District 15
 Henderson, 1923
 Marquette, 1926
 Morrill, 1926
 O'Toole, 1927
 McKay, 1928
 Hubbard High School, 1929
District 16
 Cook, 1925
 Calumet High School, 1926
 Barton, 1928
 Bennett, 1928
 Cook, Foster Park Church Branch, 1928
 Fort Dearborn, 1928
 Hookway, 1928
 Simeon Vocational High School, 1928
District 17
 Bright, 1922
 Taylor, 1923
District 18
 Brenan, 1925
 Fenger High School, 1926
 Gompers, 1926
 Shoop, 1926
 Sutherland, 1926

 Mount Vernon, 1928
 Barnard, 1929
 Clissold, 1930
District 19
 Hess Upper Grade, 1922
District 20
 Bond Upper Grade, 1926
 Parker High School, 1930
District 21
 None
District 22
 O'Keefe, 1925
 Coles, 1926
 Mann, 1926
District 23
 None
District 24
 Stockton, 1925
 Stone, 1928
District 25
 Delano, West Branch, 1922
 Westinghouse Vocational High School, 1922
 Flower Vocational High School, 1927
District 26
 None
District 27
 Ruggles, 1925
 Hirsch High School, 1926
 Dixon, 1929
Total Built 1921–30   88

V. Schools Built 1931-40
District 1
 Volta, 1931
 Garvy, 1936
 Sauganash, 1936
 Edgebrook, 1939
 Taft High School, 1939
District 2
 Kilmer, 1931
 Jamieson, 1937
 Rogers, 1937
District 3
 Lane Technical High School, 1934
 Chappell, 1937
District 4
 Smyser, 1932
 Steinmetz High School, 1934
 Dever, 1935
 Canty, 1936

TABLE 5—*Continued*

District 5
  None
District 6
  Wells High School, 1935
District 7
  Alcott, 1937
  Newberry, 1937
District 8
  None
District 9
  None
District 10
  None
District 11
  None
District 12
  Byrne, Michael, 1936
  Gage Park High School, 1939
District 13
  Du Sable High School, 1935
District 14
  Harte, 1931
District 15
  None
District 16
  Gillespie Primary and Intermediate, 1937
  Kellogg, Foster Park Branch, 1937
District 17
  Caldwell, 1936
District 18
  Mount Greenwood, 1936
  Kellogg, 1937
  Scanlan, Riverdale Branch, 1937
District 19
  None
District 20
  None
District 21
  None
District 22
  South Shore High School, 1940
District 23
  Doniat, 1935
  Oakenwald North Primary Grade, 1935
  Forrestville High School, 1938
District 24
  Goudy, 1937
District 25
  None
District 26
  Sherman, 1937

District 27
  Madison, 1939
Total Built 1931–40   34

VI. Schools Built 1941-50
District 1
  Oriole Park, 1943
  Wildwood, 1944
  Edison, 1945
District 2
  None
District 3
  Berteau-Hermitage, 1948
District 4
  None
District 5
  None
District 6
  Pulaski, 1949
District 7
  Manierre, 1947
District 8
  Marshall High School, Dante Branch, 1948
District 9
  None
District 10
  None
District 11
  Raymond, 1944
  Abbott, 1949
District 12
  None
District 13
  None
District 14
  None
District 15
  Owen, 1949
District 16
  Perry, Schmid Branch, 1948
District 17
  Chicago Vocational High School, 1941
  Luella, 1945
  Addams, 1948
District 18
  Carver Primary Grade, 1945
  Carver Upper Grade, 1946
  Carver High School, 1950
District 19
  None

TABLE 5—*Continued*

District 20
None
District 21
None
District 22
Black, 1948
District 23
Fuller, 1942
District 24
None
District 25
Goldblatt, 1941
District 26
None
District 27
None
Total Built 1941–50   20

VII. Schools Built 1951-60
District 1
Solomon, 1953
Ebinger, Stock Branch 1955
Beard, 1958
Sauganash, Thoreau Branch, 1959
Beard, Perkins Branch, 1960
District 2
Green, William, 1954
Armstrong, Bartelme Branch, 1957
Decatur, 1958
Mather High School, 1959
District 3
None
District 4
None
District 5
Reinberg, Hanson Branch, 1959
District 6
Andersen, 1955
Carpenter, 1957
District 7
Ogden, 1953
Cooley Upper Grade, 1958
Mayer, 1959
Byrd, 1960
District 8
King Elementary, 1959
District 9
Skinner, 1954
Brown, 1956
Gladstone, Allen Branch, 1958
Skinner, Sousa Branch, 1958

Medill Primary Grade, 1959
Suder, 1959
Birney, 1960
Montefiore Social Adjustment, 1960
District 10
Mason Primary Grades, 1958
Hughes, 1960
District 11
Williams, 1952
Dunbar Vocational High School, 1956
Attucks, 1957
Pershing, 1958
Einstein, 1960
District 12
Heart, 1952
Grimes, 1953
Hale, 1953
Dore, 1957
Kinzie, 1957
Peck, Nelson Branch, 1958
District 13
None
District 14
Murray, Philip, 1954
Carnegie, 1957
Reavis, 1958
Fermi, 1959
Tesla, 1960
District 15
Dawes, 1954
Hurley, 1954
Stevenson, 1954
Carroll, Rosenwald Branch, 1955
Pasteur, Lee Branch, 1956
Carroll, 1958
Hancock, 1958
Bogan High School, 1959
Hurley, Tarkington Branch, 1960
District 16
Fernwood, Wacker Branch, 1954
Drew, 1957
Harlan High School, 1958
District 17
Burnham, 1954
Burnham, Goldsmith Branch, 1954
Caldwell, McDowell Branch, 1954
Hoyne, 1955
Burnham, Anthony Branch, 1957
Washington High School, 1957
Hoyne, Earhart Branch, 1958

TABLE 5—*Continued*

District 18
  Nansen, 1953
  Mount Vernon, Dunne Branch, 1954
  Newton, 1955
  Cassell, Keller Branch, 1956
  Clissold, Sheldon Branch, 1957
  Whistler, 1958
  Aldridge, 1960
  Cassell, 1960
District 19
  Chalmers, 1959
District 20
  Yale Primary and Intermediate, 1951
  Deneen, 1955
District 21
  Beale Primary and Intermediate, 1958
  Moseley Social Adjustment, 1959
  McCosh Primary Grade, 1960
District 22
  None
District 23
  Oakenwald South Intermediate and Upper, 1955
  Judd, 1959
District 24
  None
District 25
  None
District 26
  Sherwood, 1951
  Hendricks, 1954
  Holmes, 1960
District 27
  Neil, 1953
Total Built 1951–60   82

VIII. Schools Built 1961-70
District 1
  None
District 2
  None
District 3
  None
District 4
  Spencer, 1968
District 5
  None
District 6
  Wicker, 1961
  Yates Upper Grade, 1962

District 7
  LaSalle, 1961
  Schiller, 1961
  Arnold Upper Grade, 1962
  Jones Commercial High School, 1967
District 8
  Calhoun, North, 1961
  Hefferan, 1961
  Ericson, 1962
  Jensen, 1962
  Marconi, 1962
  Webster, 1962
  Faraday, 1964
  Melody, 1965
  Marshall High School, Dante Branch, 1968
  Bethune, 1969
  Frazier, 1970
District 9
  Dodge, 1961
  Herbert, 1961
  Dett, 1963
District 10
  Crown, 1961
  Henson, 1961
  Dvorak, 1963
  Mason Intermediate Grade, 1964
  Paderewski, 1964
District 11
  Drake, 1961
  Mayo, 1961
  Doolittle Primary Grade, 1962
  Donoghue, 1963
District 12
  Dore, Blair Branch, 1961
  Grimes, Fleming Branch, 1961
  Twain, Baum Branch, 1961
  Kennedy High School, 1965
District 13
  Hartigan, 1961
  Beethoven, 1962
  Du Sable Upper Grade, 1962
  McCorkly, 1963
  Overton, 1963
  Terrell, 1963
District 14
  Shoesmith, 1961
  Dumas, 1963
  Wadsworth Upper Grade, 1963
  Hyde Park High School, Phase I, 1969
  Kenwood High School, 1969

TABLE 5—*Continued*

District 15
  Dawes, Michelson Branch, 1961
  Hancock, Crerar Branch, 1961
  Altgeld, 1968
District 16
  Bennett, Shedd Branch, 1961
  Gillespie Upper Grade, 1961
  Kipling, 1961
  McDade, 1961
  Gresham, 1968
  Ryder, 1968
  Evers, 1969
District 17
  Thorp, J. N., 1961
  Warren, Buckingham Branch, 1962
  Bowen High School, 1969
  Grissom, 1970
District 18
  Bates, 1961
  Mount Greenwood, Wiggin Branch, 1961
  Higgings, 1965
  Mount Greenwood, Duffy Branch, 1965
  Du Bois, 1969
District 19
  Cooper Upper Grade, 1962
  Johnson, 1963
  Lathrop, 1963
District 20
  Brownell, 1961
  Low Upper Grade, 1961
  Yale Upper Grade, 1963

  Banneker, 1963
  Hinton, 1965
  Stagg, 1967
District 21
  Dulles, 1962
  Reed, 1963
  Gershwin, 1965
District 22
  South Shore High School II, 1970
District 23
  Mollison, 1962
  Price, 1964
  Woodson, North, 1965
  Woodson, South, 1966
District 24
  Brennemann, 1963
  McCutcheon, 1964
District 25
  Cather, 1963
  Morton Upper Grade, 1964
District 26
  Healy, 1962
  Holmes, 1968
District 27
  Pirie, 1962
  Sbarbaro, 1963
  Tanner, 1963
Total Built 1961–70   90
Grand Total 1872–1970   616
Total Less Number Razed   564

TABLE 6

Railroads of the Chicago Switching District, 1910 to 1970

I. **Passenger-carrying Steam Railroads by Station**
   Central (Michigan Avenue at 11th Place; 1892–93)
   1. Illinois Central (owner)
   2. Chesapeake and Ohio (tenant; abandoned passenger service on the Chicago Division west of Hammond, Indiana, 1932)[a]
   3. Cleveland, Cincinnati, Chicago and Saint Louis (Big Four; tenant; leased to and merged with the New York Central 1930)
   4. Michigan Central (tenant; leased to and merged with the New York Central 1930; operations progressively transferred to LaSalle Street Station 1934 et seq., then to Union Station 1969)
   Dearborn (Polk and Dearborn streets; 1883–85)
   1. Chicago and Western Indiana (terminal company and owner; abandoned passenger service 1965)[b]
   2. Atchinson, Topeka and Santa Fe (Santa Fe; transferred operations to Union Station 1971)
   3. Chicago and Eastern Illinois (Evansville line acquired by the Louisville and Nashville 1969; remainder of property controlled by the Missouri Pacific; abandoned passenger service 1971)
   4. Chicago, Indianapolis and Louisville (Monon; abandoned passenger service 1967)
   5. Erie (merged with the Delaware, Lackawanna and Western to form the Erie-Lackawanna, 1960; abandoned passenger service 1970)[c]
   6. Grand Trunk Western (abandoned passenger service 1971)
   7. Wabash (leased to and merged with the Norfolk and Western 1964)
   Grand Central (Harrison and Wells streets; 1889–90; demolished 1971)
   1. Baltimore and Ohio (owner; see under terminal companies; transferred operations to North Western Station 1969; abandoned passenger service 1971)
   2. Chicago Great Western (Great Western or Corn Belt Route; abandoned passenger service 1956; merged with the Chicago and North Western 1968)
   3. Pere Marquette (merged with the Chesapeake and Ohio 1947; latter company abandoned passenger service 1971)
   4. Wisconsin Central (merged with the Minneapolis, Saint Paul and Sault Sainte Marie [Soo Line] 1961; abandoned passenger service in 1965)[d]
   Illinois Central Suburban (Michigan Avenue and Randolph Street; 1930–31)
   Illinois Central
   LaSalle Street (Van Buren at LaSalle Street; 1901–3)
   1. Chicago, Rock Island and Pacific (Rock Island; joint owner)
   2. New York Central (joint owner; merged with the Pennsylvania to form the Penn Central, 1968; transferred operations to Union Station 1969)[e]
   3. New York, Chicago and Saint Louis (Nickel Plate Road; tenant; merged with the Norfolk and Western and abandoned passenger service 1964)
   North Western (Canal and Madison streets; 1906–11)
   Chicago and North Western (North Western)
   Union (Canal Street between Adams Street and Jackson Boulevard; 1916–25)
   1. Chicago, Burlington and Quincy (Burlington; joint owner)

[a] Before July 1910 the Chicago Division of the C. and O. was a separate company, the Chicago, Cincinnati and Louisville Railroad.
[b] All railroads using Dearborn Station except the Chicago and Western Indiana were tenant companies.
[c] Before 1960 the Erie main line between Chicago and Marion, Ohio, was a separate but controlled and merged subsidiary company, the Chicago and Erie Railroad.
[d] All railroads using Grand Central Station except the B. and O. were tenant companies.
[e] Before 1914 the lines of the New York Central terminating at Chicago were divided between the Lake Shore and Michigan Southern and the Chicago, Indiana and Southern railroads.

TABLE 6—*Continued*

---

2. Chicago, Milwaukee, Saint Paul and Pacific (Milwaukee Road; joint owner)[f]
3. Pittsburgh, Cincinnati, Chicago and Saint Louis (joint owner; leased to the Pennsylvania 1921; latter company merged with the New York Central to form the Penn Central, 1968)
4. Pittsburgh, Fort Wayne and Chicago (joint owner; same history as the P.C.C. and St. L. except that present lease dates from 1918)
5. Chicago and Alton (tenant; merged with the Gulf, Mobile and Ohio 1947)[g]

II. **Switching, Belt, Transfer, and Line-haul Freight-carrying Railroads**
1. Baltimore and Ohio Chicago Terminal (owned by the B. and O.)
2. Belt Railway Company of Chicago (jointly owned by the A. T. and S. F., C. B. and Q., C. and O., C. and E. I., C. I. and L., C. R. I. and P., Erie, G. T. W., I. C., M. St. P. and S. Ste. M., Penna., P. M., and Wabash, and by the various later successors of these companies)
3. Chicago Junction (leased to the Chicago River and Indiana and operated by the New York Central)
4. Chicago River and Indiana (controlled and operated by the New York Central)
5. Elgin, Joliet and Eastern (line-haul carrier; owned by the United States Steel Corporation)
6. Indiana Harbor Belt (jointly owned by the Milwaukee and the New York Central)

III. **Industrial Switching Railroads**
1. Chicago and Calumet River
2. Chicago and Illinois Western
3. Chicago Short Line
4. Chicago, West Pullman and Southern
5. Illinois Northern
6. Manufacturers Junction
7. Pullman

IV. **Terminal Railroads**
1. Baltimore and Ohio Chicago Terminal (proprietary company of Grand Central Station and a switching and transfer line; owned by the B. and O.)
2. Chicago and Western Indiana (proprietary company of Dearborn Station and a switching and transfer line; owned by the Dearborn tenant companies)

V. **Electric Interurban Railroads**
1. Chicago, Aurora and Elgin; terminal at Quincy and Wells streets (operated by trackage rights over the Chicago Rapid Transit and the Chicago Transit Authority, city limits to Market Street [Wacker Drive]; passenger carrier only; abandoned service 1957)
2. Chicago, North Shore and Milwaukee; terminal at Roosevelt Road elevated station (operated by trackage rights over the Chicago Rapid Transit and the Chicago Transit Authority, south city limit of Wilmette to terminal; freight and passenger carrier; abandoned service on the Shore Line 1955, and on the remainder of trackage 1963)
3. Chicago, South Shore and South Bend; tenant company in the Illinois Central Suburban Station, Michigan Avenue and Randolph Street (operated by trackage rights over the Illinois Central from 115th Street to terminal; freight and passenger carrier; controlled by the Chesapeake and Ohio Railway since 1967)

---

f Before 1927 the corporate title of the Milwaukee was Chicago, Milwaukee and Saint Paul Railroad.
g All tenant companies of the various stations operated their trains by trackage rights over the lines of the proprietary companies for varying distances within the Chicago Switching District with the following exceptions: the Big Four operated trains by trackage rights over the Illinois Central Railroad from Kankakee, Illinois, to Central Station, a distance of fifty-four miles, and the Pere Marquette operated in similar fashion over the New York Central, Baltimore and Ohio, Rock Island, and Baltimore and Ohio Chicago Terminal railroads, in succession, from Porter, Indiana, to Grand Central Station, a distance of forty-eight miles.

TABLE 7

Revenue Passengers Carried by Chicago Transit Authority and Predecessor Companies, 1906 to 1970

Year	Chicago Surface Lines[a]	Chicago Rapid Transit Company	Chicago Motor Coach Company	Combined	Population of Chicago	Rides per Capita	Passenger Automobile Registration (Chicago)	Population per Passenger Automobile
1906	373,900,000	131,958,605		505,858,605	1,990,600	254		
1907	372,123,199	147,263,985		519,387,184	2,039,271	255		
1908	396,073,965	150,371,374		546,445,339	2,087,942	262	5,475b	381.4
1909	442,511,273	152,423,961		594,935,234	2,136,613	278	7,110	300.5
1910	481,822,110	164,875,974		646,698,084	2,185,283	296	9,963	219.3
1911	561,517,222	162,866,136		724,383,358	2,236,926	324	11,876	188.4
1912	589,178,708	164,314,524		753,493,232	2,288,568	329	16,857	135.7
1913	634,026,040	164,164,225		798,190,265	2,340,210	341	22,136	105.7
1914	629,931,909	165,770,135		795,702,044	2,391,852	333	26,814	89.2
1915	619,547,956	164,678,900		784,226,856	2,443,494	321	34,441	70.9
1916	681,583,470	180,649,694		862,233,164	2,495,136	346	48,358	51.6
1917	700,462,712	193,119,829	3,077,558	896,660,099	2,546,778	352	59,382	42.9
1918	676,263,883	197,436,736	4,571,374	878,271,993	2,598,420	338	58,505	44.4
1919	741,252,551	184,667,604	6,060,365	931,980,520	2,650,063	352	75,241	35.2
1920	768,042,418	190,636,873	6,395,472	965,074,763	2,701,705	357	106,500c	25.4
1921	750,386,454	180,626,990	7,774,953	938,788,397	2,769,178	339	137,750	20.1
1922	758,040,458	181,283,785	9,619,558	948,943,801	2,836,652	335	172,655	16.4
1923	821,409,074	203,943,551	21,916,485	1,047,269,110	2,904,126	361	218,991	13.3
1924	829,700,944	213,006,798	49,268,427	1,091,976,169	2,971,599	367	260,887	11.4
1925	840,972,623	216,045,575	57,492,529	1,114,510,727	3,039,072	367	289,948	10.5
1926	874,242,057	228,812,766	55,838,927	1,158,893,750	3,106,545	373	317,433	9.8
1927	881,948,268	226,212,172	59,270,849	1,167,431,289	3,174,018	368	335,263	9.5
1928	890,960,073	207,864,238	61,836,233	1,160,660,544	3,241,490	358	360,985	9.0
1929	899,878,161	196,774,395	69,001,990	1,165,654,546	3,308,962	352	402,078	8.2
1930	821,166,771	182,954,846	58,310,208	1,062,431,825	3,376,438	315	406,916	8.3
1931	739,903,327	152,414,248	49,571,371	941,888,946	3,378,475	279	423,786	8.0
1932	641,101,119.	126,989,541	40,799,663	808,890,323	3,380,512	239	396,783	8.5
1933	645,576,749	124,855,354	49,298,578	819,730,681	3,382,549	242	367,402	9.2
1934	676,906,698	127,276,803	43,698,473	847,881,974	3,384,586	251	368,585	9.2
1935	664,742,602	123,497,788	40,019,162	828,259,552	3,386,623	245	397,023	8.5
1936	706,631,957	129,578,269	47,827,417	884,037,643	3,388,660	261	461,527	7.3

Source: Public Information Department, Chicago Transit Authority.

a Chicago Surface Lines includes former Chicago Motor Coach Company passengers for 1953 et seq.

b Automobile registration based on fiscal years ending 30 April of the following year.

c Figure for 1920 estimated by averaging registrations for the fiscal year ended 30 April 1920 and the calendar year of 1921.

TABLE 7—*Continued*

REVENUE PASSENGERS CARRIED BY CHICAGO TRANSIT AUTHORITY AND PREDECESSOR COMPANIES, 1906 TO 1970

Year	Chicago Surface Lines	Chicago Rapid Transit Company	Chicago Motor Coach Company	Combined	Population of Chicago	Rides per Capita	Passenger Automobile Registration (Chicago)	Population per Passenger Automobile
1937	709,304,031	128,005,374	55,618,162	892,927,567	3,390,697	263	504,207	6.7
1938	663,673,976	121,702,897	54,812,976	840,189,849	3,392,734	248	506,071	6.7
1939	660,324,561	121,426,629	55,386,336	837,137,526	3,394,771	247	516,128	6.6
1940	672,205,539	123,704,810	57,410,265	853,320,614	3,396,808	251	549,537	6.2
1941	690,592,406	127,133,614	60,304,813	878,030,833	3,419,224	257	585,219	5.8
1942	747,407,420	133,208,577	69,189,952	949,805,949	3,441,638	276	545,777	6.3
1943	818,117,640	140,905,171	67,835,380	1,026,858,191	3,464,054	296	467,423	7.4
1944	842,862,953	151,062,563	70,986,197	1,064,911,713	3,486,468	305	433,880	8.0
1945	844,844,660	157,344,085	75,018,686	1,077,207,431	3,508,884	307	427,779	8.2
1946	917,002,050	157,876,421	72,732,022	1,147,610,493	3,531,298	325	461,721	7.6
1947	888,533,148	145,755,514	85,835,806	1,120,124,468	3,553,714	315	512,810	6.4
1948	825,379,675	137,621,520	89,210,955	1,052,212,150	3,576,128	294	567,726	6.3
1949	724,851,315	122,259,827	82,841,920	929,953,062	3,598,543	258	634,352	5.7
1950	641,597,249	110,603,719	80,911,483	833,112,451	3,620,962	230	705,197	5.1
1951	584,141,163	112,807,016	82,297,751	779,245,930	3,613,907	216	734,785	4.9
1952	525,415,421	112,687,227	82,796,043	720,898,691	3,606,851	200	725,746	5.0
1953	574,821,563	111,738,503		686,560,066	3,599,795	191	764,942	4.7
1954	529,934,199	111,232,302		641,166,501	3,592,740	178	792,940	4.5
1955	510,603,672	112,889,976		623,493,648	3,585,684	174	831,418	4.3
1956	505,623,461	115,659,105		621,282,566	3,578,628	174	870,487	4.1
1957	469,785,257	112,280,610		582,065,867	3,571,572	163	874,797	4.1
1958	426,226,629	107,067,414		533,294,043	3,564,516	150	856,443	4.2
1959	432,684,329	113,330,994		546,015,323	3,557,460	153	857,547	4.1
1960	421,832,145	112,924,491		534,756,636	3,550,404	151	854,572	4.2
1961	395,405,445	110,126,318		505,531,763	3,540,000	143	851,073	4.2
1962	390,842,961	114,068,016		504,910,977	3,534,000	143	859,096	4.1
1963	381,166,527	111,065,005		492,231,532	3,534,000	139	861,702	4.1
1964	379,251,204	111,218,011		490,469,215	3,534,000	139	867,399	4.1
1965	388,076,702	114,597,086		502,673,788	3,534,000	142	888,969	4.0
1966	405,728,973	117,562,012		523,290,985	3,466,000	151	913,939	3.8
1967	389,770,830	120,737,566		510,508,396	3,466,000	147	927,210	3.7
1968	346,976,958	110,792,832		457,769,790	3,520,000	130	942,959	3.7
1969	317,024,210	103,071,290		420,095,500	3,470,000	121	957,212	3.6
1970	296,176,300d	105,598,382		401,774,682	3,366,951	119	972,000d	3.5

d Estimate.

Bibliography

General Works

Abbott, Edith. *The Tenements of Chicago, 1908–1935*. Chicago: University of Chicago Press, 1936.

Andrews, Wayne. *Architecture in Chicago and Mid-America: A Photographic Essay*. New York: Atheneum, 1968.

Bach, Ira J. *Chicago on Foot*. Chicago and New York: Follett Publishing Company, 1969.

Banham, Reyner. *The Architecture of the Well-Tempered Environment*. London: Architectural Press, 1969.

Brooks, H. Allen. *The Prairie School: Frank Lloyd Wright and His Midwest Contemporaries*. Toronto: University of Toronto Press, 1972.

Burchard, John, and Bush-Brown, Albert. *The Architecture of America: A Social and Cultural History*. Boston: Little, Brown and Company, 1961.

Butler, Rush C., Jr. *Chicago*. Chicago: American Publishers Corporation, 1929.

Condit, Carl W. *American Building Art: The Twentieth Century*. New York: Oxford University Press, 1961.

——. *American Building: Materials and Techniques from the Beginning of the Colonial Settlements to the Present*. Chicago: University of Chicago Press, 1968.

——. *The Chicago School of Architecture: A History of Commercial and Public Building in the Chicago Area, 1875–1925*. Chicago: University of Chicago Press, 1964.

Corplan Associates, IIT Research Institute. *Technological Change: Its Impact on Industry in Metropolitan Chicago*. 8 vols. Chicago: IIT Research Institue, 1964.

Cutler, Irving. *The Chicago-Milwaukee Corridor: A Geographic Study of Intermetropolitan Coalescence*. Northwestern University Studies in Geography, no. 9. Evanston, Ill.: Northwestern University, 1965.

Ericsson, Henry, and Myers, Lewis E. *Sixty Years a Builder*. Chicago: A. Kroch and Son, 1942.

Giedion, Sigfried. *Space, Time and Architecture*, 3d ed. Cambridge, Mass.: Harvard University Press, 1954.

Gilbert, Paul, and Bryson, Charles Lee. *Chicago and Its Makers*. Chicago: Felix Mendelsohn, 1929.

Hitchcock, Henry-Russell. *In the Nature of Materials, 1887–1941: The Buildings of Frank Lloyd Wright*. New York: Duell, Sloan and Pearce, 1942.

Hoyt, Homer. *One Hundred Years of Land Values in Chicago*. Chicago: University of Chicago Press, 1933.

Jones, Cranston. *Architecture Today and Tomorrow*. New York: McGraw-Hill Book Company, 1961.

Jordy, William H. "The Commercial and the 'Chicago School.' " In *Perspectives in American History* (Cambridge, Mass.: Charles Warren Center for Studies in American History, 1967), 1:390–400.

Kranzberg, Melvin, and Pursell, Carroll W., Jr., eds. *Technology in Western Civilization*. 2 vols. New York: Oxford University Press, 1967.

Manson, Grant Carpenter. *Frank Lloyd Wright to 1910: The First Golden Age*. New York: Reinhold Publishing Corporation, 1958.

Mayer, Harold, and Wade, Richard. *Chicago: Growth of a Metropolis*. Chicago: University of Chicago Press, 1969.

Mendelsohn, Felix. *Chicago: Yesterday and Today*. Chicago: Felix Mendelsohn, 1932.

Merriam, Charles Edward. *Chicago: A More Intimate View of Urban Politics*. New York: Macmillan Company, 1929.

"Metals Review." *Progressive Architecture* 50 (October 1969):132–204.

Mujica, Francisco. *The History of the Skyscraper*. New York: Archaeology and Architecture Press, 1930.

Museum of Modern Art. *Built in USA, 1932–1944*. New York: Museum of Modern Art, 1944.

———. *Built in USA: Post-War Architecture*. New York: Museum of Modern Art, 1952.

One Hundred and Twenty Five Photographic Views of Chicago. Chicago and New York: Rand McNally and Company, 1902.

Ousley, Steve. "Engineering Chicago's Buildings." *Actual Specifying Engineer* 13 (January 1965):86–87, 134–38.

Peisch, Mark L. *The Chicago School of Architecture*. New York: Random House, 1964.

Pierce, Bessie Louise. *A History of Chicago*. 3 vols. New York: Alfred A. Knopf, 1937–57.

Randall, Frank A. *History of the Development of Building Construction in Chicago*. Urbana: University of Illinois Press, 1949.

Royko, Mike. *Boss: Richard J. Daley of Chicago*. New York: E. P. Dutton and Company, 1971.

Scully, Vincent. *American Architecture and Urbanism*. New York: Frederick A. Praeger, 1969.

Sexton, R. W. *American Apartment Houses, Hotels, and Apartment Hotels of Today*. New York: Architectural Book Publishing Company, 1929.

Short, James F., Jr. *The Social Fabric of the Metropolis: Contributions of the "Chicago School of Urban Sociology."* Chicago: University of Chicago Press, 1971.

Siegel, Arthur, ed. *Chicago's Famous Buildings*. Chicago: University of Chicago Press, 1969.

Spear, Allan H. *Black Chicago: The Making of a Negro Ghetto, 1890–1920*. Chicago: University of Chicago Press, 1967.

Taylor, Nicholas. "Chicago: America's German Miracle." *Sunday Times Magazine* (London), 1 September 1968, pp. 24–29.

"The Ups and Downs of Chicago Real Estate." *Architectural Forum* 59 (August 1933):141–43, 149.

Chapter 1. The City in Its Natural Setting

"A Comprehensive Sewage Treatment Program for the Sanitary District of Chicago." *Engineering News* 66 (30 November 1911):650–54.

Cooley, Lyman E. *The Diversion of the Waters of the Great Lakes by Way of the Sanitary and Ship Canal of Chicago*. Chicago: Sanitary District, 1913.

Eaton, Leonard K. *Landscape Artist in America: The Life and Work of Jens Jensen*. Chicago: University of Chicago Press, 1964.

Ericson, John. "Chicago Water Works." *Journal of the Western Society of Engineers* 18 (October 1913):763–96.

Fryxell, F. M. *The Physiography of the Region of Chicago*. Chicago: University of Chicago Press, 1927.

Garfield Park Conservatory. Chicago: Chicago Park District, undated leaflet.

Illinois Department of Public Works and Buildings. *Documentary History of the Illinois and Michigan Canal*. Springfield: Division of Waterways, 1956.

Lincoln Park Commissioners. *Annual Report of the Lincoln Park Commission*. Chicago: Lincoln Park Commission, 1894–1933.

Rand McNally Chicago Street Guide and Transportation Directory. Chicago: Rand McNally and Company, 1968.

"The Reclamation of an Extension to Lincoln Park, Chicago." *Engineering Record* 59 (27 February 1909):243–44.

South Park Commissioners. *Annual Report of the South Park Commission*. Chicago: South Park Commission, 1869–1933.

United States Works Progress Administration. *Historical Register of the Twenty-Two Superseded Park Districts*. 2 vols., typescript. Chicago: Chicago Park District and Works Progress Administration, 1941.

The Water System of Chicago. Chicago: Department of Water and Sewers, 1966.

West Chicago Park Commissioners. *The West Parks and Boulevards of Chicago*. Chicago: West Chicago Park Commissioners, [1914].

Chapter 2. The Transportation Network

"Central Station at Twelfth Street, Chicago, Illinois Central Railroad." *Railroad Gazette* 24 (14 October 1892):758–59.

The Chicago Freight Tunnels. Chicago: Chicago Tunnel Terminal Corporation, 1928.

"The Chicago, North Shore and Milwaukee Railroad." *Baldwin Locomotives* 2 (April 1924):28–33.

Chicago Subway Commission. *A Report on an Underground Rapid Transit System for Chicago.* Chicago: Chicago Subway Commission, 1911.

Droege, John A. *Passenger Terminals and Trains.* New York: McGraw-Hill Book Company, 1916.

Foreman, Milton J. *The Electrification of Railway Terminals in Chicago.* Chicago: R. R. Donnelley and Sons Company, 1908.

Gaskill, Charles H. "The Chicago Rapid Transit Company." *Baldwin Locomotives* 6 (October 1927):28–35.

Hilton, George W. "What Was Grand about Grand Central?" *Trains* 29 (September 1969):20–28.

Hilton, George W., and Due, John F. *The Electric Interurban Railway in America.* Stanford: Stanford University Press, 1960.

"History of Chicago Passenger Stations." *Journal of the Western Society of Engineers* 42 (April 1937):78–82; 42 (June 1937):124–32; 42 (October 1937):250–61.

Mayer, Harold M. "The Railway Pattern of Metropolitan Chicago." Ph.D. diss., Geography Department, University of Chicago, 1943.

Meeks, Carroll L. V. *The Railroad Station: An Architectural History.* New Haven: Yale University Press, 1956.

Middleton, William D. *The Interurban Era.* Milwaukee: Kalmbach Publishing Company, 1961.

"The New General Passenger Depot in Chicago." *Railroad Gazette* 13 (13 May 1881):257–59.

"New Terminal Station at Chicago for the C. R. I. & P. Ry. and the L. S. & M. S. Ry." *Engineering News* 50 (6 August 1903):114–19.

Official Guide to the Steam Railways of the United States, Mexico and Canada. New York: National Railway Publication Company, 1868 et seq.

Pinkepank, Jerry A. "The Belt Railway of Chicago: A Railroad's Railroad." *Trains* 26 (September 1966):36–46.

———. "How the Belt Came to Be." *Trains* 26 (October 1966):42–49.

Poor's Manual of the Railroads of the United States. New York: Poor's Railroad Manual Company, 1867 et seq.

Stover, John F. *American Railroads.* Chicago: University of Chicago Press, 1961.

————. *The Life and Decline of the American Railroad.* New York: Oxford University Press, 1970.

White, Linn. "Park Drives and Boulevards." *Municipal Engineering* 44 (February 1913):89–95.

Wilcox, R. B. "The River and Harbor of Chicago." *Journal of the Western Society of Engineers* 5 (November–December 1900):499–535.

Wisner, George M. "A Description of the Opening of the Chicago Drainage Canal." *Journal of the Western Society of Engineers* 5 (January–February 1900):8–11.

Chapter 3. The Chicago Plan

Burnham, Daniel H., and Bennett, Edward H. *The Plan of Chicago.* Edited by Charles H. Moore. Chicago: Commercial Club, 1909.

McLean, Robert Craik. "The Gookins' Plan for Chicago's Reconstruction." *Western Architect* 35 (January 1926):8, 11.

Moody, Walter D. "The Chicago Plan." *Municipal Engineering* 43 (September 1912):136–45.

————. *Wacker's Manual of the Plan of Chicago.* Chicago: Chicago Plan Commission, 1912.

Moore, Charles H. *Daniel Hudson Burnham. Architect, Planner of Cities.* 2 vols. Boston: Houghton Mifflin Company, 1921.

Moulton, R. H. "Plan of Chicago." *Architectural Record* 46 (November 1919):457–70.

Saarinen, Eliel. "Illuminating Example: Chicago," in *The City: Its Growth, Its Decay, Its Future,* pp. 300–316. New York: Reinhold Publishing Corporation, 1943.

Wacker, Charles H. "Chicago: 'A City Set in a Garden.' " *Municipal Engineering* 44 (January 1913):45–47.

Chapter 4. Buildings of the Commercial City

"Air Rights Office Building in Chicago." *Engineering News-Record* 102 (25 April 1929):664–67.

"Architectural News in Photographs." *Architecture* 56 (October 1927):196; 57 (May 1928):262; 59 (February 1929):86; 61 (January 1930):51.

The Architectural Work of Graham, Anderson, Probst and White, Chicago. 2 vols. London: B. T. Batsford, 1933.

"Architecture and Illumination." *Architectural Forum* 35 (October 1921):135.

"Barry, Marlboro, 1120 Lake Shore Drive, Jackson Towers, Devonshire, Sheridan-Brompton, 440 Belmont Avenue, 507 Aldine Apartments, Chicago." *Western Architect,* vol. 35 (April 1926), pls. 49–64.

Berkenbilt, S. E. "Chicago Concrete Building Presents Difficult Foundation Problems." *Engineering News-Record* 104 (10 April 1930):619–22.

Berry, R. D. "[Civic Opera House] Stage Equipment and Lighting." *Architectural Forum* 52 (April 1930):605–8.

"Beverly Theater, Chicago." *Architectural Forum* 64 (January 1936):45–48.

"Building Details and Equipment of Tribune Tower, Chicago." *Engineering News-Record* 94 (19 February 1925):310–11.

Burt, H. J. "Growth of Steel Frame Buildings." *Engineering News-Record* 92 (17 April 1924):680–84.

Chase, Al. "Michigan Avenue Building Sold for 4 Million." *Chicago Tribune*, 5 November 1946, sect. 1, pp. 1, 5.

"Chicago Board of Trade Building." *Architecture and Building* 62 (June 1930):162–63, 174–76.

"Chicago Theater, Chicago." *Architectural Forum*, vol. 42 (June 1925), pl. 75.

Dubin, Henry. "Constructing the Battledeck House." *Architectural Forum* 55 (August 1931):227–31.

————. "Welding Extensively Employed in Steel House." *Welding* 1 (January 1932):3–8.

Eberson, John. "A Description of the Capitol Theater, Chicago." *Architectural Forum* 42 (June 1925):373–76, pl. 80.

"The Estate of Marshall Field Is Completing Its Largest Project." *Architectural Forum* 59 (December 1933):508–11.

Frazier, C. A. "Mechanical Equipment of the Chicago Civic Opera Building." *Architectural Forum* 52 (April 1930):610–14.

Fuller, Ernest. "Famous Chicago Buildings." *Chicago Tribune:*
  "American Furniture Mart," 28 February 1959, part 2, p. 5.
  "Board of Trade Building," 29 November 1958, part 2, p. 5.
  "Carbide and Carbon Building," 31 January 1959 part 2, p. 5.
  "Chicago Temple Building," 25 April 1959, part 2, p. 5.
  "City National Bank Building," 21 March 1959, part 2, p. 5.
  "Conrad Hilton Hotel," 28 March 1959, part 2, p. 5.
  "Continental Companies Building," 2 May 1959, part 2, p. 5.
  "Field Building," 3 January 1959, part 2, p. 5.
  "Insurance Exchange," 9 May 1959, part 2, p. 5.
  "International Harvester Building," 16 May 1959, part 2, p. 5.
  "Kemper Insurance Building," 10 January 1959, part 2, p. 5.
  "London Guarantee Building," 24 January 1959, part 2, p. 5.
  "Merchandise Mart," 13 December 1958, part 2, p. 5.
  "One LaSalle Street," 30 May 1959, part 2, p. 5.
  "120 South LaSalle Street," 18 April 1959, Sports–Business sect., p. 5.

"Palmolive Building," 21 February 1959, part 2, p. 5.

"Pittsfield Building," 7 February 1959, part 2, p. 5.

"Pure Oil Building," 11 April 1959, Sports–Business section, p. 5.

"333 North Michigan Avenue," 23 May 1959, part 2, p. 5.

"The Tribune Tower," 7 March 1959, part 2, p. 5.

"Wrigley Building," 27 December 1958, part 2, p. 4.

Granger, Alfred. "The Tribune Tower as a Work of Architecture." *Western Architect* 34 (November 1925):111–13.

Gray, W. B. "Engineering Features of the Daily News Building." *American Architect and Architecture* 137 (January 1930):60–61.

Gunderson, Magnus. "The Structural Design of the Chicago Civic Opera Building." *Architectural Forum* 52 (April 1930):595–98.

"Handling the Excavation and Concrete Materials for a Large Steel Cage Building." *Engineering Record* 58 (28 November 1908):609–11.

Hood, Raymond M. "Exterior Architecture of Office Buildings." *Architectural Forum* 41 (September 1924):97–99.

———. "The Tribune Tower: The Architect's Problem." *Western Architect* 34 (November 1925):114.

Hoskins, Henry J. B. "The Palmolive Building, Chicago." *Architectural Forum* 52 (May 1930):655–66.

———. "Structure and Equipment of the Palmolive Building." *Architectural Forum* 52 (May 1930):731–36.

The International Competition for a New Administration Building for the Chicago Tribune, MCMXXII. Chicago: Chicago Tribune Company, 1923.

Joy, S. Scott. "The Central Manufacturing District, Chicago, Ill. Part I. General Features of Operation." *Architectural Forum* 34 (April 1921):123–28; "Part II. Architectural and Construction Features." *Architectural Forum* 34 (May 1921): 177–82.

"LaSalle Hotel." *Architectural Review* 2 (new series, March 1913):88–89, 163–69.

Lee, Anne. "The Chicago Civic Opera Building." *Architectural Forum* 52 (April 1930):490–514.

———. "Chicago Daily News Building." *Architectural Forum* 52 (January 1930): 21–59.

"London Guarantee and Accident Building." *Architectural Forum*, vol. 41 (September 1924), pls. 38–40.

Loucks, F. "Electrical Installations, 20 Wacker Drive Building." *Architectural Forum* 52 (April 1930):608–9.

Magurn, E. A. "Two Theaters in Chicago Office Building." *Engineering News-Record* 103 (14 November 1929):758–62.

The Marshall Field Garden Apartment Homes. Chicago: Marshall Field Estates, [1929].

McCormick, Robert R. "The Tribune Tower: The Owner's View." *Western Architect* 34 (November 1925):115.

Mumford, Lewis. "Is the Skyscraper Tolerable?" *Architecture* 55 (February 1927):69.

———. "New York vs. Chicago in Architecture." *Architecture* 56 (November 1927):242.

"The New American Furniture Mart, Chicago." *Western Architect* 34 (April 1925): 36–38, pls. 1–9.

Ogden, Palmer H. "The Chicago Allerton House." *Architectural Forum* 42 (May 1925):313–16, pls. 58–60.

"Rapid Progress Made on 32-Story Office Building at Chicago." *Engineering News-Record* 92 (27 March 1924):541.

Rebori, A. N. "The Straus Building, Chicago." *Architectural Record* 57 (May 1925): 385–94, 417–24.

———. "The Work of Burnham and Root, D. H. Burnham, D. H. Burnham and Co., and Graham, Burnham and Co." *Architectural Record* 38 (July 1915):9–168.

Reed, Earl H., Jr. "Some Recent Work of Holabird and Root, Architects." *Architecture* 61 (January 1930): 13–15, 27–32.

"Roosevelt Theater, Chicago." *Architectural Forum*, vol. 42 (June 1925), pls. 78–79.

Sabine, Paul E. "Acoustics of the Chicago Civic Opera House." *Architectural Forum* 52 (April 1930):599–604.

Sheridan, Leo J., and Clark, W. C. "The Straus Building, Chicago." *Architectural Forum* 42 (April 1925):225–28, pls. 45–47.

Solon, Leon V. "The Evolution of an Architectural Design: The Tribune Building Tower, Chicago." *Architectural Record* 59 (March 1926):215–25.

"Some Industrial Buildings by George C. Nimmons." *Architectural Record* 38 (August 1915):229–45.

"Steelwork in the LaSalle Hotel, Chicago." *Engineering Record* 59 (5 June 1909): 713–16.

Stowell, Kenneth K. "Structure and Equipment of the Chicago Daily News Building." *Architectural Forum* 52 (January 1930, part 2):107–14.

Sullivan, Louis H. "The Chicago Tribune Competition." *Architectural Record* 53 (February 1923):151–57.

"A Thirty-Four-Story Steel Frame Tower Building in Chicago." *Engineering News-Record* 94 (21 May 1925):848–50.

"Tower 256 Ft. High Tops Twenty-Four-Story Building." *Engineering News-Record* 99 (24 November 1927):824–27.

"Trains of Portable Conveyors Place Concrete for Large Building." *Engineering News-Record* 103 (12 September 1929):420–21.

" 'The Tribune' Building, Chicago, Ill." *American Architect* 128 (5 October 1925):20, pls. 264–71.

"The Tribune Tower Building, Chicago." *Architectural Forum* 41 (September 1924): 100.

"Trustees System Service Building, Chicago." *Architectural Forum:*1 (January 1931): 9–20.

"Underpinning Printing Plant for New Deep Foundations." *Engineering News-Record* 93 (18 December 1924):982–85.

Westcott, C. H. "Covered Stadium at Chicago with Long-Span Roof Trusses." *Engineering News-Record* 103 (17 October 1929):610–12.

Winkler, Franz. "Some Chicago Buildings Represented by the Work of Holabird and Roche." *Architectural Record* 31 (April 1912):313–70.

Chapter 5. Public Buildings and Parks

"The Alexander McKinlock Memorial Campus, Northwestern University, Chicago." *Architecture* 55 (June 1927):300–19.

"Architectural News in Photographs." *Architecture* 61 (January 1930):51.

"Art Gallery Built on 200-Ft. Bridge." *Engineering News* 77 (22 March 1917):460–61.

Bach, Richard F. "The Field Museum of Natural History, Chicago, Illinois; Graham, Anderson, Probst and White, Architects." *Architectural Record* 56 (July 1924):1–15.

The Brookfield Zoo, 1934–54. Chicago: Chicago Zoological Society, 1954.

Chicago Board of Education. *Annual Report.* Chicago: Board of Education, 1905–6 et seq.

Chicago Park District. *Annual Report of the Chicago Park District.* Chicago: Chicago Park District, 1934 et seq.

Chicago Public Schools. Chicago: Board of Education, 1938.

Chute, Walter H. *The John G. Shedd Aquarium.* Chicago: John G. Shedd Aquarium Society, [1932].

"The Evanston, Illinois, Township High School." *American Architect* 128 (5 October 1925):323–24, pls. 272–74.

Fokert, O. Maurice, and Angle, Paula. *City in a Garden: Homes in the Lincoln Park Community.* Chicago: Coach House Press, 1963.

Forest Preserve District. *Land Policy.* River Forest: Forest Preserve District of Chicago and Cook County, 1950.

"The Foundation for the New City Hall in Chicago." *Engineering Record* 59 (12 June 1909):745–47.

"The Grant Park Stadium, Chicago." *Architectural Forum* 42 (February 1925):79–80, pls. 9–10.

Grunsfeld, Ernest A., Jr. "The Construction and Equipment of Adler Planetarium." *Architectural Forum* 54 (February 1931):225–28.

Haas, Joseph. "Shedd Aquarium: Asleep in the Deep for Much Too Long." *Chicago Daily News Panorama*, 9 May 1970, pp. 4–6.

"Heating Plant for Professional Schools of Northwestern University." *Power* 65 (8 February 1927):199–202, 213.

Howatt, John. *Notes on the First Hundred Years of Chicago School History*. Chicago: John Howatt and Washburne Trade School Press, 1940.

"Independent Frames Support Exterior and Interior Surfaces of Temple Dome." *Engineering News-Record* 106 (8 January 1931):75–76.

"Let's Go to the Field Museum." *Chicago Daily News Panorama*, 29 March 1969, pp. 4–5.

Maher, George W. "The Restoration of the Fine Arts Building of the World's Columbian Exposition, Chicago." *Architectural Forum* 35 (July 1921):35–37.

[McLean, Robert Craik]. "The Chicago Plan after Fifteen Years." *Western Architect* 35 (January 1926):1.

Murphy, C. F. "The Field Museum of Natural History, Chicago." *Architectural Forum* 42 (February 1925):65–68, pls. 11–12.

National Spiritual Assembly of the Baha'is. *The Baha'i House of Worship*. Wilmette: National Spiritual Assembly of the Baha'is, 1953.

North, A. T. "The Adler Planetarium, Chicago." *Architectural Forum* 54 (February 1931):140–50.

Official Guide Book, Chicago Zoological Park, Brookfield, Illinois. Chicago: Chicago Zoological Society, 1955.

Official Guide Book of the Lincoln Park Zoo. Chicago: Lincoln Park Zoological Society, 1963.

O'Hara, Frank Hurlburt. *The University of Chicago: An Official Guide*. Chicago: University of Chicago Press, 1930.

"Statistics of the Construction of Chicago's Big Municipal Building." *Architectural Record* 31 (April 1912):371–80.

Williams, Patricia M. "The Burnham Plan and Field Museum." *Bulletin of the Field Museum of Natural History* 39 (May 1968):8–12.

Woodbury County Court House, Sioux City, Iowa. Sioux City: Woodbury County Court House, n.d.

"Wrecking the Old City Hall in Chicago." *Engineering Record* 59 (15 May 1909): 634–35.

Chapter 6. The Structures and Arteries of Transportation

Arnold, Bion J. *Report on the Re-Arrangement and Development of the Steam Railroad Terminals of the City of Chicago*. Chicago: Citizens' Terminal Plan Committee, 1913.

Baker, M. N. "Activated Sludge in America: An Editorial Survey." *Engineering News* 74 (22 July 1915):164–71.

"Belt Lines of the Chicago and North Western at Chicago and Milwaukee." *Railway Age Gazette* 50 (24 February 1911):355.

Brock, E. "Mechanical Features of the Chicago Union Station." *Journal of the Western Society of Engineers* 30 (December 1925):527–43.

Brumley, Daniel J. "Terminal Improvement and Electrification of the Illinois Central Railroad at Chicago." *Railway Review* 73 (1 September 1923):299–303.

Brumley, Daniel J.; Morrow, Frederick E.; and Ford, Robert H. P. "Chicago Terminal Improvements. . . ." *Transactions of the American Society of Civil Engineers* 87 (1924):802–20.

"Busiest Railway Crossing Is No More." *Railway Age* 91 (15 August 1931):241–44, 251.

Cain, Louis P., III. "The Sanitary District of Chicago: A Case Study of Water Use and Conservation." Ph.D. diss., Economics Department, Northwestern University, 1969.

"[Chicago and North Western] Opens Notable Freight House on Air Rights Property." *Railway Age* 91 (26 September 1931):471–73, 478.

Chicago and North Western Railway. *North Western Passenger Terminal.* Chicago: Chicago and North Western Railway Company, [1910?].

Chicago Citizens' Committee on River Straightening. *The Straightening of the Chicago River.* Chicago: City Council Committee on Railway Terminals, 1926.

Chicago Department of Water and Sewers. *The Water System of Chicago.* Chicago: Department of Water and Sewers, 1966.

"Chicago Double Deck Street for Congested District," *Engineering News-Record,* 85 (22 July 1920):173–75.

"Chicago Municipal Pier." *Engineering News* 74 (29 July 1915):193–97.

"Chicago Passenger Terminal of the Chicago and North Western." *Railway Age Gazette* 50 (9 June 1911):1311–15.

Chicago Terminal Committee. *Report on Railroad Terminal Coordination, Chicago, Illinois, and Vicinity.* [Chicago]: Western Regional Coordination Committee, 1936.

Chicago Traction and Subway Commission. *Report . . . on a Unified System of Surface, Elevated and Subway Lines.* Chicago: Traction and Subway Commission, 1916.

Chicago Transit Authority. *Horses to Horsepower: A Pictorial Review of Local Transportation in Chicago since 1859.* Chicago: Chicago Transit Authority, 1970.

Crane, Jacob L., Jr. "Street Development in Relation to Railroad Terminals." *Transactions of the American Society of Civil Engineers* 87 (1924):795–801.

"The Des Plaines River Activated Sludge Plant." *Engineering News-Record* 85 (9 December 1920):1134–38.

D'Esposito, Joshua. "Chicago Union Station." *Journal of the Western Society of Engineers* 30 (November 1925):447–60.

———. "The Chicago Union Station Development." *Transactions of the American Society of Civil Engineers* 87 (1924):821–27.

"Double Deck Freight Station in Six-Story Building." *Engineering News-Record* 85 (14 October 1920):732–36.

Drummond, William. *The Railway Terminal Problem of Chicago*. Chicago: City Club, 1915.

"Foundations of the Northwestern [sic] Railway Terminal, Chicago." *Engineering Record* 59 (8 May 1909):595–97.

"Freight Station with Air Rights Warehouse at Chicago." *Engineering News-Record* 103 (29 August 1929):325–26.

Haines, William L. R. "The Modern Freight Terminal of the Pennsylvania Railroad System in Chicago, Illinois." *Transactions of the American Society of Civil Engineers* 87 (1924):861–82.

Harrington, Phillip; Kelker, R. F., Jr.; and De Leuw, Charles E. *A Comprehensive Local Transportation Plan for the City of Chicago*. Chicago: Council Committee on Local Transportation, 1937.

Holt, T. "Signals and Interlocking in the Chicago Union Station." *Journal of the Western Society of Engineers* 30 (November 1925):489–500.

Howard, D. H. "Construction of the Skokie Valley Line." *Journal of the Western Society of Engineers* 32 (June 1927):182–90.

"Huge Chicago Freight Station for Pennsylvania Lines." *Engineering News* 77 (25 January 1917):129–32.

Illinois Central Railroad Research and Development Bureau. *Organization and Traffic of the Illinois Central System*. Chicago: Illinois Central Railroad Company, 1938.

Jenkins, Carter, "Inland Waterway Development in Illinois." *Journal of the Western Society of Engineers* 43 (June 1938):136–40.

Karrick, S. N. "Description of the Interior Waterway Projects in the Chicago District." *Journal of the Western Society of Engineers* 43 (June 1938):140–43.

Lacher, Walter S. "Noteworthy Passenger Station Completed at Chicago." *Railway Age* 79 (4 July 1925):7–28.

"Large Suburban Terminal Built for Illinois Central Railroad." *Engineering News-Record* 107 (3 September 1931):306–62.

Map of the Metropolitan Sanitary District of Greater Chicago Showing Annexations and Municipalities. Chicago: Metropolitan Sanitary District, 1966.

Map of the Metropolitan Sanitary District of Greater Chicago Showing Sewage Treatment Works, Pumping Stations, Channels and Sewers. Chicago: Metropolitan Sanitary District, 1966.

"Methods Used in Making New Lands and Boulevards on Chicago Waterfront."
  Engineer and Contractor 67 (July 1928):337–42; 67 (August 1928):387–92.

Metropolitan Sanitary District of Greater Chicago. *The Growth and Development
  of a Modern City.* Chicago: Metropolitan Sanitary District, 1962.

"The Metropolitan Sanitary District of Greater Chicago." *Chicago Daily News,*
  26 September 1964, special supplement.

"New Chicago Freight Terminal of the Alton Railroad." *Engineering News-Record*
  85 (14 October 1920):728–31.

"The New Chicago Passenger Terminal of the Chicago and North Western Railway."
  Engineering Record 58 (15 August 1908):177–78.

"The New Chicago Station of the Chicago and North Western Railway." *Engineering
  Record* 61 (18 June 1910):774–78.

Newcomb, Rexford. "The New Chicago Union Station." *Western Architect* 35
  (January 1926):3–7, pls. 1–16.

"The New Terminal Station of the Chicago and Northwestern [sic] Railway." *Engineering News* 66 (17 August 1911):191–97.

Noonan, Edward J. *The Railway Passenger Terminal Problem at Chicago.* Chicago:
  Committee on Railway Terminals, 1933.

"Northwestern [sic] Terminal in Chicago: Lighting, Heating, Ventilation, Motor
  Applications. . . ." *Electrical World* 58 (26 August 1911):483–88.

Post, C. W. "Electrical Equipment in the Chicago Union Station." *Journal of the
  Western Society of Engineers* 30 (December 1925):543–59.

Putnam, Rufus W. "Modern Rail and Water Terminals, with Particular Reference
  to the Situation at Chicago." *Transactions of the American Society of Civil Engineers* 87 (1924):828–60.

"Railway Terminal Power Plant . . . in New Northwestern [sic] Passenger Station in
  Chicago." *Electrical World* 58 (19 August 1911):435–41.

"The Railway Traffic of the Chicago Terminal." *Railway Age Gazette* 60 (14 January
  1916):49–51.

Ramey, H. P. "Chicago River Controlling Works." *Journal of the Western Society
  of Engineers* 42 (February 1937):3–15.

"A Record Size Bascule." *Engineering News-Record* 118 (22 April 1937):583–87.

Sawyer, Clair N. "Milestones in the Activated Sludge Process." *Water Pollution
  Control Federation Journal* 37 (February 1965):151–62.

Shaw, Alfred. "The Chicago Union Station; Graham, Anderson, Probst and White,
  Architects." *Architectural Forum* 44 (February 1926):85–88, pls. 17–24.

South Park District. *Photographic Record of the Placing of the Burnham Park Fill.*
  Chicago: South Park District, ca. 1920 et seq.

"Structural Design of U. S. Mail Terminal at Chicago," *Engineering News-Record*
  87 (22 December 1921):1010–13.

Sundry Proposals and Plans for the Development of Local Transportation Facilities in the City of Chicago. Chicago: City Clerk, 1924.

"Superstructure of Chicago Municipal Pier." *Engineering News* 74 (12 August 1915):306–8.

"Text of Supreme Court Decision in Chicago Lake Diversion Case." *Engineering News-Record* 104 (24 April 1930):696–97.

Vandersluis, W. M. "Electrification of the Illinois Central Surburban Service in Chicago." *Journal of the Western Society of Engineers* 31 (March 1926):75–93.

Wallace, John F. *Report of . . . Chicago Railway Terminal Commission*. Chicago: Chicago Railway Terminal Commission, 1921.

Weidemann, E. "Some Features of the Structural Design of Chicago Union Station." *Journal of the Western Society of Engineers* 30 (December 1925):501–26.

Young, Hugh E. "Lakefront Boulevard Link Forms Milestone in Chicago Plan: Joining of Park Systems on North and South Side." *Engineering News-Record* 118 (15 April 1937):546–48.

Credits for Illustrations

1. Chicago Department of Development and Planning, *Community Renewal Program Report*, 1964.
2. Map by *Chicago Daily News*; courtesy Forest Preserve District.
3. Chicago Transit Authority, *Chicago Transit Map*.
4. R. G. Raasch, *Official Map of the Chicago Terminal District* (Chicago: Illinois Freight Association, 1961).
5. Raasch, *Official Map of the Chicago Terminal District*.
6. Daniel H. Burnham and Edward H. Bennett, *The Plan of Chicago* (Chicago: Commercial Club, 1909).
7. Courtesy Insurance Exchange Building.
8. Photo by Bill Engdahl, Hedrich-Blessing.
9. Photo by Bill Engdahl, Hedrich-Blessing.
10. *Engineering News-Record*.
11. *The International Competition for a New Administration Building for the Chicago Tribune,MCMXXII* (Chicago: Tribune Company, 1923).
12. Photo by Bill Engdahl, Hedrich-Blessing.
13. Photo by Bill Engdahl, Hedrich-Blessing.
14. Courtesy Chicago Historical Society.
15. *Engineering News-Record*.
16. Photo by Brandt and Associates; courtesy Kemper Insurance Company.
17. *Architectural Forum*.
18. *Engineering News-Record*.
19. Photo by Bill Engdahl, Hedrich-Blessing.
20. Photo by Bill Engdahl, Hedrich-Blessing.
21. *Engineering News-Record*.
22. Photo by Hedrich-Blessing.
23. Photo by Richard Nickel.
24. Courtesy Chicago Historical Society.
25. *Engineering Record*.
26. Photo by Richard Nickel.
27. Courtesy Chicago Historical Society.
28. *Architectural Record*.
29. Photo by Woodworth Commercial Photos.
30. Photo by Woodworth Commercial Photos.
31. Photo by Woodworth Commercial Photos.
32. Photo by Woodworth Commercial Photos.
33. Photo by Chicago Park District.
34. *Architectural Record*.
35. Photo by Chicago Park District.
36. Walter E. Chute, *John G. Shedd Aquarium* (Chicago: Shedd Aquarium Society, [1932]).
37. Photo by Chicago Park District.
38. Courtesy Talman Federal Savings and Loan Association.
39. Photo by Chicago Park District.
40. Photo by Jacques Mittendorf, Chicago Zoological Park.
41. Photo by Ralph Graham, Chicago Zoological Park.
42. Photo by Richard Nickel.
43. Photo by Chicago Aerial Industries, Incorporated; courtesy University of Chicago.
44. Photo by Chicago Aerial Industries, Incorporated; courtesy University of Chicago.
45. Courtesy Chicago Historical Society.
46. Photo by Kaufmann, Weimar and Fabry Company; courtesy Chicago Historical Society.
47. *Engineering News*.
48. Collection of Arthur Dubin.
49. Courtesy General Products of Ohio, Incorporated.
50. Photo by Richard Nickel.
51. *Architectural Record*.
52. Courtesy Pennsylvania Railroad Company.
53. *Architectural Record*.
54. *Railway Age*.
55. Photo by Chicago, Burlington and Quincy Railroad Company; courtesy Chicago Historical Society.
56. *Railway Age*.
57. Photo by Richard Nickel.
58. Collection of Arthur Dubin.
59. *Chicago Sun-Times*.

Index